THE CORK ANTHOLOGY

edited by

Seán Dunne

CORK UNIVERSITY PRESS

First published in 1993 by
Cork University Press
University College
Cork
Ireland

Reprinted 1995

British Library Cataloguing in Publication Data
A CIP catalogue record is available from the British Library.

ISBN 0 902561 87 1 Hardcover
0 902561 88 X Paperback

Typeset by Seton Music Graphics, Bantry, Co. Cork
Printed by ColourBooks, Baldoyle, Dublin

Once we see our place, our part of the world, as *surrounding* us, we have already made a profound division between it and ourselves. We have given up the understanding . . . that we and our country create one another, depend on one another, are literally part of one another, that our land passes in and out of our bodies just as our bodies pass in and out of our land; that as we and our land are part of one another; so all who are living as neighbors here, human and plant and animal, are part of one another, and so cannot possibly flourish alone; that, therefore, our culture must be our response to our place, our culture and our place are images of each other and inseparable from each other, and so neither can be better than the other.

(Wendell Berry, *The Unsettling of America*)

Contents

III HILLSIDES AND CITY MARSH

IV ONE DAY FOR RECREATION . . .

V PEOPLE APART

VI THE WEIGHT OF HISTORY

Acknowledgements

I am happy to acknowledge the assistance I received from the following in compiling this anthology: Dr Michael Mortell, UCC; Virginia Teehan, UCC; Carole Quinn, UCC; Helen Davis, UCC; Pat Donnelly, UCC; Kieran Burke, Cork City Library; John Loesberg; Peter Murray; *The Irish Times* library; *The Cork Examiner* library; the staff of Cork University Press; the staff of the National Library of Ireland. Liam Moher provided material, encouragement and humour; Trish Edelstein, as ever, provided encouragement, ideas, patience and enthusiasm.

S.D.

Cork University Press has made every effort to trace the copyright-holders of the work in this anthology. If there are omissions, Cork University Press will happily correct this in reprints or future editions of the book.

Grateful acknowledgement is made to the following: Appletree Press for 'Cape Clear' by Peter Somerville-Large, from *The Coast of West Cork* (Belfast, 1985); Anvil Press (London) for permission to use the following poems by Thomas McCarthy: 'Toast' from *The Non-Aligned Storyteller* (1984); 'The Dying Synagogue at South Terrace' from *Seven Winters in Paris* (1989); 'The Provincial Writers' Diary' from *The Sorrow Garden* (1981); Anvil Press (Dublin) for an excerpt from *Guerilla Days in Ireland* by Tom Barry (Dublin, 1949; 1961); Blackstaff Press (Belfast) for '"Windfall", 8 Parnell Hill Cork' by Paul Durcan from *The Berlin Wall Café* (Belfast, 1985); Dermot Bolger for two extracts from *Song For a Poor Boy* by Patrick Galvin; Máire Bradshaw for her poem 'high time for all the marys' from *high time for all the marys* (1992); Brandon Books (Dingle) for 'Tea in the Meadow' from *To School Through The Fields* (1988) by Alice Taylor; Burns & Oates Ltd for an excerpt from *Terence MacSwiney* (1961) by Moirin Chavasse; Ciaran Carson and Liam Ó Muirthile for 'Portrait of Youth III', a translation by Ciaran Carson of Liam Ó Muirthile's poem 'Portráid Óige III'; Collins Press (Cork) for an extract from *The Life of Other Days* (1992) by Tim Cramer; Constable Ltd for 'Up The Bare Stairs' from the *Collected Stories of Seán O'Faoláin* (London, 1980); Cork Historical And Archaeological

Society for a number of articles from the *Journal of the Cork Historical and Archaeological Society*, Cork University Press for 'The Famine In Cork' which appeared as 'The Great Irish Famine' in *Some Chapters of Cork Medical History* (Cork, 1957); and 'Heffernan's Cow' from *Unusual Medical Cases: A Cork Physician's Memoirs* (Cork, 1962); Roz Cowman for her poem 'The Old Clerk' from *The Goose Herd* (Galway, 1989); Curtis Brown and the estate of Elizabeth Bowen for 'The Most Unforgettable Character I've Met' from '*The Mulberry Tree*' (1986); Greg Delanty for his poem 'Setting the Type' from *Southward* (Dublin, 1992); Dedalus Press (Dublin) for 'The Tomb of Michael Collins' by Denis Devlin from *Collected Poems of Denis Devlin* (Dublin 1989) and for 'On Dunkettle Bridge' by Gerry Murphy from *Rio de la Plata and all that* (1993); Eilís Dillon for her translation 'The Lament for Art O'Leary' (1971); Theo Dorgan for his poem 'Nocturne for Blackpool' from *The Ordinary House Of Love* (Galway, 1990); Faber & Faber Ltd and Michael Davitt for 'The Mirror', a translation by Paul Muldoon of Michael Davitt's poem 'An Scathán' published in Paul Muldoon's book *Quoof* (London 1983); John Farquharson Ltd, London, for 'Trinket's Colt' from *Some Experiences of an Irish R.M.* by Somerville and Ross; Gallery Press (Loughcrew, Co. Meath) for 'Tea Ceremony' by John Montague from *Mount Eagle* (1987); Patrick Galvin for his poem 'The Madwoman of Cork' (Dublin, 1973); John Goodby for his poem 'Namesakes'; Lillian Hall for an excerpt from *Dr. E. Œ. Somerville* by Geraldine Cummins (1952); Molly Keane for her essay, 'Elizabeth of Bowen's Court'; Lilliput Press (Dublin) for permission to reproduce 'Eoin "Pope" O'Mahony' by Hubert Butler from *Escape From The Anthill* (Mullingar, 1985); Nell McCafferty for permission to reproduce 'The Vegetable Seller'; Bryan MacMahon for his ballad 'A Song for Christy Ring'; Martin Secker and Warburg Ltd for an extract from *Helsingør Station and Other Departures* by Aidan Higgins (London, 1989); Mercier Press (Cork) for an excerpt from *The Tailor and Ansty* by Eric Cross (Dublin, 1942; Cork, 1972); Liam Moher for an excerpt from the journals of P.F. Quinlan; John Montague for his poem 'A New Litany' from *The Dead Kingdom* (Dolmen Press, 1984) and for his translation 'The Hag of Beare'; John A. Murphy for his autobiographical essay 'The Piano In Macroom'; Oxford University Press for 'A Garage In County Cork' by Derek Mahon from *The Hunt By Night* (Oxford, 1982); Cyril Ó Céirín translator of *Mo Scéal Féin* (1915) by Peter O'Leary, published as *My Story* (Cork, 1970; Oxford, 1987); Tomás Ó Canainn for his essay 'Seán Ó Riada in Cúil Aodha' which first appeared as 'In The West Cork Gaeltacht' in *Integrating Tradition: The Achievement of Seán Ó Riada* (Ballina, 1981); Gregory O'Donoghue for his poem 'Shadow Play'; Peters Fraser & Dunlop and Harriet Sheehy for excerpts from two books by Frank O'Connor: *Leinster, Munster and Connaught* and *An Only Child* (London, 1961); Laurence Pollinger Ltd and the estate of Robert Gibbings for an excerpt from *Lovely Is The Lee* (London, 1945); Poolbeg Press (Dublin) and David Marcus for an extract from *A Land Not Theirs* by David Marcus (London, 1986); Quartet Books (London) for an extract from *Cockburn Sums Up* (1981) by Claud Cockburn; Raven Arts Press for two excerpts from *Song For A Poor Boy* (1990) by Patrick Galvin; Rogers, Coleridge & White Ltd for two extracts from *Vive Moi!* by Seán O'Faoláin; Routledge & Kegan Paul (London) for two excerpts from *Stone Mad* by Séamus Murphy (London, 1966); William Trevor for an excerpt from *Excursions in The Real World* (London, 1993); University College, Cork for permission to reproduce excerpts from the letters of George Boole and from a journal kept by Daniel Corkery; Virago Press Ltd (London) for an excerpt from *Bowen's Court* by Elizabeth Bowen (1984 edition); A.P. Watt Ltd for the story 'Just Fine' by Mary Leland from *The Little Galloway Girls* (London, 1987).

Introduction

There is a sense in which every place has two geographies. The first is the familiar geography which we learned in school. This is a world of flat maps; the names of rivers; the patterns of population and the distribution of crops; the outline of coasts; the crayon colours of mountain range and veldt. With such old-fashioned geography, one is always outside a certain place, perched over it like a hawk whose steady eye scans its every detail. With such geography, place is reduced to paper and landscape is confined to geological and topographical definitions. If one searches beneath those surfaces, it is only to discover rock formations.

There is a second type of geography which is harder to define. Each place contains its own version. It is an inner geography which is formed over a long period. It is a map shaped by memory, culture and experience. This geography varies from person to person and evolves over generations. It includes songs, stories, jokes, poems, politics, works of art, sporting events, local loyalties, parochial enthusiasms — the entire paraphernalia of a particular place. It is more than that vague thing, the spirit of place. It is a sense of the life lived in a particular area, and of the way that life is expressed.

This book is an effort to present a map of this other geography as it relates to County Cork. Like all such maps, it is personal and incomplete. It includes history and autobiography; ballads and journals; letters; stories and poems. The anthology's compass is wide enough to include, in one section, a ballad about a famous dog and, in another, a great writer's memory of the last garden party held in Mitchelstown Castle before the outbreak of World War I. Like all maps, it contains areas that are radically different from each other, but which nonetheless are part of the same place. It has its jagged areas and its smooth corners. Like all anthologies, it is also the personal definition of a theme.

That definition changed as I worked on the book. At the outset, I tried to include everything and quickly accumulated six hundred pages of material. I imagined how incomplete it would seem if such-and-such an item was omitted, or if such-and-such a writer was never mentioned. With two anthologies already on my curriculum vitae, I thought of critics waiting with pens poised between ink and acid. I thought of experts who know far more about the history of Cork than I can ever claim and of academics who have written more than I would ever want to of work by Cork writers. They were waiting in the wings as I assembled my book; the more I thought of them, the more my book became not mine but theirs. I realized that I had forgotten a statement of Madame de Sévigné which I once had written on a card and pinned above my writing-table: 'When I listen only to myself, I find it works wonders.'

After listening to these imaginary others for some time, I threw the whole thing to one side. I needed to find some other way of working. One day, in great excitement, I cracked it and found that, at last, I was listening to myself. I had been studying the work of two men, Hubert Butler and Tim Robinson, whose example is pivotal for me. Butler was a liberal-minded essayist who spent most of his life in County Kilkenny and who combined a sense of local involvement with a global view. One of his guiding principles was exemplified in a quotation from the English historian William Camden. These sentences fit this anthology as easily as they fitted Hubert Butler's life:

> If any there be which are desirous to be strangers in their own soile and forrainers in their own cities, they may so continue and therein flatter themselves. For such like I have not written these lines nor taken these pains.

Butler's life and work were the opposite of that narrow focus which finds a depressing shape in many works of Irish literature and which guided the country's political and social affairs for many decades. He lived in the provinces but he was not provincial. For him, Bennettsbridge was no valley of the squinting windows, but of windows open on local affairs and also on the wider world. His life in County Kilkenny was a form of exemplary engagement with the local. It was the opposite of a point of view held by those who cut themselves off from much of local life and who look on the world of the provinces with contempt, even while still living there. 'You should come to work in Dublin. After all, it's the capital', a journalist once told me. In the light of what I felt about Hubert Butler, such an attitude, masked as cosmopolitanism, seemed provincial. Butler had translated Chekhov, but there was nothing about him akin to the desire of those sisters who wished to travel to Moscow. Instead, in ways that preceded others who promulgated the importance of working in small areas outside the main, centralized focus of power, his mind ranged over varied issues as he put into practice the belief that too high a price can be paid for tranquility.

In the work of Tim Robinson, I found another guide to the way a writer and artist can engage with a place. Robinson is the author of *Stones of Aran*, one of the most interesting and important books produced in Ireland in the twentieth century. I saw the book as a metaphor for the involvement of one person with a place. In it, Robinson walks the coastline of one of the Aran Islands and delves into its geography, its folklore, its place-names, its geology and many other features. In prose that is as layered and rich as the area he explores, Robinson deals with space in the way Proust deals with time. For him, the local is not just a set of prejudices and superficial assumptions. It is infinite. In his world, there is no end to exploration, a theory which, as he once explained to Michael Viney in an interview in *The Irish Times*, can be illustrated by the way even the leaves of a tree, when set under a microscope, are revealed as similar to small trees themselves, and so on into infinity.

Tim Robinson is also a map-maker whose cartography has achieved acclaim and awards. He has mapped Connemara, the Aran Islands, and the Burren. His maps are not simply old-fashioned depictions of place. I have spent hours poring over them, reading them like books, and learning not merely the contours of a landscape but its very history and the marks which men and women have made upon it. He has walked alone through these places and has experienced them not just as a physical surface but as an accretion of disciplines and multiple expressions. At their richest, his maps are not images to which one refers in order to get from one place to the next. They transmit the richness of the place. He encompasses both traditional geography and a certain element of that inner geography which comes not from paper and compass, but from the experience of life in a particular place.

When I applied these two examples to my work as an anthologist, I realized that I myself had undergone a radical shift in my own relationship with Cork. For many years, I had kept my distance. I was fond of quoting Seán O'Faoláin's comment that no writer or artist could thrive in Cork without frequently getting out of it for refreshment. I was wary of provincialism and saw myself as a semi-detached, uneasy inhabitant. With Butler and Robinson, however,

I found a form of engagement with a place that is more satisfying. It is also, at this point in this troubled century, part of a widespread movement that calls for a new definition of the relationship between human beings and the places in which they live, and that finds in small places not an escape from the wider world, but a series of networks that connect us to it, and that may even draw the wider world to us, as readers from around the world have been drawn to the work of Tim Robinson or have been startled into thought by some sentence written decades ago near a Kilkenny village by Hubert Butler. On a schoolroom map of Ireland, one could cover with the tips of a few fingers the small spaces in which these two have worked. Mentally, however, the space over which they ranged is immeasurable.

I determined, then, to shape my anthology as a map of the way I myself experienced Cork. I would no longer try to include every-thing, nor would I listen to what I imagined to be the demands of others. When I started work, I was amazed by the amount of good material that presented itself. Gradually, I cut swathes through it all.

At that stage, I thought mainly in terms of writers. Anthologies are most easily criticized for what they exclude. With my new way of working, I found that this did not matter because I was no longer concerned with being representative in an all-inclusive sense. If something felt as if it belonged to a map other than the one I had charted, I simply left it to one side. I thought in terms of themes, and found that the book slowly came together. Like facing mirrors, certain pieces reflected each other. As a form it felt closer to music than to writing.

An example occurred when I was working in the archives in University College, Cork, and transcribed some lines from Daniel Corkery's journal. He describes walking through poorer parts of Cork and visiting Guy's printing works. As if setting tesserae on a mosaic, I set this extract between Greg Delanty's poem about a printing works, and Thomas McCarthy's poem, 'The Provincial Writer's Diary', which is itself based on Corkery's diary. The three pieces span eighty years, yet, when read in conjunction, they gain the force of a musical phrase and present a theme within the memory of a city and its writers. Other examples are not always so obvious, but this one serves to illustrate the impulse and method. And in each case, these pieces of writing were part of the life of Cork. I had absorbed them and set them on my inner map of the place. Set next to each other in an anthology, they create that fourth dimension of which Tim Robinson has written, that dimension 'which extends deep into the self of the cartographer'. I had come a long way from my first awareness of Cork.

II

Long before all this, that first awareness had to do with sport. Defeat in sport was an integral part of my Waterford childhood. Local hurling teams were beaten year after year. When Waterford won the All-Ireland, it was an occasion so rare that the county went wild. This happened in 1948 and again in 1959. In the latter year, the winning team was welcomed home to a civic reception at which the Mayor of Waterford spoke. He was known as the Bullyman Power and his words were cut into the crystal of local memory: 'Not only are Waterford the best hurling team in Ireland. They're the best hurling team in *the world*.' It was a moment of hyperbole to which he was entitled, its defiant exaggeration part of the inevitable excitement in a place where defeat came around year after year like a dog to a door.

Often, that defeat occurred at the hands of Cork. And of all the great hurlers whose names filled the newspapers and surfaced in everyday talk, one name stood out: Christy Ring. Over the border in the next county from Cork, I heard his name spoken with admiration and, sometimes, with resentment, for he had been at the helm of too many defeats which other teams had endured. In so far as I had any mental picture of Cork, Ring was its shape and its achievement.

Years later, in 1973, I left Waterford and became a student at UCC. Among my experiences over the next few years, I remember standing on the footpath in Patrick Street one Monday night in September. At a window across the road, Christy Ring stood above a cheering crowd gathered outside the Victoria Hotel. With a grin on his round face, he raised the All-Ireland trophy like booty over his head. I felt an exile in that crowd, but was still touched by the electricity of the event. At any rate, I was busy trying to be a poet, and poets, I had read, were not supposed to feel, or be, part of crowds.

In my last year at school and in the year before I went to UCC, I had borrowed Seán O'Faoláin's autobiography *Vive Moi!* from the city library in Waterford. It went through me like a dye. It was full of practical advice for anyone who wished, as I did, to become a writer. It had a lot to say about County Cork. In places, it idolized the countryside which O'Faoláin in a wild moment had called the

Land of the Free. It made the city itself seem attractive and repulsive, a place that one minute teemed with life but the next was weighed down by the force of a suffocating provincialism. It was years before I realized that O'Faoláin was projecting his family circumstances onto the shape of his city, and that in fact it was these circumstances which he most desired to escape.

As I walked for the first time from the bus station in Parnell Place towards UCC, I felt that I was entering a landscape with which I was familiar but of which I was a little wary. The bus station itself is one of the places I remember most from those years. Around that bleak building, I waited for the bus to Waterford on Friday evenings or stepped from the bus to Cork on Sunday nights. I felt neither wholly of one place nor of the other and, while this was not a matter of great importance, the bleakness of the bus station seemed a proper expression of my state. All bus and train stations are a manifestation of limbo.

In the college, I walked, as O'Faoláin had done (in late adolescence such comparisons are important, if pretentious) along the avenue from the Western Road, and I leaned against the railings to watch students playing tennis in the courts below. Near them lay a circular, stagnant pond. Back in town, I walked through streets of large shopfronts and past the river that flowed through the first sentence of O'Faoláin's autobiography. I had done a dangerous thing: I had entered a book about a place, instead of entering the place itself. More to the point, the book was set in a period when the city was far different to the place where I now lived. I carried in my head as well a picture of Daniel Corkery, whose book *The Hidden Ireland* could still stir me, despite the suburban world in which I grew up and a childhood spent against the background of the Kennedy assassination and the Beatles. O'Faoláin had paid his respects to Corkery, but his estimate was a rose with more thorns than petals: 'Why did he not write more? The answer is as simple as it is frustrating. His environment and his circumstances exhausted him.' Corkery, O'Faoláin added, suffered from the dehydrating nature of provincial life. Dreading dehydration (whatever it was), I kept a cool distance.

Still, I was glad to be in a milieu where writing and books were considered important. There were a number of writers in the university and all of them were poets. John Montague and Seán Lucy were prominent among them. Paul Durcan lived in Montenotte, and there were a number of student poets in the city as well. I found the literature courses dull and stultifying, and thankfully discovered that it was not necessary to attend lectures in order to pass exams. The real excitement was to be found in conversation and in shared books. Thomas McCarthy seemed to have the *Collected Poems* of Yeats glued to his hand. Others, influenced by John Montague, spoke of American poets like John Berryman and William Carlos Williams. In the APCK bookshop in Cook Street, I found shelves of poetry more exciting than any I had ever seen. Here, like a child loose in a sweet-shop, I bought books from the Penguin Modern European Poets series, edited by A. Alvarez. I studied the Hungarian Ferenc Juhász (whose work was later translated into Irish by Michael Hartnett) and the work of two great women writers whose poems remain central to my life: Nelly Sachs and Anna Akhmatova.

Elsewhere in the city, I loved the smells in shops like Madden's delicatessen in Bridge Street or Maher's in Marlboro Street. It was all new: the smell of ground coffee or of strange spices; the translated voices of poets from a far corner of the Continent; the heady excitement of new friendships and books. There was also the poet Seán Ó Ríordáin, *l'homme seul*. He was a shy figure in a raincoat, his head bowed as if against a permanent gust, his wheezy breath rattling as he searched for his glasses before reading his poems to university audiences which always seemed to include a good many nuns. Isolated and ill, he became, more by reputation than acquaintance, a kind of exemplar: separate, sharp-eyed, odd, bothered, cantankerous, humorous. I went to his office in the Irish Department in UCC, but could not muster the courage to knock. Had he answered, I would probably have had nothing to say. His presence was a stimulus in itself.

Outside the university, there were others who gradually became known to me as writers. Through them, I learned more about the city. They included Robert O'Donoghue, who worked in *The Cork Examiner* and who always seemed to have a cigarette, a theory and, if I needed it, a fiver. He later told me that I was the only poet who had returned money borrowed from him. Instead of making me feel virtuous, this made me feel that in fact I might not be a poet at all. Now and then, there was O'Donoghue's friend Patrick Galvin. His poem 'The Madwoman of Cork' holds for many Cork people the place that Wordsworth's 'The Daffodils' holds for the rest of the world.

In the Long Valley Bar in Winthrop Street, poets gathered, drank and argued. The atmosphere was convivial but, with O'Faoláin's autobiography in my head, I considered it a conviviality which came from other writers rather than from the city itself. Cork, said John Montague, is good for your writing and bad for your career. Though great writers like Hugh MacDiarmid and Robert Graves came to visit, it still felt far from the centre of things.

Yet with time I realized that, for a writer, the centre is wherever he or she finds himself. I was more provincial than I wanted to admit, for I thought that, while Cork was fine, the centre was elsewhere. Cork was obviously not like O'Faoláin's city: places like the Triskel Arts Centre and the presence of many writers and artists put paid to that. Yet instead of feeling a sense of place, I felt only a sense of displacement. I was a long way from that sense of unity with one's surroundings which exemplifies the maps of Tim Robinson or the clear-minded, honed brilliance of Hubert Butler's essays.

III

That unity came later. In 1986, I started work with *The Cork Examiner*. Gradually, I came to know County Cork in a new way, but — more importantly — the job freed me from the continual company of writers, a company that is best measured in occasional doses rather than in a permanent intake. Travelling to small towns and villages, I met people whose stories became part of a cumulative store of memories that have influenced my choices in this book. I worked on a series called *Places Apart*, in which each article presented my impressions of particular places. Simply by watching and listening in towns that included Youghal and Skibbereen, I gathered stories and memories. In a way that suited my temperament, and in a way that is unusual in newspapers, the editor of *The Cork Examiner*, Fergus O'Callaghan, gave me my head. I made my own choices and wrote about anything that interested me. In time, there was hardly an area in County Cork to which I had not travelled. This is a pattern which I maintained long after the series itself was complete. Two of these journeys influenced me profoundly. They deal with different worlds, but each was a lesson in the impact of locale on history, and each became a strand in the web of connecting experiences that shaped my inner map of Cork.

The first occurred in north Cork in 1987, the second in mid-Cork, just a few miles outside Macroom, in the late summer of 1992. Each reflected a different world and, while these worlds were poles apart in social terms, each was epitomized by destruction as a historical circumstance. One was represented by a great house that had been destroyed; the other by the outline of a tiny cabin on a bleak hillside.

For a writer, north Cork is rich in associations. It is the country-side where Canon Sheehan wrote his novels and where Edmund Spenser wrote his poems. It hosted the boyhood of Edmund Burke and was a home to many Gaelic poets. It was also the home of Elizabeth Bowen. I absorbed her books and read most of *Bowen's Court*, her story of the big house where her family had lived since the seventeenth century. I was more impressed by her use of words than by her creation of character. As if to make a personal pilgrimage to the place where those words had their origins, I decided to visit the demesne where Bowen's Court had stood. I went there one Saturday in July 1987. In the village of Kildorrery, a man told me how to get to the estate. There was nothing at all there now, he told me; he also told me how local people knew Elizabeth Bowen as Mrs Cameron.

I drove on and soon arrived at Farahy where the lower gates of Bowen's Court still stand near a small graveyard and a tidy lodge. I found the grave of Elizabeth Bowen and her husband, Alan Cameron, and observed how the space where they lie is elevated above the level of others that surround them. On another headstone, I noticed the beautiful place-name Glenanaar, a word I knew from the title of a novel by Canon Sheehan.

Outside the graveyard, I walked along the avenue and, by using a photograph of the house set against the Ballyhoura hills, I worked out where Bowen's Court had stood. It had been a box-like, simply designed house made mostly of local limestone. Elizabeth Bowen recalled it as a place with friezes in Italian plasterwork; old furniture; large rooms with windows where trapped birds and butterflies banged against the glass. There were also, wrote crotchety Virginia Woolf, heavy carpets full of holes.

On the morning Elizabeth Bowen was born in 1899, servants danced a jig on the kitchen table. As an adult, she realized that those who had built the house were also building an idea: 'They began to feel and exert the European idea — to seek what was humanistic, classic and disciplined.' In 1959, circumstances forced her to put the house up for sale. She hoped that the man who bought it would live there with his family. He knocked it down. 'It was a clean end', she wrote: 'Bowen's Court never lived to be a ruin.' After the house was sold, a friend of Elizabeth Bowen's said to Molly Keane that Elizabeth looked like someone who had attended her own execution. As a young girl, she heard herons cry at night and they seemed to be the voices of lost souls. Yet there were no ghosts in the great house itself.

As I walked in the grass where the house had stood, I felt as if Bowen's Court had itself become a ghost. I could hear a dog bark among the hills and the sound of a tractor chugging near Farahy churchyard. In a house on the main road, I talked to Molly O'Brien, who had once worked in Bowen's Court. On her first day there, she told me, she was confused when she was told that members of the family wanted coffee for their tea. She spoke of Elizabeth Bowen's death in 1973, and of how the locals went to Cork Airport to meet the coffin, which then lay in the small church for a night before the burial.

Others spoke of the family and gradually I built a picture of this small part of north Cork. It was a day to which I returned in articles and poems, culminating in a poem set in Doneraile Court, where I imagined Elizabeth Bowen on a visit, home from London where the Blitz had devastated the streets and homes where her friends lived. Her intense way with words was part of the intensity with which she invested her life and, as I walked the fields at Farahy, I felt her story, and the local memory of her life, like a presence in the place itself. She is represented in this anthology with two pieces, each of them connected with north Cork, while Molly Keane — a more friendly witness than Virginia Woolf — recalls the world of Bowen's Court itself. Places are peopled with such stories and that long day in the grounds of Bowen's Court was far different from most of the days I had spent in Cork as a student and hopeful writer. Freed at last from O'Faoláin's dated strictures, I felt as if I was meeting with the landscape rather than setting myself up in opposition to it. Such meetings, akin to Tim Robinson's slow exploration of the Connemara coastline, grew more frequent.

The other experience was of a different kind, but it too stands out as a point on my map. It is represented by two of the pieces in this book, the first by Peadar Ó Laoghaire and the second by N. Marshall Cummins. It concerns the death of an entire family, the

Buckleys, during the Famine. They were found dead in their small cabin high in the hills above Macroom. Before she died, the woman shivered with cold and the man held her feet against his chest to warm them. The couple died in that posture. Earlier, they had fled the workhouse in Macroom when they heard that their two children had died. So many people died of hunger at that time that the bodies were simply collected from the banks of the Sullane near the bridge at Macroom. The children's bodies, like all the others, were buried in the Famine grave at Carrigastyra.

I decided to follow the road the family had travelled. Guided by my friend, Seán MacSuibhne, I began at a small building at the back of the hospital in Macroom. This was all that remained of the old workhouse where the Buckleys and thousands of others were sent when there was nowhere left to go and no food could be found by the poor. As Peadar Ó Laoghaire tells it, the family were kept in different sections of the workhouse. I followed the route they took to the mass grave at Carrigastyra. There, they stopped to mourn their children.

When I went there, it turned out to be a sad, haunted place. The grave was overgrown and I was unable to make my way through brambles and briars. Instead, along a nettle-covered path, I got as far as an ugly monument standing between four yew trees, with a metal frame around it.

Afterwards, we drove through Clondrohid and then went along narrow roads rising higher and higher until we were nearly level with the tall mast at Mullaghinish across the mountains. We travelled about six miles in all. When the Buckleys had taken that road, they walked all the way. They were hungry, grief-stricken and exhausted. Eventually the journey became too much for the woman. Her husband took her in his arms and carried her the rest of the way. The people they met were afraid to go near them because typhus was everywhere and no one would risk infection.

We stopped at a gate and went up through some fields. In winter, Derryleigh is a bitter place where the wind whips across the ditches. On the August day I was there, the air was rinsed and clear. I could see across to Cill na Martra; to the pass of Céim an Fhia; to a thin bog road like a ribbon in the distance. I could see the house where Peadar Ó Laoghaire was born.

Cattle stood in the first field where we walked and a dead sheep lay in the second. Thistles grew abundantly in the ruins of a cabin.

We climbed higher, past a small cairn. Near it, we came to the spot where the Buckleys had died. Up to a short time before, the place had been covered in gorse, but, when the gorse was burned, the ruins of an old settlement became visible. I could clearly make out the outlines of cabins. They seemed incredibly small, some of them no bigger than what would pass for a sitting-room nowadays. Stones and boulders were scattered around the site. The rectangular outline of one house is clearly visible and it is said locally that this is the house where the Buckleys died.

It was a simple, stark place without monument or signpost. The outline of potato ridges could be made out. The rotted crop which grew there led to the family's journey to the workhouse. We left the stones behind, walked past the ruins and then went back to the road. It was a place with ghosts as plentiful as those that haunted the fields of Bowen's Court: ghosts of a bitter, hurtful history. It was another experience that became part of the inner geography of County Cork and that therefore finds its place in this anthology. It is, I think, the saddest fragment in the book.

IV

And so, marked by these and other experiences, and by the simple experience of living an ordinary life in an ordinary place, I shaped this anthology towards what Seamus Heaney, in a felicitous phrase, called the 'equable, assenting marriage between the geographical country and the country of the mind.'

There have been similar books from other places in the past few years. Macdara Woods edited the *Kilkenny Anthology*; Dermot Bolger edited others which reflect the work of writers from Dublin and Wexford; Richard Murphy edited an anthology for Mayo. Breandán and Ruairí Ó hEithir edited *An Aran Reader*, while the novelist Dermot Healy gave a voice to the North-West in the magazine *Force 10*. These have all been part of an energy that reveals the richness of the local. It is as if all those clichés about the global village, and those Cassandra-like warnings about the growing uniformity of the world, have come to nothing. The world seems to have become smaller, yet our sense of the parish has grown and deepened. To twist E.F. Schumacher's phrase, small is meaningful. And small, as I discovered, can also be limitless.

The sheer extent of material surprised me. Whether through the eyes of nineteenth-century travellers or twentieth-century poets, County Cork has been a source for many writers. Some of them — Eilís Dillon, Isabel Healy, Paddy Woodworth and Dermot Keogh — have written specifically for this anthology. Various aspects have interested these many writers — a figure in a street, a legend, a great hurler, a vegetable-seller in the market — and these have found their way into words. This book, this inner map of a place, presents a single selection of their work.

Seán Dunne
Cork, August 1993

I THE LARGEST COUNTY

County Cork

Mr and Mrs Hall

from: *Hall's Ireland* (1841)

The county of Cork in the province of Munster is the largest county in Ireland and larger than any English county with the exception of York; from east to west it extends above ninety English miles, with its greatest breadth being about forty. It is bounded on the north by Tipperary and Limerick; on the north-east by Waterford; on the north-west by Kerry and on the south by the ocean.

The county is divided into the East and West Ridings, the East comprising eleven baronies, with the liberties of the city of Cork and the port of Kinsale, and the West, eight baronies.

The baronies in the East Riding are: Duhallow, Orrery and Kilmore, Condons and Clongibbons, Fermoy, Kinsale, Imokilly, Kerrycurrihy, Kinnalea, Barrymore, Barretts and East Muskerry.

In the West Riding they are: Ibane and Barryroe, Bere, Bantry, West Muskerry, Kinameaky, Courcies, East and West Carbery.

The principal towns of the county, besides the city of Cork, are Youghall, Kinsale, Bandon, Mallow, Cove, Bantry, Fermoy, Skibbereen, Macroom and Dunmanway.

North Cork

Arthur Young

from: *A Tour in Ireland* (1780)

Oct. 10th. Left Castle Lloyd, and took the road by Galbally to Mitchelstown [Co. Cork], through a country part of it a rich grazing tract; but from near Galbally, to the Galtee mountains, there are large spaces of flat lands, covered with heath and furze, that are exceedingly improvable, yet seem as neglected as if nothing could be made of them. The road leads immediately at the northern foot of the Galtees, which form the most formidable and romantic boundary imaginable; the sides are almost perpendicular, and reach a height, which, piercing the clouds, seem formed rather for the boundaries of two conflicting empires, than the property of private persons. The variety of the scenery exhibited by these mountains is great; the road, after passing some miles parallel with them, turns over a hill, a continuation of their chain, and commands an oblique view of their southern side, which has much more variety than the northern; it looks down at the same time upon a long plain, bounded by these and other mountains, several rivers winding through it, which join in the centre near Mitchelstown. I had been informed that this was a miserable place; it has at least a situation worthy of the proudest capital.

Upon my arrival, Lord Kingsborough, who possesses almost the whole country, procured me the information I requested in the most liberal manner, and a residence since has enabled me to perfect it. His Lordship's vast property extends from Kildorrery to Clogheen, beyond Ballyporeen [Co. Tipperary], a line of more than sixteen Irish miles, and it spreads in breadth from five to ten miles. It contains every variety of land, from the fertility of grazing large bullocks to the mountain heath the cover of grouse. The profitable land lets from 8s. to 25s. an acre, but the whole does not on average yield more than 2s. 6d. Such a field for future improvements is therefore rarely to be found. On the cold and bleak hills of Scotland estates of greater extent may be found, but lying within twenty miles of Cork, the most southerly part of Ireland, admits a rational prophesy that it will become one of the first properties in Europe.

The size of farms held by occupying tenants is in general very small, Lord Kingsborough having released them from the bondage of the middlemen. Great tracts are held in partnership; and the amounts held by single farmers rise from £5 to £50 a year, with a very few large farms. The soils are as various as in such a great extent they may be supposed: the worst is the wet morassy land, on a whitish gravel, the spontaneous growth, rushes and heath; this yields a scanty nourishment to cows and half-starved young cattle. Large tracts of wet land have a black peat or a turf surface; this is very reclaimable, and there are immense tracts of it. The profitable soil is in general a sandy or a gravelly loam, of a reddish brown colour; and the principal distinction is its being on lime or grit stone, the former generally the best. It declines in value from having a yellow sand or a yellow clay near the surface under it. There are tracts of such incomparable land that I have seen very little equal to it, except in Tipperary, Limerick, and Roscommon. A deep friable

18

loam, moist enough for the spontaneous growth to fat a bullock, and dry enough to be perfectly under command in tillage. If I was to name the characteristics of an excellent soil, I should say *that* upon which you may fat an ox, and feed off a crop of turnips. By the way I recollect little or no such land in England, yet it is not uncommon in Ireland. Quarries of the finest limestone are found in almost every part of the estate.

The tracts of mountain are of a prodigious extent; the Galtees only are six or seven miles long, from one to four miles across, and more improvable upon the whole than any land I have seen, turf and limestone being on the spot, and a gentle exposure hanging on the south. In every inaccessible cliff there are mountain ash, oak, holly, birch, willow, hazel, and white thorn, and even to a considerable height up the mountain, which, with the many old stumps scattered about them, prove that the whole was once a forest, an observation applicable to every part of the estate.

The tillage here extends no farther than what depends on potatoes, on which root they subsist as elsewhere. They sometimes manure the grass for them, and take a second crop; after which they follow them with oats, till the soil is so exhausted as to bear no longer, when they leave it to weeds and trumpery, which vile system has spread itself so generally over all the old meadow and pasture of the estate, that it has given it a face of desolation — furze, broom, fern, and rushes, owing to this and to neglect, occupy seven-eights of it. The melancholy appearance of the lands arising from this, which, with miserable and unplanted mounds for fences, with no gate but a furze bush stuck in a gap, or some stones piled on each other, altogether form a scene the more dreary, as an oak, an ash or an elm, are almost as great a rarity (save in the plantations of the present Lord) as an olive, an orange, or mulberry. There is no wheat, and very little barley. Clover and turnips, rape, beans, and peas, quite unknown.

The rents are paid by cattle, and of these dairy cows are the chief stock. The little farmers manage their own; the larger ones let them to dairymen for one cwt. of butter each cow, and 12s. to 15s. horn money; but the man has a privilege of four *collops*, and an acre of land and cabin to every twenty cows. Sheep are kept in very small numbers; a man will have two, or even one, and he thinks it worth his while to walk ten or twelve miles to a fair, with a straw band tied to the leg of the lamb, in order to sell it for 3s. 6d., an undoubted proof of the poverty of the country. Markets are crowded for this reason, for there is nothing too trifling to carry; a yard of linen, a fleece of wool, a couple of chickens, will carry an unemployed pair of hands ten miles. Hogs are kept in such numbers that the little towns and villages swarm with them; pigs and children bask and roll about, and often resemble one another so much, that it is necessary to look twice before the *human face divine* is confessed. I believe there are more pigs in Mitchelstown than human beings; and yet propagation is the only trade that flourished here for ages.

Labour is chiefly done in the cottier system, which has been so often explained. There are here every gradation of the lower classes, from the *spalpeens*, many among them strangers, who build themselves a wretched cabin in the road, and have neither land, cattle, nor turf, rising to the regular cottier, and from him to the little joint-tenant, who, united with many others, take some large farm in partnership; still rising to the greater farmer. The population is very great. It is but few districts in the North that would equal the proportion that holds on this estate; the cabins are innumerable, and, like most Irish cabins, swarm with children. Wherever there are many people, and little employment, idleness and its attendants must abound.

It is not to be expected that so young a man as Lord Kingsborough, just come from the various gaiety of Italy, Paris, and London, should, in so short a space as two years, do much in a region so wild as Mitchelstown; a very short narrative, however, will convince the reader that the time he has spent there has not been thrown away. He found his immense property in the hands of that species of tenant which we know so little of in England, but which in Ireland have flourished almost to the destruction of the kingdom, the *middleman*, whose business and whose industry consists in hiring great tracts of land as cheap as he can, and re-letting them to others as dear as he can, by which means that beautiful gradation of the pyramid, which connects the broad base of the poor people with the great nobleman they support, is broken; he deals only with his own tenant, the multitude is abandoned to the humanity and feelings of others, which to be sure may prompt a just and tender conduct; whether it does or not, let the misery and poverty of the lower classes speak, who are thus assigned over. This was the situation of nine-tenths of his property. Many leases being out, he rejected the trading tenant, and let every man's land to him, who occupied it at the rent he had himself received before. During a year that I was employed in letting his farms, I never omitted any opportunity of confirming him in this system, as far as was in my power, from a conviction that he was equally serving himself and the public in it; he will never quit it without having reason afterwards for regret.

In a country changing from licentious barbarity into civilized order, building is an object of perhaps greater consequence than may at first be apparent. In a wild, or but half cultivated tract, with no better edifice than a mud cabin, what are the objects that can impress a love of order on the mind of man? He must be wild as the roaming herds; savage as his rocky mountains; confusion, disorder, riot, have nothing better than himself to damage or destroy: but when edifices of a different solidity and character arise; when great sums are expended, and numbers employed to rear more expressive monuments of industry and order, it is impossible but new ideas must arise, even in the uncultivated mind; it must feel something, first to respect, and afterwards to love; gradually seeing that in proportion as the country becomes more decorated and valuable, licentiousness will be less profitable, and more odious. Mitchelstown, till his Lordship made it the place of his residence, was a den of vagabonds, thieves, rioters, and Whiteboys; but I can witness to its being now as orderly and peaceable as any other Irish town, much owing to this circumstance of building, and thereby employing such numbers of the people. Lord Kingsborough, in a short space of time, has raised considerable edifices; a large mansion for himself, beautifully situated on a bold rock; a quadrangle of offices; a garden of 5 English acres, surrounded with a wall, hothouses, etc. Besides this, three good stone and slate houses upon three farms, and engaged for three others, more considerable, which are begun; others repaired, and several cabins built substantially.

So naked a country as he found his estate, called for other exertions. He brought a skilful nurseryman from England, and formed 12 acres of nursery. It begins to shew itself; above 10,000 perch of hedges are made, planted with quick and trees; and several acres, filled with young and thriving plantations. Trees were given, gratis, to the tenantry, and premiums begun for those who plant most, and preserve them best, besides fourscore pounds a year offered for a variety of improvements in agriculture the most wanted upon the estate.

Those who are fond of scenes in which nature reigns in all her wild magnificence should visit the stupendous chain (of the Galtees). It consists of many vast mountains, thrown together in an assemblage of the most interesting features, from boldness and height of the declivities, freedom of outline, and variety of parts; filling a space of about six miles by three or four. Galtymore [3015 ft.] is the highest point, and rises like the lord and father of the surrounding progeny. From the top you look down upon a great extent of mountain, which shelves away to the south, east, and west; but to the north, the ridge is almost a perpendicular declivity. On that side the famous Golden Vale of Limerick and Tipperary spreads a rich level to the eye, bounded by the mountains of Clare, King's and Queen's counties, with the course of the Shannon, for many miles below Limerick. To the south you look over alternate ridges of mountains, which rise one beyond another, till in a clear day the eye meets the ocean near Dungarvan. The mountains of Waterford and Knockmealdown fill up the space to the south-east. The western is the most extensive view; for nothing stops the eye till Mangerton and Macgillicuddy's Reeks point out the spot where Killarney's Lake calls for a farther excursion. The prospect extends into eight counties, Cork, Kerry, Waterford, Limerick, Clare, Queen's, Tipperary, King's. Nor are these immense outlines the whole of what is to be seen in this great range of mountains. Every glen has its beauties; there is a considerable mountain river, or rather torrent, in every one of them. Nothing can exceed the beauty of the water. Its lucid transparency shews, at considerable depths, every pebble no bigger than a pin, every rocky basin alive with trout and eels, that play and dash among the rocks, as if endowed with that native vigour which animates, in a superior degree, every inhabitant of the mountains, from the bounding red deer, and the soaring eagle, down even to the fishes of the brook. Every five minutes you have a waterfall in these glens, which in any other region would stop every traveller to admire it. Sometimes the vale takes a gentler declivity, and presents to the eye, at one stroke, twenty or thirty falls, which render the scenery all alive with the motion; the rocks are tossed about in the wildest confusion, and the torrent bursts by turns from above, beneath, and under them; while the background is always gilled up with the mountains which stretch around.

Castle Hyde

Anonymous

As I roved out on a summer's morning
Down by the banks of Blackwater side,
To view the groves and the meadows charming,
The pleasant gardens of Castle Hyde;
'Tis there I heard the thrushes warbling,
The dove and partridge I now describe;
The lambkins sporting on ev'ry morning,
All to adorn sweet Castle Hyde.

The richest groves throughout this nation
And fine plantations you will see there;
The rose, the tulip, the rich carnation,
All vying with the lily fair.
The buck, the doe, the fox, the eagle,
They skip and play by the river side;
The trout and salmon are always sporting
In the clear streams of sweet Castle Hyde.

There are fine walks in these pleasant gardens,
And seats most charming in shady bowers.
The gladiators both bold and darling
Each night and morning do watch the flowers.
There's a church for service in this fine arbour
Where nobles often in coaches ride
To view the groves and the meadow charming,
The pleasant gardens of Castle Hyde.

There are fine horses and stall-fed oxes,
And dens for foxes to play and hide;
Fine mares for breeding and foreign sheep there
With snowy fleeces in Castle Hyde.
The grand improvements they would amuse you,
The trees are drooping with fruit of all kind;
The bees perfuming the fields with music,
Which yields more beauty to Castle Hyde.

If noble princes from foreign nations
Should chance to sail to this Irish shore,
'Tis in this valley they would be feasted
As often heroes have been before.
The wholesome air of this habitation
Would recreate your heart with pride.
There is no valley throughout this nation
In beauty equal to Castle Hyde.

I rose from Blarney to Castlebarnet,
To Thomastown, and sweet Doneraile,
To Kilshannick that joins Rathcormack,
Besides Killarney and Abbeyfeale;
The flowing Nore and the rapid Boyne,
The river Shannon and pleasant Clyde;
In all my ranging and serenading
I met no equal to Castle Hyde.

from: **The Faerie Queene**
Edmund Spenser, (1596)
Book IV, Canto XI, 40–44

Ne thence the Irishe Riuers absent were,
Sith no lesse famous then the rest they bee,
And ioyne in neighbourhood of kingdome nere,
Why should they not likewise in loue agree,
And ioy likewise this solemne day to see.
They saw it all, and present were in place;
Though I them all according their degree,
Cannot recount, nor tell their hidden race,
Nor read the saluage cuntreis, thorough which they pace.

There was the Liffy rolling downe the lea,
The sandy Slane, the stony Aubrian,
The spacious Shenan spreading like a sea,
The pleasant Boyne, the fishy fruitfull Ban,
Swift Awniduff, which of the English man
Is cal'de Blacke water, and the Liffar deep,
Sad Trowis, that once his people ouerran,
Strong *Allo* tombling from Slewlogher steep,
And *Mulla* mine, whose waues I whilom taught to weep.

And there the three renowned brethren were,
Which that great Gyant *Blomius* begot,
Of the faire Nimph *Rheusa* wandring there.
One day, as she to shunne the season whot,
Vnder Slewbloome in shady groue was got,
This Gyant found her, and by force deflowr'd,
Whereof conceiuing, she in time forth brought
These three faire sons, which being thence forth powrd
In three great riuers ran, and many countries scowrd.
The first, the gentle Shure that making way
By sweet Clonmell, adornes rich Waterford;
The next, the stubborne Newre, whose waters gray
By faire Kilkenny and Rosseponte boord,
The third, the goodly Barow, which doth hoord
Great heapes of Salmons in his deepe bosome:
All which long sundred, doe at last accord
To ioyne in one, ere to the sea they come,
So flowing all from one, all one at last become.

There also was the wide embayed Mayre,
The pleasaunt Bandon crownd with many a wood,
The spreading Lee, that like an Island fayre
Encloseth Cork with his deuided flood;
And balefull Oure, late staind with English blood:
With many more, whose names no tongue can tell.
All which that day in order seemly good
Did on the Thamis attend, and waited well
To doe their duefull seruice, as to them befell.

Out from the City

George Boole

George Boole (1815–64) became professor of mathematics at Queen's College, Cork in 1849. His work in mathematics and logic was enormously influential for subsequent generations. While in Cork, he wrote a number of letters to his sister, Maryann Boole, who lived in Lincoln in England. These letters are now kept in the Boole Library at University College, Cork. [Ed.]

Strawberry Hill, Cork
April 23rd. 1850

Took steamer for Aghada a few miles below Cove then outside car to Cloyne residence of Berkeley. . . saw a fine round tower there, noticed 12 ruined cabins in a row on entering the town, was told afterwards that they had been residences of the Cloyne brogue-makers, an extinguished branch of Irish industry. Brogues are a kind of shoe made of half-tanned leather. From Cloyne to Ballycotton. Struck with the extreme beauty of furze bushes on either side of the road, a sheet of golden blossoms. Reached Ballycotton about 7 o'clock pm. Spent the evening in the house of the Protestant clergyman the Rev. G. Kingston . . . .

Took possession of my house in the village and set up housekeeping with a piece of roast beef brought by me from Cork, and two pots of jam, and the coffee sent without my knowledge by the mother of two of our students who went down with me and took up their abode with the clergyman. My accommodation not very good, cleanliness not the household virtue of them who had the letting of the house. My servant Sarah a barefooted but apparently modest and well-taught maiden arranged to purchase bread, milk, tea etc. in the village.

Saturday morning, took a long walk over the cliffs, scenery very savage — rocks black and sharp-edged, perpendicular and slaty in texture and nowhere rounded but made acute and pointed by the action of the sea. Found people in every direction collecting seaweed for manure.

Sunday received a call from a Capt. Mervey, a gentleman who has some place in history having been one of three men who closed the door of the farmhouse on the field of Waterloo.

Visited on succeeding days the houses of the weavers and spinners in the village, inspected some of their native frieze and ordered for myself an outside coat to be made thereof. Those little manufactories, which employed about 90 people during the famine year by

Mr Kingston with the assistance of some Quakers, have kept the people out of the Unions where they would most certainly have died.

Glengarriff,
June 11th. 1850

Yesterday we travelled to Cork over the mountains. It was a delightful day and some of the scenery was very beautiful. From Bantry we came across the bog this morning. Nothing can exceed the beauty of this part of the bog surrounded by mountains and studded with islands. It deserves all that has been said of it.

The plants of this region would interest you greatly. The little flora called London Pride grows everywhere on the rocks. Spurges of great size are most abundant and ferns and foxgloves line the sides of the roads. The bogs are in many places white with the bog cotton, a very pretty plant of which I enclose a specimen, and irises etc. meet you everywhere. The weather is precisely of that kind which is most agreeable for travelling, a mixture of shade and sunshine.

Youghal Harbour
Anonymous

As I roved out on a summer's morning,
Early as the day did dawn,
When Sol appeared in pomp and glory,
I took my way through a pleasant lawn.
Where pinks and violets were sweetly blooming,
And linnets warbling in each shade,
I've been alarmed by a killing charmer.
Near Youghal Harbour I met this maid.

Her aspect pleasing, her smiles engaging,
I thought really she would distract my mind,
When I viewed her features, I thought on the fair one
That in Rathangan I left behind.
Her glancing eyes seemed most pleasing,
I think, young man, I saw you before,
Here in your absence in grief I languish,
My dear, you're welcome to me once more.

Don't you remember when once you deceived me,
And of me you did your will,
But at your returning I'll now quit mourning,
In hopes your promise you will fulfil.
It's a darling babe for you I'm rearing,
As in your travels you have never seen,
If you will agree, love, and come with me,
We will all live happy in Cappoquin.

Oh no, fair maid, I'll tell you plainly,
Here to remain I will not agree,
For when your parents would not receive me,
It made me for to quit this country.
And when your parents would not receive me,
It's then to Leinster I did repair,
Where I fell a courting another fair one,
In sweet Rathangan, near to Kildare.

It's to her I'll go, and leave off roving,
'Tis her favors I'm in hopes to win,
To tell her I'll go, and I'll bid adieu,
Saying farewell to sweet Cappoquin.
But now he has left me in grief to mourn,
Although my tender young heart he won.
So all fair maidens, beware of young men,
And think on Nancy of Cappoquin.

Some Strange Phenomena

Charles Smith

from: *The Ancient and Present State of the County and
City of Cork* (1774)

*An account of some Phenomena observed in the air, and of the effects produced by
Lightning in this County; with some general observations on the weather.*

Histories of the state of the air and weather, in different periods of
time, have always had a place in works of this kind; for which reason,
the following instances are laid before the reader. In the winter of

1695, and a good part of the following spring, there fell, in several places, of this province, a kind of thick dew, which the country people called butter, from its colour and consistence, being soft, clammy, and of a dark yellow, as doctor St. George Ash, then lord bishop of Cloyne, has recorded in the Philosophical Transactions; it fell always in the night, and chiefly in marshy low grounds, on the top of the grass, and on the thatch of cabins, seldom twice in the same place; it commonly lay a fortnight without changing colour, but then dried, and turned black; cattle fed as well where it lay, as in other fields; it often fell in lumps, as big as the end of one's finger, thin and scatteringly; it had a strong ill scent, somewhat like that of church-yards and graves; and there were most of that season very stinking fogs, some sediment of which the bishop thought might possibly have occasioned this stinking dew; it was not kept long, nor did it breed worms or other insects; yet the country people, who had scald or sore heads, rubbed them with this substance, and said it healed them.

In the summer of 1748, a shower fell in and about the town of Doneraile, of a yellowish substance, resembling brimstone, and had (as I was informed by those who saw it) a sulphurous smell; it lay but thin on the ground, and soon dissolved; this is all the account I could procure of this phenomenon from those who took notice of it.

The following odd effects of lightning may be worth mentioning. A ship, riding in the bay of Bantry, about thirty-four years ago, had her masts split in a strange manner, by a flash of lightning, part of them being twisted like a rope, whilst other parts were burned to a cinder; and the hulk was burst asunder, by the internal pressure of the air, against the sides of the vessel, the external air being greatly rarified. At another time, a small ship of war, riding in the same bay, had her masts shattered in the like manner; and the crew of another vessel had their bodies marked with stars, like the cracks in a glass-bottle; all these effects happened in winter, at which time there were strong gales of westerly winds.

In the parish of Kilmoloda, in East-Carbery, on the 27th of January 1746-7, one Robert Barry, a labouring man, being in bed with his wife and two children, in a close room, the door, which was opposite to a chimney in an outward room, being shut, a flash of lightning broke down some part of the top of the chimney, and split the chamber door, forcing one half of it into the room where the people lay. The man had his breast burned, and a small streak from his shoulder to his stomach; the woman had the side of her face, on which she lay, very much blasted and swelled; the daughter had her hair burned close to her temples; and the boy was scorched on the back of his neck. The lightning, in going out, made an hole, behind the fire-place, through the wall, which hole was larger without the house than within. A pig was found dead near the chimney. The people being fast asleep, did not hear the thunder, though there were very loud claps; nor did they know what had happened to them, till the neighbours came in the next morning, who waked and raised them up. They were all well the next day, except the woman, who kept her bed; the man said, that when he was awake he found a stone on his breast. . . .

After several weeks of tempestuous weather, and continual violent rain, on Monday night, being the 9th of January, 1748–9, were seen several flashes of lightning, attended with frequent claps of thunder, which considerably increasing, on the following night, a flash of lightning passed from west to east, in a direct line through this county; it first killed some cows to the south of Cork, and, in its progress, struck the round tower of the cathedral of Cloyne. It rent the vaulted arch at the top, tumbled down the bell and three lofts, and passing perpendicularly to the internal floor, which is about eight feet higher than the outward foundation, the protruded column of air, or lightning, or both together, by the igneous matter bursting and expanding, and not finding sufficient room, vented itself by a violent explosion, forced its way through one side of the tower, and drove the stones, which were admirably well jointed and locked into each other, through the roof of an adjacent stable; the door, though secured by a strong iron lock, was thrown above sixty yards distant into the church-yard, and shattered to pieces, which passage for the air greatly contributed to the saving of the tower. A few pigeons that frequented the top of the steeple, were scorched to death, not a feather of them being left unsinged.

On Monday June 18th, 1748, about four of the clock in the afternoon, happened the most violent storm of hail that was known in the memory of man, attended with lightning and thunder, which held above a quarter of an hour; several hail-stones measured five inches square, and others had five or six forks from the main body, of an inch long each, which broke several windows, and did other considerable damages in and about Cork.

I shall conclude this chapter with some general observations on the state of the air and weather, in this part of the kingdom.

It is observable from a regular diary of the weather, kept for several years in Cork, that the winds blow from the south to the north-west, at least three-fourths of the year: that the greatest height the mercury ascended, for the space of thirteen years past, was at 30 inches 4 tenths, and that but once only; and its lowest at 28 inches 2 tenths. It often rises to near 30 inches, and frequently falls to 28 inches 6 tenths, both which points it has rarely passed. The depth of rain, in 1738, in Cork, was 54 inches 5 tenths, and nearly the same in 1739. In 1740, but 21 inches 5 tenths. In 1741, 33 inches 6 tenths. In 1742, 38 inches 1 tenth. In 1743, 39 inches 3 tenths. In 1744, 33 inches 6 tenths. In 1745, 48 inches 4 tenths. In 1746, 30 inches. The same nearly in 1747; and in 1748, 37 inches 4 tenths. The late ingenious colonel Rye, in the year 1721, went through a course of statical experiments in this county. His observations, which relate to the effects of different seasons on the human body, are as follows.

Perspiration in winter, during the twenty-four hours, in a quite posture, within the house, was equal to the urine secreted in the same space of time, which was at least thirty-eight ounces. In summer, perspiration was double to the secretion by urine, or, at least, a third more; and when assisted by exercise, it was to what we eat and drink in proportion of five to eight nearly. In the autumn, the air being mild, perspiration was a third part more than the urine, otherwise not more than one-fifth part. In December, perspiration was a fifth part more than the urine; but in January it was as five to three. In winter, when the spirit in the thermometer stood at sixty-five, though the perspiration by day, promoted by exercise, did not exceed fifteen ounces, yet the perspiration, by being nine hours in bed, hath been forty ounces, and sometimes sixty; so that vigorous exercise by day is scarce a balance to the lying ten hours in bed in a long winter's night.

Gone West
Robert Gibbings
from: *Lovely is the Lee* (1945)

At Inchigeela the character of the country changes abruptly. No longer the swift river among broad meadows; now it is wide lakes and wild moorland, with crowded mountain peaks on all horizons. I spent a day on those lakes in early September. The boat was a small one, so short that it was almost circular, and it had but two seats, one in the bow and the other in the stern. If I sat in the stern the bow went up in the air and the water lapped the gunwale beside me. If I sat in the bow it was the stern that reared itself like the quarter of a fifteenth-century caravel.

'Stay where you are now, till I get a few stones,' said Teigue, the owner of the boat, as I balanced in the bow. He went to a wall and brought back a large boulder. 'You should have been here for the regatta,' he said, as he lifted it on to the stern seat. 'Paddy Jack Murphy and Paddy Tim Casey had the hell of a fine race. Paddy Jack had a sailor from Bantry in the boat with him, and Paddy Tim had a garda from Macroom, and the two pairs of them was old rivals.'

Teigue went for another stone. When he came back he continued the story.

'The two boats were below at the start waiting for the gun when all of a sudden Paddy Jack and the sailor started rowing. "Go on. What's keeping ye?" yelled the crowd at Paddy Tim. "We're waiting for the shot," said Paddy Tim. "Yerra never mind the shot, the gun is stuck." With that Paddy Tim and the garda started. You never saw such rowing in your life. They lifted the boat out of the water with the dint of their strokes, and they won the race.'

Teigue collected some more stones, piled them in the stern, and pushed me from the bank. The gunwale was about four inches above the water. It seemed much less.

The narrow stream, whence I sailed, soon widened into the lake. The boat moved with the current. The surface of the lake was like glass. Rich, lowland fields, backed by heather-clad hills, were mirrored in the water. Corn stooks stood on their own reflections. The edge of the lake was carpeted with white lilies. Mallard rose from a fringe of weeds. A man in a white jacket, with two black horses at the plough, was turning the green velvet of a field into brown furrows.

Faint whiffs of breeze rippled the water, lifting the edges of the lily leaves. Grey clouds were gathering on the hills to the west. While I stopped to make a drawing the wind increased. Squalls hit the lake and water splashed over the gunwale. I landed to shelter under a holly-tree while a shower swept across the valley. A man came and spoke to me. I asked him if he knew the time. He said: 'What with new time and old time and God's time it is hard to say what time it is.' He took from his pocket the works of a clock. 'It will be midday, just, by old time, but that's half an hour ahead of the sun,' he said. Then we talked for a while, and he asked: 'Are you the man is writing a book?'

'I am,' I said.

'Have you seen the Mass Rock, where they said mass when the priests was hunted?'

'I have not.'

'Come, and I'll show it to you.'

We followed the road for about half a mile, to where, under a low cliff, we found this relic of penal times, rough slabs of stone built to form an altar. 'Mass was said here 1640–1800' was inscribed on a metal disk beside it.

'Yerra there's lots of them about the country,' he said. 'There's one west at Coomataggart and there's another three miles to the south at Kilnadur. Tell me,' he added, 'did I see you with your shirt off in the boat?'

'You probably did.'

''Tis the best in the world for the rheumatics. There was a man east there beyond Clonmoyle, and he doubled up in the bed and unable to move. And the priest comes in to him, and he says: "Will you do what I tell you," he says. "I will," he said. "Go out in the sun," says the priest, "and let it roast ye." Faith a March hare couldn't catch him ever since.'

Back in the boat, the lake was calm again. I couldn't help thinking of those rough altars and of all that they implied, and the curious fact that when peoples or individuals inflict great injury on their fellow creatures they generally do so believing their actions to be right. Even Cromwell thought himself to be an instrument of God. Today the same is happening, not only in the wider spheres of life, but in our private lives. Right and wrong can be so easily defined to ourselves by what we would like to be right and wrong. It is difficult to disentangle self-interest from our politics.

Now the wind was rising again, and the lake was being whipped to silver. Wind and water were joined in wisps of spray, and waves were again coming on board. Glints of sunlight lit the cornfields, as a match flares and fades. A cormorant, so black, flew across the lake. Fifteen pounds of fish is the normal daily consumption of one of these birds.

But I was getting wet, and it became a question of me or the stones. I gave the stones the honour. Over the side they went, and

33

up went the stern. There was just clearance when I knelt amidships. And so I sailed into shelter.

'Begod 'twas on a tea-tray I thought you were,' said a man to me, as I stepped ashore.

It was on a road through this valley, to the north, that, one night, a man by the name of Patsy Kerrigan was on his way home. He was walking fast for there was a chill on the night, and, as he went, he came upon three men, and they carrying a coffin. Thinking to help them he took the fourth place, but no sooner had his shoulder touched the wood than the three men let down the coffin on the road and disappeared.

It seemed strange to Patsy. He waited a while, and a while longer, hoping they would return, but no sight or sign of them coming back. And there he was on the road, alone, with a coffin. After a while he remembered a cottage near by, where friends of his lived. So, leaving the coffin where they'd put it, he went along to his friends and he told them what had happened. They didn't know what to think of it either, for none of them knew of any one that was after dying. But they went along with Patsy, and the coffin was there on the road. And after a while they unscrewed the lid, and they opened it, and inside was a foxy-haired girl. And it seemed as if she mightn't be dead at all, for she was sweating. So they lifted her out and they took her home and, sure enough, by next morning she was able to talk to them. And she told them who she was and who were her parents and where she came from. So Patsy and one of the men in the cottage went off to tell her father, and when they found him he was digging spuds in the field below his house, and he wouldn't believe them. 'My daughter is above in bed, sick, this fortnight,' he said. Still and all, he went and had a look at her, and she was there in the bed right enough. So they had great trouble in persuading the father to go with them. But, in the latter end, he went, and, as sure as he did, it was his daughter that he found before him. You may say he was puzzled. But there was no doubt about it at all. There could be no mistake. So he took her home with him. And when he got home he took her into the bedroom, and the bed was empty. The other girl had gone. She was a changeling, d'you see. So the girl that was rescued married the man that was after taking her from the fairies, and she was sister to the grandmother of Dan Clancy who told me this.

On the other side of the lakes, in the hills to the south, there was a man by the name of Kelleher, and his wife died, and one night, a year after she died, he was in bed, in the settle-bed in the kitchen where he used to sleep, and he saw her come in and sit down at the table where she used to sit. But she said nothing. And after a while she got up and she went out. And the next night she came again, and she sat down again, and she went out again without ever a word. So the third night he prepared a meal for her and laid it on the table for her, and she came in again and she sat down in the same seat. But she never touched the meal. She didn't say a word to him, and he didn't say a word to her until, when he saw her getting up to go out, he jumped in front of her and stood in the door before her.

'Don't touch me! Don't touch me!' she said. 'Don't touch me at all!' she said.

'What can I do for you?' he said. 'Is there anything at all I can do for you?'

'There is,' she said, 'and if you want to save me you must do as I tell you. Tomorrow night,' she said, 'I'll be passing in a procession of horsemen, and I'll be up on a black horse, behind a man. You must have a ring of mountain ash on the road, with the bark peeled off, and the bare twigs sprinkled with holy water. And you must have a March cock inside, made fast with a string to your leg.' (A March cock is a bird from an egg laid and hatched in March.) 'And when you see me you must make a spring at me, and lift me down from the horse into the middle of the ring of ash, without you ever touching the horse, or the rider that's on it, or me touching a twig of the ash. And you must hold me tightly,' she said, 'when you've got a hold of me. And if you do that you'll save me.'

So Kelleher did as he was told, and he was there with the circle of ash on the road, with the bark peeled, and it all sprinkled with holy water, and the procession came along, and there was his wife, up behind another fellow, on the back of a dark slippery horse. When he seen her he made a spring at her, and he lifted her right into the circle of twigs, and no sooner did her feet touch the ground than the cock crew. And when they looked around them there wasn't a sight of the procession or the ash-twigs. So the two of them went home together, and she bore three children to him in the years that came after.

Cape Clear

Peter Somerville-Large

from: *The Coast of West Cork* (1975)

From Baltimore I took the mailboat to Cape Clear. Most times passengers face the Gascanane with dread, and are swept through white and bilious, Atlantic rollers pounding behind them. In the old days those who made the passage for the first time were expected to improvise a short poem to bring them luck and to distract them from sea-sickness. Today, even though it was early March, the weather was admirable, and the *Naomh Ciaran* made the journey under blue sky with only the suggestion of a roll. The long hump of Cape Clear rose out of the sea like a blowing whale, its steep sides scored with the pattern of fields that faded into bracken and gorse.

The Cape and Sherkin are roughly the same size, but quite different in atmosphere. The Capers have a unity which the islanders on Sherkin lack; they are remoter, proud of their isolation, and consider themselves to be living in a country of their own, where they have been able to preserve vestiges of traditional ways of life. They call the mainland 'Ireland'. Their houses, even after they are empty, are not sold to outsiders, and recent plans for a tourist hotel have been scrapped. Even the Youth Hostel is disapproved of; stories abound about unlicensed behaviour by hitch-hikers, but one feels that they may be exaggerated and that possibly the islanders resent them as intruders.

The Irish College, however, does flourish. Cape Clear, one of the few places in West Cork where Irish is widely spoken, has been classed as a Gaeltacht area. In 1966 President de Valera was flown here by helicopter to open the college, which takes in batches of students during the summer months. But the strength of the language remains in doubt. Contact with the English-speaking mainland and the summer visitors pouring in on day trips erodes the importance of Irish. As a result, the eastern end of Cape, centred around the church and the wooden bungalow of the college, has become the Irish-speaking area, whilst at the west end, where the main harbour is situated, English is largely spoken.

Coming up from the east I encountered the postman going on his rounds; he walked all round the island four days a week with the mail. Since so many islanders were named O'Driscoll or Cadogan, much time had to be spent sorting out which letters were for whom. (The name *Cadogan* is supposed to derive from a nickname bestowed upon an O'Driscoll who in one year reared a hundred calves – *céad gamhna*.) He told me that thirty-two of the houses on the east side were still occupied. They were sprinkled over green fields that sparkled in the sun with the same brilliance as the sea, divided by stone walls and continuing right down to the cliffs above the water.

In one field stood three standing stones, the largest of which had a hole cut through its centre where lovers used to pledge their vows by holding hands, a custom that probably echoed the stone's ancient cult significance. Stones elsewhere on the island had traces of Ogham writing. When I met Denis Hamish who 'spoke the English strong', he pointed out a number of little lengths of stone with curious marks that formed part of the wall in a lane. They had recently been discovered when the lane was widened to accommodate the island's cars.

Hamish could remember when Irish was spoken generally not only all over the Cape, but as far away as Macroom. Like all men of his generation he had seen the slow eclipse of the old way of life, so many houses empty, so many fields gone back to gorse. In spite of Gaeltacht grants, the population had declined to a little under two hundred, a tenth of the number here in the days before the famine. What one sees today is a ghost of the life there used to be. Once, the Capers had their own king and their own code of law which it was his duty to administer. If we are to believe Smith, they were bigger stronger men than those elsewhere, of noble character, living an ideal existence, rather like the Houyhnhnms. 'The inhabitants here are generally very simple honest people, thieving being a vice unknown among them. If a person has been found guilty of a crime, he is directly banished to the continent, which is the greatest punishment they can inflict on a criminal who endeavours all he can to remain on the island.'

Pococke, visiting Cape Clear in 1758, had less flattering impressions. 'The great vice here is drinking spirits which they do excessively even some of them say to a gallon a day. . . . They were alarm'd at seeing our boat thinking it was the Kings as they had laid in great store of Rum from the West India fleet which had lately pass'd.'

Geographically the island is almost divided into two parts by the sea. An isthmus, overlooked by the main village of Cummer, divides the north and south harbours. The north harbour, by far the most sheltered, is mainly used now. But a century ago the south harbour was the scene of immense activity. During the American Civil War there was a telegraph station there with a submarine cable linked to Sherkin, Baltimore and Europe. Ships from America would stop off at the harbour, their first landfall after the Atlantic crossing, and throw the mails into the sea wrapped in waterproof cases. These would be picked up by the islanders' boats, the first there usually receiving a guinea. The latest bulletins about the war, or the assassination of Lincoln, would then be sent by cable to London.

The Protestant church and rectory also overlooked the south harbour. The rectory, now the Youth Hostel, survives, but the church was demolished some time after 1917 when the Protestant congregation was reduced to two families. The stones were carted over to Schull, where they were used to build the Munster and Leinster Bank, alternatively serving God and Mammon. The church had been built in 1850 by the Reverend Edward Rice, who had arrived on the Cape in 1846 when the distress caused by the famine had just begun. During the following years he made a number of converts. 'They took the soup and ate hairy bacon', a Caper told me. The question of 'souping' is a delicate and emotional one; many proselytizing clergymen have been unjustly accused of this unpleasant form of pressure. But Mr Rice's reputation as a souper has been maintained over the years.

The north harbour is an inlet completely hidden from the storms outside; boats slip through a narrow passage into the heart of the cliffs. Here is the centre of island life, a tranquil haven completely protected by a wall of gorse-covered cliff, its waters gently lapping against the little beach and the shrine of St Kieran. An inner harbour, constructed by the old Fishery Board, was for many years a safe anchorage for trawlers to weather out winter storms.

On the edge of the inner harbour stands the bird observatory established in 1959. The island's situation in the centre of a number of migratory routes makes it an ideal place for watching birds, and a detailed record of sightings has been kept for over a decade. The observatory, converted from a farmhouse, is not a luxurious establishment. Bunks are provided upstairs with blankets as rough as hair shirts. Outside the privy is tacked a notice: 'Gentlemen. . . . If Possible Use the Bushes at the East End of the House. Not the Elsan, Thank-you.' In the main room downstairs are kept the items of equipment indispensable to the ornithologist — nets, rings, weighing scales, clippers, maps — and the attractive postcards of birds and island landscapes, designed by Robert Gilmore, which are on sale to visitors. Reports and registers are filled in each day — the seawatch log, the daily census, the rarity log which shows the more unusual birds that have been sighted. A tin collecting box marked *New Species* has a label: 'We hope that observers will join in the tradition of donating 6*d*. for each new species they see on the island.'

Many of the ornithologists who come to the Cape are English, bird-watching being very much an Anglo-Saxon pastime. They record the passing of each day in minute detail. 'A bout of gastritis put the Major out of action on the second. . . .' 'The arrival of John Dixon and myself coincided neatly with the arrival of one of the most interesting birds of the period — a buff-breasted sandpiper which spent nine days on the island. . . .'

I stayed with Tom and Stephanie Green, who were the first ornithologists to spend a complete year on Cape Clear. Their enthusiasm might be gauged from the fact that during the first months of their stay Stephanie was expecting the birth of her first child. They did not live in the observatory, but away to the east in 'The Glen', a valley once densely populated, but now full of empty houses and bracken-covered fields. The cottage they had found possessed the comfort of a bathroom. Outside on the balcony were strings of rabbit skins intended to be used for making clothes for the baby. The rabbits provided an unending substitute for the Sunday joint.

Tom worked from early dawn until the lack of light made bird-watching impossible. On successive days a different part of the island would be explored. Bogs, bushes, the few trees were minutely examined and each sighting tabulated. Robins, yellowhammers, wheatears, choughs. Occasionally a rarity would be sighted that sent a *frisson* through the ornithologist's world. Unusual birds seen on the island have included a rustic bunting, a blackbrowed albatross, a great shearwater, and once five eagles were observed flying in a group. In the evening Tom had further work filling up log books and adding to the collection of ticks which were being sent to a researching professor. Most of them came from the neck of a large grey cat.

For several mornings I accompanied him on his expeditions, setting off at dawn. Spring comes early in this south-west corner of the country; there were primroses already in the grassy banks and bird song everywhere. Above the cottage a track led to the ruined lighthouse and signal tower. The tower had been built at the same time as the one above Baltimore, and formed part of the same system of communication. The lighthouse, which came a few years later, was completed by 1810; its light could be seen for twenty-eight miles out to sea. Unfortunately the site proved unsatisfactory. It was too far inland and in foggy weather the light could not be seen clearly by passing ships. Its inadequacy was emphasized in 1847, when an American ship, the *Stephen Whitney*, struck a rock and went down with the loss of a hundred lives. Shortly after this tragedy, work began on the construction of a lighthouse on the Fastnet Rock.

The broken coastline was particularly dangerous, and in the nineteenth century hardly a year went by without some notable shipwreck on the cliffs of the island. In one year, 1867, for example, the *Cork Advertiser* reported two such wrecks. 'The ship, *Czar*, of Glasgow was a few days ago found deserted off Cape Clear. She was loaded with iron and coal, and when picked up bore traces of having sustained a severe gale. Not a living creature was on board.' A few weeks later: 'Since Sunday 8th, several boxes and pieces of wreck have been picked up at sea by the owners of boats belonging to Long Island and Cape Clear, and it is feared from papers also found, that the vessel wrecked was the *Enoch Ebner* of Boston, commanded by Captain Jefferson Ebner. . . .'

Down the steep track to the west we passed through the village of Cummer, straddled between the north and south harbours, where among the line of whitewashed cottages were two pubs where groceries could be bought. On one day we made a detour to the north-west, past the observatory across the fields to Dunanore. The Golden Fort is perhaps the most dramatically sited of the O'Driscoll castles, set among cliffs and sea birds on what is virtually a small island. At one time a narrow causeway linked it to the mainland; now it can just be reached by a hazardous climb over tumbled rocks. Built in the thirteenth century, it was a typical three-storeyed structure placed in a seemingly impregnable look-out position over the bay and the mainland. In later times, however, its situation proved no adequate defence from attack by land, and after the Battle of Kinsale, Captain Roger Harvey captured it by placing his guns on the high ground above it. Only the shattered tower and part of the original walls remain, while chunks of masonry dislodged by cannon and by centuries of storm are scattered among the rocks.

According to Donovan, there are many stories of treasure about Dunanore, as its name would imply. A ghost ship arrives there at night and a ghostly crew fills up the castle with treasure. In the early eighteenth century a soldier stationed on the island, excited by the stories he had heard, dug at the foot of the castle for gold. The pit can still be seen.

A few years later, a famous giant, Cruathuir O'Careavaun, retired here as a hermit, dying in the castle. He was over eight feet high and had great strength; once in Cork harbour he lifted up a ship's anchor which the whole crew had been unable to budge, even with the aid of a windlass.

On another day we took the path to the south-west past Lough Errul, on the edge of whose placid waters are a number of stone basins once used for cleaning flax. The lake is supposed to have special cleansing properties. At the far side of the hill overlooking the Atlantic are lines of stones known as the *Fir Breaga*, or False Men. *Fir Breaga* is a general term for standing stones; throughout the country many are known as False Men, possibly an indication of phallic associations. On Cape Clear the tradition goes further, and this line of unimpressive stones, so the story goes, was set up literally as false men to give the impression that the island was guarded. They look directly out to sea and, either painted red or dressed in red tunics and hats to resemble soldiers, they frightened off the French who were on their way to Bantry.

Below them were jagged cliffs speckled with yellow lichen and the droppings of innumerable birds that nested there. The steep gully of Foildermotycronacane dividing us from the long Bill of Cape was swept by shrieking gulls. At Breen rock, another bare promontory, Tom had his hide, consisting of a wall of stones overlooking the sea. Here he settled to watch the birds. A line of gannets making a purposeful flight, their long white wings tipped with black almost touching the sea, disappeared due south. There were auks, terns and squalling herring gulls. In a few weeks the great westward passage would begin, when the migrating flights would pass in great numbers. On some days one or two thousand fulmars an hour pass this way.

In summer, in July, this would be a good place for watching the Fastnet race, when the expanse of sea is covered with yachts tacking towards the rock. After they wheel around the lighthouse, their multicoloured spinnakers are set to catch the west wind which will carry them past the Cape once more on their way home to Plymouth.

I left Tom and made my way to the north harbour where the arrival of the mailboat caused the daily flutter of activity. Bales of straw and corrugated roofing were unloaded and the few passengers stumped uphill towards Cummer. Loaves of bread were transferred into a donkey-cart and taken away and within a few minutes the harbour was deserted as before.

Against the pier lay the rotting hulls of the *Carbery Lass* and the smaller *St. Patrick*. Once this small harbour was packed with ships. In 1920 there had been forty-three trawlers based on the island, including a schooner of a hundred and thirty tons. As elsewhere, the cessation of fishing sadly emphasizes the steady decline in population.

The majority of islanders always relied on fishing to augment their income from farming. They were equally at home on the rolling deck of a ship or behind a plough on their land. The famine was the first break in this pattern of life, and many of the emigrants who left the island after 1847 made their way to Newfoundland where they continued to employ their fishing skills by working on the dories. Thirty years afterwards fishing revived on Cape Clear and became a thriving trade. With the aid of grants men could buy new ships and fish on a commercial basis. The first fleet of new mackerel vessels arrived here in 1877 from the Isle of Man where they had been built. They were substantial ships compared to those formerly used, weighing twenty-four tons and carrying a crew of eight men. Their sails included a topsail, mainsail, foresail and mizen. Without engines the task of slipping through the walls of the cliff into the shelter of the harbour must have been formidable.

> The harbour of Trawkieran
> I saw it in its pride
> With its fleet of yacht-like fishing boats
> Awaiting for the tide.

The men would fish mainly for mackerel and herring, which were caught in long drift nets or by the obsolete long lines, laid out in distant locations as far away as Dursey and the Bull Rock. It was slow and laborious work in an open boat. Lewis, writing in his *Topographical History of Ireland* of the previous generation of Capers in 1837, considered that 'the men are expert and resolute fishermen, and the best pilots on the coast; they are remarkable for discerning land at a distance in snowy or foggy weather, possessing an uncommon sagacity in discovering the approach of bad weather and are exceedingly skilful in the management of their vessels.' Even today the old fishermen are remembered with something like reverence: 'Giants of men . . . not like those of today. One of them could throw Cassius Clay over his shoulder.' As for their appetites: 'For breakfast one would eat two pounds of butter, six oranges, between nine and sixteen herrings and a large crock of jam.' In the evenings a man would swallow down a bucketful of potatoes.

The Cape, along with the rest of West Cork, was hit by the American tariffs discouraging the export of mackerel. This move, coupled with factors like emigration and the change in fishing methods — trawling taking the place of drift nets — killed the old way of life. Some people blame part of the decline on injurious government policy. 'The wholesale neglect of the pelegaic fisheries,' wrote John Boland, a Skibbereen man, in 1948, 'robs the part-time fisherman of a source of income which was essential to his well-being.' On the Cape there are four fishing boats left; all of these use Bearhaven as their base and return to the island at the weekends.

But in the evening in the pubs the talk is still all about boats and fishing. Nearly all Capers have a connection with the sea. Many became merchant seamen and sailed all over the world before retiring here. An old sailor showed me his souvenirs which included a pile of pamphlets he had obtained on Hong Kong depicting Chairman Mao, whose bland features gazed up quizzically at the Sacred Heart and St Patrick which adorned his little kitchen.

Drifts of conversation come across the bar in Cotter's pub. 'I was seven hundred miles off the Cape when the last war started. . . .' '. . . the man who built that boat had no conscience — it was designed like a submarine. . . .' Mick Donoghue, a big red-headed sailor, can remember the names of all the mackerel boats and who owned them . . . the *Gabriel*, *St Ultan*, *St Agnes*, and the *St Patrick* which he himself still owns and has completely rebuilt during the last few years. A man at the back complains that in England he was charged two shillings and sixpence for a mackerel, when once he used to sell them for one and six a hundred. He had asked the waitress for a receipt to prove it to his friends living here. . . .

Cape Clear is held to be the birthplace of St Kieran, whose feast day is celebrated on the fifth of March, a fortnight before the festival of St Patrick. Possibly the choice of an earlier date was made deliberately by those who believed that St Kieran preceded St Patrick in bringing Christianity to Ireland. He is said to have been born in A.D. 352, and therefore to have been thirty years older than the country's patron, with a good head start for missionary activities.

But speculation about his life is unreliable. The dictionary of saints declares emphatically that 'most of what is related about him, however entertaining or edifying, has no value as sober history'.

On the Cape such austere rulings of scholars have been ignored. The island is filled with traces of him. Behind the strand of Kieran or 'Trawkieran' in the south harbour is his holy well and beside it a standing stone engraved with a cross, said to have been incised by the saint's own hand. If this were so, the stone would be the earliest Christian relic in Ireland. A short distance away the shell of a Romanesque church, also called after St Kieran, stands on the site of a much older building. The islanders claim that on this spot was celebrated the first mass ever held in Ireland. In 1969 mass was said here again after a gap of four hundred and fifty years. Anyone buried within the walls of the churchyard goes straight to heaven. From the amount of tombstones that crowd every inch of space it would seem that the islanders have left little to chance. The giant, Cruathuir O'Careavaun, is buried here in a large grave.

On the evening of the fourth of March the first pilgrimage is made to the shrine. Up until Marian year this spot consisted simply of the stone and the well. But now the white figure of the Virgin stands under a wing of concrete, and the wall beneath her feet through which water trickles down to the beach has been boxed in. Around her are clustered some tins of flowers. She holds a battery and bulb in her outstretched hand, and a bicycle lamp shines up from the ground.

Pilgrims used to walk to the well from all over the island. Today many of them come in cars. On the one narrow tarred road, the islanders' cars and tractors tend to get congested. There are no policemen, and regulations about road taxation, maintenance and safety are not too stringently observed. Cars, which would have been sent to the scrap heap long ago, find a new lease of life when they are shipped over the Gascanane. This evening all peace is shattered by the crackle of exhausts, as ancient Fords and Volkswagens drive down the hill from Cummer to the strand. On one the mudguards flap wildly as if at any moment it might take off and fly; another has a new plywood door, and a third hurtles through the dusk guided only by a pale flickering amber light. All are eaten away with rust, so that some fenders and mudguards look like old lace. Tonight they are parked near the shrine and families walk down to pray for a few moments. Beyond Cummer there is a flash from the Fastnet, and a ship, all lighted up, is swallowed by the sea.

Next morning another pilgrimage takes place before sunrise, but by the time I get down at nine o'clock only one man is kneeling by the standing stone, which is decorated with limp arum-lily leaves held down by pebbles. His name is O'Driscoll like so many of the islanders, and he has a thin hatchet face like an early saint.

After he has prayed I watch him fill up a bottle of water from the well. He says that it is used as a cure by most people, and moreover, because it is holy, it never goes bad. He has a bottle at home which was collected twenty years ago and is as fresh and sweet as the day it was taken. He tells me the story of the fishermen, from neighbouring Long Island, who drew some of this water for their kettle.

'Naturally it wouldn't boil. And for months afterwards, as a punishment for them, their kettle wouldn't boil up any water at all.'

The Groves of Blarney
Richard Millikin

I

The groves of Blarney,
They look so charming,
Down by the purlings
Of sweet silent brooks,
All decked by posies
That spontaneous grow there,
Planted in order,
In the rocky nooks.
'Tis there the daisy,
And the sweet carnation,
The blooming pink,
And the rose so fair;
Likewise the lily,
And the daffodilly —
All flowers that scent
The sweet open air.

II

'Tis Lady Jeffers
Owns this plantation;
Like Alexander,
Or like Helen fair;
There's no commander
In all the nation,
For regulation
Can with her compare.
Such walls surround her,
That no nine-pounder
Could ever plunder
Her place of strength;
But Oliver Cromwell,
Her he did pommel,
And made a breach
In her battlement.

III

There is a cave where
No daylight enters,
But cats and badgers
Are for ever bred;
And mossed by nature
Makes it completer
Than a coach-and-six,
Or a downy-bed.
'Tis there the lake is
Well stored with fishes,
And comely eels in
The verdant mud;
Besides the leeches,
And groves of beeches,
Standing in order
To guard the flood.

IV

There gravel walks are
For recreation,
And meditation
In sweet solitude.
'Tis there the lover
May hear the dove, or
The gentle plover,
In the afternoon;
And if a lady
Would be so engaging
As for to walk in
Those shady groves,
'Tis there the courtier
Might soon transport her
Into some 'fort,' or
The 'sweet rock-close.'

V

There are statues gracing
This noble place in —
All heathen gods,
And nymphs so fair;
Bold Neptune, Caesar,
And Nebuchadnezzar,
All standing naked
In the open air!
There is a boat on
The lake to float on,
And lots of beauties
Which I can't entwine;
But were I a preacher,
Or a classic teacher,
In every feature
I'd make 'em shine!

VI

There is a stone there,
That whoever kisses,
Oh! he never misses
To grow eloquent.
'Tis he may clamber
To a lady's chamber,
Or become a member
Of parliament:
A clever spouter
He'll sure turn out, or
An out-an-outer,
'To be let alone',
Don't hope to hinder him,
Or to bewilder him;
Sure he's a pilgrim
From the Blarney stone![1]

[1]. *The last verse is said to have been composed by Francis Sylvester Mahony (Father Prout).*

Gougane Barra

J. J. Callanan

There is a green island in lone Gougane Barra,
Where Allua of songs rushes forth as an arrow;
In deep-vallied Desmond — a thousand wild fountains
Come down to that lake, from their home in the mountains.
There grows the wild ash, and a time-stricken willow
Looks chidingly down on the mirth of the billow;
As, like some gay child, that sad monitor scorning,
It lightly laughs back to the laugh of the morning.

And its zone of dark hills — oh! to see them all bright'ning,
When the tempest flings out its red banner of lightning;
And the waters rush down, 'mid the thunder's deep rattle,
Like clans from their hills at the voice of the battle;
And brightly the fire-crested billows are gleaming,
And wildly from Mullagh the eagles are screaming.
Oh! where is the dwelling in valley, or highland,
So meet for a bard as this lone little island!

How oft when the summer sun rested on Clara,
And lit the dark heath on the hills of Ivera,
Have I sought thee, sweet spot, from my home by the ocean,
And trod all thy wilds with a Minstrel's devotion,
And thought of thy bards, when assembling together
In the cleft of thy rocks, or the depth of thy heather,
They fled from the Saxon's dark bondage and slaughter,
And waked their last song by the rush of thy water.

High sons of the lyre, oh! how proud was the feeling,
To think while alone through that solitude stealing,
Though loftier Minstrels green Erin can number,
I only awoke your wild harp from its slumber,
And mingled once more with the voice of those fountains,
The songs even echo forgot on her mountains,
And gleaned each grey legend, that darkly was sleeping
Where the mist and the rain o'er their beauty was creeping.

Least bard of the hills! were it mine to inherit
The fire of thy harp, and the wing of thy spirit,
With the wrongs which like thee to our country has bound me,
Did your mantle of song fling its radiance around me,
Still, still in those wilds may young liberty rally,
And send her strong shout over mountain and valley,
The star of the west may yet rise in its glory,
And the land that was darkest, be brightest in story.

I too shall be gone; but my name shall be spoken
When Erin awakens, and her fetters are broken;
Some Minstrel will come, in the summer eve's gleaming,
When Freedom's young light on his spirit is beaming,
And bend o'er my grave with a tear of emotion,
Where calm Avon Buee seeks the kisses of ocean,
Or plant a wild wreath, from the banks of that river,
O'er the heart, and the harp, that are sleeping for ever.

A Letter from Kinsale, 1747

Henry Pringle

Kinsale, 5th Feby., 1747

'This place is become by use a little more familiar to me, yet really it is a very vile hole, and yet I'm told there are many much worse quarters, and more lonely in this part of Ireland: however it is no small comfort to me that we are pretty well assur'd we shall go to Dublin in June, tho' the Regt. was there last Winter, but they say Genl. Otway, being an Invalid, has made an exchange with Genl. Irwin, whose Regt. was to succeed Folliott's there: Others tell us we shall go to Flanders. You complain I did not send the account of the Fire to Dublin, which I really did by the first following post; it happen'd on Wednesday and on Friday — I was in bed when the drum beat to arms between eleven and twelve, and you may imagine my thoughts when, from my window, the Town seem'd all on fire. The distance from the Barrack to the Prison is about the same as from Cork Hill (Dublin) to the College, but you can't form to yourself the least idea of the kind of street it is; on one side all rocks, and on t'other holes and dunghills: there are perpetual springs from those rocks, which make them slippery and very dangerous, the place where the guard is reliev'd is like the steepest in Wine Tavern Street, but as narrow and dirty again: it was down this street I ran that night without buckles or garters and in my Night Cap — I was told the French Prisoners were all thro' the streets, but when I got there, the officer of the Guard was removing them into another prison, where Spaniards are kept — All was done that possibly could be to save the poor Creatures, but those that were lost, being 54 in number, perish'd before it was possible to relieve them, the fire beginning with great fury at the Door, and they had no other passage out. I do not remember to have seen so dreadful a Night both of Wind and rain, and if it had blown but the smallest degree on either side of that it did, the whole town would have been burn't. With the utmost difficulty it was at last extinguish'd by the help of two fire-engines, when it had burn't the Prison and had seiz'd the adjoining Houses. The muster of the Prisoners next day was a melancholy sight, most of them having lost Relations or friends, and the smell from the ruins of the fire was intolerable.

It was a Portugueze set it on fire by making a Candle-stick of Straw, and the room being cover'd with their straw beds, as dry as tinder, it was in a blaze in an instant, and the House being slated kept it longer undiscover'd for it was not known until a Frenchman, to avoid the Flames, broke thro' the Slates and leap't down: the Centinel fir'd at him not knowing the reason of his coming out, which gave the Alarm.'

A Dream of Munster's Arcadia
William Trevor
from: *Excursions in the Real World* (1993)

All memory is grist to the fiction-writer's mill. The pleasure and the pain experienced by any storyteller's characters, the euphoria of happiness, the ache of grief, must of course be the storyteller's own. It cannot be otherwise, and in that sense all fiction has its autobiographical roots, spreading through — in my case — a provincial world, limited and claustrophobic.

I grew up in what John Betjeman called 'the small towns of Ireland' — in my case, Mitchelstown, cut down to size by the towering Galtee mountains and the Knockmealdowns, Youghal by the sea, Skibbereen lost somewhere in the back of beyond.

There were others besides, but to these three in County Cork I return most frequently. Mitchelstown is still famous for its martyrs and its processed cheese, a squat little town, looking as though someone has sat on it. A good business town, my father used to say.

Youghal, smartly elegant in my memory, is tatty on a wet afternoon. A carful of German tourists crawls along the seafront, the misty beach is empty. Once, people pointed here and remarked: I listened and my eavesdroppings told of an afternoon love affair conducted on that brief promenade, he a married doctor, she a lady in disgrace. I see them now as I made them in my fascination: she is thin, and dressed in red, laughing, with pale long hair; he is Ronald Coleman with a greyer moustache. They smile at one another; defiantly he touches her hand. They are breathtaking in their sinning, and all their conversation is beautiful; they are the world's most exciting people.

I walk away from their romance, not wanting to tell myself that they were not like that. On the sands where old seaside artists sprinkled garish colours the rain is chilly. Pierrots performed here, and the man and woman who rode the Wall of Death sunned themselves at midday. From the Loreto Convent we trooped down here to run the end-of-term races, Sister Therese in charge. The sands haven't changed, nor have the concrete façades of the holiday boarding-houses, nor the Protestant church with its holes for lepers to peer through. But Horgan's Picture House is not at all as it was. It has two screens now and a different name, and there are sexual fantasies instead of Jack Hulbert in Round the Washtub.

In Youghal there was a man who shot himself in a henhouse. Life had been hell for this man, the voices whispered, and the henhouse, quite near the back of our garden, developed an eeriness that the chatter of birds made even more sinister. The henhouse isn't there any more, but even so as I stand where it was I shudder, and remember other deaths.

Youghal itself died in a way, for yellow furniture vans — Nat Ross of Cork — carted our possessions off, through Cork itself, westward through the town that people call Clonakilty God Help Us, to Skibbereen, at the back of beyond.

Memory focuses here, the images are clearer. Horses and carts in the narrow streets, with milk churns for the creamery. On fair-days farmers with sticks standing by their animals, their shirts clean for the occasion, without collar or tie. A smell of whiskey, and sawdust and stout and dung. Pots of geraniums among chops and ribs in the small windows of butchers' shops. A sun-burnt poster advertising the arrival of Duffy's Circus a year ago.

It was a mile and a half, the journey to school through the town, past Driscoll's sweetshop and Murphy's Medical Hall and Power's drapery, where you could buy oilcloth as well as dresses. In Shannon's grocery there was a man who bred smooth-haired fox-terriers. He gave us one once, a strange animal, infatuated by our cat.

In the town's approximate centre, where four streets meet, a grey woman still stands, a statue of the Maid of Erin. E O'Donovan, undertaker, still sells ice-cream and chocolate. The brass plate of Redmond O'Regan, solicitor, once awkwardly high, is now below eye-level. In the grocers' shops the big-jawed West Cork women buy bread and sausages and tins of plums, but no longer wear the heavy black cloaks that made them seem like figures from another century. They still speak in the same West Cork lisp, a swift voice, difficult for strangers. I ask one if she could tell me the way to a house I half remember. 'Ah, I could tell you grand,' she replies. 'It's dead and buried, sir.'

The door beside the Methodist church, once green, is purple. The church, small and red-brick, stands behind high iron railings and gates, with gravel in front of it. Beyond the door that used to be green is the dank passage that leads to Miss Willoughby's schoolroom, where first I learnt that the world is not an easy-going place. Miss Willoughby was stern and young, in love with the cashier from the Provincial Bank.

On the gravel in front of the red-brick church I vividly recall Miss Willoughby. Terribly, she appears. Severe and beautiful, she pedals against the wind on her huge black bicycle. 'Someone laughed during prayers,' she accuses, and you feel at once that it was you although you know it wasn't. 'V poor' she writes in your headline book when you've done your best to reproduce, four times, perfectly, 'Pride goeth before destruction'.

As I stand on the gravel, her evangelical eyes seem again to dart over me without pleasure. Once I took the valves out of the tyres of her bicycle. Once I looked in her answer book.

I am late, I am stupid. I cannot write 20 sentences on A Day in the Life of an Old Shoe. I cannot do simple arithmetic or geography. I am always fighting with Jasper Swanton. I move swiftly on the gravel, out on to the street and into the bar of the Eldon Hotel: in spectral form or otherwise, Miss Willoughby will not be there.

Illusions fall fast in the narrow streets of Skibbereen, as elsewhere they have fallen. Yet for me, once there was something more enduring, nicest thing of all. Going to Cork it was called, 52 miles in the old Renault, 30 miles an hour because my mother wouldn't permit speed. On St Stephen's Day to the pantomime in the Opera House, and on some other occasion to see the White Horse Inn, which my father had heard was good. In Cork my appendix was removed because Cork's surgical skill was second to none. In Cork my tongue was cut to rid me of my incoherent manner of speaking. *To* Cork, every day of my childhood, I planned to run away.

Twice a year perhaps, on Saturday afternoons, there was going to Cork to the pictures. Clark Gable and Myrna Loy in Too Hot to Handle. Mr. Deeds Goes to Town. No experience in my whole childhood, and no memory, has remained as deeply etched as these escapes to the paradise that was Cork. Nothing was more lovely or more wondrous than Cork itself, with its magnificent array of cinemas, the Pavilion, the Savoy, the Palace, the Ritz, the Lee, and the Hadji Bey's Turkish Delight factory. Tea in the Pavilion or the Savoy, the waitresses with silver-plated tea-pots and buttered bread and cakes, and other people eating fried eggs with rashers and chipped potatoes at half-past four in the afternoon. The sheer sophistication of the Pavilion or the Savoy could never be adequately conveyed to a friend in Skibbereen who had not had the good fortune to experience it. The gentleman's lavatory in the Victoria Hotel had to be seen to be believed, the Munster Arcade left you gasping. For ever and for ever you could sit in the middle stalls of the Pavilion watching Claudette Colbert, or Spencer Tracy as a priest, and the earthquake in San Francisco. And for ever afterwards you could sit while a green-clad waitress carried the silver-plated tea-pot to you, with cakes and buttered bread. All around you was the clatter of life and of the city, and men of the world conversing and girls' laughter tinkling. Happiness was everywhere.

The Rakes of Mallow
Edward Lysaght

Beauing, belleing, dancing, drinking,
Breaking windows, damning, sinking,
Ever raking, never thinking,
            Live the rakes of Mallow.

Spending faster than it comes,
Beating waiters, bailiffs, duns,
Bacchus' true begotten sons,
            Live the rakes of Mallow.

One time naught but claret drinking,
Then like politicians thinking
To raise the sinking funds when sinking,
            Live the rakes of Mallow.

When at home with dadda dying,
Still for Mallow water crying;
But where there's good claret plying
            Live the rakes of Mallow.

Living short but merry lives;
Going where the devil drives;
Having sweethearts, but no wives,
                Live the rakes of Mallow.

Racking tenants, stewards teasing,
Swiftly spending, slowly raising,
Wishing to spend all their days in
                Raking as at Mallow.

Then to end this raking life
They get sober, take a wife,
Ever after live in strife,
                And wish again for Mallow.

A Garage in Co. Cork

Derek Mahon

from: *Selected Poems* (1991)

Surely you paused at this roadside oasis
In your nomadic youth, and saw the mound
Of never-used cement, the curious faces,
The soft-drink ads and the uneven ground
Rainbowed with oily puddles, where a snail
Had scrawled its slimy, phosphorescent trail.

Like a frontier store-front in an old western
It might have nothing behind it but thin air,
Building materials, fruit boxes, scrap iron,
Dust-laden shrubs and coils of rusty wire,
A cabbage white fluttering in the sodden
Silence of an untended kitchen garden —

Nirvana! But the cracked panes reveal a dark
Interior echoing with the cries of children.
Here in this quiet corner of Co. Cork
A family ate, slept, and watched the rain
Dance clean and cobalt the exhausted grit
So that the mind shrank from the glare of it.

Where did they go? South Boston? Cricklewood?
Somebody somewhere thinks of this as home,
Remembering the old pumps where they stood,
Antique now, squirting juice into a chrome
Lagonda or a dung-caked tractor while
A cloud swam on a cloud-reflecting tile.

Surely a whitewashed sun-trap at the back
Gave way to hens, wild thyme, and the first few
Shadowy yards of an overgrown cart track,
Tyres in the branches such as Noah knew —
Beyond, a swoop of mountain where you heard,
Disconsolate in the haze, a single blackbird.

Left to itself, the functional will cast
A death-bed glow of picturesque abandon.
The intact antiquities of the recent past,
Dropped from the retail catalogues, return
To the materials that gave rise to them
And shine with a late sacramental gleam.

A god who spent the night here once rewarded
Natural courtesy with eternal life —
Changing to petrol pumps, that they be spared
For ever there, an old man and his wife.
The virgin who escaped his dark design
Sanctions the townland from her prickly shrine.

We might be anywhere but are in one place only,
One of the milestones of earth-residence
Unique in each particular, the thinly
Peopled hinterland serenely tense —
Not in the hope of a resplendent future
But with a sure sense of its intrinsic nature.

Bantry Bay and Glengarriff

Mr and Mrs Hall

from: *Hall's Ireland* (1841)

The far-famed Bay of Bantry is perhaps unsurpassed by any harbour of the kingdom for natural advantages combined with natural beauties. As we approach it along the dreary road from Skibbereen, a sudden turn at the base of a rugged hill brings us suddenly within view of the most striking objects which make up the glorious scene. Far and away in the distance tower the lofty Mangerton and Macgillicuddy's Reeks; nearer, rises Hungry Hill, the Sugar Loaf and at long range, the Caha mountains among which it is said there are no fewer than three hundred and sixty-five lakes — the number having of course suggested a legend that some holy saint prayed for a lake to supply water for each day of the year.

Little flat and fertile islands lie at the feet of the spectator and nearly facing the town is Whiddy Island with its fierce-looking fortifications and its fields rich with promised harvest.

The road into the town — a town that has been truly described as a seaport without trade, a harbour without shipping and a coast with a failing fishery — runs immediately under the fine demesne of the Earl of Bantry, and all the way it is one continued line of beauty, where one never loses sight of the distant mountains or the foreground of green islands.

There are not many islands in this vast expanse of water; Whiddy is the largest, but there are also Hog, Horse, Coney and Chapel flung into the glorious bay. The bay is memorable in history as having been twice entered by a French force for the invasion of Ireland: the first time in 1689 in aid of James II, the next in 1796.

To visit Glengarriff, the tourist may proceed either by land or by water across the bay. It is obvious that the best mode is to go by one and return by the other, and both offer strong temptations to the lover of the picturesque. Those however who take it in their route to Killarney and do not design to make any stay at Bantry had better continue on by road, for the Bay may be seen fully from the hills above either Bantry or Glengarriff, or at all events by taking a boat a mile or two from the shores of either.

The road is exceedingly wild and picturesque. A short distance from the town the Mialloch, 'the murmuring river', is crossed by a small bridge, a little way below which is the Fall of Dunamarc, a precipice of some thirty or forty feet over rocks of the most fantastic forms. Close to it we saw a water-mill in full work, driven by the diverted current from the cataract.

In this immediate vicinity, according to one of the fanciful traditions, the first human foot trod upon Irish ground, Ladra having effected a landing in Ireland exactly forty days before the flood.

After passing three or four miles of good road and comparatively cultivated land, we entered a rough and rugged district with barren hills towering over us at either side and among them rapid streams rushing over gigantic stones down into the valleys. We passed on the right an interesting object — a little chapel nestling among the barren hills, and a short way further on we passed one of those singular dwelling places that are by no means rare in this part of the country. We were startled by a human form issuing from a huge mass of rocks and, upon inquiry, learned that a family actually lived in a hole which the rocks protected and sheltered; the rocks had evidently fallen ages ago in the position which they retained, enclosing and covering a natural chamber.

On entering we found a woman with three children; the man was at work in the adjacent 'garden' and here they contrived to exist during the summer months, for we ascertained that in winter they quitted it for some neighbouring town where they worked or begged according to their circumstances. The woman replied to our few questions with cheerfulness and civility, and to an expression approaching condolence as to the misery of her lot, replied, 'It's bad enough sure yer honour, but there's many have worse places to lay their four bones in.'

Language utterly fails to convey even a limited idea of the exceeding beauty of Glengarriff — the rough glen — which merits to the full the enthusiastic praise that has been lavished on it by every traveller by whom it has been visited.

It is a deep alpine valley, enclosed by precipitous hills, about three miles in length and seldom exceeding a quarter of a mile in breadth. Black and savage rocks enclose a scene of surpassing loveliness; beyond is the magnificent bay with its numerous islands, by one of which it is so guarded and sheltered as to give it the aspect of a serene lake.

The mountains are of all forms, altitudes and outlines; the most prominent amongst them is the Sugar-loaf, Slieve-na-goil, 'the mountain of the wild people', with its conical head soaring up into the clouds and to the rear, but at a considerable distance, Hungry Hill, with its naked and meagre sides down which runs a stream from the lake on its summit, which, gathering as it goes, breaks into a tremendous cataract of eight hundred feet, and flings out a spray around it that seems to cover a third part of the hill with a thick mist.

From the road to Kenmare the surpassing loveliness of the valley and the full glory of the bay will be seen to perfection. For three or four miles the traveller winds around the side of mountain along a steep and weary road barren of interest. Suddenly he arrives on the brow of the hill; he is over the glen, many thousands of feet above the ocean which he beholds stretching out into space, while the islands appear as dots around it; the river that runs through the valley has dwindled to a white thread, the trees have gathered into masses and the hill upon which he stood a while ago now seems no bigger than a fairy mound. Midway down are scattered cottages which only the pale smoke distinguishes from mole heaps. Thin and narrow streams, like snow wreaths, are running from the mountains into the lakes that send them forth again to fertilise the valley.

The village of Glengarriff consists of but a few houses; there is a little inn, happily situated at the head of the bay, and the glen is divided between two proprietors — Lord Bantry, and the widow of his brother, Colonel White. His lordship has a small lodge where he generally resides, in a valley away from a view of the sea, but the other seat skirts the left of the bay, is cultivated to the water's edge and commands a view of the principal island on which is built a Martello Tower — as if for the express purpose of giving interest and value to the demesne.

The old bridge, now a ruin, which in ancient times was on the high road to Berehaven, is called Cromwell's Bridge, and as history is silent as to the origin of the name we must have recourse to tradition.

When Oliver was passing through the glen to visit the O'Sullivans, he had so much trouble in getting across the narrow but rushing river that he told the inhabitants if they did not build him a bridge by the time he returned he would hang up a man for every hour's delay he met with.

'So the bridge was ready agin he came back,' quoth our informant, 'for they knew the ould villain to be a man of his word.'

West of Glengarriff is the promontory of Berehaven, separating Bantry Bay from the Kenmare River. It is a wild and primitive district, abounding in picturesque and romantic scenery, full of legends, with historical associations of great interest and possessing the ruins of many castles of the O'Sullivans, who were for centuries the lords of the soil, although their descendants are now but the hewers of stone and the drawers of water; of the castle of Dunboy, the ancient stronghold of the O'Sullivans, only a few walls remain, barely sufficient to point out its locality.

In the parish of Berehaven is worked one of the few profitable mines of Ireland. It is situated on the property of a Mr. Puxley and was discovered some thirty years ago, by a very minute scrutiny of the estate by Colonel Hall, who was at the period working his own mines in the neighbouring districts of the county.

The Attractions of a Fashionable Irish Watering-Place
Francis Sylvester Mahony
(Father Prout)

The town of Passage
Is both large and spacious,
And situated
Upon the say.
'Tis nate and dacent,
And quite adjacent
To come from Cork
On a summer's day;
There you may slip in
To take a dipping,
Fornent the shipping
That at anchor ride;
Or in a wherry
Cross o'er the ferry
To Carrigaloe,
On the other side.

Mud cabins swarm in
This place so charming,
With sailor garments
Hung out to dry;
And each abode is
Snug and commodious,
With pigs melodious
In their straw-built sty.
'Tis there the turf is,
And lots of murphies,
Dead sprats and herrings,
And oyster shells;
Nor any lack, O!
Of good tobacco —
Though what is smuggled
By far excels.

There are ships from Cadiz,
And from Barbadoes,
But the leading trade is
In whisky-punch;
And you may go in
Where one Molly Bowen
Keeps a nate hotel
For a quite lunch.
But land or deck on,
You may safely reckon,
Whatsoever country
You come hither from,
On an invitation
To a jollification,
With a parish priest
That's called 'Father Tom'.

Of ships there's one fixt
For lodging convicts,
A floating 'stone Jug'
Of amazing bulk;
The hake and salmon,
Playing at bagammon,
Swim for divarsion

All round this 'hulk';
There 'Saxon' jailors
Keep brave repailors,
Who soon with sailors
Must anchor weigh
From th' em'rald island,
Ne'er to see dry land,
Until they spy land
In sweet Bot'ny Bay.

On Dunkettle Bridge

Gerry Murphy

from: *Rio de la Plata and All That* (1993)

Quiet again
as the planet springs back
in the wake
of the Cobh Express,
the evening sun
gleaming by rail
into the city.

II PERSONAL MATTERS

The Hag of Beare

Anonymous

Translated by: John Montague

Ebb tide has come for me:
My life drifts downwards
Like a retreating sea
With no tidal turn.

I am the Hag of Beare,
Fine petticoats I used to wear,
Today, gaunt with poverty,
I hunt for rags to cover me.

Girls nowadays
Dream only of money —
When we were young
We cared more for our men.

Riding over their lands
We remember how, like nobles,
They treated us well;
Courted, but didn't tell.

Today every upstart
Is a master of graft;
Skinflint, yet sure to boast
Of being a lavish host.

But I bless my King who gave —
Balanced briefly on time's wave —
Largesse of speedy chariots
And champion thoroughbreds.

These arms, now bony, thin
And useless to younger men,
Once caressed with skill
The limbs of princes!

Sadly my body seeks to join
Them soon in their dark home —
When God wishes to claim it,
He can have back his deposit.

No more gamy teasing
For me, no wedding feast:
Scant grey hair is best
Shadowed by a veil.

Why should I care?
Many's the bright scarf
Adorned my hair in the days
When I drank with the gentry.

So God be praised
That I mis-spent my days!
Whether the plunge be bold
Or timid, the blood runs cold.

After spring and autumn
Come age's frost and body's chill:
Even in bright sunlight
I carry my shawl.

Lovely the mantle of green
Our Lord spreads on the hillside!
Every spring the divine craftsman
Plumps its worn fleece.

But my cloak is mottled with age —
No, I'm beginning to dote —
It's only grey hair straggling
Over my skin like a lichened oak.

And my right eye has been taken away
As down-payment on heaven's estate;
Likewise the ray in the left
That I may grope to heaven's gate.

No storm has overthrown
The royal standing stone.
Every year the fertile plain
Bears its crop of yellow grain.

But I, who feasted royally
By candlelight, now pray
In this darkened oratory.
Instead of heady mead

And wine, high on the bench
With kings, I sup whey
In a nest of hags:
God pity me!

Yet may this cup of whey
O! Lord, serve as my ale-feast —
Fathoming its bitterness
I'll learn that you know best.

Alas, I cannot
Again sail youth's sea;
The days of my beauty
Are departed, and desire spent.

I hear the fierce cry of the wave
Whipped by the wintry wind.
No one will visit me today
Neither nobleman nor slave.

I hear their phantom oars
As ceaselessly they row
And row to the chill ford,
Or fall asleep by its side.

Flood tide
And the ebb dwindling on the sand!
What the flood rides ashore
The ebb snatches from your hand.

Flood tide
And the sucking ebb to follow!
Both I have come to know
Pouring down my body.

Flood tide
Has not yet rifled my pantry
But a chill hand has been laid
On many who in darkness visited me.

Well might the Son of Mary
Take their place under my roof-tree
For if I lack other hospitality
I never say 'No' to anybody —

Man being of all
Creatures the most miserable —
His flooding pride always seen
But never his tidal turn.

Happy the island in mid-ocean
Washed by the returning flood
But my ageing blood
Slows to final ebb.

I have hardly a dwelling
Today, upon this earth.
Where once was life's flood
All is ebb.

from: Epithalamion
Edmund Spenser, (1594)

*Edmund Spenser (1552–99), who travelled to Ireland with Lord Grey of Wilton
for whom he worked as a secretary, acquired Kilcolman Castle near Doneraile,
County Cork in 1588 or 1589. While there, he worked on* The Faerie Queene
(see page 24). In 1594, he married Elizabeth Boyle and, to mark the occasion,

wrote his Epithalamion, *from which this excerpt is taken. They are said to have been married in a church in South Main Street in Cork, where Christ Church now stands. [Ed.]*

Ye Nymphes of Mulla which with careful heed,
The silver scaly trouts doe tend full well,
And greedy pikes which use therein to feed,
(Those trouts and pikes all others doo excell)
And ye likewise which keepe the rushy lake,
Where none doo fishes take,
Bynd up the locks the which hang scatterd light,
And in his waters which your mirror make,
Behold your faces as the christall bright,
That when you come whereas my love doth lie,
No blemish she may spie.
And eke ye lightfoot mayds which keepe the deere,
That on the hoary mountayne use to towre,
And the wylde wolves, which seeke them to devoure,
With your steele darts doo chace from comming neer,
Be also present heere,
To helpe to decke her, and to help to sing,
That all the woods may answer, and your eccho ring.

Wake now, my love, awake! for it is time:
The rosy Morne long since left Tithones bed,
All ready to her silver coche to clyme,
And Phoebus gins to shew his glorious hed.
Hark how the cheerefull birds do chaunt theyr laies,
And carroll of loves praise!
The merry larke hir mattins sings aloft,
The thrush replyes the mavis descant playes,
The ouzell shrills, the ruddock warbles soft,
So goodly all agree, with sweet consent,
To this dayes merriment.
Ah! my deere love, why doe ye sleepe thus long,
When meeter were that ye should now awake,
T' awayt the comming of your joyous make,
And hearken to the birds love-learned song,
The deawy leaves among?
For they of joy and pleasance to you sing,
That all the woods them answer, and theyr eccho ring.

My love is now awake out of her dreame,
And her fayre eyes, like stars that dimmed were
With darksome cloud, now shew theyr goodly beams
More bright then Hesperus his head doth rere.
Come now, ye damzels, daughters of delight,
Helpe quickly her to dight.
But first come ye, fayre Houres, which were begot,
In Joves sweet paradice, of Day and Night,
Which doe the seasons of the year allot,
And al that ever in this world is fayre
Do make and still repayre.
And ye three handmayds of the Cyprian Queene,
The which doe still adorne her beauties pride,
Helpe to addorne my beautifullest bride:
And as ye her array, still throw betweene
Some graces to be seene:
And as ye use to Venus, to her sing,
The whiles the woods shal answer, and your eccho ring.

Now is my love all ready forth to come:
Let all the virgins therefore well awayt,
And ye fresh boyes, that tend upon her groome,
Prepare your selves, for he is comming strayt.
Set all your things in seemely good aray,
Fit for so joyfull day,
The joyfulst day that ever sunne did see.
Faire Sun, shew forth thy favourable ray,
And let thy lifull heat not fervent be,
For feare of burning her sunshyny face,
Her beauty to disgrace.
O fayrest Phoebus, father of the Muse,
If ever I did honour thee aright,
Or sing the thing that mote thy mind delight,
Doe not thy servants simple boone refuse,
But let this day, let this one day be myne,
Let all the rest be thine.
Then I thy soverayne prayses loud wil sing,
That all the woods shal answer, and theyr eccho ring.

Harke how the minstrels gin to shrill aloud
Their merry musick that resounds from far,
The pipe, the tabor, and the trembling croud,
That well agree withouten breach or jar.
But most of all the damzels doe delite,
When they their tymbrels smyte,
And thereunto doe daunce and carrol sweet,
That all the sences they doe ravish quite,
The whyles the boyes run up and downe the street,
Crying aloud with strong confused noyce,
As if it were one voyce.
'Hymen, Iö Hymen, Hymen,' they do shout,
That even to the heavens theyr shouting shrill
Doth reach, and all the firmament doth fill;
To which the people, standing all about,
As in approvance doe thereto applaud,
And loud advaunce her laud,
And evermore they 'Hymen, Hymen' sing,
That al the woods them answer, and theyr eccho ring.

Aunt Bridget

Patrick Galvin

from: *Song for a Poor Boy* (1990)

I suppose, in some ways, you could say that my Aunt Bridget was a little mad. Certainly, many people thought so. She wore a flaming red blouse, a billowing black skirt, a pair of men's boots — and she told stories to children. It was night when I met her.

I was sitting on the pavement outside Miss Mac's sweet shop in Mary Street when she appeared round the corner carrying all her worldly possessions in a paper bag. She asked who I was. And when I told her she said 'I'm your Aunt Bridget'.

'The mad one?'

'That's what they say. Is your father at home?'

'No. They're all out.'

'I'll sit with you then till they come back.'

She sat beside me on the pavement and opened her bag. She removed a handful of sweets and offered me one.

'I'm not supposed to take sweets from strangers.'

'I'm not a stranger' she said. 'I'm your Aunt.'

'My father said you were mad. You ran away from home and joined the gipsies. You were all right before that.'

'Was I?'

'I don't know. They don't talk about you now. Have you come home?'

'I think so.'

'I'll take the sweet so. You can live with us.' And so she did — until she found her own house at the bottom of Evergreen Street.

In her youth, my father said, Aunt Bridget was known as a very respectable girl. She went to Mass regularly, was educated in a convent and learned to bow her head demurely in the presence of the opposite sex. She spoke, but only when she was asked, and never interrupted when her elders and betters were engaged in serious conversation.

When she reached the age of forty, however, she took what my father described as a desperate turn for the worst. No one knows how it happened but, one day, she looked at herself in the mirror and said — no. And the following day she changed her clothes, bought herself a pair of men's boots, and announced that from now on she was going to wander the roads of Ireland and tell stories to children. She kept her word — and the stories she told were magic.

There was the joyous story of a young girl who found a butterfly who had lost its colours. The girl painted new colours on the butterfly and the butterfly flew away to create a rainbow over the city. And listening to my Aunt I could see that rainbow. It arced its way through the Autumn skies and I could see its reflection in my Aunt's eyes.

Then there was the story of the young boy who climbed the highest mountain in the world and when he reached the peak he found the portrait of a woman etched deep in the rock. And the strange thing about that story was that no one had climbed that mountain before — or so it was said.

Oh, my Aunt could tell a story all right and leave it hanging there at the end to make you wonder at the mystery of it.

And there were other stories, too. Like the time she saw a woman buried in ice — or the time she saw a tree walking along the road, its branches filled with a myriad of clouds and its leaves glittering with blue stars. And she thought to herself: 'What's a tree doing walking along the road when it could just as easily fly?' For trees could fly when they were not standing still and holding the world together with their roots.

Her technique was simple. The stories were true and they were filled with wonder. Not the kind of wonder that would be understood by an adult, but a child certainly. My Aunt had faith in children, and when she saw one in the street she'd hold out her hand and the child would respond when it might never have responded to another human being.

In my Aunt's mind children were unique. You didn't have to tell them that the world rested on the back of a giant turtle. Any child could see that — and that's why the world wobbled all the time and you had earthquakes and plagues and famine and whooping cough and chicken pox and measles. If it wasn't for the trees, who held the whole thing together with their roots, the world would have collapsed years ago and sunk into an abyss. My Aunt said so. And she was right.

She said the sky wasn't always blue either. It could be any colour you wanted it to be. She once saw a pink sky and she liked it so much she kept it that way for a week in spite of people telling her she was mad. The children didn't think she was mad. The sky belonged to my Aunt — and when she'd finished with it she'd pass it on to them and they could paint it any colour they liked.

When my Aunt wasn't telling stories to children, she made children's clothes and sold them to the neighbours for whatever they could afford. Sometimes, all they could afford was — thanks. But, that was all right, too. She'd manage.

And she made dolls — paper dolls from string and newspaper and glue she'd prepared herself. You could see it bubbling in the pot that hung precariously over the fire in the back yard of her house in Evergreen Street. She stood tall. She held a large potstick in her hand and as she stirred the glue I could hear her singing softly to herself — 'If I was a witch now, I could change the world'. But she wasn't a witch. She was my lone Aunt Bridget. An artist, a storyteller and a lover of children. When she died the sky turned a bright pink and it remained that way for a long time.

Mother

Frank O'Connor

from: *An Only Child* (1961)

Whenever I read about juvenile delinquents, I find myself thinking of Mother, because she was whatever the opposite of a juvenile delinquent is, and this was not due to her upbringing in a Catholic orphanage, since whatever it was in her that was the opposite of a juvenile delinquent was too strong to have been due to the effect of any environment, and, indeed, resisted a number of environments to which no reasonable person would subject a child; the gutter where life had thrown her was deep and dirty. One way of describing this quality is to call it gaiety; another is to say that she was a woman who passionately believed in the world of appearances. If something appeared to be so, or if she had been told it was so, then she believed it to be so. This, as every psychologist knows, leads to disillusionments, and when a juvenile delinquent is disillusioned we describe it as a traumatic experience. So far as I could see, up to her death practically all Mother's experiences were traumatic, including, I am afraid, her experience with me. And some small portion of her simple-mindedness she did pass on to me.

She was small and dainty, with long dark hair that she was very proud of. She had only two faults that I ever knew of — she was vain and she was obstinate — and the fact that these qualities were masked by humility and gentleness prevented my recognizing them till I was a grown man. Father, who was as grey as a badger at thirty-five, and in danger of growing bald, in spite of his clippers, was very jealous of her beautiful dark hair, and whenever he wanted to make her mad he would affect to discover white strands in it. Being an orphan, she had no notion of her own age, and had never known a birthday, but Father had discussed it with my Uncle Tim and satisfied himself that she was several years older than himself. When he believed she was seventy, he got really angry because he was sure she was going to let her vanity deprive her of a perfectly good pension. Mother shrugged this off as another example of his jealousy. To tell the truth, that was what I thought myself. She looked, at the time, like a well-preserved fifty-five. However, to put his mind at rest, I had the date of her birth looked up in the

Customs House in Dublin, and discovered that she was only a few months short of seventy. Father was triumphant, but I felt guilty because I feared that the knowledge of her real age would make her become old. I needn't have worried. I think she probably decided finally that though the Registrar of Births and Deaths was a well-intentioned man, he was not particularly bright.

She had a lordly way with any sort of record she could get her hands on that conflicted with her own view of herself — she merely tore it up. Once, the poet George Russell did a charming pencil drawing of her, which I had framed. The next time I came home on holiday, I found the frame filled with snapshots of me, and my heart sank, because I knew what must have happened. 'What did you do with that drawing?' I asked, hoping she might at least have preserved it, and she replied firmly: 'Now, I'm just as fond of AE as you are, but I could not have that picture round the house. He made me look like a poisoner.' When she was eighty-five, and we were leaving to live in England, I discovered that she had done the same thing with the photograph in her passport. She was entirely unaffected by my anger. 'The sergeant of the police at Saint Luke's said it,' she proclaimed firmly. 'The man who took that picture should be tried for his life.' I think she was glad to have official authority for her personal view that I had been very remiss in not bringing proceedings against the photographer. When my wife and I separated, the only indication I had of Mother's feelings was when I looked at my photograph album one day and saw that every single photograph of my wife had been destroyed. Where she had been photographed with me or the children her picture had been cut away. It was not all malice, any more than the destruction of her own pictures was all vanity. I am certain it went back to some childish technique of endurance by obliterating impressions she had found too terrible to entertain, as though, believing as she did in the world of appearances, she found it necessary to alter the world of appearances to make it seem right, but in time it came to affect almost everything she did. It even worked in reverse, for one Christmas an old friend, Stan Stewart, sent her a book, but because it came straight from his bookseller, it did not contain an inscription, as books that were sent to me did. After her death, I found the book with a charming inscription from Stan, written in by herself. Her affection for him made her give herself away, for she wrote 'From dear Stan'.

She was beautiful, and — in later life at least — she knew it. Once a well-known woman writer came to the house, and when she was introduced to Mother, she threw her arms about her neck and hugged her. 'But she's so beautiful!' she said to me later in apology, and Mother accepted the tribute modestly as indicating that our visitor showed nice feelings. She had a long, pale, eager face that lit up as though there had been an electric torch behind it, and whenever people told her anything interesting, she studied their faces with a delighted or grieved expression. It was part of her belief in the reality of the objective world. She knew that when people were happy they laughed, and she laughed with them — not so much at what they said, because sometimes she didn't understand what they were saying, as in sympathy with their happiness. In the same way, when they were sad she looked grieved. It never occurred to her that people could be happy and wear a mournful face. From her point of view, this would have been a mere waste of good happiness. For the same reason, she never teased and could never understand teasing, which was the amusement of people like Father, who do not believe in the world of appearances, and though she was clever and sometimes profound, she went through life burdened with the most extraordinary misapprehensions, which she clung to with gentle persistence.

When I was a child, our walks often took us to the Good Shepherd Convent, in the orphanage of which she had grown up. I liked it because it had trees and steep lawns and pleasant avenues. On fine days we sat with one of her old friends on the lawn that overlooked the valley of the river, or, on showery ones, in the grotto of the nuns' cemetery, and Mother of Perpetual Succour, who was in charge of the garden, took me round and picked me fruit, and I suspect that sometimes, when things were not going well at home, Mother Blessed Margaret gave Mother small gifts of money and clothes. In the convent cemetery, among the tiny crosses of the nuns, was a big monument to one of the orphans, an infant known as Little Nellie of Holy God, who had suffered and died in a particularly edifying way, and about whom, at the time, a certain cult was growing up. I had a deep personal interest in her, because not only was I rather in that line myself, but Father had assisted at her exhumation when her body was removed from a city cemetery, and verified the story that it was perfectly preserved. Having attended several funerals, seen the broken coffins and the bones that were heaped on the side, and heard my relatives say knowingly: 'That was Eugene now. The one below him was Mary,' I was strongly in favour of the saintly life. When they dug me up, I wanted to be intact.

But much as I enjoyed the elegance of the convent gardens and avenues, it was there that I picked up the fragments of Mother's past life that have never ceased to haunt me. At that time, of course, they were merely a few hints, but they were sufficient to sustain my interest through the years, and later I wrote down and got her to write down as many of the facts as she remembered — or cared to remember. I stopped doing this one day when she put down her pen with a look of horror and said: 'I can't write any more — it's too terrible!'

It was. She had been the oldest of four children whose parents lived in a tiny cabin at the top of Blarney Lane beyond the point where I grew up. After her had come Margaret, then Tim, and then Nora, the baby. My grandmother was a country girl from Donoughmore, and had been married in the hood cloak, the traditional dress of country women of her day. My grandfather was a labourer in Arnott's Brewery, which was near St Mary's of the Isle Convent, at the other side of the city. Mother was his pet, and sometimes when he went to work he carried her with him in his arms, left her in the playground of the convent to amuse herself, and then came back later to carry her home again. He was a powerful man, a bowls player and athlete, and one day, for a bet, he began lifting heavy casks and injured his back. While he was in Mercy Hospital Mother was not allowed to visit him — I fancy because my grandmother had to work and Mother looked after the children — and, being his pet, she resented it. One day she left the children behind and ran all the way down Sunday's Well and Wyse's Hill and across the old wooden bridge where St Vincent's Bridge now stands to the hospital. She found him, fully dressed, sitting on his bed in the men's ward upstairs, with a group of men about him who played with her and gave her sweets. When she was leaving he came down the stairs with her, and at the front door, asked if she knew her way home. She said that she did, but he realized that she was confused, caught her up in his arms and made off with her for home. Mother told that part of the story in a rather tentative way, and I suspect that, with a child's belief in magic, she had always felt that her visit had cured him, and could not face the possibility that it might have been the cause of his death. Anyhow, I doubt if it was. I think he knew he was dying, and wanted to die at home. He lingered only a short while, and Mother remembered how he reported the stages of dying to my grandmother. 'The end is coming Julia,' he said once. 'The hearing is going on me now.'

After his death, neighbours and friends took the children in. My grandmother's people in Donoughmore, who were comfortably off, refused to do anything for her. Nora, taken by one couple, was never heard of again in this world, though in later years Mother tried hard to track her down. Someone else took Tim. Margaret, I fancy, remained on with Grandmother. Mother fell to the lot of a foreman in the Brewery named O'Regan, who lived with his childless wife in a place called Brandy Lane on the south side of the city. They were a good-natured couple, but with no comprehension of a child's needs. After the intimacy of the little cabin, Mother was terrified of her own tall solitary bedroom and the streetlamp outside that threw its light up on to the ceiling, and in the daytime Mrs O'Regan went out and left her alone in the house. One day she dragged a chair into the hall and managed to lift the latch. Then she ran wild through the city streets till a policeman picked her up and brought her home by the hand.

It was only a brief respite, because a couple of days later they were evicted for not paying the rent, and Mother and Margaret sat for hours on the roadside with the remains of their little home: the tester bed, the picture of Sir John Arnott, the brewer, and the picture of the Guardian Angel — the two protectors who had done so little for them. After that, Grandmother took Mother and Margaret to the Good Shepherd Orphanage, and when Mother realized that they were being left behind, she rushed after my grandmother, clinging to her skirts and screaming to be taken home. My grandmother's whispered reply is one of the phrases that haunted my childhood — indeed, it haunts me still. 'But my store, I have no home now.' For me, there has always been in imagination a stage beyond death — a stage where one says 'I have no home now.'

My grandmother went mad under the strain and was for a time in the Lunatic Asylum. When she came out, she worked for a few months as a maid. She used to visit Mother and Aunt Margaret at the orphanage, and once she brought Tim, then two, who was on his way to an infants' orphanage in Waterford. To begin with, the two little girls were comfortable enough. They were too young to dress themselves, so they were dispensed from the necessity for going to Mass, and for the same reason they didn't attend classes and were left in the kitchen with the older girls who did the cooking. Their cots were side by side in the dormitory, and sometimes Mother got into Margaret's bed and was caught there at 6.30 when Mother Cecilia came into the dormitory, clapping her hands and reciting the morning offering.

By the time Mother was attending classes, fever broke out in the school and a temporary hospital had to be erected in the grounds. Margaret disappeared with many of the others, but by this time Mother was growing used to disappearances. One day two girls entered the classroom, carrying a third whose legs dragged dead behind her.

'Minnie,' they said. 'Here's your sister.'

Mother ran away, and then the tall, thin girl they were carrying began to cry. Margaret was now a cripple for life and lived in the infirmary. It was Mother who carried her to and from the classrooms, where she could move about fairly well by swinging on the desks. She had developed into something of a pet and a tyrant. She was precocious, and read everything that came her way. Whatever poetry she read, she immediately memorized. She developed a hatred of injustice, and attacked even the nuns when she thought they were doing wrong. She despised Mother's timidity, and when Mother peered in the infirmary door to see if any nuns were round, Margaret called out to her not to be such a coward. The owner of the Queen's Old Castle, one of the big city stores, who sometimes visited the convent, had a wheelchair made for her so that she could be pushed round.

When Grandmother was dying in the workhouse, only Mother could make the journey to say goodbye to her. Grandmother wept, and Mother took out her own handkerchief to dry her tears. As she left the workhouse, she remembered the handkerchief. It was school property, and she might be punished for the loss of it, so she rushed back to the ward. Grandmother was still weeping, but Mother could not keep the lay sister waiting in the convent cab.

Grandmother's gentleness and humility had endeared her to some of the nuns, and when she died, Reverend Mother decided to save her from what was considered the shame of the paupers' hole, where the unclaimed bodies of the dead were thrown. Mother Mary Magdalen was a lady, and did not allow the other nuns to forget it. Her family had been of Isaac Butt's party, as opposed to the popular party of Parnell. 'My brothers were in Parliament when there were none but gentlemen there,' she told the children. She also told them that she had found her vocation at the age of twenty-eight, while attending a performance of *The Colleen Bawn* at the Opera House in Cork. I wonder whether the subject of the play, which deals with the seduction of an innocent Irish girl, and her peculiar choice of a name in religion do not imply that she considered herself to have been flighty. She sent for Mother to find out where Grandfather was buried, but Mother did not know. So Grandmother was buried in a city graveyard and Reverend Mother ordered a hearse and two covered cars — the old-fashioned two-wheeled vehicles known only in Cork. In one rode Mother with a lay sister, and in the other a couple of orphans.

There was little of the agony of the orphan child that Mother did not know, either through her own experience or the experiences of the other children, which she observed in her sympathetic way. It was the height of the Land War, and all over Ireland poor cottagers were being thrown on to the roadside by police and British troops. One frightened little girl went about for days asking: 'Will the men with the wed wousers (red trousers) come here too?' Once, a baby girl called Lynch, from Kerry, whose family had been drowned, was missing for hours, and was finally discovered in the empty chapel, patiently knocking on the altar and calling: 'Holy God! Holy God! Are 'oo there? Will 'oo send up my Daddy?' Some of the children did not realize for days the immensity of the change that had come over their lives. For a whole week one little girl called Anne Dorgan patiently watched the clock till it came to half past three and then stood up and raised her hand, asking meekly: 'Please, ma'am, can I go home now?' 'Sit down, Anne Dorgan,' the nun would say gently, but Anne would stick to her point. 'But, ma'am, 'tis half past three. 'Tis time to go home, ma'am.'

In time she too realized as Mother had done that she had no home now, and tried to divert her feeling for home to the convent, and for her parents to some nun. In some girls that switch was never affected at all and they remained to the end of their lives aloof and cold and conscious of some lack of warmth in themselves, like Kate Gaynor, a friend of Mother's whom I knew in later years and who said bitterly that every orphanage in the world should be torn down because they robbed a child of natural affection, but others were luckier or maybe less exacting. Mother used to quote a snatch of conversation that she had overheard between two infants sitting on the ground under a window, the one eager and serious, the other bored and pompous.

'Do you love God?'

'I won't tell you.'

'Do you love Mother Saint Paul?'

'I won't tell you.'

'Do you rather God or Mother Saint Paul?'

'I won't tell you.'

'I think I rather God, and then Mother Saint Paul.'

Then there was silence. Perhaps the child who would not tell was one whose natural affection was being killed.

Mother herself did not see my Uncle Tim for five years, and in the meantime he had been transferred to the Boys' Orphanage at Greenmount on the south side of the river. On her feast day, Reverend Mother decided that girls who had brothers there should be allowed to entertain them in Sunday's Well. Mother was now quite an important person, and she allowed one of her friends to join her in collecting candies and biscuits for the expected visit. My Aunt Margaret in the infirmary had a hoard. When the orphan boys marched up the convent avenue behind their band, Mother and her friend ran screaming through the ranks calling 'O'Connor! Tim O'Connor!' A small boy said modestly 'That's me,' and the two little girls stuffed his pockets with sweets and marched him off in triumph to the infirmary. But another little girl, called Eileen O'Connor, rushed after them weeping and crying that they had stolen her brother. When they realized their mistake, Mother and her friend beat the pretender and took back the sweets before returning to look for the real Tim O'Connor. After that, the experiment of allowing brothers and sisters to meet for one afternoon in the year was not repeated.

Meanwhile, Mother had her living to earn. She had been trained as a bookbinder, and was neat and skilful at this, as she was at almost anything she tackled, but she was always getting into trouble for reading the books she should have been binding. Maria Condon, who was in charge of the bookbinding class and was a gentle, grave, responsible girl, used to smile sadly and shake her head over Mother's tendency to be distracted by printed pages. She was the daughter of one of the 'fallen' women in the penitentiary and was allowed to see her mother once a week in a convent parlour. One of Mother Mary Magdalen's reforms had been to make a clean sweep of illegitimate girls from the school on the plea that it was unfair to the orphans to have an additional presumption of illegitimacy against them, but an exception had been made of Maria because her mother, who had been seduced by a well-known doctor, had taken vows and become what was known as a 'dedicated penitent', serving a life term by choice in atonement for her fall. There was a moving sequel to the story of Maria and her mother which disturbed me greatly when I was an adolescent and caused endless argument between Mother and myself.

When Maria was sixteen or seventeen she had to be sent out to work as a maid, but the nuns decided that it was unsafe for her to work in Ireland, where people would get to know of her illegitimacy. Maria, who had been told nothing about this, wanted to remain in Cork, where she could be close to her mother, but instead the nuns sent her to New York as maid in a rough Irish boarding house. An older girl who was also a maid in New York was told to look after her. Maria was homesick; she wanted to save her wages to earn her fare back to Ireland, and finally the older girl told her why she could not go back. Maria returned to the horrible boarding house, packed her few possessions, and was not heard of again for a long time. She had been so horrified at her mother's 'sin' and her own illegitimacy that she had decided to break off all connexion with her mother and the convent.

After the revelation, she had gone out and taken the first job she was offered. Fortunately for her, this was with an old American family who soon realized that she was a superior and intelligent girl. But they could not understand why she never received or wrote letters. Finally, the mistress of the house questioned her, and Maria, believing that since she was illegitimate she would be dismissed, broke down and told her everything. Her employers were shocked, and they insisted on her writing at once to her mother. Correspondence with her was resumed, but the nuns were hostile — Maria had left the good Catholic home they had found for her. Her employers encouraged Maria to get a better job and save for a little home of her own to which she could bring her mother. When she had saved enough she returned to Cork, but she found the nuns openly hostile to her plans, and her mother refused to go back to her. She had taken her vows and would end her days as an unpaid trusty in a penitentiary.

As was only natural, when I learned the truth about Maria, I had no sympathy for anyone but her, but Mother refused to let me criticize the nuns. 'They did what they thought was right,' she said obstinately and that settled it for her. But it didn't settle it for me, and I have never ceased to be haunted by the images of Maria and her mother, whose innocent lives had been blasted by an introverted religion.

Mother must have been a dreamy, sensitive child, because she had spells of somnambulism, and once she was found walking up and down a convent corridor in her nightdress, reciting Wolsey's speech from *Henry VIII* — 'Farewell, a long farewell, to all my greatness!'

She was not sent to a bookbinder's to work. One winter evening, when she was fourteen or fifteen, the Mistress of Studies came to her in the orphanage workroom where she was sewing and told her she had found a nice home for her with two ladies who had called to inquire for a maid. The Mistress of Studies then went out and returned with a regular convent outfit for girls who were leaving school — a black straw sailor hat and black coat, a pair of gloves, and a parcel of clean aprons. Mother gathered up her own possessions — a statue of the Blessed Virgin and a couple of holy pictures — said goodbye to her friends, and went off in the darkness down Sunday's Well in a covered car with the two ladies, a Mrs Bowen, who was a widow, and her daughter-in-law. The car stopped outside a terrace of new two-storey houses on Gardiner's Hill.

Mother thought the Mistress of Studies had probably been mistaken, because it didn't seem a very good home. The younger of the two women lit a candle and showed her her room, which was a little cubbyhole with a fireplace, a bed, and two or three framed Bible texts. Mother unpacked her belongings and ranged the statue of the Blessed Virgin and the holy pictures on the mantelpiece to keep her company. After her tea she sat in the kitchen till Mrs Bowen told her it was time for her to go to bed. Then she lit her candle and went up to her room. That night all her old fears came back. Since she had been taken by the O'Regan's she had never slept alone in a room. She had become used to the big classrooms and dormitories, the voices and the loud footsteps along the corridors, and she was terrified. When she left her room, she stooped for fear of knocking her head on the lintel, which was so much lower than in the big doorways she was used to, and dreaded to move lest she knock something over.

The Bowens were poor, and Mother got no wages, but the younger woman was a dressmaker, and made Mother some clothes of her own, which she liked just as well. Anyhow, she was not accustomed to money. (One of the orphans had once stolen a pound and gone straight to a sweet store, where she ordered 'a pound's worth of sweets' — as though a child of our own time should ask for twenty dollars' worth of candies.) The Bowens kept two lodgers, and the younger woman waited on them. She was an eager, earnest housekeeper, forever on the rush, and so careful of the scraps that she sometimes kept bread till it turned green. Once, Mother was throwing it out, but Mrs Bowen gave her a lecture on waste and explained that bread was healthier that way. Being a great believer in the world of appearances, Mother tried to like it, but couldn't. She decided that, like the view that the Mistress of Studies held of the Bowen's house, this was just a mistake.

Mr Bowen had a job in a wine store on Merchant's Quay, but his health was poor, and Mother was frequently sent into town to explain his absences. She was very sorry about his bad health, but she enjoyed the trips into town. At nights she was allowed to read in the parlour while the Bowens sang sentimental or comic songs, or, on Sunday, hymns — Protestant hymns of course. Mother's own favourites were always the old Latin hymns like *Ave Maris Stella* and *Stabat Mater*, but she thoroughly enjoyed the Protestant ones, having, like her son, an open mind on the subject of anything with a tune. The books at her disposal were limited in appeal, boys' school stories with a strongly sectarian bias and standard editions of the poets, but at least she was able to read Shakespeare right through.

When she was hanging out the washing, she became friendly with the sour-faced maid next door, one Betty, who kept house for two old maids called Bennett. Mother talked to her at great length about the convent and about Mother Blessed Margaret, her favourite among the nuns, but Betty hinted darkly that there was nothing she did not know about nuns and chaplains and the dark goings on in convents, and Mother realized, to her great astonishment, that Betty was a Protestant as well. Nobody had ever explained to Mother that Protestants could also be poor. I have a strong impression that from this moment Mother was bent on converting Betty. Betty told Mother that Mr Bowen was a drunkard, and Mother denied this indignantly, and explained that it was just bad health.

Mother, with her belief in the world of appearances, was always being impressed by the curious mistakes that people made. The Mistress of Studies had been mistaken about the Bowens' house, Betty thought that Mr Bowen was a drunkard, and Mr Bowen himself made mistakes that were nearly as bad. One evening his wife, who usually opened the front door when he knocked, was upstairs; Mother opened it instead, and Mr Bowen beamed on her, put his arm about her waist, and kissed her. She was taken by such a fit of giggling that she was ashamed. 'Oh, sir, I'm only Minnie,' she explained, and then went off to the kitchen to laugh in peace at the notion that anybody could take *her* for Mrs Bowen. She was longing to tell the joke to the mistress, but finally decided that it might seem forward.

But his mistake was nothing to that of Mr Daly, one of the lodgers, who was a reporter on the *Cork Examiner*. He had a blue overcoat with a velvet collar that Mother thought the height of elegance and which she stroked every time she passed it hanging in the hall. One night she woke and felt a hand on her throat. Her first impulse was to reach for the statue of the Blessed Virgin, which was on the mantelpiece over her bed, but what she grabbed instead was the velvet collar she knew so well.

'Oh, Mr Daly, is that you?' she cried in relief.

'Don't shout, Minnie!' he whispered crossly. 'I'm only looking for the candle.'

'But what are you doing in here?' she asked. 'Your room is the other way.'

'I lost my way in the darkness, that's all,' he said with a sigh, and after a couple of minutes went out quietly.

It was only then that Mother, having got over the shock, could laugh in comfort. Here was an educated man with a big job on the *Cork Examiner* who could not even find his own way upstairs in the dark! And she knew from the way he had sighed that this was something that must often happen to him and cause him a great deal of concern.

Next morning, she simply could not resist reporting his mistake to the younger Mrs Bowen, and then she wished she hadn't, because Mrs Bowen did not laugh at all. Instead, she rushed upstairs to her husband, who was still in bed, and repeated the story to him. He jumped out of bed in his nightshirt and went and threw open the door of Daly's room. Mrs Bowen was still angry when she came downstairs.

'His bed hasn't even been slept in,' she said bitterly. 'I don't think you need worry, Minnie. I fancy he won't trouble us again.'

She was right about that, because in the afternoon a messenger came from the *Examiner* for Daly's clothes, and Mrs Bowen was still so furious that she hurled them at him from the head of the stairs. She even refused to let Mother parcel them for him. Mother was full of pity for the poor little messenger, who sat at the front gate trying to fold the shirts and suits, but, indeed, I think she was sorrier for poor Mr Daly, who had been so ashamed of his own mistake that he had walked blindly out of the house and probably got no sleep at all that night. She thought it was very unforeseen of him not to explain to her how seriously Protestants regarded mistakes.

Then the Bowens had a baby, and Mother had one of her many traumatic experiences about him. She made the midwife promise that when she bought the baby, before giving it over to the mother, she would let her see it first, and when Mr Bowen invited her up to the bedroom to see the new arrival, Mother, after a stunned silence, turned to the midwife and called her a false and wicked woman. Mother hardly ever lost her temper, and never except under what she regarded as intolerable provocation, but when she did, she was magnificent. She reduced everybody to silence. The midwife apologized and excused herself on the ground of the baby's having no clothes, but Mother regarded this as a very lame excuse.

Mother, of course, was enchanted with the baby, and insisted on showing him off to Betty next door. She had no idea of the emotions she was rousing both in Betty and the two old maids she worked for. One Sunday morning the Bowens stormed back from church and denounced Mother for having said of herself and the baby that she was 'bringing up a heretic for Hell'. Mother found it difficult to deny this accusation, because she didn't know what a heretic was, even when the Bowens explained that it was something Catholics called Protestants. Mother, weeping, explained that she had never heard Protestants called that by anyone she knew, and finally the Bowens apologized, realizing that they had been victims of a plot of the Bennetts and Betty, but Mother did not lightly recover from the scene. It was quite plain now that Betty would never be a Catholic.

Mother went a few times to the convent to visit my Aunt Margaret, who was seriously ill, her two arms swathed in cotton wool. One day she was sent for, and when she arrived my aunt was dead. The nun who brought her in to see the body told her she should not cry. Margaret was better off. The nun may have been right. It was bad enough to be an orphan, but to be a cripple as well! Margaret's confession had to be heard after that of all the other children because the chaplain had to leave the confession box and sit beside her in her wheelchair. A little while before she died, one of the girls had pushed her wheelchair into the chapel in the evening, and then forgot all about her. The chaplain, too, forgot and it was only at bedtime that they discovered her missing and found her at last, having sobbed herself to sleep in the deserted chapel.

But the Mistress of Studies, who always seemed to have Mother's best interests at heart, did not forget her, and, deciding that it was bad for her to be in a Protestant home, found her a place in a respectable Catholic lodging house on Richmond Hill. It was kept by a Mrs Joyce, who had five daughters. The eldest, Kathleen, was Mother's age, and a good-natured girl, but foolish and affected. She spent her life reading sentimental novelettes. As in the Bowens' there were two lodgers, Mannix and Healy — both medical students of a violently patriotic temperament who sometimes came in covered in blood after some political riot — and when Kathleen waited on them they ridiculed her affected airs, but both were fond of Mother and brought her presents of sweets and fruit. Neither of them realized the damage they were doing her in the eyes of her mistress, a coarse and ignorant woman with a violent temper. Every little gift they brought Mother became a further slight on Mrs Joyce's fine, educated daughter, and she harried Mother relentlessly, shouting 'Gerril, do this!' and 'Gerril, do that!' One evening she came into the sitting room and saw Mannix pull Mother's pigtail. This was sufficient to put her in one of her usual furies.

'Aha, Gerril!' she said. 'The same thing will happen you as happened Madge Murphy.'

'What happened her?' Mother asked with genuine interest.

'She had a baby!'

'Well, that isn't true, anyway,' Mother said heatedly. (She never liked people to flout her intelligence.) 'How could she have a baby when she isn't even married?'

Joyce, who was eating his supper, looked up at his wife as she was about to reply, and said shortly: 'Let the child alone! She's better off as she is.'

However, that could not keep Mother off the subject of sex, on which her experience with the Bowens had made her an expert. Mrs Joyce was having her sixth, and Mother, who was nothing if not conscientious, decided to enlighten Patricia, the youngest but one of the children, about the facts of life and the untrustworthiness of midwives. She explained to Patricia that she had personally known a midwife who had promised to show her the baby as soon as she bought it, and, instead of that, had taken it straight up to the mother, concealed. Patricia, who wasn't much more than a baby herself, listened with growing stupefaction and then said: 'But you don't *buy* babies.'

'Don't you, indeed?' Mother asked good-naturedly. 'And how do you get them?'

'You make them, of course,' cried Patricia indignantly, and Mother laughed heartily at this example of childish innocence. Her laughter made the little girl furious, and when they reached home she rushed in to her eldest sister, and, pointing an accusing finger at Mother, yelled: 'She says you buy babies!'

'Ah, she only says that because you're so young,' Kathleen replied good-humouredly.

'She doesn't!' screamed the infant. 'She believes it!'

I never had the heart to ask Mother if she had taken example by the child and really learned the facts of life. The one dirty story she knew suggested that she had, but I was never quite certain that she knew what it meant. My impression is that she accepted the evidence in the spirit in which she accepted the evidence of her birth certificate and marked the case 'Not Proven'. Once in Geneva I overheard an extraordinary conversation between her and a Swiss manufacturer's wife whose son was leaving for Paris and who was very concerned about the sort of women he might meet there.

'It is such a dangerous place for a young man,' said the Swiss woman.

'Oh, the traffic!' exclaimed Mother, delighted to have found a kindred spirit. 'It took the sight from my eyes.'

'And it isn't only the traffic, is it?' the Swiss woman asked gently. 'We send them away healthy and we wish them to come back healthy.'

'I said it!' Mother cried passionately. 'My boy's digestion is never the same.'

A certain simplicity of mind that is characteristic of all noble natures, says some old Greek author whose name I cannot remember.

The real nightmare began only after the Joyces moved to a house on Mulgrave Road, near the North Cathedral. Mother no longer had a bedroom, and slept on a trestle bed in the corridor. The painters were still at work in the house, and one of them, after trying in vain to get Mother to walk out with him, proposed to her.

He told her he thought she'd make 'a damn nice little wife'. Mother didn't mind the proposal so much, but she thought his language was terrible.

'What was that fellow saying to you?' Mrs Joyce asked suspiciously when the painter left the room.

'Ah, nothing, only asking me to marry him,' Mother replied lightly, not realizing what she was doing to a woman with five daughters and a probable sixth on the way.

'A queer one he'd be marrying!' growled Mrs Joyce.

A few days later some nuns of a city order called and addressed Mother, under the impression that she was the eldest of the family, which seemed such a good joke to Patricia that she told her mother. It drove Mrs Joyce into a tempest of fury.

'A nice daughter, indeed!' snarled Mrs Joyce. 'A creature that doesn't know who she is or where she came from. She doesn't even know who her own mother was.'

This was too much for Mother. Insults directed against herself she could stand, but not insults to her mother's memory.

'My mother was a lady, anyhow,' she said. 'You're not a lady.'

After that, Mrs Joyce made her life a hell. The clothes her previous employer had made fell into rags, and Mrs Joyce refused to replace them. Instead, she gave Mother a ragged coatee, which she had bought from a dealing woman for a few pence, and an old skirt of her sister's who had just died in the Incurable Hospital. After each meal served to the lodgers, Mrs Joyce rushed in to gather up the scraps, so that there was nothing left to eat. Hunger was no new thing to any of the orphanage children, but starvation was a new thing to Mother. Instead of candies and biscuits, the medical students now gave her an occasional sixpence, and she bought a loaf of bread, which she concealed, and from which she cut a slice when Mrs Joyce went out. At night she was so tired that sometimes she never reached her trestle bed in the corridor. Once, walking across the yard with the lamp, she fell asleep and was wakened only by the crash of the falling lamp. Another time, she fell asleep crossing the Joyces' bedroom with a lighted candle, and when she woke up the curtains were in flames about her.

Then her long beautiful hair grew lousy, and Mrs Joyce ordered her to cut it off. Mother did not perceive that this was the chance the woman had been waiting for all the time. Slight her beautiful, educated daughter indeed! She would show the medical students what a girl looked like when she was ragged and starved and without hair.

That evening, when Mother served the dinner, Mannix looked at her in astonishment. 'What the hell did you do that to yourself for?' he shouted, and when she had told him he went on: 'For God's sake, girl, will you get out of this house before that woman does something worse to you? Can't you see yourself that she hates you?'

'But why would she hate me?' asked Mother.

'Because she's jealous of you. That's why.'

But Mother could not see why anyone should be jealous of somebody as poor and friendless as herself. I doubt if it occurred to her to the day of her death that the Mistress of Studies was also jealous of her. With that simplicity of mind the old author praised, she never really understood the hatred that common natures entertain for refined ones.

She was now ashamed to leave the house, even to buy food. And then something happened that showed how far she had really sunk. The Good Shepherd nuns had at last learned that the lodgers in the house were medical students, and medical students were notorious for their depravity, though this instantly ceased the moment they got a degree. It is a superstition from the early days of scientific medicine, and it has not yet died out. One day two nuns came to the house in a covered car, and ordered Mother to return to the orphanage with them. She refused, and they reminded her of the penalty she was incurring. Any girl who left one of the pleasant homes provided by the nuns without permission was not allowed to return to the orphanage, which was the only home most of the girls had. In the same way, one who refused to leave immediately when ordered was not allowed to return. Mother still refused to go back with them, and when they left in anger, she knew she had now no place in the world to go. When I tried to get her to explain this extraordinary conduct, she said, almost impatiently, that she could not go back in that state among clean, well-dressed girls. Possibly behind her refusal to return there was an element of almost hysterical vanity, but that cannot be the real explanation. My own guess is that it was despair, rather than vanity. Children, and adolescents who have retained their childish innocence have little hold on life. They have no method of defending themselves against the things that are not in their own nature. I think that, without knowing it, Mother hated the nuns for what they had made of her innocent life, and had already decided to commit suicide. Her parents were dead, Margaret had died while she was at Bowens', Tim she had seen only once for a few hours in all the years, and she had nothing left to live for.

For eight or nine months longer, it dragged on like that. The eldest girl took pity on her, helped with the housework when her mother wasn't looking, and even checked her mother when her scurrility went too far. The youngest also helped in her own enlightened way, hiding Mother's brushes and mops and dusters in order to be able to ask: 'Minnie, what are you looking for? I get it for you.' Even in her own misery, Mother laughed at the baby's goodwill. But one winter day Joyce came in at one o'clock for his dinner and it wasn't ready. His wife ordered Mother out of the house. She put off the apron she had been wearing, put on her black straw hat, threw the ragged old coatee over her shoulders — the hat, jacket and skirt were all the possessions she had left in the world — and went out onto Mulgrave Road. She saw people stop and stare at her, and realized the extraordinary figure she cut. She ran up a laneway by the North Infirmary and threw the ragged jacket there, but people still continued to look. She ran for shelter to the Dominican Church on the Sand Quay, and prayed.

She knew now that only one hope remained to her, and that a miracle. None of the nuns — not even her favourite, Mother Blessed Margaret — could overrule the Mistress of Studies, and if she went to the orphanage she would be turned away. She knew too many to whom it had happened. The only one who could overrule the Mistress of Studies was Reverend Mother. It was she who had arranged for my grandmother's funeral. But lay sisters, not Reverend Mothers, answer convent door bells, and from one o'clock until darkness fell Mother waited in the church, most of the time on her knees, praying for a miracle to happen. She had decided that if it didn't she would return to the river and drown herself. It was only when she was telling me about this period of her life that I ever heard her use such an expression in any matter that concerned herself, for not only did she believe suicide was wrong, she thought it demonstrative, and she was almost fiercely undemonstrative in grief or pain. Nor, when she talked of that afternoon, as an old woman, did she exaggerate it. Father and I, with our deep streak of melancholia, would have added something to it that, by making it more dramatic, would also have made it less terrible. It is an awful moment when gaiety dies in those who have no other hold on life.

On the dark, stepped pathway up to the convent, she met two ladies who were coming away from it, chattering, and paid no heed to them. She went up the steps to the front door and rang, and immediately the door opened and Reverend Mother stood inside. In sheer relief, Mother broke down and began to sob out her story. Reverend Mother did not recognize her at first; then something seemed to strike her. 'Aren't you the girl we told to come back from that terrible house?' she asked.

'Yes,' said Mother.

'And why *didn't* you come?'

'I had no clothes. I was ashamed.'

'It's strange I should have answered the door,' said Reverend Mother. 'I was just seeing off some friends, and something kept me here thinking. I was just walking up and down the corridor.' Clearly, she was aware of the coincidence, but Mother knew it was something more.

She brought Mother into her own parlour, sat her before the fire to warm herself, and rang the bell for the Mistress of Studies.

'Minnie O'Connor has come back from that terrible house to stay,' she said quietly, and then as the Mistress of Studies burst into a stream of abuse she added: 'Don't scold, Mother!'

Turning to Mother, the Mistress of Studies cried: 'If you're in that state, you can go to the workhouse. You will not stay here!'

'She is not in that state, and she will stay here,' Reverend Mother said firmly, and that night, for the first time in years, Mother had enough to eat, and bathed, and slept in a clean bed.

She never made much of her own misery. Other girls, as she said, had had a worse time. But she never ceased to speak of what happened as a miracle, and, in the way of those to whom miracles occur, never by so much as a harsh word attempted to blame the Mistress of Studies. Not that she did not realize that for the future she must be on her guard. I feel sure it was significant that when, a week later, the Mistress of Studies found her another nice home, in a public house off Blarney Lane that was a lodging house for cattle dealers, Mother, without even unpacking her bag, returned to the convent and told the Mistress of Studies that it was not a suitable place for a young woman. It was also significant that, a few days later, the Mistress of Studies was replaced by Mother's great friend, Mother Blessed Margaret, whom I knew and loved when she was an old lady. Old or young, she, like Reverend Mother, was a lady.

My First Morning at Work

Séamus Murphy

from: *Stone Mad* (1950)

I remember well the first morning I went to work. I was fourteen years old and small for my age (one of the men came over to me afterwards and said he thought 'it was in after a ball' I had come!). I must have looked particularly small in the company of my father who was six foot three. He was an engine-driver and had no knowledge of or interest in stonecarving. I was selected out of a group of boys in the School of Art as a lad who had possibilities but long before that I had the wish to become a sculptor.

When my father left I was given a large block of stone to serve as a bench (this is called a 'banker'). One of the carvers got me a block of soft stone and I was asked to carve a tulip. I was given a lovely red tulip as a model and I was on my way to becoming a stonecarver — the only legitimate stonecarver turned out in Cork for twenty-five years!

You can imagine my delight the first time I caught a chisel in my hand. Needless to say, it wobbled in all directions and I was nervous and began to be doubtful of ever learning to carve. I was making no progress at all; and there was the tulip wilting! Maybe it would be dead in the morning and what would I do then? But to my relief one of the carvers came and showed me how to hold the chisel. 'Keep all the pressure on your small finger, boy. Like this, and you'll find it'll come easy to you in a few days. And don't worry about the tulip, there's more where that came from.'

This put me in great form and I began to carve with zest. Every now and then one of the men would come up to me and ask me how I was getting on and give me all sorts of advice which used to confuse and frighten me.

I remember one of the carvers taking up the tulip and examining it and then saying to me: 'There's no regularity in Nature. Remember that now! No two leaves or flowers are the same. You will find different kinks and serrations in every one you take up. It's the same with men's faces, no two the same.'

With that he left me and I must say it opened up a new world for me. Ever after I used to examine all plants and flowers to see if they were regular. I liked the phrase too, 'there's no regularity in Nature'.

It had a finality about it and when I used to quote it to people later on, I always felt it was the last word on the subject.

When I got settled down and was no longer shy of the men I had a great time. I was the bane of their lives, asking questions about this type of marble and that; where it came from; if it was easy to work and a hundred other questions.

I was given a whole series of flowers to carve and make sketches of: lily-of-the-valley, columbine, roses and bunches of ivy leaves. I used to study them with great interest but I could never carve them to my own satisfaction or the satisfaction of the men. I would be working away, all concentration, when I would become aware of someone behind me and there would be one of the carvers looking at my job. He would have his head sideways and his eyes half-closed, peering at it. I would step aside and await his verdict. . . .

'You're going on well, boy. But watch the background, you're inclined to go too deep here and there.'

Then he would take the mallet and chisel and level up a bit for me.

'That's very nice indeed. Do you like the work?'

The Gargoyle made friends with me from the start, although at first I used to resent the way he used to look at me and say:

'How old are ye? . . . You're small for it. Tell me, d'ye roll a hoop in the evenings?'

I used to explain to him that I went to the School of Art for modelling and he used to say: 'Ah, you're a great boy.'

Danny Melt used to come clearing away the spalls from around the bankers.

'Take no notice of what the Gargoyle says, boy,' he would say. 'He's a great blackguard. . . . Will I put a little board under your feet? Is the job a bit high for you? 'Tis many the boy I bankered in this shed. . . . Now, don't start calling me "sir". I'm Danny Melt, and if anyone says anything to you come and tell me. I'm the man for 'em.' Then he would take off his hat and smile and say: 'If I lost me hair, I didn't lose me brains.'

'Go 'way out of that and leave the young fella alone,' Stun would say, strolling up. Stun was very good to me. He used to enquire all about my family and tell me that I was the best boy they had had in the shed for years.

'But you get no encouragement here,' he'd say. 'Now you are worth a few shillings a week and you should be getting it. But keep at it and you'll earn good money yet.'

I was to serve my apprenticeship of seven years for which a fee of eighty pounds was required. Of course that was out of the question. We were a big family and eighty pounds in cash were not to be had, so it was arranged that I go to work on a month's trial and if I was considered good an agreement might be possible.

Well, I worked for the month and was regarded by the boss as a success so it was agreed that I should work the first year for nothing.

However, I got on so well with everyone in the place that when they found out that I was getting no wages they said it was a case for a 'national', so every week one of the men collected threepence a man for me.

When I came home in the evenings my tea used to be ready for me and I felt very important as I was the first member of the family to go to work. And I used to tell my mother in great detail what I did for the day, and what the men said. She used to listen carefully to all my talk and say that I would get on well if I did what I was told and worked hard.

The Old Grenadier
Seán O'Faoláin
from: *Vive Moi!* (1965)

I

My father, whose name was Denis Whelan, was a police constable in the Royal Irish Constabulary. He came from a small farm near the hamlet of Stradbally, about fifty miles southeast of Dublin in what was then known as the Queen's County, a region named after Queen Mary, the wife of Philip of Spain, when it was first planted and shired by English settlers. It is known today by its old Gaelic name of Laois.

When I first became consciously aware of my father I chose to see him (being at the time very much under the influence of the Baroness Orczy) as a Napoleonic grenadier, tall, finely built, his back straight as a musket, his air distinguished, his eyes grey-blue and clear as if they forever reflected the snows of Moscow, his greying hair soft as dust, his neatly brushed moustache gone white before its time. I was not far wrong in romanticising him as a grenadier. He was a modest, pious, trusting man, upright, honest as daylight, and absolutely loyal to the Empire as only a born hero-worshipper can be. I have no doubt at all that certain rebellious people today would call him a square, and that, if he had ever met a couple of beats, he would have quietly advised them to go home to their mothers. He would not have raised a finger to them, least of all have tried to make or fake a charge against them — I do not believe he ever charged anybody in his life; he was too gentle. I am not idealising him. He always evoked my respect, and sometimes my admiration, but, although I am sure he loved me with a father's love, he rarely warmed me to love him. Not that I thought about it while he lived, but now I know why it was so. He was the humble but priceless foundation-stuff on which all great states and empires have raised themselves, deviously, to power and glory, and I was a natural, if mild, rebel.

I believe my father's humility was really a form of proud reverence growing out of his job. Because of this, I have occasionally told my English friends in my later years that he was a product of Sandhurst, which would be like a gendarme's son saying his papa had been through Saint-Cyr. Then I would entertain myself by explaining just what I meant. I meant that the Royal Irish Constabulary, or the Force as it was popularly called, was mainly officered by Sandhurst types — in religion mostly Anglicans, or what we called Protestants; in politics Anglo-Irish imperialists to a man — whose great ambition was to infuse and inspire the lowest ranks of the Force with the officers-and-gentlemen traditions of the crack regiments of the British Army. Only those who have known, or can imagine, the earthy simplicity of the Irish youths recruited into the Force, practically all of them poor, inexperienced young men of Catholic peasant stock, will realise the enormity of this ambition. If I may judge by my father, it succeeded absolutely; it is my impression that it also achieved a good deal of success among natives in Delhi, Colombo, Accra, Nassau, Hong Kong, Nairobi, and elsewhere.

In his dark bottle-green uniform, black leather belt with brass buckle, black helmet or peaked cap, black truncheon case and black boots, my father embodied the Law. What was far more important, he embodied all the accepted and respected values and conventions of what we would nowadays call the Establishment. In simple language, his language, he considered that the highest state in life that anyone could achieve was to be a Gentleman; and he wanted each one of his children to grow up as a Gentleman. The most easily observable effect of this on me was that, in dutiful imitation of him, I took over, holus-bolus, the accepted hierarchy of the imperial way of life.

At the top of this hierarchy was the bearded, jovial, rotund, elegant father figure of His Majesty King Edward VII. How amorally jovial he was never entered my father's devoted and loyal head. Had somebody told him the now common stories about Eddie's mistresses and concubines, about, say, Cora Pearl being brought in naked after dinner on a vast silver tray borne by six footmen, or about his gay goings-on in Balbec or Baden-Baden, or about the selfish caddishness he showed towards his friends, so painfully described by Christopher Sykes in *Three Studies in Loyalty*, my father would have thought the storyteller mad, obscene, blasphemous, a traitor and a blackguard; or else he would not have understood a word of it; or it would all have floated in and out of his ears as happened to me when The-Girl-Sawn-In-Half told me all those other wonderful and, alas, forgotten stories about 'dear Eddie.'

From His Majesty my father would trace what he called 'the line of precedence' from the First Lord of the Admiralty and the Chief of the Imperial General Staff to the First, Second, Third and Fourth Sea Lords and their corresponding Field Marshals and Admirals of the Fleet, generals, major generals, rear admirals, lieutenant generals, vice admirals, colonels and captains, down through the civilian galaxy of the Lord Chief Justice and all his judges of lower title, down to our own resident magistrates, our district inspectors and county inspectors, down and down to our local Lord Mayor, his sheriff, his aldermen and, I presume, his fur-hatted, red-cloaked mace-bearer. I am not sure how my father would have placed our Lord Bishop, our canon at Saint Peter's and Paul's, or certain rich city merchants and rich county folk like, say, Brigadier Winterbottom, who used to drive into the city in a grey tilbury drawn by a trotting bay, his fawn bowler on the side of his head, his white moustaches bristling, his gloved hand held high on the reins. But I feel sure that after all those my father and I began to waver. We could not really admit *all* the city councillors — they were too near to us, much too like ourselves. It would have been hard, for instance, so to uplift Danny Gamble, a vociferously eloquent tinsmith, a member of the Cork Corporation for our ward, who lived around the corner from us, who rarely wore either collar or tie, and whom we occasionally saw at Mass robed in the brown garments of the Third Order of Saint Francis, his belly wound about with a cream cincture, collecting the offerings of the faithful. Was he a Gentleman?

'Mind yourselves, now,' my father would say to us three brothers as we set out on our regular afternoon walk, always the same walk, up Wellington Road and down Saint Luke's. 'Mind you behave properly in the street. You never know who might be walking behind you. It might be Alderman Jimmy Simcox. Or the Lord Mayor. Or Brigadier Winterbottom. Or the canon. Or, the Lord between us and all harm, maybe the district inspector himself!'

Because of this hierarchy-worship, certain Sunday mornings provided me, like the theatre and the church, with some highly emotional images of the Admirable Life. On these special mornings my father would lead the three of us up our all too familiar Saint Luke's or Wellington Road, and on beyond it to Wellington Barracks, under the arch, into the barrack square, there to join other loyal citizens watching the church parade of whatever regiment was quartered on us at the time. I have forgotten now what form of drill took place. All I remember is that either the Union Jack or else the regimental flag was shown, and that at the end the regimental band solemnly played 'God Save the King.' My brothers told me in later years that they felt a little embarrassed at this point — two loyalties, to the Empire and to Ireland, conflicting. There was no such conflict in the Old Grenadier or in me. He would thrust out his chest, stand to attention like a ramrod and glare straight in front of him. I, at his knee, would whip off my cap, throw out my chest, glare, and feel almost choked with emotion at the sonorous brass blare of:

> *Send him victorious,*
> *Happy and glorious,*
> *Long to reign over us,*
> *God save the King.*

When the drums rolled and the brass shook the air I could hear the sabre clash, the hoofbeats, the rifle fire of all the adventure books I had read — mainly Henty's: *The Dash for Khartoum, With Kitchener in the Soudan, One of the Twenty-eight, Under Drake's Flag, Winning his Spurs, Saint George for England, With Wolfe to Canada,* or *Won by the Sword.* As we walked away my father would be completely silent, or he would touch a stone in a wall bearing the broad arrow and the carved letters W.D. (War Department) and nod at us sagely and proudly. We belonged.

This pride nourished in him a strong fire of ambition for his sons. He was to make his eldest son, Patrick, a priest, an ambition of high priority with all Irish parents, and he was madly proud of his second son, Augustine, who later entered the British Civil Service and became a Revenue Inspector.

'To think,' he would then muse, 'that a son of mine is examining the incomes of men as rich, aye and richer than, the judge and the district inspector!'

He nearly went out of his head with delight the day my brother, then stationed in Bournemouth, one of the wealthiest centres for rentier incomes in England, told him that he had a retired field marshal on his books.

'What next?' he moaned, throwing his hands up to heaven in delight. 'What next?'

Still later he put me through the university. After I got a fellowship that took me to Harvard he used to write me letters, in his neat copperplate handwriting, so full of humble respect that they used to make me squirm at my own ingratitude and inadequacy. Remember that all this was achieved on a policeman's salary of about fifty-two pounds a year, eked out with the few pounds my mother made on her lodgers. This ambition for their young was a universal mark of the old RIC, and its source is as obvious as its history is long. Indeed, when I think now of that regimental parade I wonder whether, among our own most ancient ancestors, living on the boundaries of another empire, another such father may not on occasion have stood watching from a hilltop, in a similar blended mood of smothered pride and parental ambition, the imperial eagles passing far below along the Aurelian and the Julian Way into nether Gaul, and wondered, like my father, whether his son might one day carry them.

My pride in my father was at its greatest when the assizes opened and he would be among those allotted to guard the judge at the Courthouse. The British managed these things well. The judge, gowned and bewigged, was always borne in a horse-drawn carriage, open if the weather was clement, through the streets of the city, accompanied by detachments of mounted police and military trotting, tinkling and clanking gallantly, fore and aft. These mounted police, now gone, were a smart body of men, dressed in tight black breeches with knee-high boots of shining leather, the belt worn diagonally across the chest over one shoulder, little black pillbox hats held gaily on the sides of their heads by patent-leather chin straps, their long truncheons dangling from the pommels. I remember that many of them had a way of affecting small waxed moustaches. As for the foreign soldiery, I recall with a special pleasure a detachment of cuirassiers with gleaming breastplates, helmets with long red plumes, and drawn swords. The foot police, my father among them, wore full-dress uniform, spiked helmets with silver chin straps, patent-leather belts and gloves. On his arrival at the Courthouse the judge would alight from his carriage and in stately grandeur climb the long flight of steps up to the entrance, where a row of officials stood waiting respectfully to receive him — all native-born Irishmen. It was an impressive sight. A political system had been established. We the people had accepted it. Our Church blessed it. Our politicians tolerated it. The law of the land was now about to apply it.

Meanwhile, downstairs in the waiting rooms, or in the cells, about to be herded into the dock, there would be another bunch of native-born Irishmen. Most of them would, under any system, have to be considered lawless men; but at that time others would have been there thanks only to inherent injustices in the law itself. One might be a peasant farmer who, in despair, had resisted eviction from his minute cottage and holding by the local agent of some landlord residing in London or on the Continent who rarely, if ever, laid eyes on his property. Another man in the dock might have got involved in some internecine feud with his neighbour because of some real or imagined injustice arising out of the same complicated land system. Another might be a youth whose hot blood had led him to knock down or wound a policeman for no better reason than that he disliked the law of the land without knowing why he disliked it. All such protestors, for whatever reason, against the established system were, I am sure, accepted by everybody present as criminal. I, certainly, thought them criminals whenever, through my father's almighty influence, I was slipped into the court to witness the drama of their trial, judgment and sentence. When I saw, hanging around the dim halls and corridors, the mothers, fathers, sisters, wives, or other relatives of the men on trial — old brown-shawled women, frieze-coated countrymen, rude denizens of the hills and the fields — whispering in corners with bewigged counsel, apparently overawed by their strange surroundings, fearful for their kin, I never felt for them anything but a sense of vicarious fear blended with awestruck wonderment at their folly in getting themselves into such a mess.

There were, now and again, undercurrents. A sense of fear and wonder used to visit me every time I drew my father's pinewood baton from its leather case. As I slowly fingered the smooth, hard weapon I felt repulsion and something bordering on disgust. There was nobody to make the mental connection for me with Henty's rattling rifle-fire, flashing sabres and galloping hooves, yet, in some dim way, I do think that I here first began to feel the unpleasant reality of power when combined with brute force. I felt something of the same sort when, a couple of times a year, my father would be on late duty in the Bridewell and I and one of my brothers would be sent down there with welcome bowls of soup for himself and his comrades. By way of reward, we would be shown over the cells with all their paraphernalia of restraint. Once, to amuse me, one of my father's colleagues locked my wrists in the cold handcuffs. Another time we were shown the straitjacket for violent prisoners, a contraption of stout canvas with heavy leather belts. The cell was cold, dirty-white, with a smelly water closet in the corner, and a yellow fan of light bubbling in an aperture over the iron door. On that evening my brother lay down in the straitjacket and they buckled him up to show how it was done. 'Get out o' that, now, Mr Houdini!' laughed one of the constables, standing over him in his grey shirt and braces. I trembled to see him lying there, trussed like a mummy, smiling boyishly up at my smiling father and his jolly friends.

I loved the weeks, not more than one a quarter, when my father was detailed as night watch in the streets from midnight on. He looked very big, powerful, and handsome in his special night duty uniform: a long black belted overcoat down to his shins, a domed helmet, if the weather were bad a black waterproof cape, and short black stubby leggings. Our small city was free of serious crime, so that he and his comrade had nothing to do all night but kill the long hours pacing the empty streets, or standing in doorways watching the rain make bubbles in the lamp-lit pools, slant in the wind, hiss and moan up the river — Cork is a notoriously wet and windy city — hearing nothing else except some late reveller or late night worker beating his lonely way home, or, on the cold gusts from the north, Shandon's tireless bell. One reason why I loved those occasions was because my father and his companions ate a special late supper of chops, potatoes and strong tea just before going on duty, and I was allowed either to stay up late or come down in my night-shirt to partake of bits and scraps from his plate like a puppy dog. No piece of chop has ever since tasted as sweet as those bits of tail-end from his piled-up plate, I sitting on his knee, wearing his belt wound twice around me, my face and head half extinguished under his vast helmet. The fire in the range would be glowing. The steel of the fender shone bayonet-bright. The red tiles of the kitchen looked as warm as their colour. The wind in the already deserted streets shook the windows. The two policemen would presently buckle on their belts and truncheons, button up their collars, hook their capes, slip baby bottles of whiskey into their pockets against colds and pneumonia, and adventure out into the darkness, emptiness, and rain of the city streets, whereas I was about to clamber between my two brothers into a nicely warmed bed. I particularly liked the nights when his companion was one Constable Jim Hedderman, a pleasant, lean-faced, redheaded fellow who had established himself as the Brains of the Bridewell. He was always full of chat and odd stories. He had ambitions to get the two stripes, that is to become an acting sergeant, and was forever studying for the necessary examination — which he never passed. His two favourite subjects were orthography and astronomy. My father said he used to pass the night producing hard words to spell, or, if it were a clear sky, reading the stars:

'That is Cassy-o-paya. How would you spell that, now, Dinny? That is Orion's Belt. I bet you think that is spelled "O'Ryan." It is not, then. I will now relate to you the story of Orion. . . .'

My mother would take the holy water bottle and bless the pair of them with a wild scatter of it. She and I would then peep down through the corner of the window as they started their slow pacing around the corner of the School of Art, encased, immense, trans-formed, no longer just Father or just Jim, padding out of sight, once again the embodied and respected Law.

One afternoon I ran into the kitchen, divesting myself of my school satchel, eager for my dinner, and was halted by my mother's pale face and pointing finger. There, on the old battered sofa in the kitchen, lay my father, his head bandaged round and round, his right hand wrapped in layers of cotton wool and more bandages, looking solemnly up at me. She told me that he had been sent out that morning to a place called Watergrasshill, a rural hamlet a few miles northeast of Cork, where he had joined a squad of police forcibly evicting a tenant farmer and his family from the small house and farm whose rent they, presumably, could or would no longer pay but which they had refused to surrender. He may have been a shiftless and worthless farmer or a hardworking and overburdened man; his landlord may have been indulgent and patient or he may have been a ruthless tyrant; all we knew was that the man had barricaded himself in his house, cottage, or hut, and that the police had come, as was usual on such occasions, to break in the door with rifle butts and a battering ram and throw him and his family out, with their belongings, on the roadside. In the mêlée my father had been hit with a heavy stone, and when somebody inside thrust an iron bar out through a hole in the window he had grasped it. The bar looked black, but it had come, one minute before, red-hot from the hearth. It had seared his hand to the bones. As I looked down at him, gazing silently up at me, I could not have felt more overcome if he had been a boxer in the ring and I had just seen him knocked on the flat of his back to the canvas. Beside me my mother was at one moment commiserating him and at the next upbraiding him for 'putting himself forward' in the fray.

'Sure, you were always a quiet man! Too quiet! Too soft altogether for this world. Never in your life summonsed a living soul. What call had you to be making a hero out of yourself? How fair it was you were the foolah to catch the blow and snatch the bar! Always a good father, and a kind husband. Oh, the blackguards! To do such a thing to such a quiet man . . . !'

And, indeed, this was all true. How often had I had not heard him at night in his little attic room, when we were all in bed, praying aloud for us all, in a soughing, undulating, pleading voice, on his knees by his bed, his hands joined, his eyes to the ceiling and, as always, his braces hanging behind him to the floor like a bifurcated tail:

'Oh please, dear kind Jesus, look after my poor children, Patrick, and Augustine, and John. Watch over my poor wife Bid. Guide them and guard them. Help me to work for them as long as I live. . . .'

It was his silence that wounded me, and the bewilderment in his eyes. Could it have been that he was shocked by this passionate clash with his own kind of small-farmer folk in that early morning tussle on those windy uplands? If so, it was well for him that his retirement age came before the revolutionary spirit after 1916 spread all over the country. During the Troubles, as we were ironically to call those not so dangerous and very happy years, the Force was to stand to its guns against the rebels almost to a man; so, I am sure, would he have done, stubbornly, however bewildered by it all, not, to be sure, after any deep conscience-searchings about the conflicting demands involved in the idea of loyalty, but for a quite simple and unarguable reason: 'Oh please, dear kind Jesus, look after my poor little children. . . . Help me to work for them as long as I live. . . .'

Men like my father were dragged out, in those years, and shot down as traitors to their country. Shot for cruel necessity — so be it. Shot to inspire necessary terror — so be it. But they were not traitors. They had their loyalties and stuck to them.

III

I feel downcast that I can only remember my father like this as a figure, almost as a type, rather than as a person. His own inner, private life is hidden from me completely. He is to me more of a myth than a man, a figure out of that time, out of that place, a symbol of childhood. Does it always happen when we live closely and long with a person or a place that we come to know them less and less, whether wife, husband, child, or town? With him this happens when I seize even on the one or two privacies of his life, such as his little brown locked box, always on a shelf in the kitchen. To my mother this was a Bluebeard's chamber about which she used to tease him, to his great annoyance, saying: 'I wonder what have you at all, at all, in that little brown box? Maybe a little roll of pound notes? Ha?'

I think it contained his razors, possibly a few family letters, possibly a couple of pound notes. I associate it with his one relaxation, a bet on a horse now and again. After all, he had been born in the Queen's County, which borders on County Kildare, both famous racing counties. Down there he had a friend who was supposed to be 'in the know', one Philly Behan, a starter or a starter's assistant on the Curragh. To Philly, now and again, he would send a present of a ham, and from Philly there would come, now and again, a letter which my father might, though rarely, leave on the shelf and which my mother would guiltily read. 'There is some talk about a promising three-year-old, Flyaway, trained by Hartigan, for the June meeting, and if Gus Hogan is up I would say that he would be worth a bet both ways.' But when I would hear those words I would not think of his tremors or expectations so much as of the green wonder of the Curragh plain, about which he often talked to us, or of the Great Heath of Maryborough, near his boyhood home, and of all that far-off country from which he, and therefore I, had come. For me the little brown box held green fields, yellow heather, and galloping horses. In this way he really was a bit of the Irish myth, and a bit also of the imperial myth, and through their blended ambitions and pieties he achieved wholeness.

He would not have understood one word of this, and if he had he might not have agreed, because he had one other precious dream. Every so often there would come in the post a copy of a local paper from Kildare or the Queen's with advertisements of forthcoming auctions of farms marked in red ink: 'Four miles from *Emo*. Thirty acres of useful grazing land. Farmhouse and outhouses. . . . *Kildangan*. Twenty-seven acres, three roods of fine arable land. . . . Near *Kiladoon* . . .'

It was the pipedream of a man who had not enough money to farm a window box, the uprooted peasant longing for his Mother Earth — incomplete, unwhole, mortally vulnerable away from it. There must have been thousands like him in the Force. He reminds me that we had a semipermanent lodger one year named Ross, a retired sergeant of the Force. He was a finely built man, now grey, though you could see by his eyelashes that he had once been redheaded, with flowing moustaches still russet, partly from his pipe but also from rude, persistent health. He was a figure of fun to us children because he was always talking aloud to himself, so loudly that even through the ceiling we could sometimes hear him in his room mixing up his memories of barrack yard and farm haggard:

'Yessir! Nosir! At once! Attention! Dismiss! Halt! Whoa, back, whee! Gee up! That's the gurl! G'wan! Pike it up there, Jim. Fine hay! Dismiss! Yessir! Nosir! At once, sir!'

He had never married. He lived and died on his two memories.

Last night I read with deep emotion this little entry in Cesare Pavese's *Il Mistiere di Vivere*, written at the height of his success as an author in Turin:

> Isn't it curious that at the moment when you first left
> your home in the country . . . it never occurred to you
> that you were starting out on a long journey through
> cities, names, adventures, pleasures, unforeseeable worlds

which would make you realise in the course of time that one of the richest parts of your Future, wherein the everlasting mystery would prove to be that childish You whom at that time you made no effort to possess.

I wonder what my father dreamed on his happy nights? When we talk about squares how we simplify! In every square is there a buried myth? I think I am trying to persuade myself that there is. I want desperately to believe that my father was larger than I must otherwise think. He was, so evidently, so accusingly, a good man, a loyal servant, an upright citizen, a pious Christian, a good father, that I cannot believe in him as a man at all unless he had, also, some purely personal dream outside those social virtues. I do not want to think of my father as a Father. By being my father he is lost to me, as, for all I know, I am lost to my children. Perhaps I must accept the truth, miserably: that he, happily, lost himself in his children. It makes me feel so ungiving, so helpless, now that it is too late to explain to him that if he had been less good I might now admire him less and might then have loved him more.

Freeze
Seán Ó Ríordáin
Translated by: Seán Dunne

One frosty morning I roved out
And a handkerchief was there
Before me on a bush.
I took it to put in my pocket
But it slipped because it was frozen.
It wasn't a living cloth that slipped
But something that died last night on a bush.
Then I searched in my mind
For this thing's equivalent —
A day I kissed a woman of my people
When she lay in her coffin, frozen.

In the Honan Hostel
Eilís Dillon

When I went to live in Cork in 1940 I already knew a great deal about universities and people who worked in them. This was because my father was professor of chemistry at Galway and I had watched him build up a large and prestigious department from very small beginnings. In the early twenties, he and his generation were committed to proving that Ireland and the Irish were able to reach world standards without the help of the British Empire. Though a peaceful man in general, he had been arrested in May 1918, and had spent a year in Gloucester jail. This had had the usual result of stiffening his resolve.

I knew other things about professors: that they don't like their desks tidied, that they keep irregular hours, that they have a high standard in the matter of quick understanding of their special problems and interests and that they enjoy foreign travel and good food, neither of which they can easily afford.

Perhaps my husband, Cormac Ó Cuilleanáin, spotted this special knowledge of mine when he decided on me as his life companion. As I have said in another place, he was pointed out to me in the dance hall of an Irish College with the remark that he had said he was going to marry me. There may have been something about me that suggested that I would know how to take care of his particular needs. At any rate, within six months I found myself in Cork, a city of which I knew nothing except that it was on the pleasant waters of the river Lee, and that my father had once applied for a job there and been turned down.

As I was very young, I was not then aware that my great-grandfather, William Kirby Sullivan, had been a noted professor of chemistry at Cork, and had been President of the College for many years. He had studied in Giessen with Liebig, the great German industrial chemist, and was very anxious to see Ireland develop industrially. His father had owned a paper-mill in Dripsey, on the river, but the story goes that the workers burned it down when he attempted to install machinery.

Sullivan's daughter Elizabeth married my grandfather, John Dillon, and it was Dillon who interested him in placing the first beet sugar factory in Tuam, in the west of Ireland. Sullivan also had some connection with the foundation of the model farm in Cork, whose purpose was to train poultry instructors. Though a Catholic — he had been professor of chemistry at Newman's university in Dublin — he was sufficiently of the Cork establishment to be quite powerful in a firmly entrenched Protestant society.

His relations with the Protestant community were always good, so that when the Reverend Mr Webster raised money and built a hostel for Protestant students, Sullivan was able to persuade him to call it Berkeley Hall, rather than naming it after a bigoted evangelical cleric of the time. When my husband became the Warden of the Honan Hostel, as it had then become, my father told me this with great delight. Mr Webster's project had been a failure, since the students preferred to live in lodgings rather than under his supervision.

My father had been a student in Cork, entering the medical faculty in 1900 at the age of sixteen. For the first year, in those days, medical students were obliged to follow courses in Latin and other liberal arts subjects, and from this experience he retained for the rest of his life the idea of the complete man. Besides, it was a family tradition that one should have at least some knowledge of the arts as well as of science. His grandfather Sullivan, while retaining his profession as a chemist, was a large contributor on Irish subjects to the 1870 edition of the Encyclopaedia Britannica, and wrote a very long preface to *Manners and Customs of the Ancient Irish*, Eugene O'Curry's seminal work.

At the time my father arrived in Cork, the total student registration was about two hundred. Sullivan was dead and was succeeded by two placemen in a row who did much to ruin the work he had done. At last a good appointment was made, in the person of Sir Bertram Windle, and his was still a name well remembered in Cork when I went to live there.

My husband was made Warden in 1949. The appointment was for a 'Catholic professor, whose wife was able and willing to help him in its administration.' I was both, having had my education cut short by the war and having done a spell of working in a menial capacity in hotels and at a higher level at the Irish College where I met my fate. I felt quite at home in the Warden's House. My parents had always lived in big ramshackle houses, cold in winter but heavenly in summer, with wild gardens and all kinds of hidey-holes where one could escape from one's own kind. The Warden's

House was a great improvement on these, and recognisable at once as an ideal house for children. The rooms were not many but they were enormous — we could and did have concerts in the drawing-room, which measured about thirty-five feet by twenty.

The hostel was contained in the adjoining building, all in single rooms with running water, short on bathrooms but with adequate central heating worked by a coke boiler. It had been bought by a very cultivated lawyer, with money left by the Honan family for charitable purposes, and it was he who included a complete set of Medici prints of great masters of the renaissance, in the corridors and in the students' rooms. The china was all stamped with the arms of the Hostel, showing St Finbarr looking out through the doorway of a church. This was incomprehensible until we discovered him in the coat of arms invented for the whole establishment, in the attic of our house. It was signed and sealed by Sir Neville Wilkinson, Ulster King at Arms, and was in a sad state of repair. We had it framed, complete with purple ribbon and seal, and hung it in the Warden's study.

The staff consisted of six women of a certain age, and one man who acted as janitor. White linen cloths were used in the dining-room and there was massive silver cutlery, carefully tended and counted by Maud, the waitress in charge of it. All six women distrusted the students deeply, with what reason I could not discover. Many of them had come on scholarships from the various southern counties and were highly intelligent and motivated. As the hostel was popular, my husband was able to make a point of choosing the most intelligent students who applied, and this meant that apart from occasional mutinies we all lived together in relative peace and mutual understanding.

Fifty people had to be fed three times a day with food to their complete satisfaction. Here was where my experience of the academic mind came in useful. I devised eight menus, so that there was always an element of surprise — not even the mathematicians worked out why they were never able to guess what would appear on the table. I further devised a plan of ordering the exact amount of food that would reasonably be eaten every day, so that there were never any leftovers. I placed all the orders early every Monday morning, specifying the day of delivery, and this pleased the suppliers. I applied the same principle to my own house, where I had to think of a house-keeper and a children's nurse and three children, including a baby who was born after we went to live in the Warden's House. When all this was in order, after a tour of inspection of the hostel, by half-past ten in the morning I was sitting at my desk beginning my other life as a professional writer, which had already got off to a good start before we moved into the College. I had exactly two and a half hours for this, because at a quarter past one my husband and I went into the students' dining-room and sat at a separate table for lunch, with the College chaplain.

It will be readily understood that this splendid chain of arrangements was only as strong as its weakest link. Cooks left, maids quarrelled, mine — who were always younger — left to get married, always a cause for rejoicing. Still somehow I managed to take children to music lessons and entertain them in various ways when they came home from school. My husband supervised their homework and taught them with endless interest if only academic patience. But I soon saw that, like myself, they took it for granted that an academic father is liable to have a short fuse and they could see the benefits to them every day of their lives. Besides, as the academic year was only thirty weeks, there were glorious periods of calm when almost the whole campus was shut down and we expanded into our borrowed territory.

During all those first years, Alfred O'Rahilly was the President of the College. He had colonized the old President's house, renaming it the Staff House, while staying on in his own. This was the adjoining, slightly smaller one, and he had lived in it during the years when he was the College Registrar. After he became President, he repeated over and over that eventually both buildings would naturally become part of the College. By the time he left, this was indeed taken for granted and the College lost something that had given it character and style. The value of the living presence of the President was too subtle for O'Rahilly's comprehension, or else he could not bear the thought of being succeeded by an inferior within the very walls of his house. To him, almost everyone was an inferior.

O'Rahilly had been in the Jesuits for thirteen years, and was within a whisker of being ordained when he or they decided that he should leave. He never lost his hankering after the clerical life, however, and always maintained a fierce interest in the religious life of the students and the faculty. He attended daily Mass in the Honan Chapel, often serving Mass in a black cassock and white surplice. This made visiting celebrants very uneasy, as according to the rules a man in an eminent position, such as a College President, should serve Mass in his ordinary clothes. O'Rahilly knew those rules: he also knew that the place of honour in the Chapel was the left-hand side of the altar, and he always grudged this position to the Warden, while he had to be content with the right.

Though the Chapel adjoined the College grounds, it was part of the Honan foundation and therefore not under O'Rahilly's jurisdiction at all. After my husband's appointment, he never came to Board meetings of the foundation, having fallen foul of the other Governors over a question of precedence and of his rights to direct the proceedings. This was a great relief, as he was a contentious member of many committees.

His interest in the Hostel had been destructive enough to be a warning to us. Just before the war, a previous Warden, Joseph Downey, had prudently stocked the store-room with chests of tea and sacks of sugar, to eke out the meagre rations allowed by the Department of Supplies. At Downey's death in office, O'Rahilly declared an interregnum, during which convenient period he quietly removed the tea and sugar to the old President's House and opened the first College restaurant. From these inglorious beginnings grew the fine amenities that are now available and the cupboard was left bare for the incoming Warden. This was Professor Donal MacCarthy, who afterwards became President of the College, and it was he who told us this story.

Oddly enough, O'Rahilly paid no attention to the affairs of the Honan Chapel, which was part of our foundation. We quickly discovered that there was a splendid set of gothic vestments, in all the liturgical colours, some of which had been designed by the Dun Emer Guild. So had the dorsals and frontals which were supposed to be used in the various seasons. One of these was in a sad state of neglect, and we were able to invite Katherine MacCormack, the designer of it, who was still alive and a friend of my family, to come and do the necessary repairs. Later she designed and embroidered the last set of vestments we bought for the Chapel, white, very beautiful. We also commissioned a set of purple vestments, which were made by Egan's in Cork to a design of Séamus Murphy's. The copes were museum pieces, and had survived well because they were kept in a special box in the attic of the Warden's House.

One hopes that these priceless things are safe somewhere. Priests used to complain about the weight of them, and one fears that advantage may have been taken of the Second Vatican Council to

111

abandon them to some unknown fate. Ireland has always been very low-church, and we never felt that they were properly appreciated.

Though O'Rahilly did some great things for Cork, including the foundation of the adult education programme, his interventions in campus life were often unfortunate. His interest in the morals of the students at one point took the form of insisting that the girl students should always wear stockings, even in hot weather. The girls, however, were displeased to find their President going about peering at their legs, and someone — perhaps the women's dean or the chaplain — intervened to put a stop to it. Girls in trousers would not have got past the front gate. Events of this kind led one bewildered professor, who had come from Dublin to take up an appointment in one of the sciences, to remark that University College, Cork, was like a convent run by a mad reverend mother.

O'Rahilly liked to take on powerful adversaries, and he specially enjoyed newspaper controversies. He prided himself on having routed Sir Bertram Windle, forcing him to resign the presidency. I never heard the details of that encounter. It may have been an easy win, since Windle belonged to the earlier Ireland of respect for the old establishment, and was probably uneasy in the new regime. O'Rahilly was a ruthless enemy, quite certain of his own rectitude and judgment. He often called up the Catholic church's teaching when he was asked to arbitrate in strikes in the city. This was an activity he enjoyed and his years in the Jesuits gave him great prestige. He had no scruples about his methods when he set out to destroy his foe.

Sometimes his methods were subtle enough. On one occasion, when my husband opposed him forcefully on the Academic Council, the revenge was monstrous. We had a much-loved cat named Tadhg, a large black tom, shining with health and vigour and a great pet with the children. Tadhg had come with us to the Warden's House and was the kind of cat who would consent to spend hours in a doll's pram, dressed in doll's clothes. To understand what happened, one should realise that my husband was a large man and the cat was small.

The day after the Governing Body meeting, the head gardener presented himself at the back door to say that the President had given him instructions to catch Tadhg and do him in. The gardener was very distressed. He had children of his own and he knew the unpleasantness of what he was being instructed to do. We asked what were the complaints against Tadhg and were told that the President said he had a habit of looking through the windows of the

President's House and disturbing the morals of the President's cat, and he had even been known to eat the President's cat's dinner.

We advised a policy of *laissez faire*, but the gardener said his experience was that when the President wanted something done, he would write him a letter every day asking if the orders had been carried out. We were naturally fascinated by this statement, as we knew he had applied the same form of terror to a professor who was a friend of ours, and who had suffered greatly under the strain. The gardener was in a state of miserable nervousness at the prospect of this assault, but at last we prevailed on him to give Tadhg a reprieve, at least for a few days. When the letters began to arrive, we felt obliged to put the feelings of the gardener before those of our children, and poor Tadhg was either executed or sent to a maximum security prison.

One of the real enjoyments of having a spacious house was that we were able to give hospitality to visiting musicians, in the certainty that the piano was up to their standard and that they could feel free to practise as long as they liked without disturbing anyone. After a number of exciting visits to Italy, my husband and I were instrumental in founding a branch of the Società Dante Alighieri in Cork, and the Centre in Rome sent us many distinguished musicians to give recitals. When these stayed with us, we enjoyed a sort of private concert while they practised. For me this is still always a pure pleasure.

When the Radio Éireann quartet was established and came to Cork, they soon took to trying out their concerts in our drawing-room, and far from wanting to be alone they needed us as a trial audience. The fact that they were there at all was entirely due to the efforts of Aloys Fleischmann. He was the prototype of all academics, in his single-minded devotion to an idea and his determination to overcome all odds to achieve it. Some of the odds would have seemed insurmountable to anyone else, but Aloys never stopped to consider them. I have seen him standing beside his bicycle with the rain pouring off his shabby felt hat, buttonholing a member of Cork Corporation and speaking to him so earnestly about music that escape was out of the question.

This was the method he used to brow-beat Radio Éireann into employing a quartet and sending it to Cork. He had worked for years to get the Light Orchestra there, without success, and compromised at last by accepting the quartet. I had played in his own symphony orchestra, which was always short of cellos and usually had to be bolstered up with musicians from afar to make it sound something like the real thing. Brass was always a problem, and the army kindly lent some of theirs, with a sergeant in charge to make sure no one slipped out to the Black Cock at the interval when we played in the City Hall.

Aloys loved choral music, and from doing Handel oratorios he moved on to Purcell's 'Faery Queen', with the assistance of the Cork ballet company and some local amateur singers. At that point I had to admit that my own patience would not run to amateur ballet, and I retired. Not so Aloys, though he must have known how painful the productions were. He went on to found the Cork Choral Festival and never hesitated to invite international celebrities to compose for it.

In spite of his name and his background, he was a total Irishman: I remember him stopping me one day to tell me in ecstatic tones that he had got Seán Ó Riada into his department, to teach Irish music. The fact that he and Ó Riada were so different never entered the question. He knew a dedicated expert when he saw one.

This insulation or protective covering is what makes it possible for professors to carry on their research and teaching in the face of fearful odds. Except for us, they all went home to their families in the evening and doubtless drew breath and sustenance enough to come back next day refreshed. Because we lived on the premises, we found that we needed variety in our company. Séamus Murphy's house became a refuge, when we had time to enjoy it. One met all kinds of people there, and Séamus and Máiréad made them all welcome. The conversation was interesting and constructive, and Séamus's tolerance pervaded the atmosphere. At his funeral Louis Marcus, who was often one of that company, described it as a kind of university — or rather, a hedge school, where one learned a mish-mash of interesting things, all the better for not being necessarily useful.

By the early 1960s it became obvious that my husband could no longer tolerate the climate of Cork. With the comment that if you could not live in Cork, you might as well live in Rome, he opted to move there and of course I was able and willing to go along with him. In Frascati, where we settled for the first year, I continued my life as a writer, using the same routine as I had done all my life, and presently my son remarked that he had thought I always put in my days waiting for him to come home from school. So much for those who occasionally expressed the view that living in official housing is bad for children. I can't see that it did ours any harm.

The Coat

Seán O'Faoláin

from: *Vive Moi!* (1965)

Let me tell you about the Coat. It is a symbol of everything I later came to hate and despise in this shabby-genteel life of ours. The Coat was sewn together for me, laboriously and painfully, by my mother out of the material of one of my father's cast-off uniforms. Now, these tough uniforms were made of a material so closely woven, and then shrunk, or felted, that they could have kept out everything except a bullet, so that in spite of all my mother's art as a seamstress she failed to control the obdurate material, with the result that when she had reduced the paternal jacket to the size of a boy's body, the Coat curved out like a church bell all around my bottom, my two shoulders peaked up like two epaulettes, and my two arms were encased in two tubes. I nearly wept when I saw it, and the next day, clad or confined in it, I went, most unwillingly, to school, where my companions laughed so mercilessly at me in the schoolroom, at playtime, in the yard, on my way home, that I refused to wear it again. My mother could not, or professed not to be able to, see what was wrong with it, holding it up, admiring it eloquently, fitting it on me again and again. To no purpose! I still looked like a sable-skirted fay, a minute South American mute. My mother begged. I insisted, obstinately and tearfully. In the end I had my way. The Coat lay around, or rather stood around, for months, until one day the Bottle Woman called.

This woman was a barefooted, beshawled shrimp of a creature who came to our door periodically to buy empty bottles and our cast-offs. (*Our* cast-offs!) The usual heap was thrown on the tiled floor of the hall and the usual bargaining began. A shilling for this. Sixpence for that. Suddenly she spied the Coat, snatched it up, held it up, turned it around and around, and then, with a wild peal of laughter, she cried: 'For God's sake, Missus Whalen, what in Heaven's name is *dat*?'

My mother snatched it from her and flung it on the heap.

'Sixpence,' she said.

The Bottle Woman shook her head sorrowfully, as if she were saying, 'Now, I'd like to be a philanthropist, Missus Whalen. But!'

She shook her head at fivepence, and at fourpence, and even at tuppence she would not have the coat. I, leaning over the balustrade, prayed that the Bottle Woman would at least give a penny for it.

My mother would not stoop that low. Preserving her dignity as a true lady, she said grandly: 'You may have it as a handsel.'

The Bottle Woman was too polite not to accept the gift, too honest to suppress a deep sigh as she took the piece of armour; and with as deep a sigh I leaned up from the balustrade and went upstairs to my attic window to inform all Cork of my blessed release from the shame of my masquerade.

For this was what our whole life was: a pretence that we were not what we were, a bobby, a bobby's wife, and a bobby's kids. We were shabby-genteels at the lowest possible social level, always living on the edge of false shames and stupid affections, caught between honourable ambitions and pathetic fears, between painful strugglings and gallant strivings, never either where we were or where we hoped to be, Janus-faced, throwing glances of desire and admiration upwards and ahead, glances of hatred or contempt downwards and behind. But I wonder, even as I talk about this life of the shabby-genteel that I saw on all sides of me as a boy and a youth, whether anybody today can form any idea of what genteelism meant in the British Isles before the Twenties began to make hay of it and the Thirties and Forties finally threw it out of the door. Certainly none of my American readers will understand the term or be able to form any feeling for what it once meant. Even their dictionaries — if the one before me is typical — do not know that the word means; for what this lexicographer says it means is: 'Belonging or suited to polite society, well-bred, refined, elegant, stylish.' The true meaning points to the effort to be all those things, and the transparent failure to be any of them. One has probably to go back to the novelists to get the tragicomic sense of the word. Thackeray gives it to us; so does Dickens; Gissing, Wells, Bennett, Italo Svevo; it outcrops in Forster; it is all over the stories of V. S. Pritchett. Of American writers, only one drew inspiration from this half-grey life of the ambitious poor, and she, being a Bostonian, had not the courage to depict more than a quarter of what she knew so well and had so painfully experienced — Louisa Alcott in that almost-great novel *Little Women*.

On my knees I thank God that I escaped from both genteelism and shabby-genteelism. I did it by escaping from the city to the country. I went behind the urban rot to the life that my father and mother had cast aside — had had to cast aside — when they first entered what we would nowadays call the rat race of the city. It was the beginning of my emancipation: the start of another me.

A Cork Girlhood
Isabel Healy

On the triangular carved milestone across the river and up the hill from our house, *3 Miles to Cork* was painted so thickly, black on yellow, that it was smooth. We lived in the country. The mile marker was a good place to sit and rest on the walk home from the number five bus. It was just down from the field where the wild gooseberries grew, and across the road from the field where the corncrake rattled. Today there is tennis twenty-four hours a day on thirteen courts in the corncrake's field. The gooseberries were dug out when they built the housing estate and the milestone has disappeared. Yet pheasants still strut low beneath the hedge at the edge of the meadow; wood pigeons the size of pheasants peck the lawn; the rooks remain in the trees by the river to announce each dusk and dawn, and the fox has held her territory.

All those — the fields and birds and animals — were an essential part of our Cork childhood, as rivers and hills are an essential part of Cork. Even now to hear or see the words 'Lee Valley' evokes more a way of life than merely scenery. As small children, we were brought out to see, for the last time, the houses, farms and roadside pub which were to be submerged with the flooding of the low-lying land to build a hydroelectric dam at Inniscarra. Sometimes in a drought, you can still see from the Macroom road their muddy skeletons, on which cruciform cormorants balance to dry their wings. The dam a-building was a favourite Sunday drive and also Gougane Barra, where it was always cold, and soft, loose-limbed red setters slept under the settle in the hotel at the water's edge.

We were an academic family, and thus of limited means, but so was everybody then, apart from the wealthy Quaker friends my parents had in Dublin, where there was a swimming pool in the garden and I saw my first bikini. My parents had to get a special dispensation from the bishop to go to their friends' weddings, and we were quite proud of them being so liberal as to have associates of another faith and to attend their ceremonies. I did not have too much pride to wear their cast-off clothes. If hand-smocked Viyella dresses were not purchased from the workshops at the Good Shepherd convent, then they were hand-me-downs from Dublin. Going barefoot in summer was a painful affectation more than a necessity, for there were always butt-toed Clark's sandals and Rubber Dollies (the white t-strap canvas shoes made at the Dunlop factory) in which every Cork child was reared.

Exceptions to the Catholic norm were rare and warranted whispers. Protestant-owned shops in town were frequented mainly by their own and tolerance towards the beliefs and failings of others was arbitrarily dispensed. When our maid got pregnant by a soldier from the barracks in Ballincollig, she was let go because of the detrimental effect the occurrence might have on our innocent psyches. Not that psyches were ever acknowledged; one was expected to be controlled and get on with it. Showing — or even feeling — emotion was rude, and was cut off with 'Sarah Bernhardt'. Tears got no sympathy. Praise was never given for fear of causing 'a swelled head', and feeling sorry for oneself was 'Kevin Barry' ('another martyr for old Ireland. . . .').

Before she was dismissed, that maid taught us to sing 'The Yellow Rose of Texas'. Radio Eireann came on air at lunch-time, and there were no portable transistor radios. Working around the house, my mother sang such songs as 'The Galway Plate' and 'Ballyjamesduff'. The words were less important than the sweeping or polishing rhythm, for we once found her singing 'It's a fatal thing to die for Ireland. . . .'

Our world was centred in the countryside and each season brought adventures — many of them culinary — from the first hedgerow violets and 'bread and butter', the edible first buds of hawthorn, through frog spawn in the ponds, pinkeens from the river in jam jars, mushrooms on grass thraneens, the corn we raided in the Model farm fields, damsons, crab apples, bitter hazelnuts and green-skinned walnuts from the wood, to winter holly. My father picked elderflower and rose hips to make Tokay, and the cloudy contents of big glass cylinders bubbled sporadically in the hot press beside the bottles of ginger pop made from a yeast and sugar culture which blew their corks with such nocturnal regularity that we grew accustomed to explosions in the night.

118

Wine was important, but the only pub I can remember was the narrow bar at the back of Rearden's Wine Importers opposite the Courthouse on Washington Street, where we bought our provisions on order each month. Shopping for groceries was civilized, my mother sitting on a high bentwood chair beside the long wooden counter. Everything seemed to be made of wood: the ceiling, the myriad of bins and drawers which lined the walls, and the clerk's glass-panelled caboose. The shop smelled of tea, ladled on demand into the firm's own bags by the staff, who wore mustard-coloured overalls and wrote each purchase in a long ledger. They treated us children with such deference that it was imperative, when I found a dead mouse, to put it in a matchbox and take it into town to show the staff of Rearden's. Often there was a tasting of some new sherry in a small schooner glass for my mother as she ordered, loose Kimberly biscuits out of bins for us and, if my father arrived for a lift home from UCC, we might be brought into the pub through the door at the back of the shop for a mineral and the froth from the top of his pint.

Free to ramble in our own wide territory of fields, woods and river, we did not feel claustrophobia in a country and a time of rigid thinking and censorship, where rules were unquestioned. We had 'cabby houses' and imaginary friends. We made up songs and stories and after each day's 'Listen With Mother' on the radio, went out to the garden to climb apple trees and re-enact each show. We lived in the stories of children's classics and contemporary Irish and American writers. Maura Laverty was spoken of with affection and we read *The Cottage in the Bog*, *The Little Red Hen* and books by Eilís Dillon, but the greatest favourites were Patricia Lynch, Laura Ingalls Wilder, *Eloise* and the 'Katy' stories. Though *The Young Visiters*, *Strewelpeter* and *Winnie the Pooh* were acceptable, the Bobsey Twins and Enid Blyton were forbidden in the house.

One sweltering summer in the mid-1950s, we spent entirely in the open, but never in public places. Children from families of all classes, rich and poor, crowded and privileged, were being struck down with a 'flu-like virus' which turned out to be polio. The fear and tragedy of those days still haunts Cork families and the evidence of that epidemic is still noticeable on the streets. They said polio spread through eating ice pops, or maybe that was only to keep us away from the tuppenny treat from the Cold Storage Rooms on the South Mall. They also said it was picked up from swimming in the

Lee at Blackrock Castle, but children who never swam anywhere but in the sea at Fountainstown also picked up the crippling disease.

That summer we did not walk the length of the Straight Road to the Lee Baths where there were different days for girls and boys. The unlucky sex could only stand on the road outside, hardly able even to see the water through the high railings, because of the concrete cabins which ringed the outdoor pool with its brown water sucked straight from the Lee. We rarely went to Fountainstown anyway, where the Cork families who did not go to Youghal went for a month or the entire summer. Low bungalows and tin shacks lined the hillside over the small beach, and transatlantic liners entering the harbour sailed along the horizon like a ship in a child's painting. Fountainstown regulars went out in row boats and were thrown sweets and cigarettes from high above by the posh folk on board.

We went more often to Myrtleville, where one summer afternoon we chatted with Daniel Corkery over a garden gate near a fuchsia hedge. You were either a Fountainstown family or you were not. We were not, and we felt outcasts, for as we grew older, it seemed to us a social paradise. If your family went to Fountainstown, you played tennis and went to 'hops'; during the winter months you went to swimming galas at the Eglington Street Baths in town. There, the excitement of mingling with the opposite sex was intensified by the competition, the volume of noise over the enclosed water.

There were traditions. On Christmas Eve my father put up a canopy of twisted coloured crepe paper streamers which gave the living room the appearance of a Bedouin tent. He went to midnight Mass and was in charge of lighting the fire and making the breakfast the next morning when we were out. The fire was always lit with the sports pages of the papers, because nobody ever read them. We went to see Santa Claus at the Munster Arcade, an exciting place with departments called Ladies Mantles, Millinery and Haberdashery, where brass canisters of money and receipts whizzed from counter to cashier above one's head on taut wire pulleys. One year we went to see 'The Wizard of Oz' and when I got a present of a doll, I called her Dorothy.

On St Stephen's Day we visited as many church cribs as we could manage and would make comparisons, though it was never really a contest with St Francis, the dazzling church in town where the figures wore real velvet cloaks and real oranges were presented to the bairn. The year of the hula hoop rage, we took the bus up to the heights of Gurranebraher, which was then a very new municipal housing estate and had a view of the whole city. I envied the children who could all go out on the streets with their hoops and play together. Our socializing as children was mainly familial, and confined to visiting neighbours, of whom there were few of our own age. Unaware of the kudos of 'detached' living, it was always our ambition to live in a park and have an endless supply of playmates outside the door. There was little formal entertaining. Students, especially foreigners, called for advice, and I remember a tall girl called Ruth walking the garden with my father, pouring out her love for a John Reidy who played in a jazz band in college. My father advised her to follow her heart, and the Ó Riadas went on to settle and rear a family in Cúil Aodha. I remember the big frame of the historian, John T. Collins, wedged into the small chairs in the study, and how my mother would be exasperated to see the long shadow of the Pope O'Mahony at the hall door, for he always came at the most inopportune times, and tended to stay. Looking at myself and my sisters, he said, 'You three girls are living proof that the Spanish Armada landed in Ireland.' Enthralled by the stories of the sculptor, Séamus Murphy, I sucked on a Christmas tree fairy light and the bulb exploded in my mouth.

We loved to visit the physicist Professor Reilly at the Hydro in Blarney. With great gentleness he would show us his aviary and goldfish and sometimes would offer us a choice from his million accumulated knick-knack treasures in a huge glass case. He lived in a house at St Anne's Hydro, where the buildings — whose owner rode in the last cavalry charge in history — were already slowly mouldering.

In town, women wore hats and gloves or fringed black shawls. There were horses and drays carrying coal through the cobbled streets where ran narrow rail tracks which later would catapult us from our bicycles. There were familiar characters such as Andy Gaw, who might give you a sixpence with his handshake, and a sweet shop called Hadji Bey's. My mother went into town to auctions and to meet her friends in Thompson's in Patrick Street, with its tiered silver cake-stands, or in the Green Door restaurant over Barter's Travel Agents, where we sat at damask-covered tables. The tables were small, to accommodate intimate conversation, and earned the utterly refined and respectable restaurant a reputation — probably spread about by men who spent their time in the male-only pubs — for the cruellest gossip.

There were many auction rooms in the city, and I was familiar with them all: Barry's, Woodwards, Marsh's, where mirrors and paintings and odd chairs hung on the walls, and every inch of space was covered in objects my mother would stroke and peer under and inspect. I sensed the thrill of gambling, picking the winner, worrying that anyone else had spotted its worth under the grime, bidding, possibly going too high, bearing the item home, maybe to find, after purchase, either its weak points or something wonderful, secreted in a drawer.

On St Patrick's Day we went to the Parade, standing on the footpath on the South Mall eating cubes of coconut ice sweets in white paper bags. The Parade consisted mainly of bands and people marching, wearing the uniform of their school or organisation. Members of the Pioneer Total Abstinence Society featured prominently, displaying their sacrifice. One national feast day, when my mother was sick in bed, my father put food colouring in the cooking water, and served us green potatoes. The Eucharistic Procession in June did not feature in our social or liturgical calendar, though it was huge in the city, nor did we ever attend a match or sport of any kind, though we would stop for the bowlers on Inchigaggin Lane or the roads near the Viaduct.

There was a children's film society in the Crawford Gallery where my brother and I went on Saturday afternoons. There I lost my innocence and was catapulted into a less protected world. I will never get over the anguish of 'Bambi'. I couldn't believe that life could be so cruel, or that such a terrible thing as a baby losing its mother to a hunter's shot could be portrayed on screen. But there were lighter moments with 'Monsieur Hulot's Holiday', and spiritual uplift with 'The Song of Bernadette'. The cinemas in Cork were legendary in their splendour, from the ornate domed boxes of the Palace, to the sweeping staircases and red velvet Ladies Room of the Savoy, to the sociable Pavilion, with its restaurant where country people ate when they came to town, and eligible young men brought city girls on their first date.

Once a year the foreigners briefly entered our lives; choirs and folk dance groups from faraway places with strange-sounding names, film stars and directors from America and Europe, people whom we regarded with awe, since they were rich and famous, Communists or black — social groupings thin on the ground in Cork of the 1950s. It was a time when festivals were popping up everywhere,

122

and my father, convinced that there would soon be a festival queen in each town or village which had an associated song, suggested a pageant for 'The Thing from Gloccamara'.

An Tostal began in the early 1950s with a week of ballet, film and choral music. The evening events warranted formal attire, my father wearing white tie, tails and an opera hat which delighted us as he slapped it open and shut on his knee. My mother would speak with affection of film directors such as Vittorio de Sica. My father would take the Byelorussians, Czechs and Poles to his heart. To us, they were merely grown-ups; sometimes funny, sometimes nice, but grown-ups *per se* were strange and exotic, always to be feared and obeyed. It was a time when the generation gap was a terrifying divide, which few had the courage to cross.

I look back with affection on the countryside of childhood, but not the state. Although life in Cork in the fifties was simple, it was a difficult, complicated business being inside the body of a child. The summers were long and hot, as all childhood summers were, and, in winter, sometimes we had snow. We grew up, though, strangely, few grew out, for many of my generation have stayed on in the place that shaped and sometimes even nurtured them. I still love Cork. There I belong and there I am secure.

Internal Exile in the Second City
Paddy Woodworth

I still thought I was enjoying living in Cork city when a phone call came from Dublin: a colleague on another newspaper casually mentioned that a particular job, which I had always thought would be interesting, was about to fall vacant. Suddenly, I realized with terrible clarity that I had been fooling myself. I hated my life in Cork with a passion, and any chance to get out of the city would be more than welcome. I was just lucky that I also wanted the job in question, and luckier still to get it.

Since then, I have occasionally wondered how I put up with living in Cork at all. I have also wondered, more pertinently to the matter in hand, to what extent my misery in Cork was of my own making, and to what degree it was imposed upon me by the place and its people. How did it come about that I came to feel like a *gastarbeiter*, albeit a well-treated one, in what I had previously regarded as a most attractive and hospitable part of my own country?

If what follows is to make any sense, the reader will have to accept two things about the writer. The first is that I have lived very happily out of Dublin, itself an adoptive native city from my home town of Bray, for long periods on several occasions. I have spent long periods in places as diverse as Northern Ireland and the Basque country. Had circumstances been different, I think I could have easily settled in Derry, San Sebastian or elsewhere, for good. I am therefore not the sort of Jackeen who knows for a fact that there is neither culture nor comfort beyond the banks of the Royal and Grand canals.

Secondly, it might help to know that I went to live in Cork by choice, and a choice which I thought at the time was well informed by experience. I travelled south impelled by the happiest memories of previous — but short — visits to the Real Capital. I was determined not to be influenced by what I regarded as poisonous prejudices about the legendary clannishness of our second city. If, as I heard, Maeve Binchy could not hack it in Cork, that was her problem, I reckoned, and was careful not to read, then or now, her stinging farewell to the Leeside. I knew better.

I knew better because I had attended several Cork Film Festivals in succession, and had come to regard the event as one of the high-points of a fledgling film critic's year. I loved the informality, the lack of pretension, the warmth of the welcome, the convivial ambience. All these homely virtues were seamlessly woven into an acute and cosmo-politan appreciation of film culture, particularly when the festival came under the joint directorship of Mick Hannigan and Theo Dorgan.

Here, I felt, was a place where pleasure and philosophy sat down easily at table together, where a gentle hedonism and slower, saner pace of life than the capital's permitted a sharper rather than a softer focus on the Big World beyond. And the atmosphere of liberalism in personal matters, at least among the cinema-going classes, seemed indistinguishable from that of Dublin. The idea that Cork was in any way 'behind' the metropolis on the east coast simply did not cross my mind.

I had fallen a little in love, in fact, with the subtle physical beauty of the city in crisp autumn sunlight. I loved the sense that every second street was bounded by water on which swans were floating, I loved the liquid colours which sometimes seemed to float in the air itself. I enjoyed the steep, unpredictable hills of the northside, and the little streets off the main, wonderfully serpentine thorough-fare of Patrick Street. I always got lost in this miniature maze, looking for a restaurant or lovely little bar remembered with pleasure from a previous year, and usually stumbling on new ones instead. It was in one of these bars that, at a time in my life when I needed to move on, I found myself being persuaded to apply for a vacancy at *The Cork Examiner*.

The colleagues who encouraged me were enormously generous in their assessment of my abilities. They spoke eloquently and lucidly of their excitement at the *Examiner's* potential for development into a truly national newspaper, and of the need for new blood and fresh ideas to assist that development. It was a flattering moment. While the vacancy concerned was not in their gift, they assured me that no-one else's name was on it either, and that an outside appli-cation would be welcome. Two months later, by early December, I had moved what little bag and baggage I had to a comfortable flat in Blackrock. It was rented to me by a family whose consistently warm hospitality took much of the pain out of the isolation I was to experience in the coming months. That hospitality, alas, finally seemed to be the exception which confirms the rule.

I had arrived in buoyant spirits, however, and I never expected to settle in without difficulty. Two years, I said to myself every day for the next ten months, I'll give it two years. My greatest appre-hension in fact concerned the job: I was plunging into an unfamiliar world of sub-editing on new technology. And, while I had had some verbal assurances that I would be given scope as an arts writer, this was not the job for which I had been hired, and I had no guarantee that my writing career might not be over.

I need not have worried on either score. The subs desk was infinitely patient and good-humoured as I fumbled my way into some sort of competence with the technology. Meanwhile Fergie O'Callaghan, one of the most approachable and charming editors I have ever encountered, was better than his word on the writing side. I was soon producing not one, but three, new weekly arts columns. Nor did such a high profile for an out-of-town newcomer seem to stir up any resentment. Looking back, the hours spent in the office above Academy Street were probably the most satisfying I spent in Cork.

My new colleagues were not backward in buying pints at break-time, either, and the printers, that most maligned group of human beings, were good crack. Regarding cameraderie at work, I have no complaints. My complaint, though it took me a long time to recognize it, was that I seemed to become socially invisible as soon as the shift was over and I headed home.

If I went through Christmas and the New Year without encountering any parties, and hardly a goodwill drink, I steadfastly put it down to bad timing. I told friends in Dublin that I was fine, never better, getting a lot of reading done. After three months, a colleague at the *Examiner* once asked me if I found Cork people as clannish as they said, and I still managed to dismiss the idea with sufficient conviction to fool even myself. After all, I told him, I would not have considered moving to Cork if I had not always found it one of the most sociable places in the world.

When I did begin to acknowledge that I was spending more time alone than I wanted to, I attributed this to the anti-social nature of working night shifts. But I slowly began to realize that I was fooling myself. Something was wrong here, something was strange. In the much more obviously alien environment of Derry, I had found myself made at home in other people's houses within days of my arrival. In the Basque country, long before I was halfways fluent in Spanish, language proved no barrier to hospitality and friendship.

In Cork, even when I went to arts events where I would always know a few people, I found that I somehow missed the surge to the pub afterwards, or, if I didn't, I often felt like a hanger-on at the bar. I never had the feeling that anyone actually disliked me. I simply did not seem to be there. The outsider, a figure who arouses interest in most cultures whether he or she is interesting in themselves or not, is at an unusual disadvantage in Cork. The native community is so self-contained that it needs nothing beyond itself to add spice or difference to its comfortable and familiar flavours, or so I secretly began to think. It does not reject newcomers; it simply does not see them.

It was after one such arts event, when I actually did end up drinking with a number of people, that someone innocently made a comment which forced me to alter my whole perspective on the situation. With a few drinks taken, I had hesitantly, and for the first time, expressed some of my emerging misgivings about Cork social life.

My companion listened with concern and sympathy, but no surprise, to what I had to say. To her, the whole process seemed entirely natural: 'You have to give people more time. They have to be able to work out your pedigree.'

That stopped me in my tracks. My *pedigree?* Was she serious? Was I a horse or a greyhound, I asked, or did Cork people go round with family trees in their wallets? She thought I was being very funny. I realized that she had no idea that I really did find the concept of human pedigree outrageous, and outlandish to the point of lunacy. To her, it was apparently as commonplace a concept as good looks or affability. And that sent me into reverse gear. I carefully picked my jaw up off the floor, where she still had not noticed that it had fallen, and dropped the subject.

Just a few days later, I met someone else who gave a frighteningly precise shape to my still rather vague misgivings. She was an intelligent, charming, and attractive single woman, who had worked in a high-profile job in Cork for two years. During a working lunch, she half-whispered, as though we needed a secret code: 'How do you *really* find it here?'

That led to my telling the pedigree story, which in turn caused floodgates to open. She had come to the city, she said, with similar hopes and expectations. In two years, however, she had never seen the inside of a Cork home. She had gradually realized that the only people she really socialized with, beyond work-related events, were other people from outside the city. Against all her better judgment, she had begun to meet a group of outsiders for lunch, specifically to let off steam by bitching about the city.

The idea of joining some sort of expats lunch club was as abhorrent to me as contemplating pedigrees, and I never became a member. It sounded too much like the groups of disgruntled TEFL teachers in Bilbao, who used to drink gin and tonics in their flats and complain endlessly about the natives they never made any effort to meet. My new friend agreed in principle that it was a bad practice, but she reckoned that I would give in sooner or later. 'I've found,' she said, 'that there is simply no alternative.'

The encounter forced me to recognize that, on the one hand, I had a problem in Cork. On the other hand, it enabled me to acknowledge that the problem was probably not personal, or at least not exclusively so. I think I had privately begun to fear that I had either suddenly started to secrete some particularly repellent body odour, or at least that whatever social skills I possessed had fallen off the car as I entered the city.

More months passed, without any significant improvement, but I still had no thought of leaving, and in fact I dedicated a week's holiday in June to looking for a house, the first I would ever have bought, had I found one suitable. I still wanted to settle in Cork, and could not believe that the sense of isolation I was experiencing was inevitable and permanent. Some day soon, I kept saying to myself, you'll find a way into this city. But I did begin to try to look at factors, outside my own personality and circumstances, which might be contributing to the situation.

I thought back to one of my earliest experiences of the city, nearly a decade earlier, when it was the last stop on Field Day's first national tour with *Translations*. I was both manager and public relations officer for the company, and was well aware that I had not had enough time to do the latter job to my own satisfaction. However, the word-of-mouth publicity for the production had been marvellous, and we had done 105 per cent business in venues ranging from the Gate Theatre to a convent hall in Ballyshannon. By the time we were approaching Cork, other aspects of the tour were winding down, and I had ample time to devote to public relations. I was puzzled that the *Examiner* had turned down offers of interviews with members of a company which included Brian Friel, Stephen Rea, Mick Lally, Ray McAnally and Liam Neeson, but very happy with the long and laudatory article they published on the show.

Everything else, too, went according to plan: extensive radio coverage, copious distribution of publicity fliers, posters up in every last pub in the city. I simply could not understand it when, on the opening night, the Opera House bookings were dismal, at least by the high standards set by this particular tour. We ended up, as I recall, with 60 per cent business over the week's run. Why, I asked a Northern poet who had settled in the city, should Cork respond so differently to every other venue?

Well, he said, there's the obvious reason, which is that you have no-one from Cork in the cast. I was aghast to realize that he was serious.

His remarks came back to me like a reverse boomerang when, nearly ten years later, I had sat down to write my first review of a Cork production in the Opera House for the *Examiner*. It turned out to be one of the worst productions I have ever seen on a big professional stage. For a moment, I wondered if I should make allowances for the fact that this was not the capital city, an idea I instantly dismissed as insultingly patronising to Cork. After all, if I reviewed a show by Druid or Red Kettle, I used exactly the same criteria in Galway or Waterford as I would in Dublin. Why should Cork be different?

I consequently wrote a scathing condemnation of its shoddy production values and excruciatingly sentimental presentation of Cork working-class 'characters'. When I handed in my review, a colleague reminded me, not entirely in jest, that I was still technically on probation. A member of the *Examiner* board was also on the board of the Opera House, and a well-worn story had it, possibly apocryphally, that he had, on at least one occasion, done a Citizen Kane job on an unfavourable review which one of his own journalists had had the temerity to write.

Not a comma was changed in my review, however, nor did I hear a whisper of adverse comment from management. Another colleague, though, did speak to me in hushed tones as though I had done something heroic, and said that 'only an outsider could get away with that'. Two or three days later, a letter arrived in from the late Aloys Fleischmann. How, he asked, could I possibly find so little to like in such a marvellous display of *local* talent? At a moment in Irish cultural life when other regional centres could confidently leapfrog Dublin and land successfully in Sydney or New York, Cork seemed content, nay proud, to wallow in the parochial values of the parish pantomime, where extended families make up a cosy circle between stage and audience.

Would I have remained a stranger in Cork generally if I had stayed longer? I really cannot say. I only know that, when that phone call came from Dublin to say that an interesting job was up for grabs, I knew that I wanted to leave Cork more than I had ever wanted to leave any other place.

It is for others to judge whether my experiences are in any way representative. Since I left the city, I have met several people with similar stories, and only one who found it easy to 'integrate'. But if the anecdotes recounted above are representative, it is tempting to speculate about what they represent.

I think it cannot be insignificant that, in recent years, Cork has failed to establish for itself the sort of strong, autonomous cultural profile that has distinguished cities like Galway, Derry, Limerick, Waterford and Sligo, particularly in such an obviously social medium as theatre. (Cork's visual arts profile is much stronger, partly thanks to lively institutions like the Triskel, the Sculpture Factory, and the Film Festival, which begs some interesting questions, which there is no space to consider here.)

The smaller cities, it seems to me, define themselves in terms of what they themselves actually are, and do not bother with comparisons, for good or ill, with the capital. Far from making them parochial or inward-looking, their nonchalant autonomy gives them the flexibility to absorb outside influences, and to create work which is at once indigenous and original and yet has an easy relationship with the cosmopolitan world.

Cork, in contrast, seems to be frozen in the iron grip of a second city complex. Terrified of the rather innocuous fact that it can never be the first city, everything in Cork is related to Dublin, even though Dublin may never be mentioned. For fear the comparison should be negative, inordinate comfort is taken from the sense of shared parochial experiences. The familiar is an endlessly self-confirming circle, a frame of self-reference which enables those who live within it, in moments of extreme self-delusion, to use phrases like 'the real capital', just as they used the phrase 'the real Taoiseach', and mistake, for the beguiling moment, the fantasy for the reality.

Cork is a mercantile port, ruled by merchant princes with pragmatic and philistine values. Having neither the metropolitan culture of a capital, nor the idiosyncratic identity of our smaller cities, the city seems consumed with resentment that its commercial prowess (now in severe decline in both cases) cannot buy it the pre-eminence it desires, and withdraws to the comforting prospect offered by the parochial mirror.

The outsider, whose simple presence may be a reproachful reminder that there are other worlds outside the parish boundaries, will perhaps need to be exceptionally lucky to find a real welcome in such a city.

Shadow Play
Gregory O'Donoghue

Nudges of dawn found us brazen — who'd loitered on
the summer slope past midnight, talking of Sean O'Faolain
until our laden, unfussed lulls diverted us.

We dusted the riverbank from our clothes;
climbed to see the day start its sly or sudden
ceaseless shadow play, sun flow on the streets and valley —

I have loved, admired, feared and hated no city so . . .
my shadow, and no man jumps off his own shadow.
He flirted his path across the Atlantic — a lonely wife

he'd later make a longish song and dance of
not having slept with: to only kiss, yet tell —
casuistic shadows ferried to the liner at Cobh,

darker steeples gloomed down our spangled river;
we'd perhaps have made cartwheels, handsprings, somersaults,
only to twist and jumble over, wound inside out.

He missed footsteps on intimate fields, alleys:
watching a chill dusk dim the Rockies, he lay
sad for the storied nooks of smaller places;

yet nothing drew him back to — Lilliput — Ireland's Venice.
In his tales he'd toil clear through; composing
the stirred shadows: creatures stepped forward, their voices

actual as though just now we'd met their children
on our way to the station — a small wind fretting the limes,
the Lee going matt moments before the teetering rain.

Tea In the Meadow

Alice Taylor

from: *To School Through the Fields* (1988)

When the summer had proved its intention of staying with us,
cutting the hay began. With his meadows ripened to a honey
coloured hue by the sun, my father went to the haggard and, taking
his old mowing machine firmly by its long shaft, he eased it slowly

from under the overhanging trees where it had sheltered throughout the long winter.

A simple, solid machine with two small wheels and drawn by a pair of horses, it had a raised seat for the driver at the back. On one side was a cutting knife which lay flat on the ground when in use and was raised up for the journey back and forth from the meadow. Inside this knife was a long blade with diamond-shaped edges called sections. At first my father oiled and greased the entire machine, which had seized up during the winter; then he sat astride the shaft of the mower and laid the long blade across his knee. There was a skill in edging the blades in which he took a particular pride. He had a long edging stone with a timber handle, which he kept on top of a high press in the kitchen. This was taken down and inspected and when found to be in perfect condition was the cause of great satisfaction. What could possibly have gone wrong with it is difficult to imagine, but I suppose he had discovered over the years that very few of his tools were safe from his energetic brood. Now, sitting in the warm, sheltered haggard, beginning at one end of the blade and taking it section by section, he edged along with a balanced rhythm, occasionally dipping his stone in a rusty gallon of water which stood on the ground beside him. Gradually the rusty, archaic blade assumed a new life, its teeth gleaming with a razor sharpness, and along its base lay a ridge of brown and grey froth like the moustache of a monster man. I sometimes sat on the ground and watched this deadly weapon come to life, in awe of its power for my father gave us strict instructions regarding the dangers of farm machinery and the use of his gun, and his commands were obeyed unquestioningly.

The following day cutting the hay did not commence until the sun was high in the sky and the gently swaying hay was well dry of the morning dew. Paddy and James were rounded up, eager for work as they were after a long rest since the spring ploughing. That had been heavy, cold work and they had come home at night with their hooves covered in mud, but the hayfield promised to be soft and pleasant underfoot, with ample juicy mouthfuls available to satisfy any pangs of hunger.

The two horses were tackled to the mowing machine and, arriving in the meadow, they cut the first swath along by the ditches and continued all day around the field, their rounds becoming gradually shorter. My father always watched out for birds' nests hidden in the hay, and the one most likely to be found was the pheasant family. If the birds rose from the hay he would halt the horses and walking into the high grass he would gently lift up the nest and carry it to the mossy ditch. Some nests, however, did not transport very well and once he brought home a few pheasant eggs to be put under a hatching hen. They hatched out along with her chickens but they were much smaller and far more active. When they grew bigger they were carried to the fort where several families of pheasants lived, and there they returned to their own lifestyle.

The blade of the mowing machine gave off a plaintive whine which carried across the valley and told of busy times. And so, hour after hour, my father and his horses worked in companionable silence while all around them lay the moist swaths of newly mown hay. Coming into the meadow in the late afternoon, bearing a jug of tea and home-made brown bread, I was enfolded in a wild, sweet essence that was moist and sensuous, stimulating some deep-rooted feelings in my inner being.

Now my father sat in a shady corner under a tree and drank his tea straight from the jug, while the horses also relaxed and sampled some freshly cut hay, flicking their long tails to keep the flies at bay. I explored the newly exposed ditches around by the headland, as we called the outer edge of the field after the first swath was cut. In some of the meadows a stream ran along by the ditch and here floated all kinds of interesting insects sheltering under the overgrown grass and ferns. Here too, earlier in the year, frogs' croak was to be found, a jelly-like substance encasing an abundance of black dots trailing little floating legs, the baby frogs in neo-natal condition. Those tiny tadpoles who had squirmed out of that quivering quagmire were now grown into frogs of all shapes and colours: there were yellow, green and sometimes black frogs to be found jumping along the moist ditches of the meadows.

The rabbit families lived on the other side of the meadow where conditions were drier. The whine of the mowing machine and all the unexpected activity in their quiet corner had sent them scurrying underground, but now, while there was a temporary lull, they ventured out to see what was going on. They stood transfixed in amazement to find their familiar scene totally changed; gone was the high sheltering grass, and now the entire meadow lay exposed before them. But then, seeing the horses and humans, they turned tail and disappeared, to return no doubt when all was finally quiet and their domain was no longer disturbed by human intruders.

One of the meadows had a complete hedge of wild honeysuckle or woodbine, as we knew it, and this sent out a soft, wild, heady perfume that mingled with the smell of new mown hay. You had to stand still and close your eyes to fully absorb this feast of fragrances.

When my father resumed cutting I usually stayed on, wandering around, exploring mossy ditches and picking wild flowers, until finally the last swath fell and the day's work was over. The long knife raised, the horses felt the sudden easing of their straining chains and set off briskly towards the gap that led to home. Here was a stream of spring water where they drank, spattering spray with their quivering nostrils. Back in the haggard they were relieved of the burden of the mowing machine and tackling; then they trotted off to the freedom of the green fields with only the dark patches where they had sweated beneath their tackling to show that they had spent a hot day working in the meadow. Oftentimes they lay down on the cool grass and rolled over on their backs, with legs cycling in the air. Then, righting themselves, they jumped up and galloped around the field, exulting in their freedom from restraining ropes and chains.

The next step in the cycle of haymaking depended on the weather and if it was less than perfect a process known as turning the hay had to be endured. This was sometimes done by hand with a hay pike: the swath of hay which was now dry on the top side had to be turned over and its damp underside exposed to the sun. It was a slow, monotonous process which could raise blisters on little hands unaccustomed to gripping pike handles for long, but the monotony was relieved by the companionship of many people working together. Oftentimes this job was done by a machine, aptly named the swath turner, and why it could not always be used I found hard to understand, but maybe on some occasions manpower was more plentiful than horsepower. The swath turner was a strange looking machine on two extremely large iron wheels with two timber shafts to the front, and to the rear two giant iron spiders that sped around tossing the hay in all directions, exposing it to the sun and air. It was drawn by one horse and the driver sat on an iron seat perched high over the twirling spiders.

When the hay was sufficiently dry it was raked into rows with the wheel raker, a machine similar in design to the swath turner which pulled a giant iron rake behind it. This gathered up the hay and then the driver pulled a lever which raised the rake, leaving the hay in a tidy row; down banged the rake again and the next row was collected. The aim was to have each row of hay parallel to the previous one and this required split-second timing and good horse control. That was the ideal, and when it was not achieved the driver of the wheel raker would be subjected to much derogatory comment from his or her fellow workers.

And so at last we arrived at the actual point of haymaking. The interval between cutting and haymaking could vary from two days to two weeks, depending on the weather, but the shorter the interval the better the hay. Hay, fast-dried in the hot sun, with all traces of green and moisture evaporated, was far superior to a dark brown version that had soaked up rain and had to be shaken out to be re-dried. Haymaking and wet weather made bad working companions and turned a pleasant experience into a long drawn-out hardship. However, when the sun shone all these difficulties were quickly forgotten. When the swaths were ready for saving the meadow was full of blond, crinkling hay. The smell of the hay had changed, becoming more aromatic and varied as it matured, and on the day of the cutting the meadow was perfumed with a wild, sweet fragrance that filled your nostrils with the essence of summer.

A day in the meadow was sunshine and sweat, hard work and happiness. Hayseeds and innumerable forms of insect life found their way into your hair and clung to your damp back. We were usually barefoot so we picked up numerous thorns, but this annoyance was relieved by the soft feel of mossy patches beneath our feet and we developed a second sense about where it was safe to tread. Luckily, some of our meadows lay by the river, and oh! the joy on a hot day to plunge into the icy water and rid yourself of all this sticky irritation.

A contraption called a tumbling paddy was used to collect the rows of hay into big heaps. Made entirely of timber it was like a giant comb with two handles at the back; when it was full to overflowing with hay the handle was thrown forward so that the comb tumbled over and all the hay fell out. This was then used as the base for the cocks of hay, or wyndes as we called them. When the butt had been made somebody stood on it and packed the hay down while the tumbling paddy collected more hay which was piked on to the wynde until gradually it grew tall and pointed.

Standing on the wyndes was a job for somebody light and agile. Pikes of hay were thrown up at you and had to be pulled in under your feet and danced on to firm this wavering creation. Sometimes the hay would hide an odd scratching briar or a soft yellow frog to stimulate an unplanned high jump. Things going to plan, however, you slid down the side of the wynde when it had reached its peak, then it was pared of loose hay at the base and finally tied down. A piece of hay with its ends firmly embedded in the base of the wynde was wound around the hay twine and knotted with it. The ball of twine was then thrown across the wynde and tied at the other side in the same way, and this process was repeated crossways.

And so it continued all day, wynde after wynde, while we got hotter and thirstier as the heat beat down on us. Then somebody would call in a voice full of elation: 'The tea is coming!'

My mother usually brought the tea in a white enamel bucket and maybe a tin sweet-gallon full as well. We made ourselves comfortable on various heaps of hay and passed around cups of tea with slices of homemade brown bread. We watched my mother's basket eagerly and usually she came up trumps with a big juicy apple cake. It is said that hunger is a good sauce but hunger and thirst certainly made the tea in the meadow a feast with a special flavour, like manna in the desert. The aroma of the sweet-smelling hay blended with the tea, funny stories and riddles made for great laughter and fun, and the whole occasion took on the atmosphere of a gay picnic.

Tea over we got back to work but there was new pep in our step and gradually the wyndes rose like mini pyramids around us. Towards evening, as the shadows lengthened across the field, we gathered up our rakes and pikes, and together with the horses made our weary way homewards. Sometimes, though, one of the more energetic members of the family would shout: 'Race you home!' and we would all take off, weariness forgotten in the challenge to be the first one home.

My father remained on to rake down the wyndes and tie them firmly with binder twine. I often saw him in the dusk of the evening standing by the gap of a field counting the cocks of hay, the satisfaction of a job well done all around him.

After the work in the meadow was finished the hay was drawn into the barn. We all enjoyed drawing in the hay; there was about it an air of achievement, a fulfilment of the basic need of man to fill the barns and prepare for winter. Next to his family's needs the welfare of his stock was closest to the heart of the farmer and it was every farmer's dread not to have enough to feed his animals in the harsh days of winter. My father had taken on the farm when he was sixteen years old, after the death of my grandfather, and his first winter had come long and harsh and left him with too little hay for the animals. It was a cruel experience for one so young and he never forgot it: at the end of every winter now our barn had a spare block of hay, a monument to my father's hard-earned lesson.

The hay was drawn home in the horse and float — a big sheet of solid timber with two iron wheels and two shafts in front. In the meadow it was tilted up in front so that the back edge lay along the base of the wynde of hay. Then the thick float ropes that were wound around an iron roller at the front of the float were unwound and tied behind the wyndes. The roller was turned, winding up the rope and bringing the cock of hay up along the float. The horse then drew home his load with the driver sitting on the setlock or on top of the wynde, while the children sat along the back of the float, their feet trailing along the fields. Drives in the float were part of their summer entertainment on the farm.

When they arrived in the barn the load was tilted out and, while the man with the horse set off for the next lot, the workers in the barn cleared the way for his return. My father usually piked the hay up and one of us took it from him and passed it back to another who packed it farther back. While the hay in the barn was low the work was very easy, but as the hay rose it became more difficult, and we had to work fast if we wanted to have a rest before the float came back. If the draw was long — coming up from the fields down by the river — we had a nice leisurely time when we could take down the books we had stored on the rafters of the barn. But when the hay was coming from a field near the house, on a hot day and the barn almost full, perspiration ran down your back clogged with dust, hayseeds got into your hair and down your throat, and the break between loads was all too short.

The day the last wynde was drawn home marked the end of the haymaking season. Now the barn was full of soft golden hay, and our animals were safe against the ravages of winter no matter how harsh it might come.

Plague

Claud Cockburn

from: *Cockburn Sums Up* (1981)

One night in London I heard one of my children calling for help. My wife being out at the time I ran to his bedroom, and found that he was calling in his sleep; an effect of nightmare, no more. Yet the immediate impression was frightening. Although there was, as the saying goes, nothing to it, it was an incident which seemed to give a sharply horrid reality to the fears everyone has about children — fears that they will have to call for help and there will be no help one can give, or one will not think of the right help to give until it is too late.

The alarm and depression I then felt continued through some hours, as though it were I that had had the nightmare and, waking, could not erase its impression. Nobody knows quite enough about extra-sensory perception or precognition to be perfectly assured on the subject. But it is a fact that people do have what used to be called a 'premonition of disaster'. I did not think of this as a premonition of anything, but the state of seemingly unmotivated depression was as marked as it would have been if I had actually supposed myself to have received a warning of unpleasant things to come.

We were living at that time in Hampstead because *Punch* wanted me to be in London for a half year or so, available for production of topical articles and reportage such as could not be written from Youghal. The house was commodious enough and full of convenient mechanical gadgets, including two television sets and a labour-saving bar in a big semi-basement room at the back. For some reason I had taken an unreasoning dislike to the place on first seeing it from the street and, once inside, I was vexed by a meaningless sense of uneasiness. It was annoying, because I had looked forward to this time in London. I was eager to experiment with numerous projects for *Punch*, and I thought, too, that, being at close quarters, I could sell articles to other papers more easily than I could from Ireland, and should be able to shore up, even perhaps establish on sound foundations, our always tottering financial structure. Nevertheless, I was no sooner in that house than I felt mysteriously less happy than I had expected and intended to be, and this *malaise* continued right through the summer.

Despite the television which, living normally in the south of Ireland, they had never seen before, and other amusements of London life, the three boys either actively hated London or could make it tolerable for themselves only by spending money like drunken little sailors. My wife, too, though she briefly enjoyed a series of parties, and visits to the theatre, was irksomely cut off from all the creative activity involved in the development of farm and garden, the breeding of horses, the raising of sheep. Also her upbringing had been such that she instinctively imagined that to be in London in August was to indulge a perverse masochism. No one, she had always been led to believe, is in London in August, and although, rationally, she agreed that the statement is nonsense, she could not help feeling horror at the prospect, and a conviction that to stay there deliberately in that month would be foolish and injurious to us all. For all these reasons we arranged that at the beginning of the school holidays — the eldest boy was at school in Perthshire, the second one at preparatory school near Dublin, and the third (then six years old) at a day school beside Hampstead Heath — we should all go to Youghal, and that I, by agreement with *Punch* — would fly back to London for one week in three.

At the last moment we hesitated because of news that a somewhat abnormal number of cases of polio had been reported in Cork City. We reflected, however, that there were certainly a good many cases in London, too, and that whereas, if things got worse, we could, at home, virtually isolate the children on the farm, in London they must be daily exposed to whatever risks of infection might exist. There was no reason why things should get worse. We set off. It was true that on the boat I heard several conversations among people who were sailing to Cork with the sort of apprehensions you encountered among people travelling to London from the country during the bombing. I thought this the talk of people trying to make life more exciting. Men who always got drunk in the bar of the *Innisfallen* said, that night, that they were drinking as a prophylactic against polio.

The boat docked late, and it was mid-morning before we loaded all the luggage — mountains of it, as there always are when one travels with young children — into a van and packed ourselves into the hired car for the thirty-mile run to Youghal. We had to visit a shop in St Patrick Street, the centre of the city, and I was suddenly surprised — pleased, at first — by the ease with which we found

139

parking space in a street where normally it is nearly impossible to park at all. The shop, too, was agreeably empty of pushers and jostlers. I remarked that we seemed to have hit on a lucky day. The driver of the car looked at me with astonishment. 'People are afraid,' he said. 'They're afraid to come into Cork. Business is going to hell. If the epidemic goes on, in a few weeks half the shops on this street will be bankrupt.' Not lingering to buy anything but essentials we drove out into the countryside and home.

Under our circumstances at Youghal that horrible summer, the boys could at least ride horses about, or bicycle in the neighbourhood. But there again I could note that there is perhaps a discrepancy between what the elders think the youth must be longing to do and the true facts of the case. The elder boys did like to ride, but they did not care to ride much. What they liked was to build hidden huts or tree houses, to lie motionless on their backs in their tents, or find a dangerous way to the roof and sit there reading, with emotion, *The Waste Land*.

In these pursuits the summer seemed to be passing away harmlessly enough. I went to London two or three times for a few days on each visit, motoring to Cork, travelling by train from there to Dublin and thence flying. Then, one day, I had a headache and the tips of my fingers pricked with pins and needles. I am unused to headaches and thus noticed this one. And the pricking in my finger-tips was so queer that I made myself tedious about it, mentioned this pricking until everyone was much bored with the information. My eldest son also felt this pricking. We thought it was either meaningless, or else he had perhaps picked it up psychosomatically from me.

Much later, several doctors confirmed to me that this combination of unusual — baseless — headache with the prick of the finger-tips is a common, almost an infallible, sign of polio. At the time we knew nothing of that. In reality, it appears, I had picked up the bug somewhere along the line between London and Cork. Even then, inevitably, Cork people had to travel in trains on their business. I recall that on the last of those journeys there was a clearly perceptible atmosphere of fear, suspicion, or perhaps simply high-grade caution on the train. Already things were at the point where Dubliners returning from some necessary trip to Cork felt that they could at least lessen the risk they had been compelled to run by not associating with Cork people longer than was absolutely necessary. We

Cork people found ourselves, without the slightest word being said — and perhaps with not much of a conscious thought being thought — sitting at one end of the bar and buffet car, with the Dubliners at the other.

As the situation deteriorated in Cork, the Cork people defensively spread terrifying stories about what was happening elsewhere. It was said, and absolutely believed by very many people, that in Dublin the epidemic was worse still than in Cork. People were dying like flies in every fever hospital in the city. But, due to the savage wiles and intrigues of the Dubliners, the newspapers had been, as the Irish saying goes, 'brought to see' that it would not be in their interests to report the state of affairs in Dublin. Instead they should concentrate on ruining poor Cork.

And in Cork itself the owners of some of the biggest stores in the city made a *démarche*. In deputation to the newspapers they threatened to withdraw advertising from such newspapers as might continue to report regularly and in detail on the polio epidemic there. They were intent on bringing the newspapers to see the justice of their viewpoint. As always, too, in the sordid backwaters of panic, there were people made to suffer by the frights of others. Some nearly bedridden people nearly died in various parts of the city because it was thought that all bedridden people must be polio victims, and in consequence nobody would go to their houses to deliver the milk and meat and vegetables they needed. The Gardai had to be called in to make the deliveries to those houses which were supposedly so dangerous but in reality — not that the delivery men had any means of knowing that — were no more dangerous than the air you breathed at the railway station or the General Post Office. And that was dangerous indeed.

Things were apparently going along well enough, and I was in London, at this increasingly hateful house in Hampstead, working fast to make enough money to take us all, I thought, to Mexico for a while: a place I much wanted to visit. I came down, one late summer night, the crooked road that let to this big squat house and heard the telephone ringing. It just chanced that I had dined early and alone, and was coming back to sleep at nine-thirty in the evening. No one with good news ever rings you at that hour. How could or would they? They are eating and drinking and if all your affairs were in proper order you would be eating and drinking too. A call at that time can only be an act of desperation, a signal of emergency.

This was such a call. My wife had been trying to call me from Youghal and finding me from home had telephoned Malcolm Muggeridge at his home in Sussex, and he had kept on calling me every ten minutes with a message.

The message was to say that the youngest child was ill. I had no doubt what the message meant. My wife is no alarmist. With Malcolm's help — there has never been a man on God's earth who would do more for you when the chips are down, and he has seen a number of chips down in his life — I flew free to Dublin and hired the needed car at three o'clock in the morning to go the couple of hundred miles to Youghal. The message had meant just what I had supposed. The youngest boy was in bed with suspected polio. In a couple of hours the doctor was coming to confirm or nullify the diagnosis. He confirmed it. Two hours later the child was in the ambulance on his way to St Finnbarr's fever hospital in Cork.

By a trick of the mind, when grief and anxiety are at, you think, their imaginable height, some factor intrudes itself to give the screw an extra turn, heighten the grief and anxiety a little more. In this case, in the agony of her distress, my poor wife conceived the idea that she, because of her love of Ireland and boredom of London, had selfishly overlooked the dangers to the children involved in a return to County Cork, and was thus actually responsible for what had happened. I recalled this, many months later, when I was talking with Kitty Muggeridge about the death of their youngest son — he was eighteen years old — in an avalanche of snow in the French Alps. She herself had been a ski champion once, and it seemed to her, after the event, that when he had mentioned to her that he was going skiing in that particular place at that particular season of the year, she should have remembered, over all those years, enough about conditions there to warn or discourage him, saying that at such a season there was danger of avalanches. And from this, by afterthought, it had been only a small step to the conviction that she had not only not tried to dissuade him from making the trip but, by some kind of implication, had actually encouraged him. She knew, when she talked about it, that all this was untrue or irrelevant. The young man had made his plans, he knew all that anyone needed to know about the possibilities and risks, and he would have taken those risks whatever anyone might have said. Just possibly — it is at least a possibility worth considering when grievous things happen to loved people — some people experience a compulsive need to assume guilt for what has happened, and this in reality is only an expression of a desire to become closer to them by involving oneself in their fate, rather than assume that they have been struck at by impersonal forces far beyond one's control.

Other than a compulsive need of that kind, there was no reason for Patricia to feel this bitterness of remorse, but she did feel it. And — again just possibly, although it did not look to me like that at the time — it may have been that what seemed to me an additional affliction for her was in reality a kind of aid; it could be that a sense of being in some way involved in the child's disaster, rather than a passive spectator of it, provided in its tortuous way a kind of balm in this gloomy Gilead. Yet in general remorse is both futile and debilitating.

Immediately after they had taken Patrick away in the ambulance I telephoned the school near Dublin where Andrew — then nine — was at work. For this had all happened at the very end of the holidays, and Andrew had been back at school for three or four days. He returned. I really thought all might still be well up to the very last moment when the diesel train pulled into the station and Andrew got out. I then saw that his body was bowed slightly forward in an awkward way and that he was moving his legs sluggishly. But this was the more terrifying because I had learned, by now, that the most dangerous period of polio is the period between the incidence of the infection and the moment of its diagnosis. The longer a person goes on leading a normally active life after the infection has struck, the more probable it is that he will quickly die of the disease or be permanently maimed by it.

By the following morning he, too, was in St Finnbarr's fever hospital.

Patrick was the first home. And when finally he came, I feared that, back in the surroundings in which he had spent almost all his short life, he would be even more aware of his disabilities than he had been in the strange world of the hospital. He had never run across the hospital lawn, or climbed a tree there, or ridden a pony on its driveway. I feared that at home the lawn, the trees, the pony and a lot besides would savagely jog his memory of things past. Nothing of the kind happened. First he was so happy to be at home that his escape from the hospital, for he had — as he later admitted — been convinced that the hospital was going on for ever, was seen by him as in itself an exhilarating achievement. And then, being now alert

143

and eager again, he became preoccupied not with the big range of things he could no longer do, but with the tiny extension, day by day and week by week of things he was learning to do again. To crawl from the bed to the floor, to walk a few more steps today than he could yesterday — these were a continuous, ascending series of triumphs, as uplifting as a succession of victories leading to membership of the team for the Olympic Games.

In the first weeks after his return home I was merely astonished and relieved by his vigour, determination and evident happiness. In my own mind, the dominant fact was the blow that had struck him. Gradually, under the influence of his attitude to these facts of life, I was aware of a shift in my own. It became possible to see the present, and the future that was now being constructed, as being of greater importance than the past.

The Mirror

in memory of my father

Michael Davitt

from: *Bligeard Sráide* (1983)

Translated by: Paul Muldoon

I

He was no longer my father
but I was still his son;
I would get to grips with that cold paradox,
the remote figure in his Sunday best
who was buried the next day.

A great day for tears, snifters of sherry,
whiskey, beef sandwiches, tea.
An old mate of his was recounting
their day excursion
to Youghal in the Thirties,
how he was his first partner
on the Cork/Skibbereen route
in the late Forties.

There was a splay of Mass cards
on the sitting-room mantelpiece
which formed a crescent round a glass vase,
his retirement present from C.I.E.

I I

I didn't realize till two days later
it was the mirror took his breath away.

The monstrous old Victorian mirror
with the ornate gilt frame
we had found in the three-storey house
when we moved in from the country.
I was afraid that it would sneak
down from the wall and swallow me up
in one gulp in the middle of the night.

While he was decorating the bedroom
he had taken down the mirror
without asking for help;
soon he turned the colour of terracotta
and his heart broke that night.

I I I

There was nothing for it
but to set about finishing the job,
papering over the cracks,
painting the high window,
stripping the door, like the door of a crypt.
When I took hold of the mirror
I had a fright. I imagined him breathing through it.
I heard him say in a reassuring whisper:
I'll give you a hand, here.
And we lifted the mirror back in position
above the fireplace,
my father holding it steady
while I drove home
the two nails.

In The Country

Tim Cramer

from: *The Life of Other Days* (1992)

If the Glen was our Valhalla, it was in reality only the jumping-off
point for further adventure, because immediately beyond it was the
country proper, the rural hinterland of the city. On the Ballyvolane
road, the city stopped abruptly at Rice's house, a rather stately
building with a large, high-walled garden in front and to the side,
and a small farm behind, to which was attached a little dairy where
the lush milk from the few cows was daily processed and distributed.
There the urban housing ended, but the city boundary itself was
several hundred yards further out, near the Fox and Hounds pub, a
little inscribed tablet set into a low wall on which old men would sit
smoking their pipes and chatting, with one foot literally in the city
and the other in the country. When the time came to go, they would
rise and jokingly say: 'Well, I suppose we'd better go to Cork'.

If you climbed the steep Rice's Lane, past the old barn and up
through the fields on either side which constituted the main part of
the farm, you arrived at the high Mayfield Road and St Joseph's
church, beyond which the fields were laid out in war-time plots,
cultivated by the people from the locality. Mayfield was a totally
separate village, about a mile further out, but from the top of the
hill, on a clear day, you could see the hazy blue mountains near
Macroom to the far west, and nearer, the Ballyhoura hills of north
Cork. In between lay the verdant countryside of rolling hills and
small farms, laid out like an aerial photograph. It was the sort of
view that made you want to get up and go, to travel into these far-
off landscapes.

Meanwhile, bereft of anything in the way of transport but shank's
mare, it was necessary to confine ramblings to nearer home, to the
black hills of Banduff, where the gorse blazed its deep yellow flames
across the hillside, and where the blackberries offered an abundance
of rich eating on the hedgerows along the way. Or to high Rath-
cooney, up the steep hill where the lads played the game of road
bowling — almost unique to Cork, being practised elsewhere only
in County Armagh — with 28-ounce iron bowls which they drove
with great skill along the rough surface, the aim being to complete

146

the course in the least amount of throws. The sport had — and has — a vocabulary of its own, with phrases like 'lofting the bend' (hurling the bowl across the projecting arm of a corner so that it landed in mid-road on the other side), or gaining 'a bowl of odds' (going further in one throw than the opponent in two), or 'aiming for the sod' (a wisp of grass placed on the roadway as a marker for the player).

It was all very hectic stuff, and physically demanding, as the heavy bowl was thrown with an under-arm swing that threatened to tear the arm from its socket by sheer force of velocity. Heavy gambling was part and parcel of the whole affair, so that a considerable amount of money might hang on the strong arms and shoulders of the players, each of whom had their own following, vociferous and extremely critical. It also demanded considerable vigilance on the part of the spectators: to be struck by a veritable cannonball in which mass and velocity combined to prove the theory of irresistible force was anything but amusing and could, indeed sometimes did, result in severe maiming.

While it was always diverting to watch the bowl players, our more usual trek was through the fields with our dogs, sniffing and diving into hedges after elusive rabbits, barking excitedly at each scent, and rarely disturbing any living creature besides a few birds. Provided we behaved ourselves and did not plough across fields of standing crops, the freedom of the wide acres was ours. The local farmers, most of whom we knew anyway, were tolerant of our comings and goings, and I can never remember an occasion when we were summarily ordered off the land. Instead, if they happened to be about, we would stop for a chat, or to have a drink of water, while we admired their workhorses and they in turn would have a kind word about our dogs.

Often they would direct us to distant hedgerows where they knew the rabbits were plentiful, their only restriction being that we let the dogs get on with it and did not attempt to tear down the earthen banks with iron bars 'like that crowd that came last week'. But it was obvious that we did not have any crowbars, and we were always careful about closing gates and generally respecting the farmers' hospitality and the land itself. This had been drummed into us in school and it paid rich dividends. Our farmer friends knew we could be trusted not to do anything careless and in turn, we had unrestricted access to their fields, so that they became almost our own, to wander where we would in God's clean air. Little wonder that we came to love the countryside in all its variegated grandeur and to recognize the slow turning of the seasons.

Undoubtedly the most exciting time to be in the country was at harvest, when the ripening corn waved and danced in the breeze so that the fields looked like golden ponds across which raced sunlight and shadow, bringing ever-changing hues to the rippling mass of stalks. We would keep a close eye on the fields behind our own house, waiting for the morning when the Doctor and his man would come to inspect the crop, taking a few ears of corn and rubbing them in their experienced hands, blowing away the chaff and perhaps chewing a few grains, as indeed we ourselves had already done, tasting the soft inner ear as well as the hard outer husk, and knowing that the harvest was really nigh. We were by no means experts, yet the appearance of the Doctor merely confirmed our own opinions.

Next morning, the peace would be shattered by the roar of the tractor-drawn reaper and binder, tackling the Top Field as a few men cleared the headlands with scythes in the two lower fields. Almost before we knew it, they would be upon us, the tractor chugging slowly around the edges of the Back Field, the binder flailing along behind, spitting out stooks of golden richness as the whole place droned with the sound of rhythmic activity. Gradually the circle of standing corn would grow smaller as little birds flew terrified away, mice scuttled out of reach of the machines, dogs barked as they chased the little creatures, and all the while the relentless machine disgorged itself of its bundles.

These we were allowed to arrange in stacks of three or four, ears uppermost, because the Doctor was above all a practical man and if there were youngsters willing to help, he was not going to object. The work was hard on young hands unaccustomed to such labour, but we carried on, happy in the knowledge that we were helping and that we were, for a little while at least, being taken seriously in a world of men. Only when it was all over, when the last few sheaves had come tumbling out of the maw of the binder, when the equipage had gone trundling away and the Doctor to his tea, did we really begin to enjoy ourselves. Then, in a world of stubble, we raced among the stooks, chasing the few remaining field mice with the dogs and catching some, dropping them down the frocks of the girls, whose screams of terror drowned our raucous laughter.

Soon, a strange quietness would descend on the shorn land and, as the evening sun shimmered on the heads of the standing sheaves, we would lie in the stubble, watching intently as the elder lads from the Cross patiently showed us how to make Harvest Knots from corn stems, twisting and looping them into heart shapes in a ritual that must have been as old as time itself. Next day we would wear our own badges in our shirt buttonholes with a certain pride. We had been to the harvest. We had worked the land. We had partaken of the richness of the good earth.

III HILLSIDES AND CITY MARSH

Prologue

Daniel Corkery

from: *The Threshold of Quiet* (1917)

Leaving us, the summer visitor says in his good-humored way that Cork is quite a busy place, considering how small it is. And he really thinks so, because whatever little we have of pastors, postmen, urchins, beggars; of squares, streets, lanes, markets; of wagons, motors, tramcars, ships; of spires, turrets, domes, towers; of bells, horns, meetings, cries; concert-halls, theatres, shops — whatever little we have all of these — as humdrum a collection of odds-and-ends as ever went by the name of city — are flung higgledy-piggledy together into a narrow, double-streamed, many-bridged river valley, jostled and jostling, so compacted that the mass throws up a froth and flurry that confuses the stray visitor, unless indeed he is set on getting at the true size and worth of things. For him this is Cork. But for us it is only the 'flat of the city.' What of the hill-sides? Go but three steps up any of those old-time, wide-sweeping, treeless, cloud-shadowed hills and you find yourself even at mid-day in silence that grows on you. You have scarce left the city, yet you raise your eyes, you look around and notice little gable ends that finish in little crosses of stone or arched gateways of sandstone or limestone or both, or far-stretching garden walls that are marked with tablets of brass on which are cut holy emblems and sacred letters — and as you look the silence seems to grow deeper and deeper; indeed you have come on the very fruitage of the spirit of contemplation — convents, monasteries, chapels, hospitals, houses of refuge. And to us these quiet hillsides also are Cork. Perhaps they are the quieter for the noise in the valley; perhaps, too, that little stir and bustle is quickened for those long slopes of quiet sunshine and peace. But both are Cork, hillsides and city marsh.

Self-knowledge is not easily won; and for me truly to know Cork is almost as difficult. Those faces I have been looking at in its streets today, how much do they know of that 'quiet desperation' in which, according to the American philosopher, most of the citizens of the world pass their lives? And if they do know something of this quiet desperation, whether is it the stillness of the hills or the busy-body chatter of the valley that gives it its local texture and

153

colour, its tenderness, its snap, its gentleness, its petulance, its prayer? . . . And once again the handful of wayfaring souls that are gathered into this story would pass before me, as if they would answer for all!

The Vision of MacConglinne

from: *Aislinge Meic Conglinne: The Vision of MacConglinne* (1892)
Translated by: Kuno Meyer

The four things to be asked of every composition must be asked of this composition, viz., place, and person, and time, and cause of invention.

The place of this composition is great Cork of Munster, and its author is Aniér MacConglinne of the Onaght Glenowra. In the time of Cathal MacFinguine, son of Cúcengairm, or son of Cúcenmáthir, it was made. The cause of its invention was to banish the demon of gluttony that was in the throat of Cathal MacFinguine.

Cathal Mac Finguine was a good king, who governed Munster; a great warrior prince was he. A warrior of this sort: with the edge of a hound, he ate like a horse. Satan, viz. a demon of gluttony that was in his throat, used to devour his rations with him. A pig and a cow and a bull-calf of three hands, with three score cakes of pure wheat, and a vat a new ale, and thirty heathpoults' eggs, that was his first dole, besides his other snack, until his great feast was ready for him. As regards the great feast, that passes account or reckoning.

The reason of the demon of gluttony being in the throat of Cathal MacFinguine was because he had, though he had never seen her, a first love for Lígach, daughter of Maeldúin, king of Ailech; and she sister to Fergal, son of Maeldúin, also king of Ailech, who was then contending for the kingship of Ireland against Cathal MacFinguine, as is plain from the quarrel of the two hags, when they had a duel in quatrains at Freshford:

'He comes from the North, comes from the North,
The son of Maeldúin, over the rocks,
Over Barrow's brink, over Barrow's brink,
Till kine he take he will not stay.'

'He shall stay, shall stay,' said the Southern hag;
'He will be thankful if he escapes.
By my father's hand, by my father's hand,
If Cathal meets him, he'll take no kine.'

Then kernels and apples and many sweets used to be brought from Lígach, Maeldúin's daughter, to Cathal MacFinguine, for his love and affection. Fergal, son of Maeldúin, heard this, and his sister was called unto him. And he gave her a blessing if she should tell him truth, and a curse if she should deny him it. The sister told him; for great as was her love and affection for Cathal MacFinguine, she feared her brother's curse reaching her. Then she told the true story.

The brother told her to send the apples to himself. And a scholar was summoned unto him, and he promised great rewards to the scholar for putting charms in those numerous sweets, to the destruction of Cathal MacFinguine. And the scholar put charms and heathen spells in those numerous sweets, and they were delivered to Fergal, who despatched messengers to convey them to Cathal. And they entreated him by each of the seven universal things, sun and moon, dew and sea, heaven and earth, day and night . . . that he would eat those apples, since it was out of love and affection for him they were brought from Lígach, daughter of Maeldúin.

Cathal thereupon ate the apples, and little creatures through the poison spells were formed of them in his inside. And those little creatures gathered in the womb of one — in that animal, so that there was formed the demon of gluttony. And this is the cause why the demon of gluttony abode in the throat of Cathal MacFinguine, to the ruin of the men of Munster during three half-years; and it is likely he would have ruined Ireland during another half-year . . . .

Aniér MacConglinne was a famous scholar, with abundance of knowledge. The reason why he was called Aniér was because he would satirise and praise all. No wonder, indeed; for there had not come before him, and came not after him, one whose satire or praise was harder to bear, wherefore he was called Anéra [i.e. Non-refusal], for that there was no refusing him.

A great longing seized the mind of the scholar, to follow poetry, and to abandon his reading. For wretched to him was his life in the shade of his studies. And he searched in his mind whither he would make his first poetical journey. The result of his search was to go to Cathal MacFinguine, who was then on a royal progress in Iveagh of

Munster. The scholar had heard that he would get plenty and enough of all kinds of whitemeats; for greedy and hungry for whitemeats was the scholar.

This came into the mind of the scholar on a Saturday eve exactly, at Roscommon; for there he was pursuing his reading. Then he sold the little stock he possessed for two wheaten cakes and a slice of old bacon with a streak across its middle. These he put in his book-satchel. And on that night two pointed shoes of hide, of seven-folded dun leather, he shaped for himself.

He arose early on the morrow, and tucked up his shirt over the rounds of his fork, and wrapped him in the folds of his white cloak, in the front of which was an iron brooch. He lifted his book-satchel on to the arched slope of his back. In his right hand he grasped his even-poised knotty staff, in which were five hands from one end to the other. Then, going right-hand-wise round the cemetery, he bade farewell to his tutor, who put gospels around him.

He set out on his way and journey, across the lands of Connaught into Aughty, to Limerick, to Carnarry, to Barna-trí-Carbad, into Slieve-Keen, into the country of the Fir-Féni, which is this day called Fermoy, across Moinmore, until he rested a short time before vespers in the guest-house of Cork. On that Saturday he had gone from Roscommon to Cork.

This was the way in which he found the guest-house on his arrival, it was open. That was one of the days of the three things, viz., wind and snow and rain about the door; so that the wind left not a wisp of thatch, nor a speck of ashes that it did not sweep with it through the other door, under the beds and couches and screens of the princely house.

The blanket of the guest-house was rolled, bundled, in the bed, and was full of lice and fleas. No wonder, truly, for it never got its sunning by day, nor its lifting at night; for it was not wont to be empty at its lifting. The bath-tub of the guest-house, with the water of the night before in it, with its stones, was by the side of the door-post.

The scholar found no one who would wash his feet. So he himself took off his shoes and washed his feet in that bath-tub, in which he afterwards dipped his shoes. He hung his book-satchel on the peg in the wall, took up his shoes, and gathered his hands into the blanket, which he tucked about his legs. But, truly, as numerous as the sand of the sea, or sparks of fire, or dew on a May morning, or the stars of heaven, were the lice and fleas nibbling his legs, so that weariness seized him. And no one came to visit him or do reverence to him.

He took down his book-satchel, and brought out his psalter, and began singing his psalms. What the learned and the books of Cork relate is, that the sound of the scholar's voice was heard a thousand paces beyond the city, as he sang his psalms, through spiritual mysteries, in lauds, and stories, and various kinds, in dia-psalms and syn-psalms and sets of ten, with paters and canticles and hymns at the conclusion of each fifty. Now, it seemed to every man in Cork that the sound of the voice was in the house next himself. This came of original sin, and MacConglinne's hereditary sin and his own plain-working bad luck; so that he was detained without drink, without food, without washing, until every man in Cork had gone to his bed . . . .

He remained there until midnight. Then an angel of God came to him on the pillar-stone, and began to manifest the vision unto him. As long as the angel was on the pillar-stone it was too hot for MacConglinne, but when he moved on a ridge away from him, it was comfortable. (Hence the 'Angel's Ridge' in the green of Cork, which was never a morning without dew.) At the end of the night the angel departed from him.

Thereupon he shaped a little rhyme of his own, which would serve to relate what had been manifested to him, and there he remained until morning with the poetical account of his vision ready . . . .

MacConglinne began to recount his vision, and it is said that from here onward is what the angel manifested to him, as he said:

> A vision that appeared to me,
> An apparition wonderful
>   I tell to all:
> A lardy coracle all of lard
> Within a port of New-milk Loch,
>   Up on the World's smooth sea.
>
> We went into the man-of-war,
> 'Twas warrior-like to take the road
>   O'er ocean's heaving waves.
> Our oar-strokes then we pulled
> Across the level sea,
> Throwing the sea's harvest up,
>   Like honey, the sea-soil.

The fort we reached was beautiful,
With works of custards thick,
   Beyond the loch.
New butter was the bridge in front,
The rubble dyke was wheaten white,
   Bacon the palisade.

Stately, pleasantly it sat,
A compact house and strong.
   Then I went in:
The door of it was dry meat,
The threshold was bare bread,
   Cheese-curds the sides.

Smooth pillars of old cheese,
And sappy bacon props
   Alternate ranged;
Fine beams of mellow cream,
White rafters — real curds,
   Kept up the house.

Behind was a wine well,
Beer and bragget in streams,
   Each full pool to the taste.
Malt in smooth wavy sea,
Over a lard-spring's brink
   Flowed through the floor.

A loch of pottage fat
Under a cream of oozy lard
   Lay 'tween it and the sea.
Hedges of butter fenced it round,
Under a blossom of white-mantling lard,
   Around the wall outside.

A row of fragrant apple-trees,
An orchard in its pink-tipped bloom,
   Between it and the hill.
A forest tall of real leeks,
Of onions and of carrots, stood
   Behind the house.

Within, a household generous,
A welcome of red, firm-fed men,
 Around the fire.
Seven bead-strings, and necklets seven,
Of cheeses and of bits of tripe,
 Hung from each neck.

The Chief in mantle of beefy fat
Beside his noble wife and fair
 I then beheld.
Below the lofty cauldron's spit
Then the Dispenser I beheld,
 His fleshfork on his back.

The good Cathal MacFinguine,
He is a good man to enjoy
 Tales tall and fine.
That is a business for an hour,
And full of delight 'tis to tell
The rowing of the man-of-war
 O'er Loch Milk's sea.

He then narrated his entire vision in the presence of the monks of
Cork until he reached its close (but this is not its close), and the
virtues of the vision were manifested unto Manchín.

 'Excellent, thou wretch,' said Manchín, 'go straight to Cathal
MacFinguine, and relate the vision to him; for it was revealed to me
last night that this evil which afflicts Cathal would be cured through
that vision.'

A Large and Extensive City
Thomas Campbell
from: *A Philosophical Survey of the South of Ireland* . . . (1778)

This is a city large and extensive beyond my expectation. I had been
taught to think worse of it in all respects, than it deserves; it was
described as the magazine of nastiness. And as it is the great

shambles of the kingdom, I was predisposed to credit these reports; but it is really as clean, in general, as the metropolis. The slaughterhouses are all in the suburbs, and there, indeed, the gale is not untainted; but in the city, properly so called, all is tolerably clean, and consequently sweet. If sufficient care were taken, even the suburbs might be purged of everything offensive, either to the sight or smell; for they stand upon the declivity of hills and down each street there is a copious flow of water perpetually washing down the filth, from the door of each slaughter-house into the river, which surrounds the town. The city is situated, as Spenser graphically describes it, in his marriage of the Thames and Medway.

> The spreading Lee, that like an island fair,
> Encloseth Cork, with his divided flood.

This island is intersected with several canals, either natural or artificial, which, being banked and quayed in, bring up ships almost to every street. The city, however, is mostly composed of lanes, cutting the main-streets at right angles, and so narrow, that one of them, which is but ten feet wide, is called Broad-lane. The houses are old, and far from being elegant in their appearance. On the new quays, indeed, there are some fair looking buildings; which they are obliged to weather slate. And this they do in a manner so neat as to render it, almost, ornamental.

There are two large stone bridges, one to the north, and the other to the south, over the grand branches of the Lee, besides several small ones, and some draw-bridges thrown over the lesser branches or canals. There are seven churches, an exchange, a custom-house, a barrack, several hospitals, and other public structures, yet none of them worth a second look. I have not seen a single monument of antiquity in the whole town, nor heard a bell in any of the churches, too good for the dinner-bell of a country squire. But here is something infinitely better. Here is the busy bustle of prosperous trade, and all its concomitant blessings; here is a most magnificent temple, erected to plenty, in the midst of a marsh. For that it was originally such, if there were no other evidence, the very name imports: the word Cork or Corrach signifying *palus* or fen, as I learn from Lhuid's dictionary.

A bookseller here has put this, and other tracts into my hands, which have been useful to me in my researches. Smith's history of

Cork, quoting Stanihurst, reports that 120 years ago, Cork was but the third city in Munster, now it is the second in the kingdom, and therefore called the Bristol of Ireland.

Except in the article of linen, its exports are more considerable than those of Dublin. The balance of Trade, I should conceive, to be against Dublin, the trade of which, chiefly, consists in the importation of luxuries; whereas Cork deals almost entirely in exporting the necessaries of life, beef, pork, butter, hides, tallow, &c.

All the wealth of Munster and Connaught passes through two or three cities, which may be said to have eaten up the surrounding country, where the wretched peasant never tastes the flesh of the cattle which he feeds; but subsists upon potatoes, generally without butter, and sometimes without milk.

What proportion the trade of this city bears to that of Bristol, I have not *data* to form an estimate. If we were to judge from the richness of the shops, there is here a vast inferiority. In some other respects, Cork appears to be the greater city. In 1754 the return of houses in Cork was 7445, in 1766 it was 8113; if we suppose them to have increased at the same rate since, they are now 8614. This is placing them low, for there are great numbers of the poor legally exempted from paying hearth-money; and it is not the interest of the collectors to exceed in their returns. In Bristol, and three miles round it, there are said to be but 9000 houses; if so, the houses in the city alone, are probably not so numerous as those of Cork.

In the reign of Edward IV there were eleven churches in Cork; now there are but seven. Yet it has ever since that time been esteemed a thriving city, and in the memory of man it is said to have been doubled. But we have already seen that the state of population cannot be ascertained from the number of churches; if our ancestors had not more religion than we have, they were certainly more addicted to building religious houses.

To see the reason, why the number of churches has decreased with increasing population, we should recollect, that in the time of Edward IV they had but one religion, that now they have many; and that the catholics outnumber all other denominations, seven to one at least.

As the Romanists adhere religiously to all their old institutions, in the number and division of parishes, and as they have now but seven mass-houses in so large and populous a city, we may fairly suppose that there were no more parishes in Edward's time; though there might have been eleven churches, reckoning in that number the chapels belonging to the four monasteries, which were then in Cork, viz. St Dominicks's, St Francis's, the Red Abbey, and the Cill Abbey.

It must too be observed, that though the monasteries are destroyed, the Monks remain to this day, and have regular service in their distinct houses, as in the parish mass-houses. In all of which they have a succession of services, on Sundays and holy-days, from early in the morning, till late at night, for the accommodation of their numerous votaries.

Beside these eleven mass-houses, there are four dissenting meeting-houses, belonging to Presbyterians, Anabaptists, Quakers, and French Protestants. The prevalence of Popish interest in Cork, may be argued from the following trivial circumstance: bidding a fellow whom I had picked up for my *ciceroni*, to conduct me from the cathedral to the bishop's house, he asked me *which bishop?* The same conclusion I drew at Kilkenny, from another trifle; I there heard the titular bishop greeted in the style of his dignity.

On Sunday morning early, I stepped into one of their mass-houses, and a spacious one it was. The priest had just finished the celebration of mass. On the altar stood six candles. A servitor came in, after the priest had withdrawn, and, kneeling before the altar, he entered the rails like those of our chancels; and, after kneeling again, he snuffed out two of the candles; then he kneeled again, and snuffed out two more; he kneeled a fourth time, and extinguished the fifth; the sixth he left burning.

There were several elegant carriages standing before the door when I entered, and a prodigious crowd of people in the street; as motley an assemblage of human creatures as I had ever seen. There was a multitude of beggars imploring alms in the Irish language, some in a high, and some in a low key. Some of them measured out tones as if singing but in accents the most unmusical that ever wounded the human ear. They were worse than all the tones in Hogarth's *Enraged Musician.* — If this be a bull, consider that I am in Ireland.

Had this Rabelais of the pencil introduced an Irish beggar, he would have set Pasquali mad. In the most perfect of human compositions, there is, you know, something still wanting to render it complete. Pity that the influence of a Cork mendicant should be wanting, to fill up the measure of discord, and thereby render one human production perfect.

Not content with what I saw at mass, I afterwards went to church, the steeple of which exactly answered Shakespear's description in *sloping to its foundation*: which argues the fenny bottom, whereon it stands. I was, however, delighted with the contrast I found here. The service was, throughout, performed with the utmost decency and propriety; they had a good organ, and the singing was remarkably good. The embellishments of the church were neither rich, nor studied; but they were neat and plain; and the audience had, truly as much the air of opulence and elegance, as most of the congregations in the city of London.

After service they generally betake themselves to a public walk, called the Mall; which is no more than a very ill-paved quay upon one of their canals with a row of trees on one side, and houses on the other. It is a pleasure, however, to see that they are filling up this canal, and several others, where the water, having no current, must have become noxious to the air in hot weather. On a bridge, thrown over this canal, is an equestrian statue of his late Majesty, executed in bronze by an artist of Dublin. This with a pedestrian of Lord Chatham, of white marble, and one in plaster of Paris, of king William III in the Mayoralty-house, are the only statues in this large city.

If this street were well paved, and the Mall flagged, it would be as ornamental to the town, as agreeable to the ladies. There is another public walk, called the Redhouse walk, west of the city, cut through very low grounds, for a mile in length, planted on each side, where the lower sort walk; and on leaving the Mall, I found it crowded with people, in general, very decently dressed. Farewell.

Toast

Thomas McCarthy

from: *The Non-Aligned Storyteller* (1984)

No lovelier city than all of this,
Cork city, your early morning kiss;
peeled oranges and white porcelain,
midsummer Sunday mists
that scatter before breakfast.

Mass bells are pealing in every district,
in the Latin quarter of St Lukes,
the butter *quartier* of Blackpool.
Each brass appeal calls to prayer
our scattered books and utensils,

the newly blessed who've put on clothes.
Why have I been as lucky as this?
to have found one so meticulous
in love, so diffident yet close
that the house is charged with kinetic peace.

Like a secret lover, I should bring
you bowls of fresh roses, knowing
that you would show them how to thrive.
Lucky it's Sunday, or I'd have
to raid the meter for spare shillings!

Or, maybe I should wash my filthy socks,
fret at the curtains, iron clothes,
like you after Sunday breakfast.
Normal things run deep, God knows,
like love in flat-land, eggs on toast.

A Teenage Town

Frank O'Connor

from: *Leinster, Munster and Connaught* (1950)

Waterford is one thing, Cork another. I once travelled in the train
from Kilkenny with an amiable lunatic. 'Could you tell me the name
of that castle?' I asked, and he put on a grave face, scratched his
head and replied slowly: 'That comes under the heading of forti-
fication.' 'But the bridge!' I urged. 'What do you call the bridge
beside it?' A look of real anguish came over the lunatic's face as
he scratched his head again. 'That,' he replied, 'comes under the
heading of navigation.'

Something of the same pain affects me when I turn to try and write of my native city. 'That comes under the heading of autobiography.' Just in flashes and for a day or two only I can see it under the heading of topography: a charming old town with the spire of Shandon, two sides of it limestone and two sandstone, rising above the river, as beautiful as any of the Wren spires in the city of London, and the bow fronts which undulate along Patrick Street and the Grand Parade, with their front doors high up as in round towers, and flights of steps so high that they go up parallel to the pavement, because the river flows beneath, and areas had to be built upon street-level. I can admire as if I were a stranger the up and down of it on the hills as though it had been built in a Cork accent. But it doesn't last. Objectively I am observing, subjectively I am observed, and in a way I know all too well.

That isn't, I think, because I am naturally melancholy or introspective, or because my memories of childhood are mainly unhappy ones. For a great part of my childhood I was very happy, but I cannot help thinking that towns need to be classified according to their maximum mental age, which should appear in every directory beside their population. It would be difficult for the average person over eighteen to be happy in Cork. Of course, there are worse towns, towns where the mental age is nearer twelve, and Dublin's own mental age is not so high — twenty-three or — four at best. In the history of the world only a few towns have existed where a man could grow old in the fullest development of his mental faculties, and one of these murdered Socrates.

Tea Ceremony
John Montague
from: *Mount Eagle* (1987)

She brings us to her secret place, behind the apple tree, on the last terrace of our garden. Ordering her little friends bossily, she leads them first up the ladder; we follow behind, bashful giants. She has set up a table, a few boards balanced on stones, where a half-broken doll sits facing a bruised teddy. One by one, large and small, we are assigned our places: 'now *you* sit there' and '*you* sit here'.

Then a fresh batch of orders arrives. 'Since I'm the Mummy I pour out the tea.' A child's hand reaches out, plucks and distributes china cups so delicate that they are invisible. Then it grasps a teapot handle out of space and leans across to each of us in turn, before settling back that solid object made of air down in front of her. 'And here are the sandwiches and biscuits.' Each of us receives a dusty twig or leaf. 'Now you all eat up and if any of you complain I'll tell Daddy on you.' She gives Teddy an affectionate poke which sends him sprawling to the ground. 'And sit up straight: no slouching when we have visitors.'

Solemnly, we lift the cups to our lips, toasting each other silently. Through the branches of the apple tree we can see the city, a pall of smoke over the docks, the opaque matt surface of the River Lee. Beyond those small hills is the airport and as we drink invisibility a plane climbs, a sliver of silver in the sunlight. Filtered through the apple blossom its sound is as distant and friendly as the hum of a honey-seeking bee.

Letters Home
George Boole

From the letters of George Boole, first Professor of Mathematics in Queen's College, Cork, to his sister, Maryann Boole, in Lincoln.

Queen's College, Cork
Oct. 25th. 1849

My dear Maryann,

I have at length arrived at the scene of my future labours and I have taken what I think will prove comfortable lodgings close by the college. The situation and the prospects around are all that could be desired. The river Lee flows in front of me through a beautiful valley the sides of which are covered with wood in many parts, an unusual sight in Ireland, and with suburban villas. Cork is as far as I have yet seen it a very pleasant and indeed a rather fine city. Like any other large hive of men it has of course its wretched abodes of misery and want, but of these I have only heard as yet in Cork. What I have seen presented nothing very repulsive. Neither have I have been annoyed by what so much complain of: the importunity of the mendicants. The weather is wet and strong and this may have kept the streets rather freer than they are usually said to be.

Of the state of cultivation in Ireland, judging from what I yesterday saw while travelling from Dublin it is impossible to speak in terms too sad. There is over the whole country an air of utter destitution and abandonment. For miles and miles you see nothing but fields overgrown with reeds and plashy with surface water, vast desolate bogs, cabins few in number and of the most wretched kind, scarcely a tree between you and the horizon, scarcely a human being by the way or a herd of cattle in the fields. I have seen nothing like it — I can conceive of nothing worse. Far better would it be to see the fresh and the plain as nature left them than to look upon scenes which only suggest the ideas of sloth, neglect and decay . . . .

Queen's College, Cork
Oct. 29th. 1849

I went this morning to church and on my return went into a street in which was a great crowd of people. It was almost entirely composed of beggars and the sight far exceeded in horror anything not only that I have ever before witnessed but that I had even read of. It is beyond all description. As it is impossible to relieve this wretchedness by any private efforts and as the sight of it is heartsickening, I must I believe absolve to avoid those quarters of the city in which it obtrudes itself upon us. If it were simply want, simply the inability to get food that drove people into the streets, something might indeed be done. But one cannot help seeing that there is an ostentation of rags and filth and squalor and an evident calculating in the effect which they will produce which is truly revolting. I think the state of mendicancy in this country a most serious drawback from any advantage which living in it may possess. Remember, however, to quiet your alarms that very little indeed of this is seen in the quarter in which I dwell. This suburb is exceedingly beautiful. I know of nothing like it in any English town.

Cork
May 9th. 1851

I am glad to tell you that I am much better than when I last wrote to you. I am free from those pains in the limbs from which I was then suffering and am stronger but still far from being strong. I should take care of myself . . . . what you say of illness in Lincoln corresponds with the experience of Cork. Almost everyone has been suffering more or less from influenza, bilious complaints etc. and I am told that typhus fever has been extremely prevalent in the city . . . .

There is no change here to relate. All goes on as usual. Cork is the quietest place on earth. Emigration seems to be its chief business now. While at Monkstown I was continually witnessing the passage of emigrant vessels down to the harbour . . . .

Charles Dickens in Cork

from: *The Cork Examiner*, 1 September 1858

On Monday evening CHARLES DICKENS, both personally and in his writings the most popular of living novelists, made his first appearance before a Cork audience. The house was well filled all through, though the cram in the galleries showed intellectual entertainment to be most favoured amongst the democracy. Almost precisely at the time appointed, the distinguished visitor made his appearance, and was greeted by a hearty cheer, which he cordially acknowledged. The platform on which he took his place had been carefully adapted to throw out into the strongest possible relief the figure of the reader, and to enable the audience to see in the most distinct manner the movements of his form, and the workings of his marked and expressive lineaments. The peculiarities of his appearance, the *extreme* elegance of his toilette, his handsome, yet care-worn features, his American moustache and beard, and those large, wonderful eyes which seem to fascinate everyone's attention, have been already fully described. Audiences must be favourably impressed with the quiet, gentlemanly manner in which he invites, the natural expression of any emotion to which the little book he is about to read 'may be fortunate enough' to give rise, and listeners and declaimer commence their intercourse with an easy feeling on both sides. The 'little book' was the Christmas Carol, one of the most exquisite prose idylls in any language. Full of strange character-sketching, of queer conversations, of genial loveable humour, of quaint, pathetic tenderness, and withal founded upon a violent improbability — the sudden conversion of a miser by a dream — those who read it rush through its pages with a fascination which works of graver import and perhaps higher merit cannot command. But those who have so perused it know comparatively little of its power, until they have heard its strange fancies, its odd whimsical conceits, its bits of thrilling pathos, its flashes of brilliant fun, proceeding from the lips of its author. Mr. DICKENS is a consummate actor. His voice is full and mellow — strong without being noisy, and of most versatile quality. Then he can speak with every muscle and line of his face, and then he does startle with somewhat vehement or fantastical action. All these aids are combined to make *Scrooge* more miserly, hard and exciting; his nephew more good-humoured and fore-bearant [sic]; the ghost of *Marley* more transparent; the buttons of his coat behind more visible through him; the once questionable fact of his having no bowels more self-evident; the chain he had forged for himself of cash-boxes, ledgers, steel purses etc. more firmly binding about him. The rich, flexible voice and the speaking glances make more droll that picture of Christmas at *Bob Cratchit's* — 'Tiny Tim and all', which is one of the drollest, pleasantest sketches that has ever been drawn. Who that looks at and listens to the author, as he details all the events of that astounding festivity, cannot see almost with his own eyes the two juvenile Cratchits thrusting their spoons into their mouths lest they could not restrain themselves until their time came to be helped, and should actually shriek for goose? Who does not sympathise in the hopes and fears regarding the well-being of the pudding, and follow almost in person its triumphant procession when it is found to be miraculously success-ful? It needs all the powers of the actors, as well as the author, to help us to realize the agility of old *Fezziwig*, whose legs shone so that at the last cut they seemed to wink. Without his reading, imagin-ation cannot picture the full absurdity of believing that *Topper* in reality was blind during that game of blind man's buff, which took place at *Scrooge's* nephew's, or had any other design than that of catching the plump sister — 'her in the lace tucker.' In fact, all that touched or amused in the written work had its merit heightened and made more vivid by thus proceeding, living as it were, out of the mouth of him who conceived it. Nor could it be forgotten that it was no mere actor was before you; no adaptable instrument that entered the music made by another; but the man who, out of his own rich imagination, had drawn all those shapes of beauty which dwell so fondly in our memories; whose exuberant wealth of

169

humour had left us the legacy of fun which has been made the property of high and low, and whose generous, warm heart had conceived all the benevolent homilies of love and charity, of which this *Christmas Carol* is one of the most touching.

It is almost needless to say that the two hours' reading held the attention of the audience rivetted, except when some passage elicited a spontaneous burst of laughter, or some generous sentiment evoked a cheer; and that at the end the gratified listeners saluted the departure of their illustrious entertainer with a hearty and cordial farewell. . . .

Our illustrious visitor availed himself of the leisure moments in the intervals of his entertainments to visit the scenery in the vicinity of Cork, having gone yesterday to Queenstown, and this day to Blarney. He spent a quarter of an hour on the top of the Castle, surveying the pleasant prospect, and before departing kissed the famous stone. Whether Mr. DICKENS thought this ceremonial necessary to increase the magic with which his tongue is tipped, we do not know; but surely it was not the opinion of the visitors to the Athenaeum on Monday and Tuesday evenings. We understand that Mr. DICKENS expressed the most intense delight at the natural aspect of the neighbourhood, and most agreeable disappointment at the outer condition of our people. We believe in a pecuniary point of view his visit has been very successful.

Up the Bare Stairs
Seán O'Faoláin

from: *Collected Stories* (1980)

A pity beyond all telling is hid in the heart of love.

All the way from Dublin my travelling companion had not spoken a dozen words. After a casual interest in the countryside as we left Kingsbridge he had wrapped a rug about his legs, settled into his corner, and dozed.

He was a bull-shouldered man, about sixty, with coarse, sallow skin stippled with pores, furrowed by deep lines on either side of his

170

mouth: I could imagine him dragging these little dikes open when shaving. He was dressed so conventionally that he might be a judge, a diplomat, a shopwalker, a shipowner, or an old-time Shakespearian actor: black coat, striped trousers, grey spats, white slip inside his waistcoat, butterfly collar folded deeply, and a black cravat held by a gold clasp with a tiny diamond.

The backs of his fingers were hairy: he wore an amethyst ring almost as big as a bishop's. His temples were greying and brushed up in two sweeping wings — wherefore the suggestion of the actor. On the rack over his head was a leather hat case with the initials F.J.N. in Gothic lettering. He was obviously an Englishman who had crossed the night before. Even when the steam of the train lifted to show the black January clouds sweeping across the Galtees, and a splash of sleet hit the window by his ear, he did not waken. Just then the ticket checker came in from the corridor and tipped his shoulder. As he received back his ticket he asked, 'What time do we arrive in Cork?' He said the word *Cork* as only a Corkman can say it, giving the *r* its distinctively delicate palatal trill, not saying 'Corrrk', or 'Cohk'. He was unmistakably a Corkonian.

At Mallow I came back from tea to find him stretching his legs on the platform and taking notice. He had bought the evening paper and was tapping his thigh with it as he watched, with a quizzical smile, two tipsy old countrymen in amiable dispute, nose to nose, outside the bar. A fine man on his feet; at least six foot two. I bought a paper, also, at the bookstall and as we went on our way we both read.

My eye floated from a heading about a licensing case — the usual long verbatim report, two men found hiding under the stairs, six men with bottles in the stable, much laughter in court, and so on — to a headline beside it: CORKMAN IN BIRTHDAY HONOURS LIST. The paragraph referred to 'Francis James Nugent, Baronet: for War Services.' I looked across at him.

'Did you say something?' he asked.

'No, no! Or, rather, I don't think so.'

'Pretty cold,' he said, in a friendly way. 'Though I will say one thing for the G.S.R., they do heat their trains.'

'Yes, it's nice and warm today. They're not, of course, the G.S.R. now, you know. They're called Coras Iompair Eireann.'

'What's that? Irish for G.S.R.?'

'More or less.'

We talked a bit about the revival of the language. Not that he was interested; but he was tolerant, or perhaps the right word is indifferent. After a bit I said:

'I see there's a Corkman in the new honours list.'

'Oh?'

I glanced up at the rack and said, with a grin:

'I see the initials on your hatbox.'

He chuckled, pleased.

'I suppose I'd better plead guilty.'

'Congratulations.'

'Thank you.'

'What does it feel like?'

He glanced out at the wheeling fields, with their lochs of water and cowering cattle, and then looked back at me with a cynical smile.

'It doesn't feel any different. By the time you get it you've pretty well enjoyed everything it stands for. Still, it helps.'

'I see from the paper that you went to the same school as myself.'

'Are you the old Red and Green, too?'

'Up the Abbey!'

He laughed, pleased again.

'Does all that go on just the same as before?'

'It goes on. Perhaps not just the same as before.'

We talked of West Abbey. I knew none of the men he knew, but he thawed out remembering them.

'Are all the old photographs still in the main hall? Chaps in the Indian Civil, the Canadian Mounted, the Navy, the Indian Police? God, I used to stare at them when I was a kid.'

'They're gone. They've been replaced by Confirmation groups all wearing holy medals.'

He made a bored face.

'I suppose in those days you little thought you'd be coming back to Cork one day as Sir Francis Nugent.'

He peered at me through his cigarette smoke and nodded sagely.

'I knew.'

'You did!'

'I shouldn't have said that. I couldn't know. But I had a pretty good idea.'

Then he leaned forward and let down all his reserves. As he began my heart sank. He was at the favourite theme of every successful man: 'How I Began.' But as he went on I felt mean and rebuked. I doubt if he had ever told anyone, and before he finished I could only guess why he chose to tell me now.

'You know, it's extraordinary the things that set a fellow going. I always knew I'd get somewhere. Not merely that, but I can tell you the very day, the very hour, I made up my mind I was going to get there. I don't think I was more than fourteen or fifteen at the time. Certainly not more than fifteen. It was as simple as that' — clicking his fingers. 'It was all on account of a little man named Angelo — one of the monks who was teaching us. He's gone to God by now. There was a time when I thought he was the nicest little man in the whole school. Very handsome. Cheeks as red as a girl's, black bristly hair, blue eyes, and the most perfect teeth I've ever seen between a man's lips. He was absolutely full of life, bursting with it. He was really just a big boy and that's probably why we got on so well with him. I've seen him get as much fun out of solving a quadratic equation or a problem in Euclid as a kid with a new toy. He had a marvellous trick of flinging his *cappa* over one shoulder, shoving his two wrists out of his sleeves like a conjurer, snapping up a bit of chalk and saying, 'Watch what I'm going to do now,' that used to make us sit bolt upright in our desks as if . . . well, as if he was going to do a conjuring trick. And if you could only have seen the way he'd kick ball with us in the yard — you know, the old yard at the back of West Abbey — all we had was a lump of paper tied with twine — shouting and racing like any of us. He really was a good chap. We were very fond of him.

'Too fond of him, I've often thought. He knew it, you see, and it made him put too much of himself into everything we did. And the result was that we were next door to helpless without him. He made us depend on him too much. Perhaps he wasn't the best kind of teacher; perhaps he was too good a teacher — I don't know — have it whichever way you like. If he was tired, or had a headache, or sagged, we sagged. If he was away sick and somebody else had to take charge of us we were a set of duffers. They could be just as cross as he was — he was very severe, he'd take no excuses from anybody — or they could be as merry as he was: it just wasn't the same thing. They had a job to do, and they did the best they could, but with him it wasn't a job, it was his life, it was his joy and his pleasure. You could tell how much the fellows liked him by the way they'd crowd around him at play hour, or at the end of the holidays to say good-bye.

'One particularly nice thing about him was that he had no favourites, no pets, as we used to call them. Did you call them that in your time? But he was — what shall I say? — more than a little partial to me. And for a very, if you like to call it, silly reason. In those days, you see, politics were very hot in Cork city; very hot, very passionate. Of course, they were the old Irish Party days, long before your time, when politics were taken much more seriously than I've ever seen them taken anywhere else. John Redmond had one party called the Molly Maguires, and William O'Brien had another party called the All for Irelanders. Mind you, if you asked me now what it was all about I'd find it very hard to tell you, because they were all the one party at Westminster, and they were all agreed about home rule, but once it came to election time they tore one another to pieces. Fights in the streets every night, baton charges, clashes between rival bands, instruments smashed on the pavements. One night, with my own eyes, I saw a big six-foot countryman take a running jump down the Grand Parade and land right on top of a big drum.

'Well, Angelo was a Molly, and I needn't tell you he was just as excited about politics as he was about everything else, and I was also a Molly and a very hot one. Not that I understood anything at all about it, but just that my father was one of the hottest Redmondites in the city of Cork. And, of course, nothing would do Angelo but to bring politics into class. He'd divide the class into Mollies and All Fors and when we'd be doing Euclid or reciting poetry he'd set one team against the other, and he'd work up the excitement until the fellows would be clambering across the desks, and if any fellow let down his side we'd glare at him until he'd want to creep away out of sight, and if he scored a point we'd cheer him as if he'd kicked a goal in an All Ireland Final.

'It was on one of these days that it happened. We were at the Eighth Problem. The Mollies wanted one point to pull even. I was the last man in — and I muffed it. And no wonder, with Angelo shouting at me like a bull, "Come on, now, Frankie. If A.B. be placed on C.D. . . . Up the Mollies! Go on, Frankie. Go on. If A.B. . . ."

'The All Fors won. Angelo laughed it off with, "Very good, very good, back to yeer places now. Work is work. This isn't the Old Market Place. Now for tomorrow," and so on.

'But he kept me in after school. There I sat, alone in the empty classroom upstairs — you know the one, near the ball alley — with the crows outside in the yard picking up the crusts, and the dusk falling over the city, and Angelo, never speaking a word, walking up and down the end of the room reading his office. As a rule we were let out at three. He kept me there until five o'clock rang. Then he told me to go home and went off himself up to the monastery.

'I walked out of the yard behind him, and at that moment if I had had a revolver in my hand I'd have shot him. I wouldn't have cared if he'd beaten me black and blue. I wouldn't have cared if he'd given me extra work to do at home. He deliberately got me into trouble with my father and mother, and what that meant he understood exactly. Perhaps you don't. You don't know my background as he knew it. When I tell you that my father was a tailor and my mother was a seamstress I needn't tell you any more. When a kid's mother has to work as hard as his father to push him through school you can guess the whole picture. I don't seem to remember an hour, except for Sundays, when one or other, or both, of these machines wasn't whirring in that little room where we lived, down by the distillery, sometimes until twelve or one o'clock at night. I remember that day as I walked home I kept saying to myself over and over again, "If only my mummy wasn't sick." All the way. Past the distillery. Around by the tannery. You possibly know the little terrace of houses. They've been there since the eighteenth century. Dark. We had only two rooms. In the hall. I can still get that stuffy smell that had been locked up there for a hundred and fifty years — up the bare stairs. On the landing there was a tap dripping into an old leaden trough that had been there since the year dot. I could hear the machine whirring. I remember I stopped at the window and picked a dead leaf from the geraniums. I went up the last few steps and I lifted the latch. My father was bent over the machine; specs on his forehead, black skeins of thread around his neck, bare arms. My mother was wrapped in shawls in the old basket chair before the fire. I could draw that room; the two machines, my bed in one corner, my dinner waiting on the table, the tailor's goose heating on the grate. The machine stopped.

'"In the name of God what happened to you, boy?" says my father. "Is there anything wrong? What kept you? Your poor mother there is out of her head worrying about you."

'"Ah, I was just kept in, sir," says I, passing it off as airily as I could. "How are you, Mummy?"

'The old man caught me by the arm.

'"Kept in?" says he, and the way he said it you'd think I was after coming out of the lockup. "Why were you kept in?"

'"Ah, 'twas just a bit of Euclid I didn't know, that's all."

'It was only then I noticed that the mother was asleep. I put my hand to my lips begging him not to waken her. He let a roar out of him.

'"A nice disgrace! Kept in because you didn't know your Euclid!"

'"What is it, what is it, Frankie?" she says, waking up in a fright. "What did they do to you, boy?"

'"'Twas nothing at all, Mummy, just that I didn't know a bit of Euclid. I had to stay back to learn it."

'"A nice how d'ye do! And why didn't you know your Euclid?" — and he had me up against the wall and his fist raised.

'"It wasn't really Euclid at all, Father. It was all Angelo's fault. It was all politics. He divided the class into All Fors and Mollies and because the All Fors won he kept me in out of spite. Honestly, that's all it was, Mummy, there was nothing else to it."

'"Holy God," whispers the old man. "So it wasn't only the Euclid, but lettin' down John Redmond in front of the whole class. That's what you did, is it?"

'"Oh, for God's sake, Billy," says the mother, "don't mind John Redmond. 'Tis little John Redmond or any other John Redmond cares about us, but 'tis the work, the work. What are we slaving for, boy, day and night, and all the rest of it? There's your poor father working himself to the bone to send you through school. And so on. Nothing matters, boy, but the work! The work!"

'"'Tisn't only the work," says the old man. "'Tisn't only the work," and he was sobbing over it. "But to think of poor John Redmond fighting night after night for Ireland, standing up there in the House of Commons, and you — you brat — couldn't even do a sum in Euclid to stand by him! In your own school! Before everybody! Look at him," he wails, with his arm up to the picture of John Redmond on the wall, with his hooked nose and his jowls like an old countrywoman. "Look at the dacent gentleman. A man that never let down his side. A gentleman to the tips of his toes if there ever was one. And you couldn't do a simple sum in Euclid to help him! Th'other fellows could do it. The All Fors could do it. But my son couldn't do it!"

'And with that he gave me a crack that nearly sent me into the fire.

176

'The end of it was that I was on my knees with my head on the mother's lap, blubbering, and the old man with his two hands up to John Redmond, and the tears flowing down his face like rain, and the mother wailing, "Won't you promise, Frankie, won't you promise to work, boy?" and I promising and promising anything if she'd only stop crying.

'That was the moment that I swore to myself to get on. But wait! You won't understand why until I've finished.

'The next day Angelo took the same problem, at the same hour, and he asked me to do it again. Now, kids are no fools. I knew by the look on his face why he asked me to do it. He wanted to make friends with me, to have everything the same as if yesterday had never happened. But he didn't know what had happened inside in me the night before. I went through the problem, step by step — I knew it perfectly — down to the Q.E.D.

'"Now, isn't it a pity, Frankie," he says, smiling at me, "that you wouldn't do that yesterday?"

'"Oh," I said, in a very lordly, tired voice, "I just didn't feel like it."

'I knew what was coming to me, and I wanted it, and to make sure that I got it I gave him that sort of insolent smile that drives grownups mad with children. I've seen that smile on my own children's faces now and again, and when I see it I have to go outside the door for fear I'd knock them the length of the room. That is what Angelo did to me. I got up off the floor and I sat back in my place and I had the same insolent smile on my face.

'"Now, if you please," says Angelo, reaching for his cane, and he was as white as his teeth, "will you kindly do the next problem?"

'I did it, step by step, calm as a breeze, down to the Q.E.D. I'd prepared it the night before.

'"Right," says Angelo, and his voice was trembling with rage. "Do the next problem."

'I had him where I wanted him. He was acting unfairly, and he knew it, and the class knew it. I had that problem prepared too. Just to tease him I made a couple of slips, but just as he'd be reaching for the cane I'd correct them. I was a beast, but he'd made me a beast. I did it, down to the Q.E.D. and I smiled at him, and he looked at me. We both knew that from that moment it was war to the knife.

'I worked that night until twelve o'clock; and I worked every night until I left school until twelve o'clock. I never gave him a chance. I had to, because until the day I left that place he followed me. He followed me into Middle Grade. And into Senior Grade. He made several efforts to make it up with me, but I wouldn't let him. He was too useful to me the other way. I sat for the Civil Service and I got first place in the British Isles in three subjects out of five, geometry, chemistry, and history, third in mathematics, fifth in German. I did worst in German because I didn't have Angelo for German. I think I can say without arrogance that I was the most brilliant student that ever passed out of West Abbey School.'

Sir Francis leaned back.

'You must have worked like a black.'

'I did.'

'Well, it was worth it!'

He looked out over the fields which were now becoming colourless in the falling dusk and his voice sank to a murmur, as if he were thinking aloud.

'I don't know. For me? Yes, perhaps, I had no youth. For them? I don't know. I didn't work to get on, I worked to get out. I didn't work to please my mother or my father. I hated my mother and I hated my father from the day they made me cry. They did the one thing to me that I couldn't stand up against. They did what that little cur Angelo planned they'd do. They broke my spirit with pity. They made me cry with pity. Oh, I needn't say I didn't go on hating them. A boy doesn't nourish hatred. He has his life before him. I was too sorry for them. But that's where they lost everything. A boy can be sorry for people who are weak and pitiable, but he can't respect them. And you can't love people if you don't respect them. I pitied them and I despised them. That's the truth.'

He leaned back again.

'You don't look like a man whose spirit was ever broken,' I laughed, a little embarrassed.

'The spirit is always broken by pity. Oh, I patched it up pretty well. I made a man of myself. Or, rather,' he said with passion, 'with what was left of myself after they'd robbed me of my youth that I spent slaving to get away from them.'

'You'd have slaved anyway. You were full of ambition.'

'If I did I'd have done it for ambition alone. I tell you I did it for pity and hate and pride and contempt and God knows what other reason. No. They broke my spirit all right. I know it. The thing I've put in its place is a very different thing. I know it. I've met plenty of men who've got along on ambition and they're whole men. I know it. I'm full of what they put into me — pity and hate and rage and pride and contempt for the weak and anger against all bullying, but, above all, pity, chock-a-block with it. I know it. Pity is the most disintegrating of all human emotions. It's the most disgusting of all human emotions. I know it.'

'What happened to Angelo?'

'I don't know. Nor care. Died, I suppose.'

'And . . . your father?'

'Fifteen years after I left Cork he died. I never saw him. I brought my mother to live with me in London.'

'That was good. You were fond of her.'

'I was sorry for her. That's what she asked me for when I was a boy. I've been sorry for her all my life. Ah!'

His eyes lit up. I looked sideways to see what had arrested him. It was the first lights of Cork, and, mingling with the smoke over the roofs, the January night. Behind the violet hills the last cinder of the sun made a saffron horizon. As the train roared into the tunnel we could see children playing in the streets below the steep embankment, and he was staring at them thirstily, and I must have imagined that I heard their happy shouts. Then the tunnel opened and swallowed us.

There were no lights in the carriage. All I could see was the occasional glow of his cigarette. Presently the glow moved and my knee was touched. His voice said:

'She's with me on this train. My mother. I'm bringing her back to Cork.'

'Will she like that?'

'She's dead.'

The train roared on through the tunnel. As we passed under the first tunnel vent a drip of water fell on the roof. The tiny glow swelled and ebbed softly.

'I'm very sorry.'

His voice said, in the darkness:

'I meant to bury her in London. But I couldn't do it. Silly, wasn't it?'

After a while another drip of water splashed on the roof. The windows were grey.

'You did the kind thing.'

His voice was so low that I barely heard it.

'Kind!'

In a few more minutes we were drawing up in steam alongside the lighted platform. He was standing up, leaning over his hatbox. From it he lifted a silk topper and a dark scarf. He put on his black frock coat. 'Good-bye,' he said politely, and beckoned for a porter.

From the platform I watched him walk down towards the luggage van where a tiny group already stood waiting. They were all poor people. There was a bent old woman there in a black shawl, and three or four humble-looking men in bowler hats and caps. As I watched him bow to them and doff his hat to the old woman and introduce himself, the yellow pine-and-brass of the coffin was already emerging from the van and the undertaker's men in their brass-buttoned coats were taking it from the porters. Among his poor relations he walked reverently, bare-headed, out into the dark stationyard.

They slid the coffin into the motor hearse; he showed his relatives into the carriages, and, stooping, he went in after them. Then the little procession moved slowly out into the streets on its way to whatever chapel would take her for the night into its mortuary.

Chant of the Quay Called Coal

(an excerpt) vernacularly versed by 'Phineas O'Gander'
from: *The Cork Examiner,* 24 December 1870

Were I sublimer than the Grecian rhymer,
Than Prisistratus or bold Bonaparte,
Could I when lyrical, like Moore, that miracle,
Endue my dialect with tuneful arte —
I'd pen a ditty of this beauteous city,
So wise and witty 'twould beget renown,
And with thrush or curlew, I'd extol that purlieu,
The Coal Quay Market of my native town.

It's there good liquor can be had on tick, or
If you'd like it quicker for the ready shot,
With high gentility to breed civility,
In every company of this famed spot;
No disputation upon sect or nation,
In this location will be ever found,
Where you'll see proud Normans and both Jews and Mormons,
With the Flynns and Gormons drinking on one round.

Did I Versailles see, or the Shams de Lazy,
Or Tsarkoe Selo, I would tell them true,
Their Boulevarding and their Mobile Garden
Is all blackguarding, the mere foreign crew;
Let god and goddess, without vest or bodice,
Display proportions in each leafy seat,
But, for sublimity of dainty dimity,
There's no extremity like Market Street.

You'll see the cook shops, with their store surprising,
Most appetizing both to sight and scent,
Each swain emerging with his favourite virgin,
Those bowers resorting for nutriment;
Oh that's the sporting with those couples courting,
Their crubeens picking between every kiss,
With the hostess smiling at their ways beguiling,
While adding cabbage to their feast of bliss.

I've seen Killarney, I have been to Blarney,
The Tower of Babel, and Sweet Convamore,
But for all wonders of convivial grandeurs,
There is no galaxy like this bright shore;
When at that ferry whence black Charon's wherry,
Shall bear me, merry, o'er the river Styx,
Could I when parting choose the point of starting,
My lovely Coal Quay is the place I'd fix!

Setting The Type
Greg Delanty
from: *Southward* (1992)

I pick a magnifying glass from your desk
& hold it to a haze of men
bowed over the jigsaw puzzles of galley trays.

You confer with Dan Hannigan.
I wonder at the results of a half century
of nicotine on his right index finger.

Through zig-zag bars of an old-fashioned elevator
I have just spotted the ascending head
& Humpty-Dumpty body of Donnie Conroy.

He will be broken by drink
& his daughter's death.
Her face is now smiling from his desk.

You turn & escort me to the letterpress.
Mr. Lane punches my name into shiny lead
& declares hereafter it is eternal.

The names of Dan Hannigan, Owen Lane, Donnie Conroy —
I could go on forever invoking the dead —
were set deep in a boy

impressed by the common raised type on the 3rd floor
of Eagle Printing Company, 15 Oliver Plunket Street,
in the summer-still, ticking heart of Cork City.

Extracts from a Journal
Daniel Corkery

18.7.07

Today a sweltering day; called into Guy's about Fr. Augustine's
programme. When I saw the printing department I thought of how
dull we live. I have been often in printing offices; Guys was not
different only the heat seemed to make it more oppressive. The
sweat ran down the faces; some bent over desks; some were setting
up type; one boy was knocking a set-up case of type asunder. Notice
the smell of the printing ink on everything. And the small gas-jet
burning in the dark corner on midsummer midday. Two girl workers
were holing labels and chatting laughingly. A pile of trays containing
types of different characters stood in a frame-work against the wall.

A hum of machinery, one saying as it went back and forward Ha-ha-ha. The old men looked fairly healthy; the young pale and delicate. The old had survived probably. Whenever I see 'printing office' I should see all this at a glance. And I won't.

5.8.07

Bank Holiday. M. Cullinane arrived from Skibbereen today. In the evening went with Cull and Breen to visit J. Long in Union. A most depressing place. We only saw the school department. The boys vilely dressed dirty sore-eyed were playing in a dry and earthy playground surrounded on two sides by high stone walls, and on the other two sides by iron railings — the railing went up for about six or seven feet. Here they play summer and winter. One wondered how there was such heart in their play. The way up to J. Long's room was dark, up stone steps, dirty, smelling. The beds in the boys' dormitory seemed somewhat little better than rags — noticed the pillow slips were torn. The beds were very close, they stood on a sort of raised platform — about six inches high. The place smelled foully.

Cullinane remarked that J. Long looked depressed. I think it was the spirit of the place.

We were shown by Miss Kenna (assistant teacher) the infants' dormitory. When we opened the door it looked like an ant-hill — the little fellows with only a very short singlet on, walking about the beds crawling over them in a perfect silence — one little fellow seemed almost nude. There were some nice little beds of flowers.

15.8.07

Tonight saw the first performance given here by the Abbey Theatre Co. The plays acted were

Hyacinth Halvey	Lady Gregory
The Rising of the Moon	"
Spreading the News	"
and Riders to the Sea by J.M. Synge	

The first three are farce more or less; the last poignant tragedy. The cast gets a good effect by sticking solely to the point. An English dramatist would have complicated matters by making someone in love with the drowned man. It would be impossible to say

183

from this whether Synge can write drama; the story is so powerful in itself that it needs only the merest telling. The reflections one made at the end of the play are really what one would make if the thing happened in real life. Is this right?

20.8.07 Tuesday

This morning went out looking up schoolchildren. Visited Paul St. Marsh. Main St. All very poor tenement houses. All had some features in common. The stairs were leaning to one side: vacant 'common' rooms seemed frequent; whitewash everywhere; intense curiosity on all the landings as to whom I might be; ashamed look on the faces of those who opened the door for me, their faces always unwashed, with hair hanging; an effort made to draw the clothes over the breast; half-naked children running round. In a house in Harpur's Lane there were in one room a middle-aged woman with bare feet, a young girl and a soldier, her brother I should say, and several children. While I was talking to a woman in Kyrls St. a neighbour came and put her head through a window. I was speaking over the half-door; she was looking through a window expecting some sensation presumably. All were very quiet. The only woman who took any interest in her child's welfare was one above the rest socially. It is such lanes as these turn out soldiers.

22.8.07

Went through the lanes this morning trying to get young fellows to schools. In one place you can look down to another landing through iron bars. In a particularly ramshackle house in Paul St. looking through a lobby window your view is filled with one of the rose windows of SS Peter and Paul's. So that the meanest places have their glimpses of lovely things. In the yard of the house high up is a white bracket carved projecting from a wall on which stands what seems to be the capital of a column. Flowers grow in it.

In Harpur's Lane — one the filthiest of all — I was told — 'Erra where are they at all — anyway their father went to hospital last night — and their good little clothes are in the pawn — and his mother bought a gansy for Jerry but Jerry wouldn't go to school with it — and Paddy wouldn't go as Jerry wouldn't go — so you see 'tisn't their mother's fault at all.'

184

Tonight was drizzling but the moon was shining. D. Harr, D. Breen and myself came by the fields from Magazine to Glasheen Road. There were lovely pictures at every hand's turn. Looking towards the moon, the corn-field was not as different from its surroundings in tone but looking from the moon it was quite bright — and egg yellow.

The Provincial Writer's Diary

Thomas McCarthy

from: *The Sorrow Garden* (1981)

On cold nights in November he read late
and worried about the gift of fiction;
he was enveloped in a shell of lethargy.
Everything was let go —
even his diary lay idle for a whole month
while he chased provincial loneliness
from the corners of his mother's house.

Everything became consumed by the Personal:
furious theatre work killed some time,
strolling with his bachelor friends, fishing,
or the steady cumulative ritual of walking
beyond the city to sketch its grey limits.
But nowhere could he find (within those limits
of thought) the zeal that would consume life.

He lived far from the heroic. On Monday
mornings he would stalk the grey ghettos
of the North side and low-lying tenements
for absentee school-children. He would be taken aback
by the oppressive stench and filth of their lives.
One morning he thought, as if explaining all misery,
that such homes were the nests of the Military.

The Bells of Shandon

Francis Sylvester Mahony (Father Prout)

With deep affection and recollection,
    I often think of those Shandon bells,
Whose sounds so wild would, in days of childhood,
    Fling round my cradle their magic spells.
On this I ponder, where'er I wander,
    And thus grow fonder, sweet Cork, of thee;
        With thy bells of Shandon,
        That sound so grand on
The pleasant waters of the river Lee.

I have heard bells chiming full many a clime in,
    Tolling sublime in cathedral shrine;
While at a glib rate brass tongues would vibrate,
    But all their music spoke nought like thine;
For memory dwelling on each proud swelling
    Of thy belfry knelling its bold notes free,
        Make the bells of Shandon
        Sound far more grand on
The pleasant waters of the river Lee.

I have heard bells tolling, 'old Adrian's Mole' in,
    Their thunder rolling from the Vatican,
With cymbals glorious, swinging uproarious,
    In the gorgeous turrets of Notre Dame;
But thy sounds were sweeter than the dome of Peter,
    Flings o'er the Tiber, pealing solemnly,
        Oh! the bells of Shandon,
        Sound far more grand on
The pleasant waters of the river Lee.

There's a bell in Moscow, while on tower and Kiosko
    In St. Sophia the Turkman gets,
And loud in air calls men to prayer,
    From the tapering summit of tall minarets.
Such empty phantom I freely grant them,
    But there's an anthem more dear to me,
        It's the bells of Shandon,
        That sounds so grand on
The pleasant waters of the river Lee.

The Legend of the Lough
Crofton Croker

from: *Researches in the South of Ireland* (1824)

A little way beyond Gallows Green of Cork, and just outside the town, there is a great lough of water, where people in winter go and skate for the sake of diversion; but the sport above the water is nothing to what is under it, for at the very bottom of this lough there are buildings and gardens, far more beautiful than any now to be seen, and how they came there was in this manner. Long before Saxon foot pressed Irish ground, there was a king called Corc, whose palace stood where the lough now is, in a round green valley, that was just a mile about. In the middle of the courtyard was a spring of fair water, so pure, and so clear, that it was the wonder of all the world. Much did the king rejoice at having so great a curiosity within his palace; but as people came in crowds from far and near to draw the precious water of this spring, he was sorely afraid that in time it might become dry; so he caused a high wall to be built up round it, and would allow nobody to have the water, which was a very great loss to the poor people living about the palace. Whenever he wanted any for himself, he would send his daughter to get it, not liking to trust his servants with the key of the well-door, fearing they might give some away.

One night the king gave a grand entertainment, and there were many great princes present, and lords and nobles without end; and there were wonderful doings throughout the palace: there were bonfires, whose blaze reached up to the very sky; and dancing was there, to such sweet music, that it ought to have waked up the dead out of their graves; and feasting was there in the greatest of plenty for all who came; nor was any one turned away from the palace gates — but 'your welcome, heartily,' was the porter's salute for all.

Now it happened at this grand entertainment there was one young prince above all the rest mighty comely to behold, and as tall and as straight as ever an eye would wish to look on. Right merrily did he dance that night with the old king's daughter, wheeling here and wheeling there, as light as a feather, and footing it away to the admiration of everyone. The musicians played the better for seeing their dancing; and they danced as if their lives depended upon it. After all this dancing, came to supper; and the young prince was

187

seated at table by the side of his beautiful partner, who smiled upon him as often as he spoke to her; and that was by no means so often as he wished, for he had constantly to turn to the company and thank them for the many compliments passed upon his fair partner and himself.

In the midst of this banquet, one of the great lords said to King Corc, 'May it please your Majesty, here is everything in abundance that heart can wish for, both to eat and drink, except water.'

'Water!' said the king, mightily pleased at some one calling for that of which purposely there was a want. 'Water shall you have my lord speedily and that of such a delicious kind, that I challenge all the world to equal it. Daughter,' said he, 'go fetch some in the golden vessel which I caused to be made for the purpose.'

The king's daughter, who was called Fior Usga (which signifies in English 'spring water') did not much like to be told to perform so menial a service before so many people, and though she did not venture to refuse the commands of her father, yet hesitated to obey him, and looked down upon the ground. The king, who loved his daughter very much, seeing this, was sorry for what he had desired her to do, but having said the word, he was never known to recall it; he therefore thought of a way to make his daughter go speedily and fetch the water, and it was by proposing that the young prince, her partner, should go along with her. Accordingly, with a loud voice, he said, 'Daughter, I wonder not at your fearing to go alone so late at night; but I doubt not the young prince at your side will go with you.' The prince was not displeased at hearing this; and taking the golden vessel in one hand, with the other led the king's daughter out of the hall so gracefully that all gazed after them with delight.

When they came to the spring of water in the courtyard of the palace, the fair Usga unlocked the door with the greatest care, and stooping down with the golden vessel and to take some of the water out of the well found the vessel so heavy that she lost her balance and fell in. The young prince tried in vain to save her, for the water rose and rose so fast that the entire courtyard was speedily covered with it and he hastened back almost in a state of distraction to the king.

The door of the well being left open, the water, which had been so long confined, rejoiced at obtaining liberty, rushed forth incessantly, every moment rising higher and higher, and was in the hall of the entertainment sooner than the young prince himself, so that when he attempted to speak to the king he was up to his neck in water. At length the water rose to such a height that it filled the entire of the green valley in which the king's palace stood, and so the present Lough of Cork was formed.

Yet the king and his guests were not drowned, as would now happen if such an awful inundation were to take place; neither was his daughter, the fair Usga, who returned to the banquet-hall the very next night after this dreadful event; and every night since the same entertainment and dancing goes on in the palace at the bottom of the lough, and will last until some one has the luck to bring up out of it the golden vessel which was the cause of all this mischief.

Nobody can doubt that it was a just judgment upon the king for his shutting up the well in the courtyard from the poor people. And if there are any who do not credit my story, they may go and see the Lough of Cork, for there it is to be seen to this day; the road to Kinsale passes at one side of it; and when its waters are low and clear, the tops of the towers and stately buildings may be plainly viewed in the bottom by those who have good eyesight, without the help of spectacles.

The Madwoman of Cork
Patrick Galvin
from: *The Wood-Burners* (1973)

Today
Is the feast day of Saint Anne
Pray for me
I am the madwoman of Cork.

Yesterday
In Castle Street
I saw two goblins at my feet
I saw a horse without a head
Carrying the dead
To the graveyard
Near Turner's Cross.

I am the madwoman of Cork
No one talks to me.

When I walk in the rain
The children throw stones at me
Old men persecute me
And women close their doors.
When I die
Believe me
They'll set me on fire.

I am the madwoman of Cork
I have no sense.

Sometimes
With an eagle in my brain
I can see a train
Crashing at the station.
If I told people that
They'd choke me —
Then where would I be?

I am the madwoman of Cork
The people hate me.

When Canon Murphy died
I wept on his grave
That was twenty-five years ago.
When I saw him just now
In Dunbar Street
He had clay in his teeth
He blest me.

I am the madwoman of Cork
The clergy pity me.

I see death
In the branches of a tree
Birth in the feathers of a bird.
To see a child with one eye
Or a woman buried in ice
Is the worst thing
And cannot be imagined.

I am the madwoman of Cork
My mind fills me.

I should like to be young
To dress up in silk
And have nine children.
I'd like to have red lips
But I'm eighty years old
I have nothing
But a small house with no windows.

I am the madwoman of Cork
Go away from me.

And if I die now
Don't touch me.
I want to sail in a long boat
From here to Roche's Point
And there I will anoint the sea
With oil of alabaster.

I am the madwoman of Cork
And today is the feast day of
Saint Anne.
Feed me.

The Old Clerk
Roz Cowman
from: *The Goose Herd* (1989)

There was a honeycomb
of redbrick lamplit terraces
which still survive around the
barrack square.

This was where his life began,
when the Old Queen was alive.
This was his boast.
Now she is gone, and only

the sweet nostalgic names
are there,
Lansdowne and Grosvenor,
Wellesley and Wellington,

the ghost of honey in an empty hive.

The Dullest Town

Chevalier De Latocnaye

from: *A Frenchman's Walk Through Ireland 1796–1797* (1798)

I arrived at Cork, the dullest and dirtiest town which can be imagined. The people met with are yawning, and one is stopped every minute by funerals, or hideous troops of beggars, or pigs which run the streets in hundreds, and yet this town is one of the richest and most commercial of Europe. The principal merchants are nearly all foreigners, Scotch for the most part, and in the short period of ten years are able sometimes to make large fortunes.

There is no town where there is so much needful to do to make the place agreeable to a great number of the poor inhabitants. The spirit of commerce and self-interest has laid hold of all branches of the administration. For example, it would be very easy to furnish the town with a public fountain, but the person or company which has the privilege of bringing water in pipes to the houses thinks that by the building of such a fountain there would be lost a number of guinea subscriptions. Therefore, in order that the avidity of an obscure individual should be satisfied, thirty thousand inhabitants must suffer the punishment of Tantalus. I have seen poor people obliged to collect the water falling from the roofs on a rainy day, or to take it even from the stream in the streets. All the time there is perhaps hardly a place which it would be so easy to supply with water as Cork, by reason of the heights which surround it. There is even a spring or fountain about a mile away, which is called Sunday's Well, which appears to me to have sufficient water for the supply of a public fountain in the centre of the town. The water supply for private houses is drawn from the bed of the river a mile above the town. Why should it be so difficult to do for the public what interest has done for the richer classes?

The dirt of the streets in the middle of the town is shameful, and as if that were not enough, it would seem as if it were wished to hinder the wind and the sun from drying the filth, for the two ends of the street are terminated by prisons, which close the way entirely and prevent the air from circulating.

The grain market in a town of such considerable size ought naturally to be much frequented. Actually it has been placed on the first floor of a building, and the crowd can only reach it by a stairway two or three feet wide, exposed to all weathers; and to make matters worse, the steps are so much worn that they are slippery and dangerous. One would imagine that there should be nobody allowed on this stairway excepting those who come to or go from the market; but the most disgusting beggars have taken possession of the wall-side and assail the passers-by with their cries, while presenting a porringer or bag in which they are nearly obliged to throw a handful of meal. I have seen a poor woman fall the whole length of the stairs, upsetting nearly everyone on them, and breaking her own arm.

The meat market is the only one which is as it ought to be. It is new, and it is to be hoped that the magistrates will, in the end, think of the other places where the public must congregate.

Although the people are very poor, nothing or no one can persuade the mothers to send their children to the poorhouse or almshouse. They are afraid that they would be sent away to other places — a thing which formerly did happen, but a less cruel system is observed now. The mothers wish that their children should not be brought up in the Protestant religion, which is professed in these establishments. A frequent sight is one of these poor unfortunates with two children on her back and another in her apron, holding another by the hand, and beseeching for the cold charity of the passers-by, who being accustomed to such sights generally turn away their eyes. The poor woman, however, also accustomed to such indifferences, consoles herself by smoking a black pipe, so short that the fire almost seems to be in her mouth.

The rich people accuse the poor of being content to live in dirt and to sleep with their cattle. They like it no better than their rich brethren and sisters; necessity, cruel necessity, is the reason for their manner of life. Their misery is such that they become indifferent to decencies. Let them be furnished with the means of changing this life. Let them be put in a position to cultivate the decencies, and know some of the comforts of life, and it will be seen how unjust are the accusations which have been made.

The peasant is idle here; but of what use would activity be to him? The price of his day's work hardly suffices to maintain him and his family. Costs of various food commodities have been multiplied by three, and yet the price of labour remains the same. Over nearly the whole of Ireland the labourer earns only sixpence a day; his wife and his children are hopeless about doing anything in a country where there are no manufactures. What can, then, such an unfortunate family do? The sixpence suffices only to furnish potatoes and water. Should the father fall sick or die, the poor mother is obliged to quit the country with her children and wander, begging a horrible subsistence. Cursed be the cruel man who first dared to make game of the misery of his fellow. It is one of the shocking artifices of the avaricious, for immediately when we have come to laugh at the ills of others, we feel ourselves freed from any necessity to help them.

I visited the Cove which is the port of Cork, ten or twelve miles lower down at the mouth of the river — it is one of the prettiest bays and one of the safest in Europe. There I was well and kindly received by the brave General Vallencey, to whom I presented the last letter I possessed of Mr. Burton Conyngham. The researches of the General in Irish antiquities are known through the whole literary world; perhaps he has pushed a little too far his enthusiasm for the Irish language, in which (although an Englishman) he has made surprising progress. He asserts, or pretends to believe, that it is as old as the world, and is perhaps the same which Adam and Eve made use of in the Garden of Eden, the general mother of all languages of the universe from the Huron to the Chinese. He quotes in his grammar singular examples of its agreement with about thirty living languages in all parts of the world.

It is certain that all the nations of Europe, the greater part of those of Asia and even of Africa, have had origin in the country from whence came the Irish. It may be that the isolated situation of these people has facilitated the preservation in its purity of the ancient language of their country of origin.

General Vallencey has travelled over Ireland for fifteen years, and has made surveys for maps of the different counties. The Government in the end, as a reward for his labours, has given him the post which he occupies at the moment, that of Commandant of the Port of Cove, which is now so strongly fortified that there is no danger that any hostile vessel can enter. It cannot be denied that he is a man of value to the State in more than one way, seeing that he has twelve children of a first marriage, ten of a second, and twenty-one of a third. There are very few men who have done their duty so well.

I presented my respects to Lady Colthurst, an amiable widow, and much too pretty to remain one for long. The General, to whom I showed the letters in my possession, planned my course towards the north, making it unnecessary for me to return immediately to Cork.

I walked the whole length of the island of Cove, and, fatigued, I sat myself down to rest in a graveyard, amusing myself by reading the epitaphs. I had often heard of Irish 'bulls,' but had not been fortunate in finding one, and there I found on a tomb, on which, after the names of the family, I read with pleasure, 'Lord, have mercy on the souls *here* interred.' And so, I said to myself, these good folk have buried under this stone both soul and body. Over nearly the whole of Ireland, but more particularly in the south, I find a peculiar manner of expression which, as far as I can judge, comes from a mixture of the two languages, and this manner accounts for the 'bull' or stupidity. The mistakes are not any greater than those made by a person speaking a language which is not his own. Here they commonly call the fosse *dyke*, the name which is given to the wall in England; and here they call the wall *ditch*, which is the name there given to the fosse.

Passing Inchiquin, the spot from which one has the finest view of the bay, I came to Castle Mary, belonging to Lord Longueville, and saw in his park a Druid's altar. This was a large one, twenty or thirty feet long by about fifteen wide, supported on three large stones. One is astonished in reflecting on the power or apparatus that was necessary to lift such weights. These great stones prove that the people who placed them knew something of mechanical science, and consequently must have attained a high degree of civilization. As to the use to which they put these stones there are doubts. Some say that the Druids offered on them human sacrifices, which may be true, but it is perhaps enough to say that they would serve on all occasions when the priests judged it necessary to expose any object to the view of the people. From here I went to Cloyne, and there attended a service of benediction which the Bishop bestowed on his clergy on the Sunday after the service. Near the cathedral is one of those round towers of which I have spoken. It is higher and bigger than the ordinary type. The peasants of the neighbourhood are persuaded that it was built by the devil in a single night, and that he brought the stones for it from a far country. I saw no difference between the stones of the tower and those at hand. All I can say is that if the devil built it, the devil is a good mason.

Cloyne is one of the principal bishoprics in Ireland in point of income. The episcopal town, however, is a little place, but rather larger than that of Ferns. Following the crowd of peasants going to mass, I took the road to Castle Martyr, and, at some distance from this pretty little town, I met a man of very respectable appearance riding on horseback and accompanied by a lady. I had a shrewd guess as to who this should be, and, by inquiring from a servant, I found that I was correct in supposing the gentleman to be Lord Shannon. I asked the domestic to say that a foreigner who had a letter for his lordship desired to speak with him. My letter was delivered on the king's highway, and, after it was read, his lordship asked me to continue my road to his house, where he would join me soon.

Castle Martyr is one of the most beautiful and one of the best cared-for places, not merely in Ireland, but, perhaps, in Europe. The garden, which Lady Shannon finds pleasure in cultivating, is a charming retreat where flowers of every species are arranged with singular skill. I spent five or six days here, and, on leaving, Lord Shannon was good enough to give me an extremely flattering general letter of recommendation. It was addressed only to his friends, but I have since shown it, practically, to everybody, and the manner in which it has been received is a testimony to the esteem in which his lordship is held by the public. Returning towards Cork I stopped at Middleton to see a large cloth manufactory. It is an entirely new manufacture in this part of Ireland, and has had a great many difficulties to surmount before attaining its present success. It is, however, not altogether as great as might be desired. Several persons in Cork have assured me that if this company could borrow £20,000 sterling for ten years, without interest, it would certainly become a very flourishing industry; but who is going to lend £20,000 without interest? Only the Government could do it, and there is a simple way of doing it. This would be to put a heavy tax on whisky, and to put the resulting revenue in the hands of manufacturers. This would produce two desirable effects at once: it would encourage industry, and arrest the progress of drunkenness.

I spent some time in the island of Foaty with a spoiled child of fortune, Mr Smith Barry. He has travelled much, is very courteous and reasonable, appears to be well educated, is good natured, and would be happy if he had only £500 a year instead of £25,000; but his riches have so surfeited him and disgusted him with the world that he has almost totally retired from society, and lives a rather melancholy life in his island, which is not the island of Calypso. Calling at the little island of Cove, I introduced myself to Mr Silver Oliver, a gentleman who has given hospitality for a long time to an old, exiled French officer, who is treated as one of the house, and with much kindness. Mr Oliver asserts that he has fulfilled all the duties that society can reasonably require from a man. He has been Member of Parliament two or three times, he has been Privy Councillor, he has been married, he has several children, &c., &c., and consequently he has a right to live according to his fancies, and these are sometimes rather original. I returned to Cork by the river, and had opportunity to observe that the boatmen here are very much of the bantering type we know on the great rivers of France. Necessity obliged me to return to this City of Yawns. This time, however, the people appeared to be animated, and bands of workers marched through the streets shouting. I asked what was the reason for the row, and was told that the apprentice-shoemakers had, by common accord, struck work, in order to force their masters to increase their wages. I followed them and saw them stop at different times before the houses of master-shoemakers, and have some warm exchanges of words with them. At last the magistrates interfered, and one of them at the head of some soldiers promenaded the streets, endeavouring to disperse the discontented apprentices; but these only made fun of him, and arranged matters so cleverly that he was always in the place where they were not. Night, as in England, made the tumult cease and sent everyone home to bed.

I had a recommendation to the Bishop, who received me very kindly, and this gave me great pleasure, for I think it proves that all animosities between the two religions are at an end. He sent me to the Catholic Bishop, Dr Moylan, who is an educated man, and much respected in the country.

On the occasion of I know not what fête the children made a fire of bones (which is a common practice all over Ireland on days of rejoicing), and they amuse themselves by dancing around the fire and even by running over it with their bare feet. This gave me occasion to make some reflections on the etymology of *bone fire* in England, which term seems to me to come from this fire of bones, rather than from the forced French of *bon feu* or *feu de joie*.

The climate of Cork is rainy in the extreme. It rains every day in life, and the temperature of the air has perhaps influenced the character of the inhabitants. It would not be incorrect to call this country 'The Land of Whim and Spleen'. There are a great number of people here who are called 'characters', and who have all sorts of strange whims and crotchets. One will never sit down to table for fear of being suffocated by the odour of the viands, and takes his meals alone in the vestibule; another spends his income on favourite animals, or 'pets', as they are called; a third, after having enchanted you by a beautiful voice and charming music, finishes up by boxing you. There is one with a red cap who gallops through the streets and enters shops on horseback, when he wants to buy anything. There is one who plays the bagpipes and who is willing to be disinherited from nearly two thousand pounds sterling per annum, rather than give up his pipes, which are at present his sole source of income. There is a man who believes that everybody wishes to poison him. He watches for the entry of any person into a baker's shop, follows him, and when the stranger has bought a loaf he seizes it and runs off with it, believing that the bakers are not anxious to poison anybody but himself. He acts the same way in butchers' shops. Another has constituted himself children's nurse, and washes, rubs, combs, and wipes them. I could mention many other examples of these 'characters', but have said enough.

There is no place of shelter for the weak-minded of Cork — it is a hideous spectacle to see them in the streets. For the greater part, it is true, they are quiet, but it is so cruel and humiliating to see human nature degraded that an effort should be made to separate them from society.

The Dying Synagogue at South Terrace

Thomas McCarthy

from: *Seven Winters in Paris* (1989)

Chocolate-colored paint and the July sun
like a blow-torch peeling off
the last efforts of love.
More than time has abandoned this,
God's abandonment, God's synagogue,
that rose out of the ocean
one hundred years from here.
The peeling paint is an immigrant's
guide to America — lost on the shore
at Cobh, to be torn and scored
by a city of *luftmenshn*;
Catholics, equally poor, equally driven.

To have been through everything,
to have suffered everything and left
a peeling door. *Yahweh* is everywhere,
wherever abandonment is needed —
a crow rising after an accident,
wearing the grey uniform
of a bird of carrion, a badger
waiting for the bones of life
to crack before letting go:
wishing the tenth cantor to die,
the Synagogue to become a damp wall,
the wailing mouths to fester.
Too small. To be a small people
aligned to nothing is to suffer blame
like a thief in the night. An activist
threw a petrol-bomb for Palestine:
the sky opened and rained hail
like snow-drops. Flowers for memory,
petrol for the far-away.
To name one's land is to be a cuckoo
pushing others, bird-like, into a pit:

until, at the end, every sacred gesture
becomes vain, soiling the Synagogue
door like the charcoal corpses

at Mauthausen Station, 1944. A few
survived in the green valley of know-
nothing: spent themselves putting boots
on the Catholic poor, counting the brown
pennies, the corncrakes on their
trade routes, and the guerilla raids.

To sit here now, in the rancid sunshine
of low tide, is to contemplate
all of the unnoticed work of love —
exquisite children fall like jewels
from an exhausted colporteur's bag:
a mid-century daughter practises piano,
an *étude* to forget terror; a brother
dreams of the artistic life, another
shall practise law and become, in time,
the Catholics' tall Lord Mayor.
Where these jewels fall beside the peeling
door, let us place the six lilies of memory;
the six wounds of David's peeling star.

Just Fine

Mary Leland

from: *The Little Galloway Girls* (1987)

'And how are you, yourself?' he asked.

The question was so unexpected that she blushed. Heat rushed through her and she turned her head towards the street, looking blindly through the grey window of the solicitor's office where they both sat in a calm of waiting, agreed on settlement, terms, undertakings, custodies, maintenance and matrimonial ownership, waiting now only for the formality of documents and signatures.

The question and its implications tipped the balance of silence between them. For Michael it was only a gesture he meant to be able to make, a sign of continuing concern about what might happen to her, how she would manage, how things were working out with the child.

For Martha it was more. Bewildered thoughts battered against each other in her head; what was it he wanted to know? Could she tell him what happened about the income tax? Or would this be the right time to mention the fees for the nursery school, or the fact that the exhaust pipe was loose, yet again, in her car? What was he *asking* her?

The panic in her head sat back into words which she did not speak, but which seemed to hurl themselves from her temples against the window through the glass, onto the street of the city where it seemed to her they bounced and recoiled and rang out again, a sounding of her rage.

'How am I? Myself? Oh, now to be truthful, to be truthful, I am fine. But lonely. Lonely. And different. That clean word rings clear, like a bell in my mind, different, yes, and glad to be. The new two of us in this long new time have found that there is less and less to be afraid of. I can climb over the rubble of mortgage repayments to find old crocus bulbs sending up their striped shafts of green in the garden. We are not afraid of the icy roads of winter without you, or of the windows rocking in the dark wind. The dark without Daddy is no more than just the dark.

'Look at the bills, the bills are smaller. One fire will do us, there is no threat in the telephone. My bed is my own, unshared, and going to sleep at night is like sliding into friendly water. The house yes, the house is yours, and like a shell you are welcome to the shape of it, for we are the flesh inside and we thrive. What can I say about our linked lives except this: we are happy together.

'And if I am lonely it is not because the man in my life is only four years old. I am lonely for something I may not have recognized when I had it, if I had it, and which I cannot describe now. The closest I can come is that these words have to stay inside here, in a new place in which I have come to live, but which I now know is not an exile, it is just somewhere else. *Me.*'

When the pattern of hidden words changed and slowed Martha's silence changed too, for with her arrival at herself she had brought one piece of luggage. Her journey had the weight of a ghost strapped to its back, the ghost of a question, what was happening to him?

Where was he living? What would they tell the boy together as their last shared undertaking for him? Oh, this was a question with a deepening range, a query which went on further, touching against corners it could not probe. Martha's greatest fear now was that a disturbance of the secrecy of this man's life might reveal, in its hollows, a space for her. And while there was a need to know something, something that could be told as 'just fine!', perhaps — she did not want to know if a room was being kept for her.

She had already established so firmly in her heart that the child which had been born of the two of them was now forever to be only his or hers, there was no 'theirs', no future fusion which could bind them to anything together ever again. In this savagery of sundering she found passion and strength, hard hot words which made sense to her and put a pattern on chaos. Once, early on, perhaps two years before this meeting of settlements, she had given herself a picture of what was happening to their marriage. She had seen herself, sitting among the ruins, numbering the bricks; Michael did not even notice the collapse.

It was then that she had realized that the boy was a brick also, a part of a structure which she had thought must remain because he was within it. Had she still loved her husband then, when it was technically 'before'? — another unasked question, or at least a silent one, easily postponed. No, something had been happening to her then as well as to him, or rather *with* him, for he had not changed, she thought, nothing had happened 'to' him. For after all, what had happened, the actual occurrence, had only been, again, a question.

'This is our last child, isn't it? Can you see any way in which we will sleep together again, as husband and wife, or have more children?'

His gentle 'no' solidified so that the air in the space between them was a wall of stone. The marriage flung itself against it and broke and died in that instant. The heavy roses on the curtains and the chairs glowed like wreaths; beyond them the garden was laden with autumn, its weighted leaning trees framing the small figure, red-anoraked, a pom-pom hat pulled far down over his ears so that eyes, nose and little pursed mouth made a small intent mask, while the small hands, with rake and brush, sculled the grass to gather and heap the drifting leaves.

The remembered picture came to her complete, and she remembered too how they had been surrounded in that conversation by the comfort they had created together, but which it then seemed they could not touch, fabrics which might blister and split at the pressure of their taut bodies. It was as though the tension had crystallized, as though everything was sharp and shining, cold and hard to the touch if they dared to touch the materials of their disappearing lives.

What had they said at that time that had brought them to this? Had it been just that question and that answer? Of all that went before, the betrayal and all she had been told, Martha found it hard to give herself accurate evidence. It was true, of course, but was it accurate? What had happened, what exactly had been the cause of this effect?

In this blaze of immediate confusion, while Michael's question rolled and broke among the rocky caves of her mind, memory made her want to say only this, to say what were the things she would never say.

'We will never say to you — come back, come back to eat at another table in another room, away from the worry of our noise; come back to read the shorter fairy tale, to give abstracted praise, to listen and not remember, to give a deeper lie.' Unuttered, these alone were the insubstantial slights her heart had listed. But these could not be all. If they were, were they all that was left?

In the office they sat on stiff chairs of ornamented wood and sharp brown leather. Outside, the Mall uncoiled its stream of traffic winding past the Imperial Hotel, down towards the bridges. Against a sky luminous with winter the spires of the Cathedral were pointed with cold. Only minutes had passed in the silence inside, but from the street the evening beat against the brick and stone of these buildings, climbing to its usual crescendo of people pounding homewards.

Michael sat in shadow, but turned his head towards her when she spoke.

'I'm just fine,' Martha said. She looked at him. His face was flushed with tears.

A Nocturne for Blackpool

Theo Dorgan

from: *The Ordinary House of Love* (1990)

Dolphins are coursing in the blue air outside the window
And the sparking stars are oxygen, bubbling to the moon.
At the end of the terrace, unicorns scuff asphalt,
One with her neck stretched on the cool roof of a car.

A key rasps in a latch, milk bottles click on a sill,
A truck heading for Mallow roars, changing gear on a hill.
The electric hum of the brewery whines, then drops in pitch —
Ground bass for the nocturne of Blackpool.

The ghost of Inspector Swanzy creeps down Hardwick Street,
MacCurtain turns down the counterpane of a bed he'll never
    sleep in,
Unquiet murmurs scold from the blue-slate rooftops
The Death-Squad no-one had thought to guard against.

The young sunburned hurlers flex in their beds, dreaming of
    glory,
Great deeds on the playing-fields, half-days from school,
While their slightly older sisters dream of men and pain,
An equation to be puzzled out again and again.

Walloo Dullea, melodious on the Commons Road, hums airs
    from Trovatore,
The recipe as before, nobody stirs from sleep
And 'Puzzle the Judge', contented, pokes at ashes —
'There's many a lawyer here today could learn from this
    man.'

North Chapel, The Assumption, Farranferris and Blackpool,
The mass of the church in stone rears like rock from the sea
But the interlaced lanes flick with submarine life
Older than priests can, or want to, understand.

This woman believed Jack Lynch stood next to God, who
  broke the Republic.
This man beyond, his face turned to the wall, stares at his
  friend
Whose face will not cease from burning in an icy sea
  — torpedoed off
Murmansk from a tanker. He shot him, now nightly he
  watches him sink.

Here is a woman the wrong side of forty, sightless in her
  kitchen
As she struggles to make sense of the redundancy notice,
Of her boorish son, just home, four years on the dole, foul-
  mouthed,
Of her husband, who has aged ten years in as many days.

The bells of Shandon jolt like electricity through lovers
In a cold-water flat beneath the attic of a house in Hatton's
  Alley,
The ghost of Frank O'Connor smiles on Fever Hospital Steps
As Mon boys go by, arguing about first pints of stout and Che
  Guevara.

The unicorns of legend are the donkeys of childhood, nobody
Knows that better than we know it ourselves, but we know
  also that
Dolphins are coursing through the blue air outside our
  windows
And the sparking stars are oxygen, bubbling to the moon.

We are who we are and what we do. We study indifference in
  a hard school
And in a hard time, but we keep the skill to make legend of
  the ordinary.
We keep an eye to the slow clock of history in Blackpool —
Jesus himself, as they say around here, was born in a stable.

  for Mick Hannigan

The Ursuline Convent

William Makepeace Thackeray

from: *The Irish Sketchbook* (1843)

There is a large Ursuline convent at Blackrock, near Cork, and a lady who had been educated there was kind enough to invite me to join a party to visit the place. Was not this a great privilege for a heretic? I have peeped into convent chapels abroad, and occasionally caught glimpses of a white veil or black gown; but to see the pious ladies in their own retreat was quite a novelty — much more exciting than the exhibition of Long Horns and Short Horns by which we had to pass on our road to Blackrock.

The three miles' ride is very pretty. As far as nature goes, she has done her best for the neighbourhood; and the noble hills on the opposite coast of the river, studded with innumerable pretty villas and garnished with fine trees and meadows, the river itself dark blue under a brilliant cloudless heaven, and lively with its multiplicity of gay craft, accompany the traveller along the road; except here and there where the view is shut out by fine avenues of trees, a beggarly row of cottages, or a villa wall. Rows of dirty cabins, and smart bankers' country-houses, meet one at every turn; nor do the latter want for fine names, you may be sure. The Irish grandiloquence displays itself finely in the invention of such; and, to the great inconvenience, I should think, of the postman, the names of the houses appear to change with the tenants: for I saw many old houses with new placards in front, setting forth the *last* title of the house.

I had the box of the carriage (a smart vehicle that would have done credit to the Ring), and found the gentleman by my side very communicative. He named the owners of the pretty mansions and lawns visible on the other side of the river: they appear almost all to be merchants, who have made their fortunes in the city. In the like manner, though the air of the town is extremely fresh and pure to a pair of London lungs, the Cork shopkeeper is not satisfied with it, but contrives for himself a place (with an euphonious name, no doubt) in the suburbs of the city. These stretch to a great extent along the beautiful, liberal-looking banks of the stream.

I asked the man about the Temperance, and whether he was a temperance man? He replied by pulling a medal out of his waistcoat pocket saying that he always carried it about with him for fear of temptation. He said that he took the pledge two years ago, before which time, as he confessed, he had been a sad sinner in the way of drink. 'I used to take,' said he, 'from eighteen to twenty glasses of whisky a day; I was always at the drink; I'd be often up all night at the public: I was turned away by my present master on account of it'; — and all of a sudden he resolved to break it off. I asked him whether he had not at first experienced ill-health from the suddenness of the change in his habits; but he said — and let all persons meditating a conversion from liquor remember the fact — that the abstinence never affected him in the least, but that he went on growing better and better in health every day, stronger and more able of mind and body.

The man was a Catholic, and in speaking of the numerous places of worship along the road as we passed, I'm sorry to confess, dealt some rude cuts with his whip regarding the Protestants. Coachman as he was, the fellow's remarks seemed to be correct: for it appears that the religious world of Cork is of so excessively enlightened a kind, that one church will not content one pious person; but that, on the contrary, they will be at church of a morning, at Independent church of an afternoon, at a Darbyite congregation of an evening, and so on, gathering excitement or information from all sources which they could come at. Is not this the case? are not some of the ultra-serious as eager after a new preacher, as the ultra-worldly for a new dancer? don't they talk and gossip about him as much? Though theology from the coach-box is rather questionable, (after all, the man was just as much authorized to propound his notions as many a fellow from an amateur pulpit,) yet he certainly had the right here as far as his charge against certain Protestants went.

The reasoning from it was quite obvious, and I am sure was in the man's mind, though he did not utter it, as we drove by this time into the convent gate. 'Here,' says coachman, 'is *our* church. *I* don't drive my master and mistress from church to chapel, from chapel to conventicle, hunting after new preachers every Sabbath. I bring them every Sunday and set them down at the same place, where they know that everything they hear *must* be right. Their fathers have done the same thing before them; and the young ladies and gentlemen will come here too; and all the new-fangled doctors and teachers may go roaring through the land, and still here we come regularly, not caring a whit for the vagaries of others, knowing that we ourselves are in the real old right original way.'

I am sure this is what the fellow meant by his sneer at the Protestants, and their gadding from one doctrine to another; but there was no call and no time to have a battle with him, as by this time we had entered a large lawn covered with haycocks, and prettily, as I think, ornamented with a border of blossoming potatoes, and drove up to the front door of the convent. It is a huge old square house, with many windows, having probably been some flaunting squire's residence; but the nuns have taken off somewhat from its rakish look, by flinging out a couple of wings with chapels, or buildings like chapels at either end.

A large, lofty, clean, trim hall was open to a flight of steps, and we found a young lady in the hall, playing, instead of a pious sonata — which I vainly thought was the practice in such godly seminaries of learning — that abominable rattling piece of music called *la Violette*, which it has been my lot to hear executed by other young ladies; and which (with its like) has always appeared to me to be constructed upon this simple fashion — to take a tune, and then, as it were, to fling it down and upstairs. As soon as the young lady playing 'the Violet' saw us, she quitted the hall and retired to an inner apartment, where she resumed that delectable piece at her leisure. Indeed there were pianos all over the educational part of the house.

We were shown into a gay parlour (where hangs a pretty drawing representing the melancholy old convent which the Sisters previously inhabited in Cork), and presently Sister No. Two-Eight made her appearance — a pretty and graceful lady, attired thus.

'Tis the prettiest nun of the whole house,' whispered the lady who had been educated at the convent: and I must own that slim, gentle, and pretty as this young lady was, and calculated with her kind smiling face and little figure to frighten no one in the world, a great six-foot Protestant could not help looking at her with a little tremble. I had never been in a nun's company before; I'm afraid of such — I don't care to own — in their black mysterious robes and awful veils. As priests in gorgeous vestments, and little rosy incense-boys in red, bob their heads and knees up and down before altars, or clatter silver pots full of smoking odours, I feel I don't know what sort of thrill and secret creeping terror. Here I was, in a room with a real live nun, pretty and pale — I wonder has she any of her sisterhood immured in *oubliettes* down below; is her poor little weak, delicate body scarred all over with scourgings, iron-collars, hair-shirts? What has she had for dinner today? — as we passed the refectory there was a faint sort of vapid nun-like vegetable smell, speaking of fasts and wooden platters; and I could picture to myself silent sisters eating their meal — a grim old yellow one in the reading-desk, croaking out an extract from a sermon for their edification.

But is it policy, or hypocrisy, or reality? These nuns affect extreme happiness and content with their condition: a smiling beatitude, which they insist belongs peculiarly to them, and about which the only doubtful point is the manner in which it is produced before strangers. Young ladies educated in convents have often mentioned this fact — how the nuns persist in declaring and proving to them their own extreme enjoyment of life.

Were all the smiles of that kind-looking Sister Two-Eight perfectly sincere? Whenever she spoke her face was lighted up with one. She seemed perfectly radiant with happiness, tripping lightly before us, and distributing kind compliments to each, which made me in a very few minutes forget the introductory fright which her poor little presence had occasioned.

She took us through the hall (where was the vegetable savour before mentioned), and showed us the contrivance by which the name of Two-Eight was ascertained. Each nun has a number, or a combination of numbers, prefixed to her name; and a bell is pulled a corresponding number of times, by which each sister knows when she is wanted. Poor souls! are they always on the look-out for that bell, that the ringing of it should be supposed infallibly to awaken their attention?

From the hall the sister conducted us through ranges of apart-ments, and I had almost said avenues of pianofortes, whence here and there a startled pensioner would rise, *hinnuleo similis*, at our approach, seeking a *pavidam matrem* in the person of a demure old stout mother hard by. We were taken through a hall decorated with a series of pictures of Pope Pius VI — wonderful adventures, truly, in the life of the gentle old man. In one you see him gracefully receiving a Prince and Princess of Russia (tremendous incident!). The Prince has a pigtail, the Princess powder and a train, the Pope a — but never mind, we shall never get through the house at this rate.

Passing through Pope Pius's gallery, we came into a long, clean, lofty passage, with many little doors on each side; and here I confess my heart began to thump again. These were the doors of the cells of the Sisters. Bon Dieu! and is it possible that I shall see a nun's cell? Do I not recollect the nun's cell in 'The Monk,' or in 'The

Romance of the Forest?' or, if not there, at any rate, in a thousand noble romances, read in early days of half-holiday perhaps — romances at twopence a volume.

Come in, in the name of the saints! Here is the cell. I took off my hat and examined the little room with much curious wonder and reverence. There was an iron bed, with comfortable curtains of green serge. There was a little clothes-chest of yellow wood, neatly cleaned, and a wooden chair beside it, and a desk on the chest, and about six pictures on the wall — little religious pictures: a saint with gilt paper round him; the Virgin showing on her breast a bleeding heart, with a sword run through it; and other sad little subjects, calculated to make the inmate of the cell think of the sufferings of the saints and martyrs the Church. Then there was a little crucifix, and a wax-candle on the ledge; and here was the place where the poor black-veiled things were to pass their lives for ever!

After having seen a couple of these little cells, we left the corridors in which they were, and were conducted, with a sort of pride on the nun's part, I thought, into the grand room of the convent — a parlour with pictures of saints, and a gay paper, and a series of small fineries, such only as women very idle know how to make. There were some portraits in the room, one an atrocious daub of an ugly old woman, surrounded by children still more hideous. Somebody had told the poor nun that this was a fine thing, and she believed it — heaven bless her! — quite implicitly: nor is the picture of the ugly old Canadian woman the first reputation that has been made this way.

Then from the fine parlour we went to the museum. I don't know how we should be curious of such trifles; but the chronicling of small-beer is the main business of life — people only differing, as Tom Moore wisely says in one of his best poems, about their own peculiar tap. The poor nun's little collection of gimcracks was displayed in great state: there were spars in one drawer; and, I think, a Chinese shoe and some Indian wares in another; and some medals of the Popes, and a couple of score of coins; and a clean glass case, full of antique works of French theology of the distant period of Louis XV., to judge by the bindings — and this formed the main part of the museum. 'The chief objects were gathered together by a single nun,' said the sister with a look of wonder, as she went prattling on, and leading us hither and thither, like a child showing her toys.

What strange mixture of pity and pleasure is it which comes over you sometimes when a child takes you by the hand, and leads you up solemnly to some little treasure of its own — a feather or a string of glass beads? I declare I have often looked at such with more delight than at diamonds; and felt the same sort of soft wonder examining the nun's little treasure-chamber. There was something touching in the very poverty of it: had it been finer, it would not have been half so good.

And now we had seen all the wonders of the house but the chapel, and thither we were conducted; all the ladies of our party kneeling down as they entered the building, and saying a short prayer.

This, as I am on sentimental confessions, I must own affected me too. It was a very pretty and tender sight. I should have liked to kneel down too, but was ashamed; our northern usages not encouraging — among men at least — that sort of abandonment of dignity. Do any of us dare to sing psalms at church? and don't we look with rather a sneer at a man who does?

The chapel had nothing remarkable in it except a very good organ, as I was told; for we were allowed only to see the exterior of that instrument, our pious guide with much pleasure removing an oil-cloth which covered the mahogany. At one side of the altar is a long high *grille*, through which you see a hall, where the nuns have their stalls, and sit in chapel time; and beyond this hall is another small chapel, with a couple of altars, and one beautiful print in one of them — a German Holy Family — a prim, mystical, tender piece, just befitting the place.

In the *grille* is a little wicket and a ledge before it. It is to this wicket that women are brought to kneel; and a bishop is in the chapel on the other side, and takes their hands in his, and receives their vows. I had never seen the like before, and own that I felt a sort of shudder at looking at the place. There rest the girl's knees as she offers herself up, and forswears the sacred affections which God gave her; there she kneels and denies for ever the beautiful duties of her being: no tender maternal yearnings, no gentle attachments are to be had for her or from her — there she kneels and commits suicide upon her heart. O Honest Martin Luther! thank God, you came to pull that infernal, wicked, unnatural altar down — that cursed Paganism! Let people, solitary, worn-out by sorrow or oppressed with extreme remorse, retire to such places; fly and beat your breasts in caverns and wildernesses, O women, if you will, but be Magdalens first. It is shameful that any young girl, with any vocation however seemingly strong, should be allowed to bury herself in this small tomb of a few acres. Look at yonder nun — pretty, smiling, graceful, and young — what has God's world done to *her*, that she should run from it, or she done to the world, that she should avoid it? What call has she to give up all her duties and affections? and would she not be best serving God with a husband at her side, and a child on her knee?

The sights in the house having been seen, the nun led us through the grounds and gardens. There was the hay in front, a fine yellow corn-field at the back of the house, and a large melancholy-looking kitchen-garden; in all of which places the nuns, for certain hours in the day, are allowed to take recreation. 'The nuns here are allowed to amuse themselves more than ours at New Hall,' said a little girl who is educated at that English convent: 'do you know that here the nuns may make hay?' What a privilege is this! We saw none of the black sisterhood availing themselves of it, however: the hay was neatly piled into cocks and ready for housing; so the poor souls must wait until next year before they can enjoy this blessed sport once more.

Turning into a narrow gate with the nun at our head, we found ourselves in a little green, quiet enclosure — it was the burial-ground of the convent. The poor things know the places where they are to lie: she who was with us talked smilingly of being stretched there one day, and pointed out the resting-place of a favourite old sister who had died three months back, and been buried in the very midst of the little ground. And here they come to live and die. The gates are open, but they never go out. All their world lies in a dozen acres of ground; and they sacrifice their lives in early youth, many of them passing from the grave upstairs in the house to the one scarcely narrower in the churchyard here; and are seemingly not unhappy.

I came out of the place quite sick; and looking before me — there, thank God! was the blue spire of Monkstown church soaring up into the free sky — a river in front rolling away to the sea — liberty, sunshine, all sorts of glad life and motion round about: and I couldn't but thank heaven for it, and the Being whose service is freedom, and who has given us affections that we may use them — not smother and kill them; and a noble world to live in, that we may admire it and Him who made it — not shrink from it, as though we dared not live there, but must turn our backs upon it and its

And in conclusion, if that most cold-blooded and precise of all personages, the respectable and respected English reader, may feel disposed to sneer at the above sentimental homily, or to fancy that it has been written for effect — let him go and see a convent for himself. I declare I think for my part that we have as much right to permit Sutteeism in India as to allow women in the United Kingdom to take these wicked vows, or Catholic Bishops to receive them; and that Government has as good a right to interpose in such cases, as the police have to prevent a man from hanging himself, or the doctor to refuse a glass of prussic-acid to any one who may have a wish to go out of the world.

On the Banks of My Own Lovely Lee

Anonymous

How oft do my thoughts in their fancy take flight,
To the home of my childhood away.
To the days when each patriot's vision seem'd bright,
'Ere I dream'd that those joys should decay.
When my heart was as light as the wild winds that blow,
Down the Mardyke through each elm tree,
Where I sported and played 'neath each green leafy shade,
On the banks of my own lovely Lee.
Where I sported and played 'neath each green leafy shade,
On the banks of my own lovely Lee.

And then in the springtime of laughter and song,
Can I ever forget the sweet hours.
With the friends of my youth, as we rambled along,
'Mongst the green mossy banks and wild flowers.
Then, too, when the evening sun sinking to rest
Sheds its golden light over the sea,
The maid with her lover the wild daisies press'd,
On the banks of my own lovely Lee.
The maid with her lover the wild daisies press'd
On the banks of my own lovely Lee.

'Tis a beautiful land this dear Isle of song
Its gems shed their light on the world,
And her faithful sons bore thro' ages of wrong
The standard St Patrick unfurled.
Oh! would I were there with the friends I love best,
And my fond bosom's partner with me
We'd roam thy banks over, and when weary we'd rest
By thy waters, my own lovely Lee.

Oh, what joys should be mine 'ere this life should decline
To seek shells on thy sea-girdled shore,
While the steel-feathered eagle, oft splashing the brine,
Brings longing for freedom once more.
Oh, all that on earth I wish for or crave
Is that my last crimson drop be for thee,
To moisten the grass of my fore-fathers' grave
On the banks of my own lovely Lee.

Namesakes

John Goodby

Although I once drank in Idle Working Men's Club
And know that names are never quite what they seem,
It would be hard to swallow Cork Button Co.,
The Iron Throat, a lane called Knapp's Square, a city
Which had awarded itself the Victoria Cross.

Had that taxi rank been a taxidermists? While one
Mouth of the river gargled under Patrick's Street
Where Father Mathew, Apostle of Temperance, palmed
Change from four hundred and forty-eight bars and the fly-
Over opened by Lord Mayor Goldberg was rumoured
To have been rechristened by locals The Passover,

I still believed we might learn how Leper's Walk
Ran to Lover's Walk, why the Quadrangle refused
To take four sides. But between the English Market
And the Root Market you slipped past the Butter Market,
Before you crossed the Shaky Bridge, broke step.

from: **A Portrait of The Artist as a Young Man**

James Joyce, (1916)

Stephen was once again seated beside his father in the corner of a railway carriage at Kingsbridge. He was travelling with his father by the night mail to Cork. As the train steamed out of the station he recalled his childish wonder of years before and every event of his first day at Clongowes. But he felt no wonder now. He saw the darkening lands slipping away past him, the silent telegraph-poles passing his window swiftly every four seconds, the little glimmering stations, manned by a few silent sentries, flung by the mail behind her and twinkling for a moment in the darkness like fiery grains flung backwards by a runner.

He listened without sympathy to his father's evocation of Cork and of scenes of his youth, a tale broken by sighs or draughts from his pocket flask whenever the image of some dead friend appeared in it or whenever the evoker remembered suddenly the purpose of his actual visit. Stephen heard but could feel no pity. The images of the dead were all strangers to him save that of uncle Charles, an image which had lately been fading out of memory. He knew, however, that his father's property was going to be sold by auction, and in the manner of his own dispossession he felt the world give the lie rudely to his phantasy.

At Maryborough he fell asleep. When he awoke the train had passed out of Mallow and his father was stretched asleep on the other seat. The cold light of the dawn lay over the country, over the unpeopled fields and the closed cottages. The terror of sleep fascinated his mind as he watched the silent country or heard from time to time his father's deep breath or sudden sleepy movement. The neighbourhood of unseen sleepers filled him with strange dread, as though they could harm him and he prayed that the day might come quickly. His prayer, addressed neither to God nor saint, began with a shiver, as the chilly morning breeze crept through the chink of the carriage door to his feet, and ended in a trail of foolish words which he made to fit the insistent rhythm of the train; and silently, at intervals of four seconds, the telegraph-poles held the galloping notes of the music between punctual bars. This furious

215

music allayed his dread and, leaning against the window-ledge, he let his eyelids close again.

They drove in a jingle across Cork while it was still early morning and Stephen finished his sleep in a bedroom of the Victoria Hotel. The bright warm sunlight was streaming through the window and he could hear the din of traffic. His father was standing before the dressing-table, examining his hair and face and moustache with great care, craning his neck across the water-jug and drawing it back sideways to see the better. While he did so he sang softly to himself with quaint accent and phrasing:

> 'Tis youth and folly
> Makes young men marry,
> So here, my love, I'll
>   No longer stay.
> What can't be cured, sure,
> Must be injured, sure,
> So I'll go to
>   Amerikay.
>
> My love she's handsome,
> My love she's bony:
> She's like good whisky
>   When it is new;
> But when 'tis old
> And growing cold
> It fades and dies like
>   The mountain dew.

The consciousness of the warm sunny city outside his window and the tender tremors with which his father's voice festooned the strange sad happy air, drove off all the mists of the night's ill humour from Stephen's brain. He got up quickly to dress and, when the song had ended, said:

—That's much prettier than any of your other *come-all-yous.*

—Do you think so? asked Mr Dedalus.

—I like it, said Stephen.

—It's a pretty old air, said Mr Dedalus, twirling the points of his moustache. Ah, but you should have heard Mick Lacy sing it! Poor Mick Lacy! He had little turns for it, grace notes that he used to put in that I haven't got. That was the boy who could sing a *come-all-you*, if you like.

216

Mr Dedalus had ordered drisheens for breakfast and during the meal he cross-examined the waiter for local news. For the most part they spoke at cross purposes when a name was mentioned, the waiter having in mind the present holder and Mr Dedalus his father or perhaps his grandfather.

—Well, I hope they haven't moved the Queen's College anyhow, said Mr Dedalus, for I want to show it to this youngster of mine.

Along the Mardyke the trees were in bloom. They entered the grounds of the college and were led by the garrulous porter across the quadrangle. But their progress across the gravel was brought to a halt after every dozen or so paces by some reply of the porter's.

—Ah, do you tell me so? And is poor Pottlebelly dead?

—Yes, sir. Dead, sir.

During this halts Stephen stood awkwardly behind the two men, weary of the subject and waiting restlessly for the slow march to begin again. By the time they had crossed the quadrangle his restlessness had risen to fever. He wondered how his father, whom he knew for a shrewd suspicious man, could be duped by the servile manners of the porter; and the lively southern speech which had entertained him all the morning now irritated his ears.

They passed into the anatomy theatre where Mr Dedalus, the porter aiding him, searched the desks for his initials. Stephen remained in the background, depressed more than ever by the darkness and silence of the theatre and by the air it wore of jaded and formal study. On the desk he read the word *Foetus* cut several times in the dark stained wood. The sudden legend startled his blood: he seemed to feel the absent students of the college about him and to shrink from their company. A vision of their life, which his father's words had been powerless to evoke, sprang up before him out of the word cut in the desk. A broad-shouldered student with a moustache was cutting in the letters with a jack-knife, seriously. Other students stood or sat near him laughing at his handiwork. One jogged his elbow. The big student turned on him, frowning. He was dressed in loose grey clothes and had tan boots.

Stephen's name was called. He hurried down the steps of the theatre so as to be as far away from the vision as he could be and, peering closely at his father's initials, hid his flushed face.

But the word and the vision capered before his eyes as he walked back across the quadrangle and towards the college gate. It shocked him to find in the outer world a trace of what he had deemed till then a brutish and individual malady of his own mind. His monstrous reveries came thronging into his memory. They too had sprung up before him, suddenly and furiously, out of mere words. He had soon given in to them and allowed them to sweep across and abase his intellect, wondering always where they came from, from what den of monstrous images, and always weak and humble towards others, restless and sickened of himself when they had swept over him.

— Ay, bedad! And there's the Groceries sure enough! cried Mr Dedalus. You often heard me speak of the Groceries, didn't you, Stephen. Many's the time we went down there when our names had been marked, a crowd of us, Harry Peard and little Jack Mountain and Bob Dyas and Maurice Moriarty, the Frenchman, and Tom O'Grady and Mick Lacy that I told you of this morning and Joey Corbet and poor little good-hearted Johnny Keevers of the Tantiles.

The leaves of the trees along the Mardyke were astir and whispering in the sunlight. A team of cricketers passed, agile young men in flannels and blazers, one of them carrying the long green wicket-bag. In a quiet bystreet a German band of five players in faded uniforms and with battered brass instruments was playing to an audience of street arabs and leisurely messenger boys. A maid in a white cap and apron was watering a box of plants on a sill which shone like a slab of limestone in the warm glare. From another window open to the air came the sound of a piano, scale after scale rising into the treble.

Stephen walked on at his father's side, listening to stories he had heard before, hearing again the names of the scattered and dead revellers who had been the companions of his father's youth. And a faint sickness sighed in his heart. He recalled his own equivocal position in Belvedere, a free boy, a leader afraid of his own authority, proud and sensitive and suspicious, battling against the squalor of his life and against the riot of his mind. The letters cut in the stained wood of the desk stared upon him, mocking his bodily weakness and futile enthusiasms and making him loathe himself for his own mad and filthy orgies. The spittle in his throat grew bitter and foul to swallow and the faint sickness climbed to his brain so that for a moment he closed his eyes and walked on in darkness.

He could still hear his father's voice —

— When you kick out for yourself, Stephen — as I daresay you will one of these days — remember, whatever you do, to mix with gentlemen. When I was a young fellow I tell you I enjoyed myself. I mixed with fine decent fellows. Everyone of us could do something. One fellow had a good voice, another fellow was a good actor, another could sing a good comic song, another was a good oarsman or a good racket player, another could tell a good story and so on. We kept the ball rolling anyhow and enjoyed ourselves and saw a bit of life and we were none the worse of it either. But we were all gentlemen, Stephen — at least I hope we were — and bloody good honest Irishmen too. That's the kind of fellows I want you to associate with, fellows of the right kidney. I'm talking to you as a friend, Stephen. I don't believe a son should be afraid of his father. No, I treat you as your grandfather treated me when I was a young chap. We were more like brothers than father and son. I'll never forget the first day he caught me smoking. I was standing at the end of the South Terrace one day with some maneens like myself and sure we thought we were grand fellows because we had pipes stuck in the corners of our mouths. Suddenly the governor passed. He didn't say a word, or stop even. But the next day, Sunday, we were out for a walk together and when we were coming home he took out his cigar case and said: — By the by, Simon, I didn't know you smoked, or something like that. — Of course I tried to carry it off as best I could. — If you want a good smoke, he said, try one of these cigars. An American captain made me a present of them last night in Queenstown.

Stephen heard his father's voice break into a laugh which was almost a sob.

He was the handsomest man in Cork at that time, by God he was! The women used to stand to look after him in the street.

He heard the sob passing loudly down his father's throat and opened his eyes with a nervous impulse. The sunlight breaking suddenly on his sight turned the sky and clouds into a fantastic world of sombre masses with lakelike spaces of dark rosy light. His very brain was sick and powerless. He could scarcely interpret the letters of the signboards of the shops. By his monstrous way of life he seemed to have put himself beyond the limits of reality. Nothing moved him or spoke to him from the real world unless he heard in it an echo of the infuriated cries within him. He could respond to no earthly or human appeal, dumb and insensible to the call of summer and gladness and companionship, wearied and dejected by his father's voice. He could scarcely recognize as his own thoughts, and repeated slowly to himself:

— I am Stephen Dedalus. I am walking beside my father whose name is Simon Dedalus. We are in Cork, in Ireland. Cork is a city. Our room is in the Victoria Hotel. Victoria and Stephen and Simon. Simon and Stephen and Victoria. Names.

The memory of his childhood suddenly grew dim. He tried to call forth some of its vivid moments but could not. He recalled only names. Dante, Parnell, Clane, Clongowes. A little boy had been taught geography by an old woman who kept two brushes in her wardrobe. Then he had been sent away from home to a college, he had made his first communion and eaten slim jam out of his cricket cap and watched the firelight leaping and dancing on the wall of a little bedroom in the infirmary and dreamed of being dead, of mass being said for him by the rector in a black and gold cope, of being buried then in the little graveyard of the community off the main avenue of limes. But he had not died then. Parnell had died. There had been no mass for the dead in the chapel and no procession. He had not died but he had faded out like a film in the sun. He had been lost or had wandered out of existence for he no longer existed. How strange to think of him passing out of existence in such a way, not by death but by fading out in the sun or by being lost and forgotten somewhere in the universe! It was strange to see his small body appear again for a moment: a little boy in a grey belted suit. His hands were in his side-pockets and his trousers were tucked in at the knees by elastic bands.

[On the evening of the day on which the property was sold Stephen followed his father meekly about the city from bar to bar. To the sellers in the market, to the barmen and barmaids, to the beggars who importuned him for a lob Mr Dedalus told the same tale — that he was an old Corkonian, that he had been trying for thirty years to get rid of his Cork accent up in Dublin and that Peter Pickackafax beside him was his eldest son but that he was only a Dublin jackeen.]

They had set out early in the morning from Newcombe's coffee-house, where Mr Dedalus's cup had rattled noisily against its saucer, and Stephen had tried to cover that shameful sign of his father's drinking bout of the night before by moving his chair and coughing. One humiliation had succeeded another — the false smiles of the market sellers, the curvetings and oglings of the barmaids with whom his father flirted, the compliments and encouraging words of his father's friends. They had told him that he had a great look of his grandfather and Mr Dedalus had agreed that he was an ugly likeness. They had unearthed traces of a Cork accent in his speech and made him admit that the Lee was a much finer river than the Liffey. One of them, in order to put his Latin to the proof, had made him translate short passages from Dilectus and asked him whether it was correct to say: *Tempora mutantur nos et mutamur in illis* or *Tempora mutantur et nos mutamur in illis.* Another, a brisk old man, whom Mr Dedalus called Johnny Cashman, had covered him with confusion by asking him to say which were prettier, the Dublin girls or the Cork girls.

— He's not that way built, said Mr Dedalus. Leave him alone. He's a level-headed thinking boy who doesn't bother his head about that kind of nonsense.

— Then he's not his father's son, said the little old man.

— I don't know, I'm sure, said Mr Dedalus, smiling complacently.

— Your father, said the little old man to Stephen, was the boldest flirt in the city of Cork in his day. Do you know that?

Stephen looked down and studied the tiled floor of the bar into which they had drifted.

— Now don't be putting ideas into his head, said Mr Dedalus. Leave him to his Maker.

— Yerra, sure I wouldn't put any ideas into his head. I'm old enough to be his grandfather. And I am a grandfather, said the little old man to Stephen. Do you know that?

— Are you? asked Stephen.

— Bedad I am, said the little old man. I have two bouncing grandchildren out at Sunday's Well. Now, then! What age do you think I am? And I remember seeing your grandfather in his red coat riding out to hounds. That was before you were born.

— Ay, or thought of, said Mr. Dedalus.

— Bedad I did, repeated the little old man. And, more than that, I can remember even your greatgrandfather, old John Stephen Dedalus, and a fierce old fire-eater he was. Now, then! There's a memory for you!

— That's three generations — four generations, said another of the company. Why, Johnny Cashman, you must be nearing the century.

— Well, I'll tell you the truth, said the little old man. I'm just twenty-seven years of age.

— We're as old as we feel, Johnny, said Mr Dedalus. And just finish what you have there and we'll have another. Here, Tim or Tom or whatever your name is, give us the same again here. By God, I don't feel more than eighteen myself. There's that son of mine there not half my age and I'm a better man than he is any day of the week.

— Draw it mild now, Dedalus. I think it's time for you to take a back seat, said the gentleman who had spoken before.

— No, by God! asserted Mr Dedalus. I'll sing a tenor song against him or I'll vault a five-barred gate against him or I'll run with him after hounds across the country as I did thirty years ago along with the Kerry Boy and the best man for it.

— But he'll beat you here, said the little old man, tapping his forehead and raising his glass to drain it.

— Well, I hope he'll be as good a man as his father. That's all I can say, said Mr Dedalus.

— If he is, he'll do, said the little old man.

— And thanks be to God, Johnny, said Mr Dedalus, that we lived so long and did so little harm.

— But did so much good, Simon, said the little old man gravely. Thanks be to God we lived so long and did so much good.

Stephen watched the three glasses being raised from the counter as his father and his two cronies drank to the memory of their past. An abyss of fortune or of temperament sundered him from them. His mind seemed older than theirs: it shone coldly on their strifes and happiness and regrets like a moon upon a younger earth. No life or youth stirred in him as it had stirred in them. He had known neither the pleasure of companionship with others nor the vigour of rude male health nor filial piety. Nothing stirred within his soul but a cold and cruel and loveless lust. His childhood was dead or lost and with it his soul capable of simple joys and he was drifting amid life like the barren shell of the moon.

> *Art thou pale for weariness*
> *Of climbing heaven and gazing on the earth,*
> *Wandering companionless . . . ?*

He repeated to himself the lines of Shelly's fragment. Its alternation of sad human ineffectiveness with vast inhuman cycles of activity chilled him and he forgot his own human and ineffectual grieving.

high time for all the marys
Máire Bradshaw

for mary robinson

This poem was written to mark the conferring of the Freedom of the City of Cork on President Mary Robinson in Cork City Hall on 23 February 1991. President Robinson was the first woman to receive this honour. She was not, however, the first woman nominated for it. The spiritualist and author Geraldine Cummins (see page 295), for example, had once tried to have the Freedom awarded to the writer Edith Somerville. To those who were in the City Hall when President Robinson was conferred, therefore, there was a sense not only of the President's presence but of others as well, and many of them had up to then been silent, ignored and unrecognized. (Ed.)

I

anna lee
is dressed
in black
tonight
wearing a
halter neckline
rucked in
velvet and gold
a swan
pinned
here and there
for decoration

a sailor's fancy
she'll dance
'til the sun rises
on dawn square
and better value
mr dunne
cuts his disco lights
to off —

chaperoned by quays
locked by bridges
north to south
poverty and class
out for a night —

II

old women darn —
holy spires
needle the
dark sky

finbarr's golden angel
wings akimbo
ready to box
the ears
of drunks
and lovers
pausing
on their way
to barrack street
for chips . . .

voices ring out
in shandon
the belfry
silent for once —
pigeons of peace
taking their ease —

III

in rte
— an angelus pause —
a different angel
declaring unto
yet another mary . . .

a woman is lifting
up her skirt
ready for a jig

she's rolling up
her sleeves
a washload of dreams
ready for ironing

a medb
of the táin
she is taking
the brown bull
through silver bells
and cockle shells
to the park . . .
young men and women
first to vote
owing no favours
cheer —
and 'here's to you
mrs robinson'

IV

for certain
women are up
off their knees

all at once
being a housewife —
a housekeeper
or pushing a trolly
in dawn square

has a certain
air about it
a moment
when mrs nobody

becomes mrs somebody
head and tail
at high doh
stepping lightly

anna lee and
anna livia plurabelle
the kissing cousins
at high tide
and high time
for all the marys . . .

'Windfall', 8 Parnell Hill, Cork
Paul Durcan
from: *The Berlin Wall Café* (1985)

But, then, at the end of the day I could always say —
Well, now, I am going home:
I felt elected, steeped, sovereign to be able to say —
I am going home.
When I was at home I liked to stay at home;
At home I stayed at home for weeks;
At home I used sit in a winged chair by the window
Overlooking the river and the factory chimneys,
The electricity power station and the car assembly works,
The fleets of trawlers and the pilot tugs,
Dreaming that life is a dream which is real,
The river a reflection on itself in its own waters,
Goya sketching Goya among the smoky mirrors.
The industrial vista was my Mont Sainte-Victoire;
While my children sat on my knees watching TV
Their mother, my wife, reclined on the couch
Knitting a bright-coloured scarf, drinking a cup of black coffee,
Smoking a cigarette — one of her own roll-ups.
I closed my eyes and breathed in and breathed out.
It is ecstasy to breathe if you are at home in the world.
What a windfall! A home of our own!

Our neighbours' houses had names like 'Con Amore',
'Sans Souci', 'Pacelli', 'Montini', 'Homesville';
But we called our home 'Windfall':
'Windfall', 8 Parnell Hill, Cork.
In the gut of my head coursed the leaf of tranquillity
Which I dreamed was known only to Buddhist Monks
In lotus monasteries high up in the Hindu Kush.
Down here in the dark depths of Ireland,
Below sea-level in the city of Cork,
In a city as intimate and homicidal as a Little Marseilles,
In a country where all the children of the nation
Are not cherished equally
And where the best go homeless, while the worst
Erect block-house palaces — self-regardingly ugly,
Having a home of your own can give to a family
A chance in a lifetime to transcend death.

At the high window, shipping from all over the world
Being borne up and down the busy, yet contemplative, river;
Skylines drifting in and out of skylines in the cloudy valley;
Firelight at dusk, and city lights in the high window,
Beyond them the control tower of the airport on the hill
— A lighthouse in the sky flashing green to white to green;
Our black-and-white cat snoozing in the corner of a chair;
Pastels and etchings on the four walls, and over the mantelpiece
Van Gogh's Grave and *Lovers in Water*;
A room wallpapered in books and family photograph albums
Chronicling the adventures and metamorphoses of family life:
In swaddling clothes in Mammy's arms on baptism day;
Being a baby of nine months and not remembering it;
Face-down in a pram, incarcerated in a high chair;
Everybody, including strangers, wearing shop-window smiles;
With Granny in Felixstowe, with Granny in Ballymaloe;
In a group photo in First Infants, on a bike at thirteen;
In the back garden in London, in the back garden in Cork;
Performing a headstand after First Holy Communion;
Getting a kiss from the Bishop on Confirmation Day;
Straw hats in the Bois de Boulogne, wearing wings at the seaside;
Mammy and Daddy holding hands on the Normandy Beaches;
Mammy and Daddy at the wedding of Jeremiah and Margot;

Mammy and Daddy queueing up for *Last Tango in Paris*;
Boating on the Shannon, climbing mountains in Kerry;
Building sandcastles in Killala, camping in Barley Cove;
Picnicking in Moone, hide-and-go-seek in Clonmacnoise;
Riding horses, cantering, jumping fences;
Pushing out toy yachts in the pond in the Tuileries;
The Irish College revisited in the Rue des Irlandais;
Sipping an *orange pressé* through a straw on the roof of the Beaubourg;
Dancing in Père Lachaise, weeping at Auvers.
Year in, year out, I pored over these albums accumulating,
My children looking over my shoulder, exhilarated as I was,
Their mother presiding at our ritual from a distance
 — The far side of the hearthrug, diffidently, proudly:
Schoolbooks on the floor and pyjamas on the couch —
Whose turn is it tonight to put the children to bed?

Our children swam about our home
As if it was their private sea,
Their own unique, symbiotic fluid
Of which their parents also partook.
Such is home — a sea of your own —
In which you hang upside down from the ceiling
With equanimity, while postcards from Thailand on the mantelpiece
Are raising their eyebrow markings benignly:
Your hands dangling their prayers to the floorboards of your home,
Sifting the sands underneath the surfaces of conversations,
The marine insect life of the family psyche.
A home of your own — or a sea of your own —
In which climbing the walls is as natural
As making love on the stairs;
In which when the telephone rings
Husband and wife are metamorphosed into smiling accomplices,
Both declining to answer it;
Initiating, instead, a yet more subversive kiss
 — A kiss they have perhaps never attempted before —
And might never have dreamed of attempting
Were it not for the telephone belling.
Through the bannisters or along the bannister rails
The pyjama-clad children solemnly watching
Their parents at play, jump up and down in support,

Race back to bed, gesticulating wordlessly:
The most subversive unit in society is the human family.

We're almost home, pet, almost home . . .
Our home is at . . .
I'll be home . . .
I have to go home now . . .
I want to go home now . . .
Are you feeling homesick? . . .
Are you anxious to get home? . . .
I can't wait to get home . . .
Let's stay at home tonight and . . .
What time will you be coming home at? . . .
If I'm not home by six at the latest, I'll phone . . .
We're nearly home, don't worry, we're nearly home . . .

But then with good reason
I was put out of my home:
By a keen wind felled.
I find myself now without a home
Having to live homeless in the alien, foreign city of Dublin.
It is an eerie enough feeling to be homesick
Yet knowing you will be going home next week;
It is an eerie feeling beyond all ornithological analysis
To be homesick knowing that there is no home to go home to:
Day by day, creeping, crawling,
Moonlighting, escaping,
Bed-and-breakfast to bed-and-breakfast;
Hostels, centres, one-night hotels.

Homeless in Dublin,
Blown about the suburban streets at evening,
Peering in the windows of other people's homes,
Wondering what it must feel like
To be sitting around a fire —
Apache or Cherokee or Bourgeoisie —
Beholding the firelit faces of your family,
Beholding their starry or their TV gaze:
Windfall to Windfall — can you hear me?
Windfall to Windfall . . .
We're almost home pet, don't worry anymore, we're almost home.

A New Litany

John Montague

from: *The Dead Kingdom* (1984)

I

The impulse in love
to name the place as
protection and solace;
an exact tenderness.
The way a room
can be so invested
with the presence
of a capable woman:
I see you bustling
around the house,
fragile and living,
tensely loving, as
long ago, my mother.
May she be granted,
this houre, her Vigill,
a certain peace.

II

That we are here
for a time, that
we make our lives
carelessly, carefully,
as we are finally
also made by them;
a chosen companion,
a home, children;
on such conditions
I place my hopes
beside yours, Evelyn,
frail rope-ladders
across fuming oblivion.

III

A new love, a new
litany of place names;
the hill city of Cork
lambent under rain,
the lamenting foghorn
at Roche's Point, hold-
ing its hoarse vigil
into a white Atlantic,
the shrouded shapes
of Mounts Brandon,
Sybil Head and Gabriel;
powers made manifest,
amulets against loneliness,
talismans for work:
a flowering presence?

IV ONE DAY FOR RECREATION . . .

The Piano in Macroom
John A. Murphy

Waiting for my mother to come from the chapel or from some household chore to play the piano: . . . whirling around and around on the stool till I became dizzy . . . 'stop that, child of grace, you'll be sick' . . . later on, lighting the butts of candles in their brass sockets . . . shadowy illumination on the music sheets . . . learning to turn the page at the right moment . . . snuggling into warm folds of sound . . . lifting childish treble to join her thin soprano . . .

My maternal grandfather was a fairly well-off (for a time at least) small-town draper, genteel in manner and Redmondite in politics. ('Ah, John Redmond was a gentleman' he would remind me, implicitly dismissing post-1916 scruff.) My mother's convent education included those musical accomplishments which were then deemed proper to a young lady's station in life. But my mother's station in life turned out to be rather more arduous than expected. She became a Sinn Féiner and Gaelic Leaguer, to the distress of her family, and married (to the never-quite-voiced disapproval of *some* of her family) a carpenter of small farmer, artisan and Fenian stock. In those days a craftsman's skills were poorly rewarded and though my father worked hard and devotedly for an unappreciative employer (and, happily, for a greatly appreciative family) we were throughout my boyhood never comfortably off. Yet we had a modest sufficiency, and contentment in those days was generally guaranteed by unchallenged dogmas and simple pieties — God was certainly in his heaven and de Valera would just as surely one day put things right with our world. In our house there was the enrichment of music, running throughout our everyday life and costing little or nothing, except the occasional visit of the piano-turner.

The piano, a wedding present from my mother's father, was the focus of our home, the shrine where we worshipped almost daily but where my mother alone officiated. My elder brother and my two sisters were sent to Miss Richardson, the chapel organist, for piano lessons (did that dedicated lady ever charge anything?) but when they failed to stay the course my potential talent was never investigated. My mother's music-making was almost entirely confined to home, with rare appearances in the town hall where she accompanied the local talent at concerts. The domestic musical sessions occasionally ran to soirées with tea and relatives. Sometimes, young teachers in digs came to join in the singing. A cousin still claims that though he had no voice my mother miraculously taught him how to sing. A hopeful candidate in a golden-voice-tenor competition used to come to our house for rehearsals: he had words and songs off by heart — of necessity, indeed, since he was illiterate and I remember that my mother once tactfully righted a music sheet that he had courteously placed upside-down in front of her.

My mother played the piano whenever the spirit moved her — a daily pentecost at the height of her form. She could be temperamental, as was her right, of course, and no amount of pleading could move her on these occasions: she would plead a bout of sickness (genuine enough in a life of chronic ill-health) or an ivory out of tune — 'a string, my child, is false' — or most heart-sinking of all, the death of a relative or neighbour. The protocol of court mourning was complicated but rigorous — several days for a nearby wake or funeral, weeks on end for a relative, even a short period on receipt of sad news about an American cousin, gone from Ireland for years and dead and buried months before. We protested loudly at these all-too-frequent silences, these stark deprivations. 'But, Mom, sure he's dead and what harm can it do him?' She was adamant, appealing to my father for moral support. 'Have the youngsters today any respect for the dead? Anyway, what would people say?'

At the piano she was a perfectionist, wincing at a false key or at a jangled chord inadvertently struck. All musical directions had to be strictly observed. 'John, if you're roaring now, how can you sing *fortissimo* later on?' She believed a good voice was such an extraordinary gift ('the greatest music is the music that comes from inside you') one had to express thanks by taking pains. She taught me how to sing 'seconds': protesting, I had to join her in intricate and sometimes appallingly bad duets (does anyone now sing 'What is the spell?' from 'The Bohemian Girl'?) which had, however, the redeeming virtue of training one to harmonize any song spontaneously. To her I owe this not inconsiderable vocal skill, at least as meritorious a social grace as doing card tricks.

The cardinal sin in singing was to go off key. In the middle of a Christmas carol or a rousing ballad, my mother would sweep her hands off the keys, clap them to her ears and emit a horrified shriek: 'Jesus, Mary and Joseph, someone is FLAT! Is it you Thade?' 'Blast it, woman', in that loud voice which belied my father's extraordinary gentleness, 'I never went flat in my life'. I was always afraid that she might think *me* capable of this heinous lapse. To this very day the fear secretly persists. Impugn my scholarship, if you will, challenge my political motivations, spread scandal about my private life, even pollute my pint, but at your gravest peril accuse me of 'going flat'.

The range of my mother's musical interests was extraordinary. There were the set piano pieces she had imbibed with her lessons. The waltz was the great dance of her girlhood and whole evenings might be taken up wordlessly with one Strauss waltz after another, while admiring citizens sat on the window-sill outside. Irish dance music would be played in the thumping *céilí* style of the pre-revival days. But it was the singing she enjoyed most — romantic Viennese; Brahms and Schubert; solos, duets and hilarious attempts at operatic quartets. Operatic gems were held in high regard, Gounod and Verdi foremost . . . 'to our fair Provence come home, peace and joy shall calm thy soul'. 'Home To Our Mountains', of course, and 'Out of the Love I Bear Thee'. In the last named, my father soulfully and melodiously bade farewell to a certain Leonora who to my childish ears took flesh as two indigenous lovelorn sisters 'Eily and Nora'. My parents' generation had a special affection for operas with an 'Irish' dimension — 'The Bohemian Girl', 'Maritana' and the artless, amateurish and much beloved 'The Lily of Killarney'. We sang not alone the stock favourites from these but obscure numbers in which my mother, but not I, could discern some musical quality. We children learned snatches from an operetta about Robin Hood, enthusiastically produced in Macroom before any of us were born and, I am convinced, never since heard of:

> Foresters free are we, are we
> Under the greenwood, greenwood tree
> Living a life of careless glee
> Shirking responsibility, yes!
> Shirking responsibility.

And my mother quickly picked up the hits from all the musicals from 'The Desert Song' to 'Oklahoma'. Gilbert and Sullivan were always gentlemen most welcome in my house, and indeed in my town, despite the prissy disapproval of Irish-language enthusiasts. 'Go bhfóire Dia orainn, príomhbhaile Ghaeltacht Mhúscraí, an baile is gallda in Éirinn!'

237

My mother had (I still have) three sedate volumes of *The World's Favourite Songs*. These drawing-room (in our case, read 'parlour') effusions could no doubt be heard in Hove or Hampstead as well as in Macroom. Again, we had staid renderings of the dully nostalgic Stephen Foster. Radio introduced my mother to the successive pop tunes of the day and I would bring out to her from Cork the appropriate music sheets which she would play off with gusto. Even in those prim days, the covers would occasionally dare to feature a hint of thigh or a suggestion of cleavage: my mother was unfailingly outraged by such depravity and, if it was particularly blatant she would have recourse to a strip of brown paper to cover the offending parts (*o sancta simplicitas!*). We learned the Edwardian music-hall songs of her girlhood, as well as quite extraordinary American ditties, communicated to us periodically by a Macrompian pastor who had struck it rich in Florida. Long years afterwards, I was genuinely astonished to find that my American hosts had never heard of these numbers. They listened uncomprehendingly as I sang while being driven through Omaha's main drag:

> *I'm going back again to old Nebraska*
> *And if anyone should ask yeh*
> *I'll be in my old Nebraska home*

And in St Louis on the grassy slope overlooking the paddle steamers, my friends there were mystified by:

> *My bones are aching, my heart is breaking*
> *No silver lining in the clouds I see*
> *For years I've loved the dear old Mississippi*
> *And look what Mississippi's done to me.*

Dead mother, never travelled at all, sharply remembered by great waters far away.

However, Irish music was always fully catered for. If she had a catholic taste it was above all an Irish catholic taste. There was an ascending order of preference but no snobbish omissions. At the vulgar end of the spectrum the Irish songs were 'stage' or syrupy, or Mother Machree-ish, brought home by returned Yanks. Moore's Melodies were rendered reverentially, and here again my mother had a strong predilection for the less hackneyed melodies. (Only recently did it strike me that 'The Mid-hour of night' is 'Bean an Fhir Rua' emasculated, if I may confuse my genders). John McCormack was her great idol, adored for his purity of tone, impeccable phrasing and precise diction (though she found him somewhat deficient in nationalist credentials). My parents proudly recalled their good fortune in once hearing him live, albeit from the back of a crowded concert hall. 'And did you once see Shelley plain?' My mother derived great amusement from my innocent use of the wrong preposition in a line of a favourite McCormack song, 'The Green Bushes', . . . 'and I'm not so poor as to marry *with* clothes'.

Both my parents had a great store of nationalist and nationalist-cum-love songs in English. A much-thumbed volume was *Songs of the Nation*, an anthology of Young Ireland ballads. *Songs of the Gael*, a poor Béarlóir's *Ceol ár Sinnsear*, proudly carries my mother's signature, Eibhlín, Bean Ua Mhurchadha.

Many of the airs in this little volume were taken down by a Macroom woman, Annie O'Reilly, whom my mother knew well. The editor, Pádraig Breathnach, appears to have had in large measure that censorious puritanism which characterized certain Gaelic Leaguers. In his footnotes to the songs, there are stern denunciations of 'anglicized music-hall rubbish' and 'the inanities of the anglicized concert hall'. I am glad to say this cultural moralizing never bothered my mother at all. But she was proud of Breathnach's reference to the Macroom district as 'that home of Irish melody'.

My parents were Sinn Féiners and Gaelic Leaguers, manifesting for the language an enthusiasm and love, typically unmatched by any great fluency. My mother was very conscious of the still vigorous culture that in her girlhood flourished in Ballyvourney and Ballingeary. Macroom (where we spoke Hiberno-English) was then to the West Muskerry Gaeltacht what Dingle is now to Dunquin. *Sean-nós* was alive, if not altogether well, and living down the road, and known to outsiders as 'having the nyaah'. My mother's songs in Irish were those native to the area like 'A Bhúrcaigh Bhuí ón gCéim', 'Cath Céim an Fhia' and 'An Capaillín Bán'. My father's was exclusively an English-language repertoire which included the great Seán Ó Duibhir an Ghleanna air beginning 'After Aughrim's great disaster' (This version is set down in *Glenanaar* in the context of a dramatic classroom incident, and the strong presumption must be that Canon Sheehan himself wrote the words). My father had a soft baritone voice, and nodded his head constantly as he sang. To the lovely tune of "'S ar Éirinn ní neosfainn ce h-í' he had sentimental English verses which I have never heard from anybody else and which I have never seen published.

> *Oh her father has riches galore*
> *Of cattle and corn and wealth*
> *And broad lands by the wild Avonmore*
> *While I have but youth and good health.*
> *But she's the fair maid I adore*
> *And her fond love she's plighted to me*
> *Without riches or bright golden store*
> *'S ar Éirinn ní neosfainn cé h-í.*

The peasant coyness of the title line had a local variant:

> *Oh, if I had Macroom and all the broad lands by the Lee*
> *And all the fine farms from Blarney to Ballinagree,*
> *I'd give them and more this comely young lassie to gain*
> *And for tons of bright gold, of course, I won't tell her name.*

We sang the songs of the Tan War and the Civil War ('The Legion of the Rearguard') but not very frequently, and my mother did not care for the vulgar braggadocio of 'The Boys of Kilmichael'. Perhaps those events were too near, too passionate, or too troubled for my parents to sing about comfortably. They preferred ballads associated with the Wild Geese and curious pseudo-Jacobite songs with bathetic endings:

> *But I do not weep for my Donal dead*
> *For he died in his jacket green.*

I am glad to say my mother greatly admired the noble Thomas Davis whose spirited but hopeless vision of Irish fraternity we often saluted — ironically, to the air of Lillibulero:

> *English deceit can rule us no more,*
> *Bigots and knaves are scattered like spray —*
> *Deep was the oath the Orangemen swore,*
> *'Orange and Green must carry the day'*
> > *Orange! Orange!*
> > *Bless the Orange!*

> *Tories and Whigs grew pale with dismay,*
> *When from the North*
> *Burst the cry forth,*
> *'Orange and Green will carry the day!'*
> > *No surrender!*
> > *No Pretender!*
> *Never to falter and never betray —*
> > *With an Amen,*
> > *We swear it again,*
> *Orange and Green shall carry the day.*

Odd now to think that for all those years, Macroom, for famous people I was to meet later, was a condescended-to 'baile gallda' on the 'bóthar na Gaeltachta', a despised stage on the pilgrimage west to the last dwindling language reservations. Similarly, I found myself spiritedly defending the piano against the purists who denounced it as a non-instrument, an abomination of un-Gaelic gentility.

Our piano no longer really functions but it still stands in mute memoriam to my mother. She lived just long enough to hear and marvel at Ó Riada's early glories but she died before everyone suddenly burst out singing and playing. Perhaps she now enjoys those Miltonic 'solemn troops and sweet societies that sing, and singing in their glory move'. I only hope they don't 'go flat'.

A few years ago I came across some verses by D.H. Lawrence. Doubtless, Mrs Lawrence's repertoire was much more limited than my mother's; *we* sang very few hymns in Macroom; and the lines are clumsy, and lack any real merit. And yet . . . .

> *Softly, in the dusk, a woman is singing to me*
> *Taking me back down the vista of years, till I see*
> *A child sitting under the piano, in the boom of the tingling*
> > *strings*
> *And pressing the small, poised feet of a mother who smiles as*
> > *she sings.*
>
> *In spite of myself, the insidious mastery of song*
> *Betrays me back till the heart of me weeps to belong*
> *To the old Sunday evenings at home, with winter outside*
> *And hymns in the cosy parlour, the tinkling piano our guide.*

The Opera Company Visit

David Marcus

from: *A Land Not Theirs* (1986)

Percy Lovitch got off the tram at the top of King Street and picked his steps carefully over the muddy road to the footpath. The Glanmire Station was only two minutes away and he still had some twenty minutes to spare before the train from Dublin was due in — if it arrived at all. And, even if it did arrive, the Carl Rosa Company might have decided not to travel and his journey would have been in vain. Reading the *Examiner* every morning with its accounts of houses and farms burned, people pulled off trains, RIC men kidnapped and shot, Black and Tans terrorizing whole villages, Flying Columns ambushing patrols, convoys blown up, hunger strikes, arrests, goodness knows what — yes, it must look quite dangerous to any outsider, especially if that outsider was English and prominent, as the members of the Carl Rosa Opera Company certainly would be. They could hardly be blamed if they decided not to risk it. But Percy Lovitch knew their manager; he had toured with him for many seasons throughout Britain and Europe in earlier days when H. Barrett Brandreth was a young tenor and, although Brandreth would probably see the safety of his company as his primary responsibility, Percy also knew that he liked a challenge. H. Barrett Brandreth was a man who met difficulties with ebullient relish, and as the company had always been very popular in Cork — well, perhaps they'd decide to take whatever risk was involved.

The weather had dried up, so Percy didn't need to hurry the last few yards to the station, and before setting off he examined the photographs in glass cases on the walls of the Coliseum cinema at the corner of the street. There was a Charlie Chaplin comedy showing: *Oh What a Night*. Charlie was a card. And not only in the pictures. Percy had read in the *Examiner* only that morning that his wife had been granted a divorce on the grounds of Charlie's adultery with his latest leading actress. Oh, he was a card all right. Always picked a stunner for his films. Percy wondered if that little contralto, Eunice Stanford, would be with the Carl Rosa this time. She was a stunner, too — and she had been quite a sport on their last visit. Good for a playful hug and peck backstage. Not a bad voice, either.

Rich in the middle register where, he felt, so many contraltos seemed to produce a hooting sound. It would be nice if she was there again. Not that Percy any longer was interested in passing flirtations. They had been pleasant diversions when he had been a young music student and later during his years on tour. But they had been only diversions. Opera and his operatic career had been the one important pursuit of his life. Religious observance had become secondary, marriage not even thought about. Now, pushing sixty, with his youth well gone and his voice no longer quite good enough for the big roles he loved, he was left with a future that in its predictability and lack of excitement was indistinguishable from his present. He had his nice little music shop in Tuckey Street; it gave him a comfortable living with no great effort — and with the growing popularity of the gramophone he could see his business expanding very profitably in coming years. So why should he even think about Palestine? Wasn't he too old to start a fresh struggle? Wasn't he happy with the Cork Jewish community? He got on with everybody and he knew that they felt really uplifted whenever he took a synagogue service and transformed the whole ritual with the richness of his voice and the sweetness of his melodies. Yes, granted he was a great improvement on Rev. Levitt, but how often did he get the chance? And in five years' time — maybe less — his voice would have deteriorated even more. What difference would it make to him where he lived if his voice became a croak?

He looked along the whole stretch of King Street, as far as his eye could see, and measured its elegance and variety against Karlinsky's picture of what *Eretz* was like and what living there — trying to live there — would entail. For Percy Lovitch, King Street had the colour, the vivacity, the contrasts of a street in any of the big European cities he had toured with the Company. It had the splendid, almost ornate façade of the Metropole Hotel with its red brick topping all that plate glass and terracotta work. Next door it had the Palace Theatre, Percy's favourite haunt, where every week he went to enjoy a programme of music-hall turns that included the best in the world. How could the cinema with its jerky silent pictures possibly compare with flesh and blood, with the wit, the talent, the appeal and aura of such stars as Harry Lauder, Vesta Tilley, Lupino Lane? And the colour — cinemas were darkened tombs whose insides might be wooden pens for all it mattered and where the person next to you could be *Malach Hamovess*, the Angel of Death himself, for all you could see of him. But the Palace, with its wall decorations of red and gold motifs, its resplendent boxes, its regal stage curtains — to Percy Lovitch that was the sort of air he had breathed for so long, that was something he'd not get in *Eretz*. They'd never have his King Street there — not in his lifetime anyway. Why, only a few doors from where he was standing were the premises of Hadji Bey, where every week before going into the Palace Theatre he bought a box of 'Hadji Bey's World Famous Turkish Delight', soft, powder-dusted sweetmeats that to Percy looked like miniature harem cushions. Not much chance of such delicacies in *Eretz*; he might find a few relatives of Hadji Bey left there since the British took over the area from the Ottomans, but it wouldn't be Turkish Delight they'd give him. If he weren't on his way to the station, he'd buy a box right now, but he didn't want the nuisance of carrying it.

He looked at his watch. Time to go. Percy Lovitch fluffed out his white silk scarf inside his dark overcoat, twirled his rolled-up umbrella and, humming 'Questa o quella' to the pace of his stride, set off. Rabbi Cohen didn't even know yet when they were leaving for *Eretz*, so he had time enough to make up his mind. Monday *Bohème*, Tuesday *Carmen*, Wednesday *Cav* and *Pag* . . . . The possibility that the Company might not arrive was unthinkable. The best week of the year was in prospect; he wasn't going to worry about anything else until it was all over.

He reached the station five minutes before the train was due and to his amazement found Platform 1, where it would be coming in, thronged with people. His face flushed with alarm at the thought that they had gathered to make trouble, but he was somewhat reassured to see that the platform was well patrolled by RIC men, and on joining the crowd his composure was fully restored by the discovery that, like him, they had come to welcome the Opera. Despite their fears — which he heard voiced on all sides — that the Company might not be on the train, they were all in the best of spirits. As he squeezed through it seemed to him that there were almost as many women as men — and not a few of the women had brought along their children, hoping, he guessed, to give them a memory they could hand down in later years to their own families. For the most part the women looked thoroughly respectable, not to say decorous, in their long coats of conservative hues, and square fur-trimmed hats like cloth boxes pulled down to their ears. Working-class youths who were presumably unemployed or else had given up their dinner hour had pushed themselves to the front, forming a line at the edge of the platform, their rough-and-ready apparel of cloth caps, mufflers and no overcoats despite the inclement weather dissuading anyone else from displacing them. The rest of the men were a mixture of middle-class merchants — distinguished by their Homburgs, heavy overcoats and large moustaches — and raffish would-be Lotharios who offered each other cigarettes from silver cases and were continually brushing specks of soot from their expensive suits.

The noise of conversation, punctuated by much laughter and snatches of song, was deafening, echoing back from the high glass roof and augmented by the repeated clamour of porters trying to make a path for themselves and their clanging barrows. When the crowd realized that the insistence of the porters indicated the imminent arrival of the train, they cleared a way for them to take up positions at the platform's edge where they could assist the passengers with their luggage. Anticipation raised the hubbub to an even higher pitch until suddenly, from one end of the station the cry arose, 'It's comin', whisht there, the train's comin'.' Everyone grew silent. Faces were turned in that direction, eyes pinned to where the gleaming tracks disappeared abruptly into the pitch-black, mile-long tunnel that had been gouged out from under the hills of North Cork to commence every journey to the capital and end every journey from it. Ears were strained to pick up the slightest sound, but some of the crowd, more accustomed, for one reason or another, to meeting the Dublin train, knowingly lifted their chins to catch the first, almost ghostly draught of cold air from the tunnel which would tell them that the huge engine was now a quarter of a mile away, somewhere under St Luke's parish. But it was the experts, the porters, who signalled the first tangible proof of arrival when one of them cocked an eye over the edge of the platform and directed the gaze of those nearby to the polished tracks which had quietly commenced vibrating as if infected with the atmosphere of excitement. Then within seconds all the signs and sounds multiplied to a deafening crescendo as with whistle screeching and steam scorching from its funnel, engine number 400 crashed out of the darkness and, couplings clanging together, pulled itself to a noisy stop.

Immediately carriage windows which had been tightly closed against the tunnel's smoke and soot clattered down and heads were thrust out. Percy Lovitch forced a way through the crowd, turning this way and that to scan the faces of as many passengers as possible. 'Barry,' he suddenly shouted. Again 'Barry,' he called, fighting his way forward, almost breathless with excitement as, eyes shining, he appealed to the milling people to make way. 'It's the manager. They've come, the Carl Rosa have come.' He might have given the signal for bedlam. The cry was taken up, cheering and shouting broke out on all sides, and Percy, despite his bulk, was almost swept off his feet as he found himself propelled towards the beaming resplendent figure standing in the open doorway of one of the carriages.

H. Barrett Brandreth affected to be unsurprised by the warmth of his welcome. He raised his silver-topped cane in salute to the crowd, his rubicund face and pointed waxed moustaches glistening as if newly polished.

Percy Lovitch struggled to seize his gloved hand and shake it enthusiastically.

'Percy,' Brandreth greeted, seeming to speak in no more than a conversational tone and yet making himself heard above the din. 'How nice of you to meet us, old man. Are these all your friends?'

'No, Barry,' Percy shouted back, 'they're yours. They've come to welcome you. We thought you mightn't come to Cork this year. We weren't certain.'

H. Barrett Brandreth ran a hand over his wavy pomaded hair, gave a few elegant touches to the dark astrakhan collar of his long brown coat, and stepped down from the carriage, turning to gather the members of his Company in behind him. But the crowd surged around, slapping his back and pumping his hands, and Percy had no time to see what old friends from the cast were still in harness before the cry of 'Rise him, boys, rise him,' was heard and the momentarily startled impresario suddenly erupted into the air to land, cane waving triumphantly, on two pairs of burly shoulders.

Percy Lovitch fought to keep in touch with the smiling Brandreth, who, his poise fully restored despite the precariousness of his situation, was being borne towards the station forecourt. Behind him the other members of the Company were being helped down from the train, the male singers struggling to maintain protective embraces around their women in case any of the young men in the crowd might, in an excess of enthusiasm, try to lift them shoulder high in the wake of their manager.

Eventually the swaying mass emerged from the station exits and Brandreth was deposited on one of two horse-drawn floats that had been brought for the occasion. There were many helping hands to push Percy Lovitch up beside him, and the floats quickly became platforms for the bemused members of the Company as the crowd closed in, still cheering and shouting in acclamation. At length there was nothing for it but for Brandreth to hold up a hand in appeal for silence.

'Speech, speech,' came the call, as if he had not already made his intention clear.

'Good friends and fellow opera-lovers,' he said, his restrained tone expertly projected to the furthest listeners, 'my Company and I have been looking forward to our annual visit to Cork for a long time. We heard there had been certain — ah — difficulties in this part of the world in recent months, and I understand there was some scepticism as to whether we would run the gauntlet of existing troubles and fulfil our engagement. Well, you see the answer before you.' He swept a hand around to include the whole Company, and as the crowds cheered and clapped Percy saw the leading tenor, Louis Dorney, was still with them, as was also Gwynne Davies, the bass, and Alice Austen, the coloratura soprano. The Manager motioned again for silence and continued. 'I made some enquiries before we set out and I believe the Carl Rosa is the first theatrical company to visit Cork for several weeks. We are proud and honoured . . . .' The rest of his words were drowned in a fresh outburst of cheering and then, as if at a signal, bands of young men went to the front of each float, unharnessed the horses and, taking their place between the shafts, pulled the floats in triumph out onto the street towards the Opera House and the theatrical lodgings nearby. Catching the mood of the occasion Louis Dorney pushed himself to the front of his float and started to sing, to be joined immediately by the rest of the Company. As the rousing strains of the Toreador's Song rang out, the crowd responded with a will. All traffic halted and drew aside, pedestrians stood still in wonderment, cheering and clapping, shopkeepers and shoppers thronged in doorways, the whole complement of the Royal Irish Constabulary in King Street Barracks poked their heads out of windows or gathered on the Barracks steps to see the cavalcade pass. As the massive chorus of sound reverberated between the tall buildings, Brandreth put an arm round Percy Lovitch's shoulders, while Percy, his face bright red and perspiration gleaming on his brow, waved his umbrella like a conductor's baton and sang with all his heart, and with all his soul, and with all his might.

247

Munster Final, 1944

P.D. Mehigan (Carbery)

from: *Vintage Carbery* (1984)

An hour after the drawn game of July 16th, I met John Quirke and Christy Ring. We thrashed out the pros and cons of a startling finish, and I told them of my friendly sporting bet with an old Limerick friend.

'Double it next time,' said John Quirke.

'Carbery boy,' says fair-haired Christy Ring of the beaming, ruddy face, 'Quirky and I won't let you down,' and the flashing Glen Rovers' winger shook my hand heartily.

Last Sunday, another glamorous day in Thurles town — same lighthearted, good tempered, 20,000 crowd. Same brisk air in the stately square. There seemed a smile of pride and triumph on the bronze face of Dr Croke as the glad throngs of young vigorous folk — and old men too! — trooped past for the Gaelic Park over the bridge. Our transport scheme worked out difficult and slow; we were late for the opening scenes of the game which will rank with the classic Munster finals of the past in its stern, naked grandeur; in its hearty, manly spirit where rival surging bloods swung ash with freedom and abandon; where scores were level three times in the hour; where Mick Mackey treated us all to his wizard artistry; where Malone (from the Hill of Fedamore) proved almost the equal of Scanlon himself in the Limerick goal; where Limerick's flag was in the ascendant through 55 pulsating minutes until they were sailing home five points in front with only broken time to play. Cork's desperate final rally, whilst the clock ticked its last fateful minutes — a rally which every man in the field from Mulcahy out seemed to share — a rally which the spearheads (Morrison and Quirke) clinched with balancing scores that sent the comparatively small but virile Cork contingent shouting hoarsely.

Then came as dramatic and brilliant a score as ever Thurles finals have recorded. Christy Ring (of the Glen) still bounding with life and energy, nosed a rolling ball to the 'boss' of his hurley, raced through on Cork's right wing and let fly a daisy-clipper — dead on the post. Five stout Limerick backs pulled and parried. That ball's pace deceived one and all. Malone shadowed in, made a despairing effort to arrest its flight, and all but succeeded. Young Kelly (the sheet-lightning boy-sprinter) sped to the ball's aid — 'twas over the line; the great game was lost and won!

John Lynch, playing confidently in his old, new and favourite place, broke away for a long-range point shortly after Mr Seamus Gardiner had led in Most Rev. Dr O'Dwyer, Superior General of Maynooth's Mission, an old All-Ireland and Tipperary hurler, to set the boys under way. In a crack Dick Stokes had balanced and McCarthy's score gave Limerick the lead. Cork were quickly down-field, and Morrison pulled hard and low for a ball to the net which gave Malone no chance.

Cork's lead was short-lived. McCarthy and Ryan were breasting the ball well and Mick Mackey was away on one of his specialities — a swerving, dodging solo run — he flashed the ball to his brother John close on the square: a deft tap and the ball was through. Limerick led now and played with abundant confidence.

Hurling on both sides was sweet and true. Sean Condon hit a beauty point, but Limerick were soon surging up and Mick Mackey was again on the job. The Ahane leader was in irresistible mood as he crashed a goal and a point home in effortless fashion — Limerick leading nine points to five and a third of the hour gone.

Alan Lotty (of 'Sars') was holding Stokes well, but Cork's tall centre-half was limping badly. That old knee had let him down again. Cork's sideline brain-trust now got busy. Mick Mackey must be held or the day was lost to the triple champions! And so the brain-wave brought a rapid switch — Din Joe Buckley down to mark Limerick's star attacker; Curly Murphy in Lotty's place and big Pat Donovan of the Glen at right-half. Stokes swung a glorious shot for a point but Condon and Lynch were dead on the mark with high drives above the bar leaving Limerick a goal clear after a gallant first half: 2-4 to 1-4.

Malone had brought down many hot shots and continued to play well. At the other net Mulcahy was watchful as a lynx between the branches of a tree. Dick Stokes, from accurate frees, put Limerick five points clear. When Lynch and Cottrell — both hurling well now — opened up Cork fireworks, Malone stopped one from 10 yards out. Ash clashed; strong men pulled hard and fierce — there was a brief flare-up by lusty bloods. 'Twas quelled at once and the great game swung on. Joe Kelly again streaked in from Cork's left wing and pulled hard and true to whip a Cork goal home. Once again the scene changed to the other goal. Mick Kennedy, brought back after several years, had been doing right well in front of Malone. He cleared again; Johnny Power helped the good work; Limerick were away in a Shannon flood; young Clohessy raced past, and John Mackey made no mistake with a glorious swerve and shot — net — Limerick still five points clear and time running on.

Another wave from the Cork brain-trust. John Quirke who saved the game last time came in to the 40 mark. He had a sweet point in a tick. Cork were now staging a most determined final assault. John Lynch and Con Cottrell were bringing down every ball and feeding their front lines. Power and Cregan swung long balls back. Limerick's big contingent roared in one voice as Mick Mackey got possession — fouled on the way as he netted after the whistle had gone. Dick Stokes missed the free for once. Young, Buckley, the Murphys, Lynch and Cottrell were all moving fast — Morrison on the ball, a lightning swing — net — Cork one point behind and broken time being played.

John Quirke's cool skill again to the aid. A lovely neat swing — ball sails over the bar for the equalizer. Referee looks at his watch — we make it one minute to go — Christy Ring gets the ball; it glues to his hurley as he sprints up the wing like a shadow — away she goes — dead straight, fast and true to the Limerick net for so sensational a win that we are silent until the whistle blows. The 1940 final, when Limerick won the replay, was reversed. Limerick had led for the bulk of the hour and may have had the rough end of the day's fortunes. But there is no mistaking Cork's determined final stand and rousing rally. Christy Ring had prophesied truly — his goal will live in hurling history.

A Song For Christy Ring
Bryan MacMahon

Come gather round me boys tonight and raise your glasses high;
Come Rockies, Barrs and Rovers Stars, let welcome hit the sky;
Let bonfires blaze in heroes' praise, let Shannon echoes fling,
For homeward bound with hurling crown comes gallant
    Christy Ring.

So all you hurlers from the Nore, you lads from Corrib's side,
From Garryowen gay and bold with Tipp's own men beside,
You may have hurlers straight and tall who can a camán
    swing,
But whose the name can play the game with Cork's own
    Christy Ring.

When we were young we read in school in the days of old
The young Setanta showed his worth with shield and spear of
    gold.
As hurling hard on royal sward he'd hurling heroes fling
— My soul today, he'd yield the sway if he met Christy Ring.

A health to faithful Wexford boys, to the Rackards and their
    team
Should Cork surrender Ireland's crown may victory on them
    gleam,
John Kelly's name we hold in fame — of '98 we sing,
But Slaney's plan must find a man to equal Christy Ring.

How oft I've watched him from the hill move here and there
    in grace,
In Cork, Killarney, Thurles town or by the Shannon's race;
'Now Cork is bet; the hay is saved!' the thousands wildly sing —
They speak too soon, my sweet garsún, for here comes
    Christy Ring.

Listening to the Captain
Patrick Galvin

from: *Song for a Poor Boy* (1990)

Every Sunday after Mass, the neighbours gathered in our tenement
flat to sing and tell stories. My father played music and, sometimes,
recited poetry he'd made up in his head. My father would never
admit to having made up these poems. He said they were the work
of great men long gone and now sadly neglected. My mother said
he was the biggest liar in Cork — and he was. But he was also a

poet. A poet is a man who tell lies, but in short lines and with style. My father had style.

Paddy Tom Kilroy also had style. He lived over in Frenches Quay and everyone called him The Captain because he wore a sailor's cap and had never been to sea. He owned a small fishing-boat, too. It was willed to him by his father and was moored near the South Gate Bridge, but Paddy had never set foot on it. He said the weather was too bad.

The weather had started to go bad fifteen years ago when Paddy's father had died and left him the boat. It was still bad and there was no sign of an improvement.

Paddy leaned over the parapet of the South Gate Bridge and stared at the boat. The timbers were rotting. The seagulls were nesting on the deck and the barnacles were choking the hull to death.

Paddy looked at the sky. If only the weather would improve — but he knew it wouldn't. He'd read in the newspaper that morning that there was a storm brewing over Cork. He buttoned his coat. The weather was killing him. He could feel it in his bones.

One Sunday, Paddy arrived at our flat in Margaret Street and said he'd changed into a seagull. He didn't look like a seagull, and he still wore his sailor's cap, but my father invited him in and asked him if he'd seen a doctor? Paddy shook his head. There was no point. Doctors knew nothing about seagulls and, besides, he was happy enough the way he was. Come to think of it — he'd always wanted to be a seagull, but the boat got in his way.

My father thought he'd gone raving mad, but my mother was more sympathetic. She offered him fish. Paddy ate the fish and said he'd never tasted anything sweeter in his life. On his way out, he thanked my mother and said he'd remember her in his will. My father almost choked. He hated fish and he was convinced that Paddy would be in the madhouse within the week.

A few days later, Paddy returned to the house. My mother found him sitting on the stairs and there were tears in his eyes. He said the police were after him, and when my mother asked him what crime he'd committed, he said he hadn't committed a crime. All he'd done was to fly in and out of the South Chapel during Mass and screech — 'More Fish'!

The congregation was terrified and the Parish Priest had a heart attack — but whose fault was that? A seagull was a perfectly harmless bird and all the congregation had to do was to say 'Sorry, Paddy, we've run out of fish' and Paddy would have been satisfied and gone elsewhere.

When the police arrived, Paddy was wheeled off to the Bridewell and he spent a week in there flapping his wings about and claiming that under International Law it was illegal to imprison a seagull.

The guards at the Bridewell knew nothing about International Law, but they insisted that under Irish Law the police could arrest anyone for anything — even if he were a seagull.

Paddy applied for bail, and my mother had to pawn my father's best suit in order to raise the money to have Paddy released.

My father was a tolerant man, but when his best suit had to be pawned to have a seagull released from jail, things were getting out of hand altogether. He had nothing against seagulls — provided they let their droppings fall on someone else — but this particular seagull was getting on his nerves. He wanted his suit back — and he said so without music.

My mother laughed. She knew that Paddy was a genius, and if he felt he was a seagull, then that's what he was. After all, there were worse things he could be — like a policeman or a Blueshirt. My father didn't agree at all and was now beginning to worry about my mother. Any minute now and she'd be sprouting wings.

She didn't. She pulled her black shawl tightly around her shoulders and went to the courthouse the following morning to hear Paddy being charged with a breach of the peace. He pleaded 'Not Guilty' and when the magistrate asked him for his full name he replied:

'Seagulls don't have full names. They're just called — Seagulls.'

The magistrate nodded his head. He understood perfectly. Paddy was a poet. He dismissed the case and Paddy winged it from the court a free bird.

He was missing for months. My mother searched around his usual haunts, but there was no trace of him. Paddy had disappeared.

Then, one day, while she was sitting in a pub in Sullivan's Quay, having her usual bottle of stout, the door opened and Paddy walked in. She offered him a drink. Paddy accepted and sat beside her in the snug.

'You've been away?' she said.

'I have' Paddy declared. 'Do you notice anything different about me?'

My mother wasn't sure. Paddy shook his head. He was no longer a seagull.

'That's a sad day for Cork, Paddy.'

'It's a sad day for me too, Maam. But the fates were against it.'

He finished his drink and turned towards the door.

'By the way' he said — 'I've willed you the boat. Maybe your son will find a use for it.'

'I'm sure he will' said my mother. 'But you'll be with us for a long time yet, Paddy.'

Paddy shrugged his shoulders. 'I'll be going now' he said. 'Thanks for the drink.'

'Are you going far?'

'I'm going for a walk on the water' Paddy replied. 'God knows when I'll be back.'

The door closed behind him and a week later Paddy's body was found floating on the water close to Blackrock Castle. My mother wept — and the seagulls carried Paddy home.

The Armoured Car
Seán O'Callaghan

Come all my good friends and around me attend, you
    can listen to my song,
You must appreciate a hound so great to the sport that
    you belong.
No land or a title did he ever own and he cared not for
    who you were,
He was bred and trained by the boys of Fair Hill and
    they called him the Armoured Car.

Now facts to you I'll disclose, he'd a check-proof nose
And he never yet lost a hunt.
He had cast iron jaws and steel padded paws —
Every nail was like an iron bar.
From one mile to ten he would never give in
If you ran him from here to Castlebar.
Small wonder gentlemen that the boys of Fair Hill
Used to call him the Armoured Car.

Now in the year of 21 when he started to run,
Having surveyed the country all round,
He sent a sworn declaration to the Harriers Association
That he cared not for man, hare or hound:
And he swore right then that if he didn't win
To Fair Hill he'd never repair:
Small wonder gentlemen that the boys of Fair Hill
Used to call him the Armoured Car.

Now he stormed Timoleague and he nearly caused the
    plague
When he fought through the playing school yard.
Spectators stood around: they were half spellbound,
For light there wasn't a spark.
The judges were growing tired but were soon inspired
When out shone the evening star.
Who'd be coming to the front and he leading the hunt —
It was Doyley's old Armoured Car.

At the battle of Waterloo sure ye know this is true
How he laid all the enemy low
When we thought he was done from the heat of the
    sun
And the armour on fire would go.
From the finish to the start he broke the Blarney dogs'
    heart
And he surpassed the evening star
When a voice from Seán 'go ahead, Ceolán, take the
    place of the Armoured Car.'

At the siege of Kileens sure he reigned supreme
O'er the Northern United foe
When passing all Saints sure their hearts down fell
When for judgment they quickly seen him go.
The spectators on Blarney rock, sure they got such a
    shock
When shouted Casey Finbar
'It's just as good to finish up
Here comes Doyley's old Armoured Car.'

Now when the Free State bill was framed and peace was
    proclaimed
And the country slumbered in repose,
North, South, East and West sure he couldn't be
    suppressed,
For he cared not for friend or foe.
And when the Black and Tans with their Saxon clans
To England sailed afar,
With all their guns and rap sure they never could capture
Doyley's Old Armoured Car.

Now here is my glass and around may it pass,
As we drink in a token of love.
Here's to every hand that mine can expand
And those up in Heaven above.
Here's to every hound who can nose the ground,
No matter where you are.
'Twould be Conny Doyle's delight if every hound here
    tonight
Had a heart like the Armoured Car.

Johnny Jump Up
Tadhg Jordan

I'll tell you a story that happened to me
One day as I went down to Youghal by the sea.
The sun it was bright and the day it was warm
So says I a quiet pint wouldn't do me no harm.

I went in and I called for a bottle of stout:
Says the barman I'm sorry, all the beer is sold out:
Try whiskey or Paddy, ten years in the wood:
Says I, I'll try cider, I heard it was good.

Oh never, O never, Oh never again
If I live to a hundred or a hundred and ten,
For I fell to the ground and I couldn't get up
After drinkin' a quart of the Johnny Jump Up.

After lowering the third I made straight for the yard,
Where I bumped into Brophy, the big Civic Guard.
Come here to me boy, don't you know I'm the law,
Well I up with me fist and I shattered his jaw.

He fell to the ground with his knees doubled up
But it wasn't I hit him, 'twas Johnny Jump Up.
The next thing I met down in Youghal by the sea
Was a cripple on crutches and says he to me:

'I'm afraid of me life I'll be hit by a car
Won't you help me across to the Railwayman's Bar.'
After drinking a quart of the cider so sweet
He threw down his crutches and he danced on his feet.

I went up the Lee Road, a friend for to see,
They call it the madhouse in Cork by the Lee.
But when I got up there the truth I do tell
They had the poor so-and-so tied up in a cell.

Said a guard testing him, say these words if you can:
'Around the rugged rocks the ragged rascal ran.'
Tell them I'm not crazy, tell them I'm not mad —
It was only a sup of the bottle I had.

A man died in the Union, by the name of McNabb.
We washed him and laid him outside on a slab,
And after O'Connor his measurements did take
His wife took him home to a bloody fine wake.

'Twas about twelve o'clock and the beer it was high:
The corpse he jumped up and says he with a sigh:
'I can't get to Heaven, they won't let me up
Till I bring 'em a quart of the Johnny Jump-up.'

Trinket's Colt

Edith Somerville and Martin Ross

from: *Some Experiences of an Irish R.M.* (1899)

It was Petty Sessions day in Skebawn, a cold, grey day of February. A case of trespass had dragged its burden of cross summonses and cross swearing far into the afternoon, and when I left the bench my head was singing from the bellowings of the attorneys, and the smell of their clients was heavy upon my palate.

The streets still testified to the fact that it was market day, and I evaded with difficulty the sinuous course of carts full of soddenly screwed people, and steered an equally devious one for myself among the groups anchored round the doors of the public-houses. Skebawn possesses, among its legion of public-houses, one establishment which timorously, and almost imperceptibly, proffers tea to the thirsty. I turned in there, as was my custom on court days, and found the little dingy den, known as the Ladies' Coffee-room, in the occupancy of my friend Mr Florence McCarthy Knox, who was drinking strong tea and eating buns with serious simplicity. It was a first and quite unexpected glimpse of that domesticity that has now become a marked feature in his character.

'You're the very man I wanted to see,' I said as I sat down beside him at the oilcloth-covered table; 'a man I know in England who is not much of a judge of character has asked me to buy him a four-year-old down here, and as I should rather be stuck by a friend than a dealer, I wish you'd take over the job.'

Flurry poured himself out another cup of tea, and dropped three lumps of sugar into it in silence.

Finally he said, 'There isn't a four-year-old in this country that I'd be seen dead with at a pig fair.'

This was discouraging, from the premier authority on horse-flesh in the district.

'But it isn't six weeks since you told me you had the finest filly in your stables that was ever foaled in the County Cork,' I protested; 'what's wrong with her?'

'Oh, is it that filly?' said Mr Knox with a lenient smile; 'she's gone these three weeks from me. I swapped her and six pounds for a three-year-old Ironmonger colt, and after that I swapped the colt and nineteen pounds for that Bandon horse I rode last week at your place, and after that again I sold the Bandon horse for seventy-five pounds to old Welply, and I had to give him back a couple of sovereigns luck-money. You see I did pretty well with the filly after all.'

'Yes, yes — oh, rather,' I assented, as one dizzily accepts the propositions of a bimetellist; 'and you don't know of anything else — ?'

The room in which we were seated was closely screened from the shop by a door with a muslin-curtained window in it; several of the panes were broken, and at this juncture two voices that had for some time carried on a discussion forced themselves upon our attention.

'Begging your pardon for contradicting you, ma'am,' said the voice of Mrs McDonald, proprietress of the tea-shop, and a leading light in Skebawn Dissenting circles, shrilly tremulous with indignation, 'if the servants I recommend you won't stop with you, it's no fault of mine. If respectable young girls are set picking grass out of your gravel, in place of their proper work, certainly they will give warning!'

The voice that replied struck me as being a notable one, well-bred and imperious.

'When I take a barefooted slut out of a cabin, I don't expect her to dictate to me what her duties are!'

Flurry jerked up his chin in a noiseless laugh. 'It's my grandmother!' he whispered. 'I bet you Mrs McDonald don't get much change out of her!'

'If I set her to clean the pigsty I expect her to obey me,' continued the voice in accents that would have made me clean forty pigsties had she desired me to do so.

'Very well, ma'am,' retorted Mrs McDonald, 'if that's the way you treat your servants, you needn't come here again looking for them. I consider your conduct is neither that of a lady nor a Christian!'

'Don't you, indeed?' replied Flurry's grandmother. 'Well, your opinion doesn't greatly distress me, for, to tell you the truth, I don't think you're much of a judge.'

'Didn't I tell you she'd score?' murmured Flurry, who was by this time applying his eye to a hole in the muslin curtain. 'She's off,' he went on, returning to his tea. 'She's a great character! She's eighty-three if she's a day, and she's as sound on her legs as a three-year-old! Did you see that old shandrydan of hers in the street a while ago, and a fellow on the box with a red beard on him like Robinson Crusoe? That old mare that was on the near side — Trinket her name is — is mighty near clean bred. I can tell you her foals are worth a bit of money.'

I had heard of old Mrs Knox of Aussolas; indeed, I had seldom dined out in the neighbourhood without hearing some new story of her and her remarkable *ménage*, but it had not yet been my privilege to meet her.

'Well, now,' went on Flurry in his slow voice, 'I'll tell you a thing that's just come into my head. My grandmother promised me a foal of Trinket's the day I was one-and-twenty, and that's five years ago, and deuce a one I've got from her yet. You never were at Aussolas? No, you were not. Well, I tell you the place there is like a circus with horses. She has a couple of score of them running wild in the woods, like deer.'

'Oh, come,' I said, 'I'm a bit of a liar myself — '

'Well, she has a dozen of them anyhow, rattling good colts too, some of them, but they might as well be donkeys, for all the good they are to me or any one. It's not once in three years she sells one, and there she has them walking after her for bits of sugar, like a lot of dirty lapdogs,' ended Flurry with disgust.

'Well, what's your plan? Do you want me to make her a bid for one of the lapdogs?'

'I was thinking,' replied Flurry, with great deliberation, 'that my birthday's this week, and maybe I could work a four-year-old colt of Trinket's she has out of her in honour of the occasion.'

'And sell your grandmother's birthday present to me?'

'Just that, I suppose,' answered Flurry with a slow wink.

A few days afterwards a letter from Mr Knox informed me that he had 'squared the old lady, and it would be all right about the colt.' He further told me that Mrs Knox had been good enough to offer me, with him, a day's snipe shooting on the celebrated Aussolas bogs, and he proposed to drive me there the following Monday, if convenient. Most people found it convenient to shoot the Aussolas snipe bog when they got the chance. Eight o'clock on the following Monday morning saw Flurry, myself, and a groom packed into a dogcart, with portmanteaus, gun-cases, and two rampant red setters.

It was a long drive, twelve miles at least, and a very cold one. We passed through long tracts of pasture country, fraught, for Flurry, with memories of runs, which were recorded for me, fence by fence, in every one of which the biggest dog-fox in the country had gone to ground, with not two feet — measured accurately on the handle of the whip — between him and the leading hound; through bogs that imperceptibly melted into lakes, and finally down and down into a valley, where the fir-trees of Aussolas clustered darkly round a glittering lake, and all but hid the grey roofs and pointed gables of Aussolas Castle.

'There's a nice stretch of a demesne for you,' remarked Flurry, pointing downwards with the whip, 'and one little old woman holding it all in the heel of her fist. Well able to hold it she is, too, and always was, and she'll live twenty years yet, if it's only to spite the whole lot of us, and when all's said and done goodness knows how she'll leave it!'

'It strikes me you were lucky to keep her up to her promise about the colt,' I said.

Flurry administered a composing kick to the ceaseless strivings of the red setters under the seat.

'I used to be rather a pet with her,' he said, after a pause; 'but mind you, I haven't got him yet, and if she gets any notion I want to sell him I'll never get him, so say nothing about the business to her.'

The tall gates of Aussolas shrieked on their hinges as they admitted us, and shut with a clang behind us, in the faces of an old mare and a couple of young horses, who, foiled in their break for the excitements of our outer world, turned and galloped defiantly on either side of us. Flurry's admirable cob hammered on, regardless of all things save his duty.

'He's the only one I have that I'd trust myself here with,' said his master, flicking him approvingly with the whip; 'there are plenty of people afraid to come here at all, and when my grandmother goes out driving she has a boy on the box with a basket full of stones to peg at them. Talk of the dickens, here she is herself!'

A short, upright old woman was approaching, preceded by a white woolly dog with sore eyes and a bark like a tin trumpet; we both got out of the trap and advanced to meet the lady of the manor.

I may summarize her attire by saying that she looked as if she had robbed a scarecrow; her face was small and incongruously refined, the skinny hand that she extended to me had the grubby tan that bespoke the professional gardener, and was decorated with a magnificent diamond ring. On her head was a massive purple velvet bonnet.

'I am very glad to meet you, Major Yeates,' she said with an old-fashioned precision of utterance; 'your grandfather was a dancing

261

partner of mine in old days at the Castle, when he was a handsome young aide-de-camp there, and I was — You may judge for yourself what I was.'

She ended with a startling little hoot of laughter, and I was aware that she quite realized the world's opinion of her, and was indifferent to it.

Our way to the bogs took us across Mrs Knox's home farm, and through a large field in which several young horses were grazing.

'There now, that's my fellow,' said Flurry, pointing to a fine-looking colt, 'the chestnut with the white diamond on his forehead. He'll run into three figures before he's done, but we'll not tell that to the old lady!'

The famous Aussolas bogs were as full of snipe as usual, and a good deal fuller of water than any bogs I had ever shot before. I was on my day, and Flurry was not, and as he is ordinarily an infinitely better snipe shot than I, I felt at peace with the world and all men as we walked back, wet through, at five o'clock.

The sunset had waned, and a big white moon was making the eastern tower of Aussolas look like a thing in a fairy tale or a play when we arrived at the hall door. An individual, whom I recognized as the Robinson Crusoe coachman, admitted us to a hall, the like of which one does not often see. The walls were panelled with dark oak up to the gallery that ran round three sides of it, the balusters of the wide staircase were heavily carved, and blackened portraits of Flurry's ancestors on the spindle side stared sourly down on their descendant as he tramped upstairs with the bog mould on his hobnailed boots.

We had just changed into dry clothes when Robinson Crusoe shoved his red beard round the corner of the door, with the information that the mistress said we were to stay for dinner. My heart sank. It was then barely half-past five. I said something about having no evening clothes and having to get home early.

'Sure the dinner'll be in another half hour,' said Robinson Crusoe, joining hospitably in the conversation; 'and as for evening clothes —— God bless ye!'

The door closed behind him.

'Never mind,' said Flurry, 'I dare say you'll be glad enough to eat another dinner by the time you get home.' He laughed. 'Poor Slipper!' he added inconsequently, and only laughed again when I asked for an explanation.

Old Mrs Knox received us in the library, where she was seated by a roaring turf fire, which lit the room a good deal more effectively than the pair of candles that stood beside her in tall silver candlesticks. Ceaseless and implacable growls from under her chair indicated the presence of the woolly dog. She talked with confounding culture of the books that rose all round her to the ceiling; her evening dress was accomplished by means of an additional white shawl, rather dirtier than its congeners; as I took her in to dinner she quoted Virgil to me, and in the same breath screeched an objurgation at a being whose matted head rose suddenly into view from behind an ancient Chinese screen, as I have seen the head of a Zulu woman peer over a bush.

Dinner was as incongruous as everything else. Detestable soup in a splendid old silver tureen that was nearly as dark in hue as Robinson Crusoe's thumb; a perfect salmon, perfectly cooked, on a chipped kitchen dish; such cut glass as is not easy to find nowadays; sherry that, as Flurry subsequently remarked, would burn the shell off an egg; and a bottle of port, draped in immemorial cobwebs, wan with age, and probably priceless. Throughout the vicissitudes of the meal Mrs Knox's conversation flowed on undismayed, directed sometimes at me — she had installed me in the position of friend of her youth — and talked to me as if I were my own grandfather — sometimes at Crusoe, with whom she had several heated arguments, and sometimes she would make a statement of remarkable frankness on the subject of her horse-farming affairs to Flurry, who, very much on his best behaviour, agreed with all she said, and risked no original remark. As I listened to them both, I remembered with infinite amusement how he had told me once that 'a pet name she had for him was "Tony Lumpkin," and no one but herself knew what she meant by it.' It seemed strange that she made no allusion to Trinket's colt or to Flurry's birthday, but, mindful of my instructions, I held my peace.

As, at about half-past eight, we drove away in the moonlight, Flurry congratulated me solemnly on my success with his grandmother. He was good enough to tell me that she would marry me tomorrow if I asked her, and he wished I would, even if it was only to see what a nice grandson he'd be for me. A sympathetic giggle behind me told me that Michael, on the back seat had heard and relished the jest.

We had left the gates of Aussolas about half a mile behind when, at the corner of a by-road, Flurry pulled up. A short squat figure arose from the black shadow of a furze bush and came out into the moonlight, swinging its arms like a cabman and cursing audibly.

'Oh murdher, oh murdher, Misther Flurry! What kept ye at all? 'Twould perish the crows to be waiting here the way I am these two hours ——'

'Ah, shut your mouth, Slipper!' said Flurry, who, to my surprise, had turned back the rug and was taking off his driving coat, 'I couldn't help it. Come on, Yeates, we've got to get out here.'

'What for?' I asked, in not unnatural bewilderment.

'It's all right. I'll tell you as we go along,' replied my companion, who was already turning to follow Slipper up the by-road. 'Take the trap on, Michael, and wait at the River's Cross.' He waited for me to come up with him, and then put his hand on my arm. 'You see, Major, this is the way it is. My grandmother's given me that colt right enough, but if I waited for her to send him over to me I'd never see a hair of his tail. So I just thought that as we were over here we might as well take him back with us, and maybe you'll give us a help with him; he'll not be altogether too handy for a first go off.'

I was staggered. An infant in arms could scarcely have failed to discern the fishiness of the transaction, and I begged Mr Knox not to put himself to this trouble on my account, as I had no doubt I could find a horse for my friend elsewhere. Mr Knox assured me that it was no trouble at all, quite the contrary, and that, since his grandmother had given him the colt, he saw no reason why he should not take him when he wanted him; also, that if I didn't want him he'd be glad enough to keep him himself; and finally, that I wasn't the chap to go back on a friend, but I was welcome to drive back to Shreelane with Michael this minute if I liked.

Of course I yielded in the end. I told Flurry I should lose my job over the business, and he said I could then marry his grandmother, and the discussion was abruptly closed by the necessity of following Slipper over a locked five-barred gate.

Our pioneer took us over about half a mile of country, knocking down stone gaps where practicable and scrambling over tall banks in the deceptive moonlight. We found ourselves at length in a field with a shed in one corner of it; in a dim group of farm buildings a little way off a light was shining.

'Wait here,' said Flurry to me in a whisper; 'the less noise the better. It's an open shed, and we'll just slip in and coax him out.'

Slipper unwound from his waist a halter, and my colleagues glided like spectres into the shadow of the shed, leaving me to meditate on my duties as Resident Magistrate, and on the questions that would be asked in the House by our local member when Slipper had given away the adventure in his cups.

In less than a minute three shadows emerged from the shed, where two had gone in. They had got the colt.

'He came out as quite as a calf when he winded the sugar,' said Flurry; 'it was well for me I filled my pockets from grandmamma's sugar basin.'

He and Slipper had a rope from each side of the colt's head; they took him quickly across a field towards a gate. The colt stepped daintily between them over the moonlit grass; he snorted occasionally, but appeared on the whole amenable.

The trouble began later, and was due, as trouble often is, to the beguilements of a short cut. Against the maturer judgment of Slipper, Flurry insisted on following a route that he assured us he knew as well as his own pocket, and the consequence was that in about five minutes I found myself standing on top of a bank hanging on to a rope, on the other end of which the colt dangled and danced, while Flurry, with the other rope, lay prone in the ditch, and Slipper administered to the bewildered colt's hind quarters such chastisement as could be ventured on.

I have no space to narrate in detail the atrocious difficulties and disasters of the short cut. How the colt set to work to buck, and went away across a field, dragging the faithful Slipper, literally *ventre à terre*, after him, while I picked myself in ignominy out of a briar patch, and Flurry cursed himself black in the face. How we were attacked by ferocious cur dogs, and I lost my eye-glass; and how, as we neared the River's Cross, Flurry espied the police patrol on the road, and we all hid behind a rick of turf while I realized in fullness what an exceptional ass I was, to have been beguiled into an enterprise that involved hiding with Slipper from the Royal Irish Constabulary.

Let it suffice to say that Trinket's infernal offspring was finally handed over on the high road to Michael and Slipper, and Flurry drove me home in a state of mental and physical overthrow.

I saw nothing of my friend Mr Knox for the next couple of days, by the end of which time I had worked up a high polish on my misgivings, and had determined to tell him that under no circumstances would I have anything to say to his grandmother's birthday present.

It was like my usual luck that, instead of writing a note to this effect, I thought it would be good for my liver to walk across the hills to Tory Cottage and tell Flurry so in person.

It was a bright, blustery morning, after a muggy day. The feeling of spring was in the air, the daffodils were already in bud, and crocuses showed purple in the grass on either side of the avenue. It was only a couple of miles to Tory Cottage by the way across the hills; I walked fast, and it was barely twelve o'clock when I saw its pink walls and clumps of evergreens below me. As I looked down at it the chiming of Flurry's hounds in the kennels came to me on the wind; I stood still to listen, and could almost have sworn that I was hearing again the clash of Magdalen bells, hard at work on May morning.

The path that I was following led downwards through a larch plantation to Flurry's back gate. Hot wafts from some hideous cauldron at the other side of a wall apprised me of the vicinity of the kennels and their cuisine, and the fir-trees round were hung with grue-some and unknown joints. I thanked heaven that I was not a master of hounds, and passed on as quickly as might be to the hall door.

I rang two or three times without response; then the door opened a couple of inches and was instantly slammed in my face. I heard the hurried paddling of bare feet on oil-cloth, and a voice, 'Hurry, Bridgie, hurry! There's quality at the door!'

Bridgie, holding a dirty cap on with one hand, presently arrived and informed me that she believed Mr Knox was out about the place. She seemed perturbed, and she cast scared glances down the drive while speaking to me.

I knew enough of Flurry's habits to shape a tolerably direct course for his whereabouts. He was, as I had expected, in the training pad-dock, a field behind the stable yard, in which he had put up practice jumps for his horses. It was a good-sized field with clumps of furze in it, and Flurry was standing near one of these with his hands in his pockets, singularly unoccupied. I supposed that he was prospecting for a place to put up another jump. He did not see me coming, and turned with a start as I spoke to him. There was a queer expression of mingled guilt and what I can only describe as divilment in his grey eyes as he greeted me. In my dealings with Flurry Knox, I have since formed the habit of sitting tight, in a general way, when I see that expression.

'Well, who's coming next, I wonder!' he said, as he shook hands with me; 'it's not ten minutes since I had two of your d —— d peelers here searching the whole place for my grandmother's colt!'

'What!' I exclaimed, feeling cold all down my back; 'do you mean the police have got hold of it?'

'They haven't got hold of the colt anyway,' said Flurry, looking sideways at me from under the peak of his cap, with the glint of the sun in his eye. 'I got word in time before they came.'

'What do you mean?' I demanded; 'where is he? For heaven's sake don't tell me you've sent the brute over to my place!'

'It's a good job for you I didn't,' replied Flurry, 'as the police are on their way to Shreelane this minute to consult you about it. *You!*' He gave utterance to one of his short diabolical fits of laughter. 'He's where they'll not find him, anyhow. Ho ho! It's the funniest hand I ever played!'

'Oh yes, it's devilish funny, I've no doubt,' I retorted, beginning to lose my temper, as is the manner of many people when they are frightened; 'but I give you fair warning that if Mrs Knox asks me any questions about it, I shall tell her the whole story.'

'All right,' responded Flurry; 'and when you do, don't forget to tell her how you flogged the colt out on to the road over her own bounds ditch.'

'Very well,' I said hotly, 'I may as well go home and send in my papers. They'll break me over this ——'

'Ah, hold on, major,' said Flurry soothingly, 'it'll be all right. No one knows anything. It's only on spec the old lady sent the bobbies here. If you'll keep quiet it'll all blow over.'

'I don't care,' I said, struggling hopelessly in the toils; 'if I meet your grandmother, and she asks me about it, I shall tell her all I know.'

'Please God you'll not meet her! After all, it's not once in a blue moon that she ——' began Flurry. Even as he said the words his face changed. 'Holy fly!' he ejaculated, 'isn't that her dog coming into the field? Look at her bonnet over the wall! Hide, hide for your life!' He caught me by the shoulder and shoved me down among the furze bushes before I realized what had happened.

'Get in there! I'll talk to her.'

I may as well confess that at the mere sight of Mrs Knox's purple bonnet my heart had turned to water. In that moment I knew what it would be like to tell her how I, having eaten her salmon, and capped her quotations, and drunk her best port, had gone forth and helped to steal her horse. I abandoned my dignity, my sense of honour; I took the furze prickles to my breast and wallowed in them.

Mrs Knox had advanced with vengeful speed; already she was in high altercation with Flurry at no great distance from where I lay; varying sounds of battle reached me, and I gathered that Flurry was not — to put it mildly — shrinking from that economy of truth that the situation required.

'Is it that curby, long-backed brute? You promised him to me long ago, but I wouldn't be bothered with him!'

The old lady uttered a laugh of shrill derision. 'Is it likely I'd promise you my best colt? And still more, is it likely that you'd refuse him if I did?'

'Very well, ma'am.' Flurry's voice was admirably indignant. 'Then I suppose I'm a liar and a thief.'

'I'd be more obliged to you for the information if I hadn't known it before,' responded his grandmother with lightning speed; 'if you swore to me on a stack of Bibles you knew nothing about my colt I wouldn't believe you! I shall go straight to Major Yeates and ask his advice. I believe *him* to be a gentleman, in spite of the company he keeps!'

I writhed deeper into the furze bushes, and thereby discovered a sandy rabbit run, along which I crawled, with my cap well over my eyes, and the furze needles stabbing me through my stockings. The ground shelved a little, promising profounder concealment, but the bushes were very thick, and I laid hold of the bare stem of one to help my progress. It lifted out of the ground in my hand, revealing a freshly cut stump. Something snorted, not a yard away; I glared through the opening, and was confronted by the long, horrified face of Mrs Knox's colt, mysteriously on a level with my own.

Even without the white diamond on his forehead I should have divined the truth; but how in the name of wonder had Flurry persuaded him to couch like a woodcock in the heart of a furze brake? For a full minute I lay as still as death for fear of frightening him, while the voices of Flurry and his grandmother raged on alarmingly close to me. The colt snorted, and blew long breaths through his wide nostrils, but he did not move. I crawled an inch or two nearer, and after a few seconds of cautious peering I grasped the position. They had buried him.

A small sandpit among the furze had been utilized as a grave; they had filled him in up to his withers with sand, and a few furze bushes, artistically disposed around the pit, had done the rest. As the depth of Flurry's guile was revealed, laughter came upon me like a

268

flood; I gurgled and shook apoplectically, and the colt gazed at me with serious surprise, until a sudden outburst of barking close to my elbow administered a fresh shock to my tottering nerves.

Mrs Knox's woolly dog had tracked me into the furze, and was now baying the colt and me with mingled terror and indignation. I addressed him in a whisper, with perfidious endearments, advancing a crafty hand towards him the while, made a snatch for the back of his neck, missed it badly, and got him by the ragged fleece of his hind quarters as he tried to flee. If I had flayed him alive he could hardly have uttered a more deafening series of yells, but, like a fool, instead of letting him go, I dragged him towards me, and tried to stifle the noise by holding his muzzle. The tussle lasted engrossingly for a few seconds, and then the climax of the nightmare arrived.

Mrs Knox's voice, close behind me, said, 'Let go my dog this instant, sir! Who are you ——'

Her voice faded away, and I knew that she also had seen the colt's head.

I positively felt sorry for her. At her age there was no knowing what effect the shock might have on her. I scrambled to my feet and confronted her.

'Major Yeates!' she said. There was a deathly pause. 'Will you kindly tell me,' said Mrs Knox slowly, 'am I in Bedlam, or are you? And *what is that?*'

She pointed to the colt, and that unfortunate animal, recognizing the voice of his mistress, uttered a hoarse and lamentable whinny. Mrs Knox felt around her for support, found only furze prickles, gazed speechlessly at me, and then, to her eternal honour, fell into wild cackles of laughter.

So, may I say, did Flurry and I. I embarked on my explanation and broke down; Flurry followed suit and broke down too. Overwhelming laughter held us all three, disintegrating our very souls. Mrs Knox pulled herself together first.

'I acquit you, Major Yeates, I acquit you, though appearances are against you. It's clear enough to me you've fallen among thieves.' She stopped and glowered at Flurry. Her purple bonnet was over one eye. 'I'll thank you, sir,' she said, 'to dig out that horse before I leave this place. And when you've dug him out you may keep him. I'll be no receiver of stolen goods!'

She broke off and shook her fist at him. 'Upon my conscience, Tony, I'd give a guinea to have thought of it myself!'

269

V PEOPLE APART

Harry Badger

C. C. W.

from: *The Journal of the Cork Historical and Archaeological Society* (1892)

The famous Harry Badger flourished during the first quarter of this century, and, to the delight of the boys of Cork, daily took his walks abroad till somewhere about the year 1830, when he met a tragic end.

Amongst a variety of things which distinguished this eminent man from the common herd was a remarkable indifference to the *quality* of his food. On one occasion a few cheerful young men met him 'by the merest accident,' and having assured him that they felt for him the highest respect, offered him a pint of porter as a token of their esteem. Harry lost not an instant in accepting so flattering an offer, and the party at once adjourned to the nearest public-house, where one of the ingenuous youths, having procured a foaming pint, handed it to Harry, and, in so doing, dropped into it (unseen by the recipient) a lively young mouse. Harry finished the beverage without drawing breath, and handed back the pint *quite empty*. The young men waited for an exclamation, but none came, he only wiped his mouth with his sleeve and looked happy. At last one of the company inquired in an insinuating kind of way whether he had met anything in the porter? 'Sure enough,' said Harry, 'so I did — *a fly.*'

Poor Harry's death was the result of a practical joke. Above all other food Harry loved tripe, and some of his friends determined that they would give him a really good dinner. With this benevolent object in view they procured an old huntsman's leather breeches, and, having cut it into pieces of the right size, they boiled it with milk and plenty of onions, and a couple of nice dusts of pepper and salt, and, having led the victim into a secluded hay-loft, set the steaming pot before him and locked him in. Harry finished the leather breeches in two days, and on the third he died, sincerely and deeply lamented by all the boys of Cork who lost the delicious pleasure of tormenting the most amusing public character our city ever possessed.

Tom Green

Robert Day

from: *The Journal of the Cork Historical and Archaeological Society* (1892)

The historical pages of our Journal have already been graced with the portraits of 'Harry Badger,' 'Bothered Dan,' and 'Foxy Norrey.' There are yet some more worthies of the same family, whose eventful lives will be forgotten, and whose names will be for ever unrecorded if not numbered in the list of those who, perchance, were often a burden to themselves, but who were sources of innocent amusement to many of their fellow-citizens, and to those with whom chance brought them into contact.

One such was Tom Green, whose father was an army tailor, and 'as fine a man, sir, as ever sat on a boord.' When the Island of Martinique was taken from the French, Tom was there with his parents, and while England was still at war with France, they returned home, and were landed in Cove. Here his father, whose name was Arthbutnot, died, and his mother married, 'for shortness,' a gentleman of one syllable named Green, whose patronymic the soft and pliant son adopted.

He had a lively recollection of the voyage round the Cape of the Dolphins, flying-fish, and the 'sherks,' and of crossing the line, of Neptune boarding the ship attended by ocean monsters and sea-nymphs, and, provided with a mixture of tar, soap, and an iron hoop, with which all those who would not 'pay their footing' were first lathered and then shaved.

Tom ranked among the light weights, although not short of stature; his face must have been unusually plump in his youth, because in his old age it was, without exception, the most remarkable make-up of folds and wrinkles, grooves and hollows, and miniature valleys, glens and mountains, that nature ever in an eccentric freak supplied to one of her sons. He used to account for his wealth of wrinkles by saying 'He fell on a gravel walk when he was a boy.' His head dress was a blue cloth cap, and in the expansive top of this he kept his pipe, match-box, and pocket-handkerchief, and stored his allowance of tobacco. He was in his person scrupulously clean. His boots, no matter how broken, always shone with the lustre of 'Day and Martin'; and his clothes, though threadbare, were ever spotless and free from dust and soil.

In his early days he was a post-boy to McDowell who kept the Imperial Hotel. Upon one winter's evening, when watering a pair of horses in the South Channel, at the slip in Hanover Street, the led horse lost his foothold, and, falling into the swollen river, dragged the companion horse, and Tom with him, and all three were carried down by the current; the horses under the South Gate Bridge and down the river until they came ashore on the green fields at Copley's Dock, and the rider to one of the bridge piers, where he was held by the force of the water until drawn up by a rope which he placed under his arms.

Tom had one failing — whiskey. In these old times a glass of whiskey, familiarly known as 'a small darby,' could be purchased for a penny; and he could always tell you whether the publican gave good or bad measure, because, as his teeth were all gone, his mouth exactly held a glass. As a boy I used to sit and watch him, with the greatest interest, eating his dinner, which he never commenced without devoutly going through the formula of grace — this was both simple, concise, comprehensive and unique, and conveyed the hope that 'God [would] bless the providers and the consumers.'

He would then select a potato of moderate size, and, putting it into his toothless mouth, would subject it to a process of rolling until it had disappeared and made room for another. His expression was so intensely comical that an eminent firm of brass founders in the city had offered him five shillings for a cast of his face, as they wanted something fresh in hall-door knockers. But he would not entertain the offer.

While in McDowell's employment as post-boy he had the oft-repeated distinction of driving condemned criminals to execution. It was then the custom to hang the culprit at, or near, the place where the crime was committed. On one occasion he drove as a postilion three such unhappy creatures in a 'calash'; they were accompanied by a priest, and Canty the hangman, and, on arriving at 'Two-pot House,' near Mallow, the first gallows was erected and the first condemned man hung: and so on, until all were 'turned off' and met their miserable doom.

These postilion rides were, however, of a varied and diversified character. On one day it was a hanging, on the next, perhaps, 'a wedding job,' with a drive to Killarney, which, in the first quarter

of the present century, was the most favoured place for the honey-
moon, Finn's Hotel, the old 'Kenmare Arms,' being the house at
which both bride and bridegroom, postilion and horses, sought
repose and found rest. His descriptions of these drives, and of the
return journeys, was full of story, when the saddle was vacated, and
the rider reclined in the comfortably cushioned carriage, after having
secured an extemporized rein which gave the horses their head, and
permitted them to instinctively follow their own way home.

On one of these return journeys Tom had laid in a supply of Old
Cork whiskey, goat's milk, household bread, and Kerry butter, and
on these he was making a frugal lunch when the horses, in an
exposed part of the road kept too close to the edge, and down went
horses, carriages and coachman, rolling over and over a steep
embankment until all were safely brought up and lodged in a bog
without hurt or harm.

But I must bring this imperfect memoir to a close. Tom lived
until he was well nigh one hundred years of age. The poor old
fellow was a pensioner of our family, and a faithful servant, 'as
honest as the sun,' but with so ardent a love of whiskey that,
although a pious Catholic, he has often assured me, in all sincerity,
that he would 'steal whiskey from the Pope.'

Cork and the Dean

John Paul Dalton

from: *The Journal of the Cork Historical and
Archaeological Society* (1892)

The life of one of the most extraordinary men that ever lived,
whether we regard his genius or his character, drew to its melancholy close in the year 1745. Jonathan Swift, conscious of his amazing
talents and knowing himself superior to nearly all the great ones of
his day, with whom he was on terms of familiarity, was yet rather
feared than admired, and those intellectual powers, which in another
generation would have advanced him to a position commensurate
with his abilities, did but serve to frustrate his desires and foil his
ambition. His character was almost as inexplicable as his genius was

great, and remains to this day a source of wide difference of opinion among the critics. The victorious champion of his country's best interests, we yet find, in the latter part of the nineteenth century, an able and delightful Irish author [Charles Gavan Duffy] who makes little of his patriotism, and implies that Swift was more actuated by his own private ends than by the public good. But be his motives what they may (and if we pry into the secret motives of all illustrious characters, the result will be found somewhat disastrous to the cause of virtue and patriotism), the good he did was great and undoubted, and deserved the warm gratitude of his countrymen, and it is gratifying to find that the Corporation of Cork were not entirely forgetful of this. The freedom of the city was conferred on the Dean in the year 1737, and acknowledged by him in a letter of which the following is a copy, which shows the miserable condition he was then in, and gives some rather amusing particulars relative to the presentation.

To the Right Worshipful the Mayor, Aldermen, Sheriffs, and Common Council of the City of Cork.

Deanery House, Dublin.
Aug. 15, 1737

GENTLEMEN, — I received from you, some weeks ago, the honour of my freedom in a silver box, by the hands of Mr. Stannard; but it was delivered to me in as many weeks; because, I suppose, he was too full of more important business. Since that time I have been wholly confined by sickness, so that I was not able to return you my acknowledgment; and, it is with much difficulty I do it now, my head continuing in great disorder. Mr Faulkner will be the bearer of my letter, who sets out this morning for Cork.

I could have wished, as I am a private man, that in the instrument of my freedom, you had pleased to assign your reasons for making choice of me. I know it is a usual compliment to bestow the freedom of the city on an archbishop, or lord chancellor, and other persons of great titles, merely upon account of their stations or power; but a private man, and a perfect stranger, without power or grandeur, may justly expect to find the motives assigned in the instrument of his freedom, on what account he is thus distinguished. And yet I cannot discover in the whole parchment scrip any one reason offered. Next, as to the silver box, there is not so much as my name upon it, nor any one syllable to show it was a present from your city. Therefore I have, by the advice of friends, agreeable with

my opinion, sent back the box and instrument of freedom by Mr
Faulkner, to be returned to you; leaving to your choice, whether to
insert the reasons for which you were pleased to give me my
freedom, or bestow the box upon some more worthy person whom
you may have an intention to honour, because it will equally fit
everybody. I am, with true esteem and gratitude, gentlemen,

Your most obedient and obliged servant.

J. SWIFT

The Mayor of Cork replied as follows to the foregoing:

Cork, *Sept.* 14, 1737

REVEREND SIR — I am favoured with yours by Mr Faulkner, and am
sorry the health of a man, the whole kingdom has at heart, should
be so much in danger.

When the box with your freedom was given the Recorder, to be
presented to you, I hoped he would, in the name of the city, have
expressed their grateful acknowledgments for the many services the
publick have received from you, which are the motives that induced
us to make you one of our citizens; and as they will ever remain
monuments to your glory, we imagined it needless to make any
inscription on the box, and especially as we have no precedents on
our books for any such. But, as so great and deserving a patriot
merits all distinction that can be made, I have, by the consent and
approbation of the Council, directed this box to you, and hope,
what is inscribed upon it, although greatly inferior to what your
merit is entitled to, will however demonstrate the great regard and
respect we have for you, on account of the many singular services
your pen and your counsel have done this your country; and am,
reverend sir, your most obedient, humble servant,

THOMAS FARREN, Mayor

The silver box above mentioned was destined to an ignoble end,
for in the Dean's will occurs the following:

Item: I bequeath to Mr John Grattan, prebendary of
Clonmethan, my silver box in which the freedom of the city
of Corke was presented to me; in which I desire the said John
to keep the tobacco he usually cheweth, called pigtail.

Father Mathew

William Makepeace Thackeray

from: *The Irish Sketchbook* (1843)

In regard of the Munster ladies, I had the pleasure to be present at two or three evening-parties at Cork, and must say that they seem to excel the English ladies not only in wit and vivacity, but in the still more important article of the toilette. They are as well dressed as Frenchwomen, and incomparably handsomer; and if ever this book reaches a thirtieth edition, and I can find out better words to express admiration, they shall be inserted here. Among the ladies' accomplishments, I may mention that I have heard in two or three private families such fine music as is rarely to be met with out of a capital. In one house we had a supper and songs afterwards, in the old honest fashion. Time was in Ireland when the custom was a common one; but the world grows languid as it grows genteel; and I fancy it required more than ordinary spirit and courage now for a good old gentleman, at the head of his kind family table, to strike up a good old family song.

The delightful old gentleman who sang the song here mentioned could not help talking of the Temperance movement with a sort of regret, and said that all the fun had gone out of Ireland since Father Mathew banished the whisky from it. Indeed, any stranger going amongst the people can perceive that they are now anything but gay. I have seen a great number of crowds and meetings of people in all parts of Ireland, and found them all gloomy. There is nothing like the merry-making one reads of in the Irish novels. Lever and Maxwell must be taken as chroniclers of the old times — the pleasant but wrong old times — for which one can't help having an antiquarian fondness.

On the day we arrived at Cork, and as the passengers decended from 'the drag,' a stout, handsome, honest-looking man, of some two-and-forty years, was passing by, and received a number of bows from the crowd around. It was Theobold Mathew with whose face a thousand little print-shop windows had already rendered me familiar. He shook hands with the master of the carriage very cordially, and just as cordially with the master's coachman, a disciple of temperance, as at least half Ireland is at present. The day after the famous dinner at MacDowall's, some of us came down rather late, perhaps in consequence of the events of the night before — (I think it was Lord Bernard's quotation from Virgil, or else the absence of the currant-jelly for the venison, that occasioned a slight headache among some of us, and an extreme longing for soda-water) — and there was the Apostle of Temperance seated at the table drinking tea. Some of us felt a little ashamed of ourselves, and did not like to ask somehow for the soda-water in such an awful presence as that. Besides, it would have been a confession to a Catholic priest, and, as a Protestant, I am above it.

The world likes to know how a great man appears even to a valet-de-chambre, and I suppose it is one's vanity that is flattered in such rare company to find the great man quite as unassuming as the very smallest personage present; and so like to other mortals, that we would not know him to be a great man at all, did we not know his name, and what he had done. There is nothing remarkable in Mr Mathew's manner, except that it is exceedingly simple, hearty, and manly, and that he does not wear the downcast, demure look which, I know not why, certainly characterizes the chief part of the gentlemen of his profession. Whence comes that general scowl which darkens the faces of the Irish priesthood? I have met a score of these reverend gentlemen in the country, and not one of them seemed to look or speak frankly, except Mr Mathew, and a couple more. He is almost the only man, too, that I have met in Ireland, who in speaking of public matters, did not talk as a partisan. With the state of the country, of landlord, tenant, and peasantry, he seemed to be most curiously and intimately acquainted; speaking of their wants, differences, and the means of bettering them, with the minutest practical knowledge. And it was impossible in hearing him to know, but from previous acquaintance with his character, whether he was Whig or Tory, Catholic, or Protestant. Why does not Government make a Privy Councillor of him? — that is, if he would honour the Right Honourable body by taking a seat amongst them. His knowledge of the people is prodigious, and their confidence in him as great; and what a touching attachment that is which these poor fellows show to any one who has their cause at heart — even to any one who says he has!

Avoiding all political questions, no man seems more eager than he for the practical improvement of this country. Leases and rents, farming improvements, reading-societies, music-societies — he was full of these, and of his schemes of temperance above all. He never misses a chance of making a convert, and has his hand ready and a pledge in his pocket for sick or poor. One of his disciples in a livery-coat came into the room with a tray — Mr Mathew recognized him, and shook him by the hand directly; so he did with the strangers who were presented to him; and not with a courtly popularity-hunting air, but, as it seemed, from sheer hearty kindness, and a desire to do every one good.

When breakfast was done — (he took but one cup of tea, and says that, from having been a great consumer of tea and refreshing liquids before, a small cup of tea, and one glass of water at dinner, now serve him for his day's beverage) — he took the ladies of our party to see his burying-ground — a new and handsome cemetery, lying a little way out of the town, and where, thank God! Protestants and Catholics may lie together, without clergymen quarrelling over their coffins.

It is a handsome piece of ground, and was formerly a botanic garden; but the funds failed for that undertaking, as they have for a thousand other public enterprises in this poor disunited country; and so it has been converted into a *hortus siccus* for us mortals. There is already a pretty large collection. In the midst is a place for Mathew himself — honour to him living or dead! Meanwhile, numerous stately monuments have been built, flowers planted here and there over dear remains, and the garden in which they lie is rich, green, and beautiful. Here is a fine statue, by Hogan, of a weeping genius that broods over the tomb of an honest merchant and clothier of the city. He took a liking to the artist, his fellow-townsman, and ordered his own monument, and had the gratification to see it arrive from Rome a few weeks before his death. A prettier thing even than the statue is the tomb of a little boy, which has been shut in by a large and curious *grille* of ironwork. The father worked it, a blacksmith, whose darling the child was, and he spent three years in hammering out this mausoleum. It is the beautiful story of the pot of ointment told again at the poor blacksmith's anvil; and who can but like him for placing this fine gilded cage over the body of his poor little one? Presently you come to a Frenchwoman's tomb, with a French epitaph by a French husband, and a pot of artificial flowers in a niche — a wig and a pot of rouge, as it were, just to make the dead look passably well. It is *his* manner of showing his sympathy for an immortal soul that has passed away.

The poor may be buried here for nothing; and here, too, once more
THANK GOD! each may rest without priests or parsons scowling hell-
fire at his neighbour unconscious under the grass.

James Hudson

Anonymous

from: *The Journal of the Cork Historical and
Archaeological Society* (1895)

'For the last hundred years no such humourist as James Hudson, of
Cork, has been known,' writes the artist-author, J. D. Herbert in his
Irish Varieties, published in 1836. 'He was the only son of a
wealthy tobacconist, and his father, anxious to have him well
educated, yet without the risk of sending him to school, had the
first tutors to attend him. Under their care, so considerable was his
improvement that he could vie with any classical scholar. To the
dead languages were added French, Spanish, Italian and German;
he had also a taste for poetry and music; wrote songs admirably, and
sang them with effect. He was, in fine, a genius of the first order,
and had a turn for mimicry and personification, unique and
unparalleled, but frolic and whim predominated, so that practical
jokes became with him the order of the day. As he grew up, he
became so entertaining in company that his parents lost the power
of keeping him at home. His contempt for domestic life and love
for social converse gradually led him into scenes the most eccentric
and inconceivable. Too late they tried coercive measures. Every
attempt of theirs failed. When his father granted him no pocket-
money he met this by borrowing; and had he been of age might
have ruined himself by *post obit* supplies. His father then had to
enforce on him early hours, telling him that unless at home by 11
o'clock he might go where he pleased. One night that he was out
until two o'clock he knocked so repeatedly at the door that his
mother opened a window and asked "Who was there?"

"Tis I, ma'am," said Jemmy.

"Oh, you unfortunate boy, why will you vex your father thus?
He won't give the key."

"Then what am I to do? He won't give me any money; and am I to walk the streets all night? I might go to the hotel, but have not means to pay for a bed."

"Oh! the Lord mend you; there is half-a-crown."

"Ah, you did not tell me in time; it has gone down into the area."

She then threw down another; and with a groan shut down the window. Jemmy picked up the two half-crowns, and rejoined his companions. Soon after this occurrence he was at a party, with his father and mother, at a friend's house, where he knew they would be induced to stay to a late hour. Slipping away unperceived he got home, and sent the servants to bed. At one o'clock a knocking awakened him, and after some time he opened the window. "Who's there?" he cried out.

"Don't you know? It is your father and mother."

"*My* father and mother! I know no such thing. *My* father and mother are in bed. If you knew *my* father you should know that he does not permit anyone to enter this house after eleven. He has locked me out after that hour. Go your way. If you make any more noise I'll call the watch, and send you to sleep in the watch-house." With these words he shut the window, and they had to sleep at an hotel. When his mother thought to keep him at home on a particular Sunday, by locking up his linen, he deliberately opened the hall door, just as the people were returning from prayers, and began to wash his nether garment before their astonished eyes. These jokes stopped his parents from contending any further with him; they found it was all in vain. Gradually freeing himself from parental control, Hudson wanted nothing now but needful supplies to enable him to pursue his favourite whim of contriving matter to excite laughter. His father kept him to a limited sum and his friends refused to lend him anything. He, therefore, applied himself to raise his finances; and by attending gentlemen at elections he became so useful that to have him at your side would nearly ensure a return; while, being of no party himself, he was free to choose, and was faithful to whatever side he was engaged.' The variety of tricks and schemes he adopted and played off, independent of squibs, crackers, speeches, satirical and humorous, songs, etc., were so numerous and vile that Herbert says he could not venture to transcribe them. 'When at one time pressed for money, Hudson wrote a song on an election then going forward in Cork, and prevailed on a friend to accompany him, both disguised as ballad singers, to sing this humorous lilt in the streets; and such an impression did it make upon the auditors that their stock of ballads was soon exhausted. They were purchased at sixpence each, and fifty shillings was realized. In this way they had a nice supper, and next day dinner and wine out of the proceeds.' Herbert relates three further instances of Hudson's audacious practical jokes, but they are too long for reproduction here. Hudson's end was a premature one. He left Cork one evening on horseback, and was found lying dead in a ditch with his skull fractured, and his horse grazing unconcernedly near him. 'Thus,' adds Herbert, 'was the witty, facetious, and admirable performer, James Hudson, whose life was a perpetual comedy, doomed to end his days tragically by a sudden and unprovided death.'

The Gargoyle and Others

Séamus Murphy

from: *Stone Mad* (1966)

The Gargoyle was always first into work in the morning. He was always waiting outside the gate for the gaffer to open up and he would be in a bad state if the gaffer happened to be a few minutes late, shifting from one foot to the other with impatience, saying: 'This is bad — this is bad! Look here, wouldn't one of ye get in the back-way and open up? We'll get nothing done today. This will put the kybosh on everything.'

Stun said to him on one occasion: 'Why do you leave the place at all? Why don't ye stay there all night and have a meal brought in to ye? If I had me way I'd chain you to the banker, you're so fond of it.'

'Now,' said the Gargoyle, 'for all your time, you're a very ignorant man. Didn't you see the job I got up yesterday? Well, I've been thinking of it all night and I have it all worked out and I'm anxious to see if the way I've decided is all right, because it often happened that I got a brainwave in bed about a tricky job and when I tried it out in the morning I discovered it wouldn't work . . . . Of course a genius like you wouldn't have any trouble about a thing like that.'

'No,' said Stun, 'when I down tools I refuse to think any more about the trade until next morning. Anyway, you get nothing for working in your sleep, so what's the use?'

'I know that, but to judge by your dial this morning you must have been working harder than me. I'd advise you to throw a basin of cold water on it before you're noticed.'

When the gate was opened the Gargoyle would rush in and off would come the coat which would be hung on a nail near his banker, on would go the apron, and his old battered hat would be shoved back on his head, exposing a troubled-looking brow. The pipe would be filled and while engaged in this ritual, which took place every morning, he would stand and survey all the men in the shed, giving them the 'once over' as he called it.

With a faint smile on his face he would look hard at Danny Melt and slowly lower his eyes until they were looking at Danny's feet. Then he would half open his mouth and look up at Danny's face in pretended wonder. Danny took an outsize in boots and was very sensitive about it, so that the Gargoyle's first approach in the morning used put him on edge. 'Isn't it awful?' he would say, 'what a man has to put up with from an ould codger like him.'

To make matters worse, if Danny went up the passage near the Gargoyle's banker, the Gargoyle would rush in a flurry to one side as he was passing, his eyes anxiously fixed on the boots. He said he suspected that Danny had iron collars on the tops of them to make sure his feet would stay in the 'floats' when he lifted them. And he said it was a wonder the Corporation allowed him to walk on the flags at all.

But one Monday morning Danny was a bit sour and he went baldheaded for the Gargoyle:

'The boots troublin' you again? Well, they're me own. Bought and paid for in the North Main Street. Not like the rags you've on ye — all bits out of a dead man's bundle!'

This hit the Gargoyle on a tender spot as he was never known to buy anything. Whenever he heard that someone connected with the craft was dead he always put in for the old clothes . . . . 'Would he call up for the bundle tonight?'

Once he arrived in the shed wearing a minister's coat and pants and a pair of light boots he had scrounged from the dead man's widow. He was the oddest thing we ever saw but he completely ignored all the remarks that were passed about his appearance. His waxen face and drooping moustache under the battered old soft hat made him look like a Chinaman. And it would be hard to describe the effect of the coat, shrunken up about his shoulders, and his trousers hitched up a few inches above the brightly polished boots.

Danny Melt said he looked like a cockroach, and someone else said he was like an old preacher and should be shouting 'Halleluiah!' We all got around him and examined the cloth and said that while it was a splendid bit of stuff, it was not suited to the trade, and that after half-an-hour he'd be like a miller with the dust. But that didn't trouble the Gargoyle, who was never known to brush his clothes, but he agreed that the boots were not in keeping with the craft. So he sold them as a Sunday pair to one of the carvers. We all said they were a bargain, except the Bish, who wanted to know if they were got honest!

'Of course not,' said Danny Melt. 'Sure, 'tis well known that he lives on plunder, and he can't deny it! When he called up to get the bundle after Nedgill's father died he put his hand in a drawer and stole a set of false teeth and flogged them for two pound ten — I heard all about it. He'd ha' been up in court if they could prove it against him. Not that 'twould make any difference to him, he'd swear blind that he didn't know what they were, that he didn't know there were such things in the world . . . . Them boots got honest? Not on your life. They walked out of some room while he was discussing poultry with the woman of the house. Did any of ye ever hear him on that subject? Ye should be out with him sometime and hear him talk. 'The Wyandotte are great laying birds but the Rhode Islands are a more serviceable and healthy fowl, and people have a weakness for brown eggs.' He would have the poor woman up in a heap in no time and he'd twist the neck of one of her pullets as soon as her back was turned. That's the Gargoyle for you!'

'Well now,' said the Gargoyle, 'you're the one to talk! You killed two ducks on the road home from Bandon and sold them when you got to Cork. And did I ask you what you got for them? Or did you offer to share with me? Oh, no! But sure, 'tis what I'd expect from an old militia man. But you lose more than you gain by trying to play the old soldier on me.'

At this Danny turned to us:

'Did ye hear that? Me playing the old soldier on him. The last time we were in Knockaderry putting up a job he did me out of a stand as nice as you like. When the people who the job was for arrived he was all about them, with his finger on his chin and he as solemn as a judge: "I got special instructions about the erection of this job, sir. The boss said that no matter what it costs or what it takes, he wanted it done well for a very particular client." Then, when he saw there was a chance of the man parting, he shouted at me to go down to the stream for a fresh bucket of water — 'twas to get me out of the way so's I wouldn't see what he got. But I could see be the way he went to work whether he got a stand or not. If he got it, 'twould be "Danny this . . . and Danny that" and "you're the best man I ever had out with me". On the other hand if he failed I could do nothing right, and he'd kick everything round him and scamp the job. And then he talks to me about being an old soldier! I was always a man!' concluded Danny, giving his head a twitch and looking at us for approval.

'You were,' said the Gargoyle, 'until Molly Mull got hold of you. I tell you she wasn't long knocking the independence outa ye.'

'Leave the wife out of it now,' said Danny, 'or I'll give the company some sidelights on Maisie and it mightn't go down so well with you. For all your scraping, you never have a tosser left after her.'

Here the Bish intervened:

'Now, Danny, don't be casting aspersions like that on your fellow-man. Remember there's a God above looking down.'

'Ah, shut up, man,' said Danny. 'The Gargoyle doesn't know how many gods there are, and I know he'll be going to a warm climate. Old Nick will give him a few years square chiselling the hobs o' hell.'

'Maybe, maybe,' said the Gargoyle, 'but I'll send for you to give me a turn, and I'll want someone to sweep the spalls out of me way.'

At this stage everyone joined in with remarks about the next world. Were the gates of heaven really gold? Or were they cut stone? Were there any quarries there? If there were not, the poor stonies would be in a bad way for want of material. Paradise for them would be plenty of the 'mealy-grey' and a shed facing south with a top light!

'Well, now,' said Stun, 'I don't know how they are going to provide for all the trades in heaven. Most of ye know poor Satan. The last time I saw him was at the finish of Cobh Cathedral. He died shortly afterwards of something inwardly. He had just come in off the road and you should have seen the get-up of him — a straw hat, a claw hammer coat, an umbrella, and on his feet a big pair of militia boots.

'Ye see, the boots were the important thing to Satan. All his life boots of all kinds had a terrible fascination for him. He was forever looking at them, examining the shape of them, the make of them, the kind of leather in them — not only his own, but everyone's boots. He was so taken up with them that when he got angels to carve, he would put boots on their feet! Not a word of a lie! I've seen those angels myself and when I joked him about them he bawled me off properly. "An' what the hell use would wings be to 'em?" said he, "aren't they serving their time here on earth? An' who knows but that they'll be on the road some day like meself . . . Anyway who the blazes told you angels haven't boots? You may be sure footwear isn't overlooked in Heaven and if it is, I, for one, have no intention of going there." So you see, Satan was more concerned with the footwear than with stone.

'So they'll have their work cut out for them in heaven trying to provide for all the trades and tastes. An' it mightn't be so pleasant to be bankered alongside some of the men that were there long ago. They'd disgrace us to judge by some of the work they left behind them on this side. We'd have to serve our time all over again.'

'It's a shame on you, Stun,' said the Bish, 'to be talking that way. Presuming to know what way affairs are conducted in Heaven!'

'Will you listen to the wet blanket,' said the Gargoyle. 'If you had your way our lives would be spent in a miserable fashion, contemplating something we know nothing at all about. Show a bit of sense sometimes, man. This "valley of tears" business gets me down. Your conversation would add years to any man, with yer "There's only the loan of us all here," and "there will come a time when we will have to make a clean breast of everything."'

'There'll come a time for a lot of other things, too,' said Danny Melt. '*I'm* waiting for the time when you'll stand a round of drinks.'

'You're welcome,' said the Gargoyle. 'Your time's your own.'

'Be the janey,' said Stun, 'how is it ye always manage to turn the conversation around to drink? They'll have to have a brewery in heaven for yeer benefit!'

'Of course they will,' said the Gargoyle, 'sure everyone knows 'tis thirsty work. Anyway there's bound to be a section of the brewery men, and without the dust they'd be idle. We'll see that the stout is in good condition! None of yer flat stout with a dash of the "Old Man" for the stonies.'

'I'm after getting an awful longing on me for a pint,' said Danny Melt, 'but I'm short tuppence.'

'A deal of a pity on you,' said Stun, 'haven't you strap at Miss O's?'

'I didn't pay her at all last week, so I wouldn't like to chance her.'

'Spin her the old yarn. Tell her you had to buy a Confirmation suit for one of the young fellas. It always works.'

'Ah, that's too old. She's fly for it. And besides I want to keep on good terms with her. She's not the worst of them at all.'

'There's sense for you!' said Stun to the Gargoyle. 'Danny doesn't want to kill the goose that lays the golden eggs. And small blame to him. Nothing like having a horse in the stable.'

'True,' said the Gargoyle, 'although there are times when you'd be tempted to slope the best of them, because between you and me, they have it well out of us.'

'They must live too,' said Danny.

'Yes; but, sure making a living out of a man's thirst is a queer business. And not alone that but they keep filling out drinks for you when you are full up, instead of lining them up against a day when a man would be broke. But, no, they're out to squeeze the last bob out of you while the going is good. They do well out of the mugs' money and of course they get to be great judges of people. Me dear man, they'd size you up in one act. When you go into one of them on a Friday night everything is done to make you feel you're doing the house an honour by calling for a drink. Yer man leaves whatever people he is talking to and comes over to welcome you. You call for a pint and he looks over his shoulder and says to the barmaid in a loud whisper: "A nice pint — and draw it fresh!" That's for your benefit and you're expected to believe that no-one else would get that special attention. Then he'll start a conversation about the craft and compliment you on whatever job you are doing — he heard about it from a man who "called at this very house last week."'

'That's them all out,' said Stun. ''Tis often I noticed the puss they have on of a Monday. You call for a drink and they get convenient deafness and you have to repeat the order while they make up their minds whether you can have it or not.'

'That,' said the Gargoyle, 'is what's known as treating you with diffidence.'

'It's about time,' said Danny Melt, 'that you treated someone to something.'

Séamus Murphy and the Tailor

Eric Cross

from: *The Tailor and Ansty* (1942)

Amongst the Tailor's many friends is Séamus Murphy, the Irish sculptor. When he proposed making a bust of the Tailor, the Tailor readily agreed, and was ready for the job on the spot.

'Damn it, man, it was ever said that two heads are better than one, and the one I have now I have had for seventy-five years and it is getting the worse for wear. Of course I'll have a new one.'

All the apparatus and materials were assembled, and the Tailor inspected them with the interest of a fellow craftsman. Ansty ignored the business in the beginning. Her only interest in it was her resentment of the invasion of the Room — 'with all the ould clay and mortar to make a new divil' — and making fresh disorder of her disorder.

The Room at last justified the Tailor's name for it, and did become for a while 'The Studio'. For an hour or so each day he posed and talked and commented. The measurements interested him and he linked this part of the business with his own craft.

'Many's the time that I have measured a man's body for a new suit of clothes, but I never thought that the day would come when I would be measured myself for a new head.'

'I think that we will have a rest for a while,' suggested Séamus during one session.

'The divil a rest do I need. Do you know that I feel it less than I did the time the whole of my body was making before I was born. There is a considerable improvement in this method. A man can smoke and take his ease and chat away for himself.'

The news soon spread that the Tailor's 'image' was being made. Even the Sheep, on his weekly visit, mentioned it.

'I did here tell, Tailor, that you are in the way of having your image made. I don't know. But I did hear tell.'

'Faith, I am,' agreed the Tailor, 'and a good strong one too. It is going to be made in bronze — the hardest metal that ever was. It was the metal that the Tuath de Danaans brought to Ireland with them, and it will last for hundreds of years.'

'Indeed!' exclaimed the Sheep, settling down a little farther on his stick. 'Tell me, Tailor,' he asked, with a show of interest, 'how will that be done?'

'Yerra, manalive. It's easy enough. You stick your head into a pot of stirabout, and when it is cold you pull out your head and melt the metal and pour it into the hole your head made. Then you eat up the stirabout and you find your new head inside the pot.'

'Indeed!' grunted the Sheep. 'Indeed, that's wonderful enough.' He settled a little more securely on his stick to absorb and digest this new information. After a while he came out of his shell again. 'They tell me that it is unlucky for a man to have his image made, Tailor. Would this be like a photograph now, could you tell me?' The Sheep has always refused to stand for his photo.

'Thon amon dieul! Unlucky! It isn't half so unlucky as going to bed. Many a man had twins as the result of going to bed, and, any-way, most people die in bed. If they had real sense they would keep out of bed, and then the death would not catch them so easily.'

'Yes. Yes. I suppose that is true,' unreadily assented the Sheep, and left very shortly after in case the Tailor might add another to his already great load of fears.

Ansty's interest was awakened when the clay began to take form. Then she was, in the beginning, afraid of it. She removed her cream pans from the Room to the cupboard under the stairs. Whatever curse may fall upon the place as the result of this latest prank of 'himself', the cream must be preserved from harm at all costs.

But, in spite of her fear, she could not resist a sally. From the safe distance of the doorway she watched the operation once or twice. 'Look at my divil! You'd think to look at him and the mug of him that he was a statoo in a chapel.' Familiarity with the sight of the 'image' gradually made her contemptuous.

Cork Echo did not like the idea at all. In the beginning it was mysterious to him, and he could not understand it. Then, when the 'image' was taking form, it roused all his religious scruples.

'It isn't right, Tailor. It isn't right, I tell you. It's a grave image and it is against the commandments. The church is against it, and all the popes.'

'Yerra, what harm! What harm can there be in a head? Didn't you make a couple of small lads, whole and entire, body, legs, head and all, yourself, and you talk about an ould head.'

Dan Bedam almost scratched his own head off in puzzlement at it. He could not understand it at all.

'Bedam, Tailor, I hear that you are having a new head made.'

'That's true enough, Dan. A brand-new head that will last a hundred years, made of bronze, the hardest substance there is. It won't be affected by the heat or the cold or the sun or the rain.'

'Bedam, that's queer. I've never heard of the likes of that before.'

'It's a new patent, Dan. They have got a new method of making people because the young people nowadays are failing at the job, and the population of the country is going down.'

'Bedam, I didn't hear that.'

'There are a lot of new wonders in the world nowadays, Dan. There's aeroplanes and cars and wireless, and now this new way of making people.'

'Bedam, but I've heard it said that wonders will never cease.'

'True for you, Dan. Wonders will never cease so long as women kiss donkeys.'

Dan disappeared on one of his errands. After a while he came back to redden his pipe and to have another look at the Tailor's own head. He did not know that the 'image' was in the other room.

'Bedam, I was thinking, Tailor, will you be able to use it? Will you be able to talk and smoke and see with it?'

'Thon amon dieul! What the hell do you think that I am having it made for? Do you think that I want to become a dummy? I tell you that when I have this head I will be a different man. You have often heard tell that you cannot put a young head on old shoulders. Well, this is what it is. I was thinking of having it done the other way at first. Of having a new body fitted to my old head, but the expense for the bronze was too much, so I am starting with the head first. Then I thought that the new brains would not be so good as the old ones. Then I thought that the old ones had done a power of thinking in their time and it would be better after all to make a start with the head.'

Dan was lost in wonderment for a while.

'Bedam, but Séamus Murphy must be a clever man.'

'Clever! I should think he is. He's as good as Daniel O'Connell and Owen Roe put together. They were good enough in the old-fashioned way, but before he's finished he'll have the whole of Ireland populated again. It's a much quicker way than the way you had of going about the business, Dan.'

'Bedam, it must be. I must tell herself about it tonight.' Dan went back to his journeying with wonder and amazement.

The daily sessions continued with interest and much verbal assistance from the Tailor. He remembered a story about a man who made a statue — but that story will not bear repetition.

'I think that if you tighten your mouth, it would be better Tailor,' suggested Séamus.

'True for you, Séamus. It's the loose mouth that does all the harm in the world. I remember a man by the name of ——' And it was another quarter of an hour before he stopped talking and the mouth was tight enough for the work to proceed.

He had one tooth left in his head. It was a very large canine which was completely useless, but of which he was very proud. It even had a name. He referred to it always as 'The Inchcape Rock'.

'I tell you that that tooth has enjoyed itself. It was no fun in its day when it had all its companions. They were the boys for you. Many's the half-gallon of porter that has swirled around that, and many is the pig that it has made mincemeat of.'

'I am going to tackle your hair now, Tailor.'

'Fire away, Séamus, my boy. Fire away. I have forgotten how many there are of them, but they are all numbered, according to the Book. But one wrong here or there won't make any difference. The divil a bit.'

Now and again Ansty peered into the room to see what progress was being made.

'Will you look at my ould shtal? Will you look at the puss on him? You'd think that he was all cream, sitting up there looking like a statoo in the chapel, and the divil doing nothing at all the time but planning lies and the shtories.'

'You'd better get yourself tidied up a bit,' commanded the Tailor in the midst of one of her commentaries.

'Whyfor should I get tidied?' she asked with surprise.

'We'll have to go and see the priest when this is done,' explained the Tailor.

'For what, you divil?'

'Thon amon dieul! don't be asking questions but do as you are told. We have to go and get married again. You were only married to the old head, and you will have to be married to the new head now, or we will be living in sin.'

'Hould, you divil!'

The day for the plaster casting arrived. The Tailor discovered all manner of possibly useful things for the job in Cornucopia. When at last the job was done he complimented Séamus. 'A damn neat job. It could not have been done better if I had done it myself.'

The cast was trimmed and carried away for the metal casting. Then Séamus brought it back to Garrynapeaka and the whole valley was invited to the exhibition of 'The Tailor's New Skull'.

It was placed on the stand in the dim light of the Studio with a dark cloth behind it. The door was closed. The guests were assembled. The stout and the beer and the whiskey were opened, and all was expectancy.

The occasion was graced by the presence of the 'Saint', another old friend of the Tailor's whom Ansty calls 'the biggest divil in Ireland — after himself', with a complete lack of reverence for the cloth. The 'Saint' made a speech on the marvels of this new wonder and opened the Studio door with a string, revealing 'The Tailor's New Skull'.

There was the rapt silence of wonder for a moment. Then Ansty, who was bored with the whole affair, and what seemed to her to be a quite unnecessary amount of fuss about nothing at all, and who had bustled and pushed through the crowd, ripped the silence asunder.

'How are the hens by ye, Johnny Mac?'

Ansty's inconsequential remark brought the assembly back to earth. The Sheep had been gazing, with eyes agog, first at the Tailor and then at the image, scarcely able to believe what he saw.

'It's devilish. It's devilish, I tell you, Tailor.' He grunted assent with his own remark, and hastened away from the house with his drink only half finished.

Dan Bedam was stirred to expression.

'Bedam!' he gasped, 'bedam, but . . . do you know . . . but it greatly resembles the Tailor!'

The Tailor himself hopped up to it and gave it a crack with his knuckles. 'There you are. A fine head. There's a head will wear out several bodies, and it will break the jaws of any flea or midge that tries to bite it!'

'Look at him, will you? Look at my ould shtal,' breaks in Ansty, seeing a chance of pricking the Tailor's latest balloon, 'my ould devil of the two heads, and the one he has already is no use by him. It's another bottom he needs, for the one he has he's nearly worn out, sitting on it in the corner all day long, and shmoking and planning lies.'

'Wouldn't you like a bust of yourself done, Mrs Buckley?' asks the 'Saint' sweetly, almost certain of the reply. 'A bust of you and the Tailor would make a grand show together.'

'Busht! Busht!' Ansty snorts with contempt. 'If you want a match for that ould devil you can make a busht of my backside!'

It was a great night. The drink flowed and the tongues were loosened. The Tailor sang and everyone sang and soon the 'busht' was forgotten. But the Tailor keeps in touch with it still. He has cuttings from the papers relating to it, and he follows it round from exhibition to exhibition in the newspapers.

Nor has Ansty forgotten. Now and again she contemplates the Tailor for a moment or two and wonders, and then expresses her thoughts. 'And to think that Séamus made a busht of that ould devil as though he was a saint in a church. The man must be half cracked. As cracked as himself. Glory be! and to think that he wouldn't settle the leak in the chimney for me, and he with the good mortar and plaster, making a "busht".'

The Death of Edith Somerville
Geraldine Cummins
from: *Dr E. Œ. Somerville* (1952)

The young and daring have not the monopoly of adventures. For the very old the mere act of living is a precarious adventure. On the journey down the nineties every physical movement taken is a hardship or an anxiety, and pain, the savage enemy, may at any moment leap from time's dark forest, clutch and kill.

About 1.15 a.m. on Tuesday morning I heard through my dreams the urgent ringing of a bell. When roused I realized there was cause for alarm — as I noted the click of lights turned on, the soft tread of footsteps, the rustle of a dress. Complete awareness registered the thought that Edith's secondary reasoning self was struggling to impose its will by holding down that other self, was striving to release the soul from the meshes of the body.

I got up, opened my door and listened. The lights were on: all was quiet. After a few minutes I returned to bed.

Time passed slowly with deep anxiety as my companion. But I heard no more sounds though I lay awake until the blue of dawn showed beneath the curtains.

Later that morning I learned from Nurse that Edith had had a heart attack during the night. 'First she breathed so loudly I thought she'd be heard at the top of the house, then her breath stopped. So I rang . . . '

Medical remedies brought her back, but it is possible that they would have been powerless if the primary self had not been strong in will and love and won.

Remarkably Edith asserted herself on the day that began with the heart attack. I spent about two hours and a half alone with her. It was the early afternoon and she was up and seated in her chair. No doze, often the refuge of boredom, was taken in that time that was occupied in a manner that pleased her and held her attention. I had reserved for this occasion a special entertainment that did not, as I had feared, fail.

Martin was uppermost in our thoughts and talk; for now 'the end of the road' seemed near.

They had travelled the same road together for twenty-nine years, and then, for thirty-four years Edith had gone on alone. But to her, Martin was an invisible presence, one within call; and this friendship and its memories remained as vivid as ever when she spoke of her to me on that last day we spent together.

My friend, Penrose Smyth, arrived in her car about five o'clock to fetch me away. I was to stay near Bantry for a few days. On her arrival Edith, in spite of the afternoon session, insisted on being wheeled in her chair to the dining-room. Ours was a cheerful, talkative tea-party, a gathering of six people, and Edith held it as the central figure towards whom the threads of the other personalities all insensibly or sensibly converged.

But Penrose fell into disfavour with her hostess when the clock made her realize it was time for good-byes. She endeavoured to sweeten the moment of leave-taking by delivering a message from a Mrs Wills about the works of Somerville and Ross.

'I have re-read your books so many times I can quote passages from them by the yard and recite them by the hour.'

Edith was not taken in by this attempted slurring over of the farewell moments. A glint of mischief came into her eyes, and was expressed in her reply.

'Will you thank Mrs Wills for her nice message and say that I am sorry she has nothing better to do than to learn my books off by heart.'

Later, Mrs Wills suitably enjoyed this unexpected response to her homage.

It was arranged that I should pay Edith a visit on Friday, 14 October as I was leaving for London late in the following week. She was apparently in good health. On Monday, 3 October, she went driving in the trap with Nurse and Mike. During the drive they met two ladies who were riding. 'Stop the pony, Mike,' said Edith, 'I want to speak to the rider of that mare.' So Mike pulled up, and she spoke to one of the two horsewomen; 'That's a very nice mare you are riding. Where did you get her? Are you going to buy her?' etc. The riders and the ex M.F.H. talked together for about five minutes, and there seemed for her a sudden clearing of sight. She showed her old, keen interest, and it was reported that she made some apt comments on the mare's points and general appearance . . . .

But a letter received from H. on Wednesday 5th informed me that Edith had been taken ill on Monday night and had 'slight congestion of the lungs.' It was not till Saturday morning that I received what seemed to be completely reassuring news. So, with my mind easy about her, I went to Cork from Glanmire by an afternoon train.

Because of the good news and owing to a busy round of shopping, Edith was not in my thoughts. But during that afternoon in spite of the need for concentration on various affairs, I was a prey to fatigue and a sombre depression; yet it was a day with a smile and not one tear — the sunshine almost continuous.

The light had a soft, caressing quality, the air was gentle and tepid in its warmth; so there was no accounting for my deepening depression as I made my way in and out among the strollers on the packed pavements. Saturday afternoon is the time for a weekly parade of people on the main street of this river-encircled city.

However, at five o'clock, as I entered a shop with the intention of making a purchase, there occurred a surprising change of mood. For no apparent reason release came to my mind. It was freed then from the heavy burden of depression, which like a great stone was rolled away.

The purchase of a beret and the paying for it is not conducive to dreamy picture making. Yet, suddenly, a mental picture displaced all else. The foreground of consciousness became filled with an animated portrait of Edith Somerville.

In appearance she looked some fifteen years younger than when I had last seen her. The silky, white hair, pink cheeks, grey-green eyes, the bright provocative glance were inexpressibly charming. The vision lingered for a few moments, then she waved her hand forwards and upwards, and the old gay radiance of her smile blessed me before she vanished. This was a strange experience in a crowded shop. But I did not associate it with death. It suggested life.

I straightened my body, and no longer walked slackly with a stoop. Now I was in a buoyant mood, freed from physical weariness and with a freed soul. This mood continued to be mine.

An hour and a half later after lightly and easily climbing the steep hill from Dunkathel station to my home, I was greeted with the news of a telephone message that had been received at six o'clock. I learned then that Edith Somerville had passed peacefully away about 3.15 p.m. that afternoon.

Was she freed from the last threads that hold the spirit to the tomb of the body, was the great stone only rolled away from the mouth of the cave at that moment in the late afternoon when I, mentally preoccupied with mundane matters, saw Edith so clearly and received from her dear self that gayest of farewells? Delusion or no, at the time the experience infused me with hope and life, with the freedom which is of the spirit that never dies.

On 11 October, an afternoon of sun and wind, her friends and her relatives filled the church of St Barrahane, and, using the local phrase she particularly fancied I said 'Goodbye now!' The 'now' conveys that the goodbye is only for the present; we would meet again at some future date.

The following extract from *The Cork Examiner*, written by Mrs Desmond Somerville, tells the last of her earthly story.

> Dr Edith Œnone Somerville, Castletownshend, great and true countrywoman of Carbery was last Saturday carried on the shoulders of her friends down the steep hill of the village she had made so much her own and up the many steps of the church. Every man of those who bore the coffin had known her all her life; every man, woman and child who followed her had grown up under

her eyes: the older men had seen her on horseback galloping after her hounds across their fields; they had
bought and sold horses and cattle with her; her roots
were as deep in the soil of her fathers as their own.

It was very right and fitting that she should go with
such simplicity, such deep affection and such true grief
to her rest high up above the harbour she had so often
painted under the Carbery skies which on the previous
evening had lit all their fires for her passing.

On Tuesday she was buried in Castlehaven Church
Yard alongside Martin Ross (Miss Violet Martin), her
beloved cousin and collaborator. On the coffin was laid
her doctor's hood, her hunting whip and horn (placed
there by her faithful and devoted friend and huntsman,
Mr Mike Hurley) and her palette and brushes — evidence
of the three great passions of her life: painting, writing
and hunting.

The service was conducted by the Bishop of Cork,
Cloyne and Ross, the Right Rev. Robert Hearn, LL.D.,
assisted by the Ven. Archdeacon Sykes.

The principal mourners were: Lady Coghill (sister),
Vice-Admiral Hugh Somerville (brother) and Mrs Hugh
Somerville; Brigadier D. H. S. Somerville, of Drishane
(nephew) and Mrs Somerville; Mrs Terence Johnston
(niece) and Mr Terence Johnston; Mr Gilbert Somerville
(nephew).

Among the many messages of condolence received
was a much appreciated telegram from Mr Eoin O
Mahony, K.M., who said: 'Heartfelt sympathy on death
of the greatest Irishwoman of her generation.'

The Most Unforgettable Character I've Met

Elizabeth Bowen

from: *The Mulberry Tree* (1986)

A great cold grey stone house, with rows upon rows of windows, ringed round with silence, approached by grass-grown avenues — has life forever turned aside from this place? So the stranger might ask today, approaching my family home in Ireland. It is miles from anywhere you have ever heard of; it is backed by woods with mountains behind them; in front, it stares over empty fields. Generations have lived out their lives and died here. But now — everybody has gone away?

No: not quite. A low wing runs out at the back of the house, and from its chimney you see, winter and summer, a plume of woodsmoke rising against the trees. And through one window, as dusk falls, the glow of firelight welcomes you. This fire never goes out; it is Sarah Barry's — or was Sarah Barry's until last spring, when she died. Since then, her son Paddy keeps it alight: he sits beside it in his chair, looking across at hers.

When Sarah, then Sarah Cartey, first arrived at Bowen's Court, County Cork, she was a girl of fourteen. She left her home in County Tipperary to become a kitchenmaid in my grandfather's house. Taking her place in the trap beside her new Master, she had set out one morning upon the fifty-mile drive. She did not know when, if ever, she would see home again. Ireland looks so small from the outside, it is hard to realize how big the distances feel: for the simple people, each county might be a different continent — and way back in the last century this was even more so. Young Sarah, face set towards County Cork, might have been driving off into Peru. Mr Bowen, towering beside her in his greatcoat, and keeping his horse along at a saving trot, was for her the one tie between the old and the new — she already knew him by sight, and by awesome name, for the Master owned large estates in both counties, and drove to and fro weekly between the two. It was on the return from one of these trips that he was bringing back with him Sarah Cartey. In his part of Tipperary, as in his part of Cork, everyone went in dread of Mr Bowen. He was a just man, but he was hard: to his wealth was added the weight of his character — choleric, dynamic and overbearing. In those days, the Protestant Irish landlord exercised more or less absolute power, and was, if he misused it, hated accordingly. Tall and heavy, bearded, genially ruddy but with rather cold blue eyes, my grandfather was typical of his class. Unlike some, he ran his estates like a man of business. Few loved him, but he was a big gun.

But so, in her way, was Sarah. From the first, it seems, they recognized this in each other, which was the reason why they got on so well. Driving along that day, she sat fearlessly upright. When he spoke she answered, cheerfully and forthright. The tears that kept pricking her violet-blue eyes were blinked back: she did not let one fall. At home, her mother and all the neighbours had told her she was a lucky girl, to get such a start — legends of Bowen's Court grandeur were current in Tipperary. So she kept her chin high, as befitted a lucky girl. If this were life, she was going to live it well. It was in the dusk, at the end of the day-long journey, that Sarah saw Bowen's Court for the first time.

When Sarah, as an old woman, told me this story, she looked at me with eyes that had never changed. Their character and their colour were set off by jet-black lashes. Laughing and ageless, these were the most perfect Irish eyes in the world. They were, I suppose, strictly her only beauty — though Sarah was as comely as you could wish. Her complexion kept into old age its vivid bloom. Her hair, curling generously round her forehead, lost no vitality as it turned white — in youth it was, like her vigorous eyebrows, dark. She was short and, since I remember her, broad and stout: she must have been thickset even as a young girl.

The Bowen's Court in which she took up her duties was unlike the silent house of today. Lavishly kept up, it was at the height of its Victorian prime. Mr and Mrs Bowen, their nine children, eight indoor servants and frequent visitors more than filled it. The eldest Bowen daughter was also called Sarah. Perhaps it was something in the tie of the name that made the two girls friends from the first, then lifelong allies. The young Bowens had been rigidly brought up: in the heart of this countryside they led formal lives. Handsome, but overgrown and pale, they lived in fear of their father. They might well have envied Sarah her spontaneity. They adored their gracious mother, but her they too seldom saw. Under the Mistress's calm rule, the household ran like clockwork.

Of the upstairs rooms — with their damasks, marbles, mirrors, mahogany — Sarah Cartey at first saw little: the basement claimed

301

her; over the dark stone-flagged floors she hurried to and fro. At first she was like a kitten, under everyone's feet, but her wits soon gave her command of the situation. Clean, strong, quick, friendly and willing — she was approved. The Bowen's Court servants, from the butler and cook down, were a hierarchy, but a good-humoured one. Some, like Sarah, were Catholics, others Protestants — 'But', Sarah told me, 'we all got on so well together, you'd never know which was which.' In that case, tempers must have been doughty, for the kitchen worked at exacting pressure: if a meal were not on his table up to the minute, the Master would 'roar aloud', at which the whole household quaked.

Except Sarah. She never quaked at the Master: she understood him. He had been out early, poor man, so needed his dinner *now*. As a rule, he ignored the servants, who for their part gave him a wide berth. But whenever he came across Sarah — staggering with her pail from the well, perhaps, or running an errand out to the garden — he would stop and ask her how she was getting on. Was she learning to like her work, did she miss her home? Looking up, she assured the Master that she was happy. The fact was, she refused stoutly to be anything else. Therefore, she kept those dear Tipperary memories locked away in her heart. But there, as a part of her inmost being, they grew in strength and power as years went by. As an old woman, she ached to go back *home*. What kept her? She stayed with us to the end. It was to Bowen's Court that she gave her genius — her genius for making all that she touched live.

Though hers was the most independent mind I have known, Sarah did not question the social order. The injustices (as they would appear now) of my grandfather's household did not strike her. Out of what might have been servitude she made for herself a creative career. Her whole personality went into what she did. I believe that 'class' to Sarah meant simply this — the division of people according to their different duties. Thus, she worked alongside the Bowens, rather than for them. She respected the Bowens because, as she saw it, they played their allotted parts in the proper way. She perceived that the Master, in his estate management, spared himself no more than he spared his men; that the Mistress's life, with so many demands upon it, was selfless; that the young gentlemen lived under discipline like cadets; that the young ladies studied, and practised the piano, as industriously as she, Sarah, scrubbed at the pots and pans. If downstairs you worked like a black, upstairs you had to 'behave' like a Spartan. Life evened up, in the long run. She envied no one, and only pitied those to whom God had given nothing to do. When she was nearly eighty, I told her she worked too hard. 'Thank God, I always enjoy myself!' she flashed out.

Clouds gathered over Bowen's Court. First, the Mistress died of smallpox — her eldest son had brought the infection home from abroad. Then, the Master married again, and his growing-up children resented the woman who had taken their mother's place. Strife and estrangements followed: all over the house one now heard angrily raised voices, or encountered sullenly shut doors. Worse was to come — it became evident that the Master was going out of his mind. The estate, lacking his grip, suffered: it began to run at a loss. When the Master died, it was found that severe retrenchments must be made; labourers were turned away from the farm, and most of the indoor servants were sent away. My father, who as eldest son had now succeeded to Bowen's Court, was hard put to it, even so, to keep things going at all. His sister, Miss Sarah, kept house for him. Need it be said that Sarah Cartey became the new young Mistress's lieutenant?

Together, the two Sarahs schemed and worked to make home what it ought to be for the others. This was always a hard and sometimes a thankless task. Miss Sarah, sensitive to the criticisms of her younger brothers and sisters, relied upon Sarah Cartey to keep her spirits up. The sorrows and terrors of the last few years had left their mark on the young Bowens; also, left will-less without their father's authority, they now hardly knew where to turn. They needed to be rallied, inspired, cheered — and it was here that Sarah Cartey came in. She became the steady dynamo of the house. From her they learned the meaning of zest for life. Her esteem built them up in their own eyes. And she understood them — her devotion was never blind. Short of money, and isolated in the great shabby house, they could easily have dropped out of society. But Sarah insisted that this should not happen; the old Master's children must keep their place. She encouraged the brothers to bring home their friends from college, and compelled the sisters to entertain. She loved to hear laughter. Meanwhile, she was doing the work of six, turning her hand to everything — cooking, laundering, scrubbing. I don't know how many times a day she plied up and down between the basement and attics. But she always had time to joke with the young gentlemen, or to help the young ladies to dress for balls. She, who had left her own mother at fourteen, never ceased to pity the motherless Miss Bowens: she supplied, in her own way, motherly pride and love. It was a lasting disappointment to her that none of the four married.

She herself did not marry till she was over thirty. Her comeliness and her fame as a cheerful worker could not fail to bring many suitors around — but she had literally no time to listen to them. When as last she did give her heart, she chose worthily. This marriage went only in one way against her dreams — it won her away forever from Tipperary. The Barrys were County Cork people: living on the estate, they were trusted employees and friends of the Master's household — and more, between Bowens and Barrys existed the foster-tie, then very strong in Ireland. One after another, the Bowen's Court babies had been sent out to nurse with Mrs Barry, who raised up alongside them a numerous family of her own. I have always heard, and can well believe, that the Barrys were descended from the Kings of Ireland — their ancestors must have been mighty over this very land before my own, Cromwellian settlers, arrived. Certainly, Patrick Barry, who became the husband of Sarah, was tall and distinguished-looking. And he was upright in character as he was in build.

The young couple set up in a colour-washed cottage on the outskirts of the estate: it faced across the road towards distant mountains, but its back window overlooked Bowen's Court, down the fields. So Sarah, even at the height of her own happiness, could still keep an eye on us — and she did. I only hope that calls from the helpless mansion did not break in too often on Sarah's years as a wife. For these, had we only known it, were to be as few as they were ideal.

At Bowen's Court there had again been changes. My father had married; his brothers and sisters had gone their different ways into the world. My mother — charming, dreamy and totally inexperienced as a housekeeper — found her new home an alarming proposition. She had been left by Miss Sarah a parting word of advice — 'Go to Sarah Barry if you are in any trouble.' At this point, I come on the scene — and as far back as *I* can remember, Sarah was with us more or less every day. To escape downstairs to the laundry where Sarah worked became my dominating idea. Happiness stays, for me, about the warm smell of soapsuds. I remember her short strong arms red from the heat of water, and the hilarious energy with which she turned the wringer — as though this were some private game of her own. Under her hand, the iron sped effortlessly over the steaming linen. I suppose all children delight in seeing a thing well done — the craftsman is their ideal grown-up. Sarah, I can see now, was divided between her love for 'the Baba' and her love for her work — one could hardly fail to get in the other's way. When I flopped into her baskets of new-bleached linen, she would haul me out with — 'Come on, now: you're too bold for me altogether!' On the best days, she used to let me 'help'. One of the pleasures of growing older was that of growing more fully into her confidence. And I grew tall fast — it was not so long before her laughter-creased eyes were on a level with mine.

Her vivid plumpness was fascinating — it went with her abundance of warmth and wit. Time was to teach me how comprehending her love could be. In those first years, as the child of a happy home, I suppose I took love for granted — it was, rather, Sarah's *amusingness* that attracted me. Her repartee could be lightning-quick — at that nobody got the better of her. And almost every day she had something for me: a surprise, a story, a secret — only for her and me.

Sarah's cottage home — with the lustre mugs on the dresser, the new-baked bread, the speckless hardwood furniture — seemed to me paradise. But, looking round it again, I found one thing missing: after that I began asking my mother, 'But why hasn't Sarah got any baby?' Other friends must have wondered the same thing — Sarah childless meant a sort of loss to the race. She herself ceased to believe that God would see to the matter — and so He did. I shall never forget the morning when Sarah called me to her in a particular tone. I could feel at once that something was in the air. She put her arms close round me; her dear breath tickled my ear as she whispered, 'Now here *is* a secret for you — God is going to send me a little parcel!'

We were away when her son was born. My father's illness kept us from Bowen's Court, so that I did not see Paddy till he was two years old. Any child of Sarah's would have seemed beautiful, but this one really was so. The sunshine of her nature seemed to have found its way into his eyes, his glowing cheeks and his golden curls. Her womanhood had been crowned as it deserved. It would have been understandable if Sarah, after her years of waiting, had been unable to bear her darling out of her sight. But in this, as in all, she was generous — she let me make off with this miracle-baby for afternoons together, climb with him up to the tops of hay-ricks, carry him off to the stream to sail paper boats. In our absence — and our visits during those years were brief — she was acting as caretaker at Bowen's Court: with small Paddy clutching her skirts she patrolled the deserted rooms. It seemed unnatural to her, then as always, that 'the Family' should be away — but she could fill the emptiness with her own summer — the radiance in which she lived with husband and child.

Then, while Paddy was still a small boy, Patrick took sick and died. I do not know how she faced out her desolation: she to whom so many had turned could now only turn to herself. Sarah was never meek; there was always a touch of fire about her goodness. Her whole being cried out against the loss. In the end she triumphed; she did not let it warp her. Only, as I grew old enough to be able to read her eyes, I could see behind their gaiety an eternal wound. For a while, her thoughts turned to Tipperary — should she not go home again, taking her child with her? But no; she was wanted at Bowen's Court — she stayed. She continued to live in the roadside cottage, though there were times when its loneliness frightened her. Often, the mountain winds roared through the trees at the back; after holidays, drunken people lurched past her door. One terrible night, she heard one man kill another — as key-witness, she had to attend the trial. Agitation made her evidence contradictory: both the victim and the prisoner had been her neighbours. 'I pitied both the poor fellows,' she said to me.

Sarah's sense of justice was strong, but personal. She felt the Law's aim should be the same as her own — good treatment for as many people as possible. What she detested in crime was its unkindness. The killing at her gate had been exceptional in being a *crime passionel*: most violence in Ireland had a political source. Her girlhood had been in the days of the Land League; she was to live through the repercussions of the 1916 Rising, through 'the bad times' that followed the Great War, through the Civil War after the Treaty, when the British had gone. Lorries crashing along with armed men rocked her house in the night; she saw horizons scarlet with burning mansions and farms; she heard reverberations from blown-up bridges. You never knew what might happen, from day to day. Through all this, Sarah never took sides. Thinking in terms of people, not of ideas, she never examined the ethics either of landlordism or British rule. When, after the Treaty, Ireland was split in twain, it was simply against *all* foolishness that she shook her head. She loved life's decent pattern of love and work — anyone who destroyed this became her enemy.

Through it all, no faction raised its hand against Sarah. Since her widowhood, she had kept herself to herself — on civil terms with all neighbours, she was on close terms with none — and she never talked: her discretion stood her in good stead. In the thick of it all, she did say, 'It would break your heart to see good time squandered away like this.'

I grew from a schoolgirl into a young woman: I married, travelled, became a writer, and enjoyed my fill of big city life. But, each time I returned to Bowen's Court and to Sarah I found that she, who had never in her life left the South of Ireland, could still make circles round me. Nothing I told her surprised her. She liked to hear about London, and, of course, about Rome — I was able to bring her back a rosary blessed by the Pope. She was alarmed when she heard I planned to go to America, for fear I should not come back — so few Irish people did. I don't think she saw much point in travel, really: why should anyone wish to move from their own place? Sarah's scepticism was good for me — like most young people, I bolted ideas whole simply because they were the ideas of my own day. Attempting to argue with her, I was forced to think.

I know that my having no children disappointed her deeply, though she was too delicate in her feeling ever to speak of this. When my father died, at the end of weeks of illness that had been agonising for him and for all of us, it was to her that I turned. Leaving his room, when it was over, I found the staircase full of spring evening light and Sarah standing there looking up, waiting for me. We sat down side by side on the stairs, and she put her arms round me — as she had not done since the day she whispered to me about her 'little parcel'. 'The poor Master . . . ' she said. Her memories of my father, reaching back, made his life complete. *I* had only known my father as my father. But she, as we sat there, saw the red-headed schoolboy, the anxious young head of the house, the proud bridegroom, the lonely man fighting breakdown for many years. Her sense of his triumphant dignity as a human being passed, without a word spoken, from her to me. It was she, a few hours later, who did the last work for him — 'You must come and see him,' she said proudly, 'He looks lovely.' She took me to see — he did. Her fingers had fluted the linen over his body into a marble-like pattern, a work of art.

I had been the only child: Bowen's Court was now mine. I could not live there altogether; our married home was in England, near my husband's work. So, in order that everything might be taken care of, Sarah and Paddy shut up their cottage and took up their quarters at the back of the house. When we *could* be there, she took charge of us and of everything. What summer holidays she gave us, and what Christmases! And what meals she cooked — once again, the big kitchen range roared, and she stood over it royally. Into those visits of a few weeks on end she helped us pack the feeling of an unbroken home life. Each time, the rooms to which we returned might have been left only yesterday. Fires burned, flowers were in the vases, and our beloved possessions (preserved by Sarah as might be the toys of children) lay where we had put them down last time.

As of old, she was all for company: to please her we could not invite too many guests. Beaming, she watched me reopen what had been dismantled bedrooms at the top of the house. She declared, 'We're like a palace again!' Sarah's idea of company, I remembered, had been formed in the stately days of my grandfather — gentlemen in tailcoats and high collars, ladies whose rustling silks swept the ground. What would she make of my friends — creatures of a changed society, of an outside world that she did not know? But at bare-limbed young women in brief skirts, at young men in slack and colourful country clothes — sunning themselves on the steps, calling out of the windows, playing wild games on wet days — she did not bat an eyelid. They were happy, they liked the house and us and her cooking — so they were all right with her. Because she loved human nature, she could move with the times. Each new guest, on arrival, came downstairs with me to be introduced to Sarah — and there were few who did not find their way down again. One was safe in tracing a missing guest to the kitchen. As one of them said to me, 'She's an education.'

What Sarah felt in her heart of hearts about my becoming a writer I do not know. Books could teach her nothing, and played no part in her life. She was used to seeing a gentleman at his desk — my grandfather at his accounts, my father over his legal documents — but she might well have considered a typewriter inhuman company for a woman. I think it was always a shock to come on me, rooted there, indoors on a fine morning or late on into the night. But her philosophy with regard to work held good: happy in hers she could not begrudge me mine. Also, I had explained to her how my affairs stood — since my grandfather's death finances had not improved: I could only afford to keep Bowen's Court if I earned money. So she saw that what I did, along with the much that she did, followed the same ideal — to keep things going.

Sarah refused to believe that this war would come. She still held the Great War had taught us the needed lesson — she was not a student of European affairs. Her optimism had kept so much trouble at bay that I think *I* almost believed it could stop Hitler. After Munich, she was all triumph — 'Didn't I tell you, now?' When, on that sunny Sunday morning, 3 September 1939, I switched off the radio after Chamberlain's voice, I hesitated at the head of the kitchen stairs. How was I to tell Sarah she had been wrong? When I had done so, she shrugged her shoulders, opened the front of the range and poked the fire. The she flashed round on me — 'Well, it won't last!'

I wish she could have lived through it. Shadows of change, anxiety, deprivation crept up on the house in her last years. I don't think she set much store by Ireland's neutral safety while my husband and I were in London, 'among those bombs'. She knew I knew she would have given the world for me to have stayed at Bowen's Court, out of it all. But her comprehension of things was too fine to allow her once to suggest that I should do so. My husband's work was in London, and my place was beside him: people she loved did not desert their posts. Beyond that, this war had for her no definable rights and wrongs, any more than a senseless family quarrel. She hated war as unkindness; she mourned it as waste.

Our visits were shorter, fewer: no friends came with us. From rooms no longer in use Sarah packed away the hangings and pictures — 'Till the good times come back.' The wing behind Bowen's Court, in which she lived with Paddy, is a row of rooms overlooking the grass-ground yard. From them in the old Master's day one had heard the clatter of horses, in my day cars being run in and out of the garage. Now all was silence. Sarah's parlour had been my grandfather's estate office: with its barred window and iron safe in the wall it was not home-like — but somehow she made it so. She hung it round with pictures that had been in my nursery, and on the hearth kept burning that constant fire. Again, she patrolled the empty block of the house, on the watch for any suspicion of damp or damage. Every day Paddy switched on the library radio, and, among sheeted furniture, he and she heard the news. Paddy, now grown up into a clever man, explained the war to his mother — but could not explain it away. Things began to run very short — coal, tea. And you had to think twice before you lit a candle.

It was in the fourth year of the war that the final assault on her came. A growth formed in her body. To her, who always had been sound from top to toe, this at first seemed a nightmare from which she must surely wake. It was weeks before she nerved herself to tell Paddy. When she did, she bound him to secrecy: *I* must not be worried — wasn't the war enough? Things got worse: she consented to see a doctor. Radium treatment in Dublin was his urgent advice. Very well: she would go, she would try it. She was not in pain, thank God.

Sarah, now nearing eighty, left Bowen's Court in the spirit in which she arrived there at fourteen — chin up, heart high, ready for what might come. Before she left she was busy: she had a great deal to see to. She went over every inch of the house — yes, it was fit for us to come back, if we chose, tomorrow. In the larder, she checked over the bottled fruit, and re-covered some dozens of jars of jam. She wished she could have made more strawberry, that was our favourite kind. The evening before she started, friends from far and near came in to bid her Godspeed. Sarah, the Tipperary woman who had always kept her heart a little detached, had to realize how well County Cork loved her. Even those who only knew her by sight, driving her donkey trap up the hill to Mass on Sundays, sent good wishes. Everyone, shyly, promised Sarah their prayers. *She* — as they all remember — was in great spirits. 'Oh, I'll be back', she laughed, 'before you can miss the time. And too grand for you altogether, after my trip to Dublin.'

She had only once — and that years ago — been to Dublin before. She said she would be a poor thing if she couldn't enjoy a journey. She and Paddy made their way down the train to the tea-car, where they declared a feast. The line, as though specially laid for her, runs through County Tipperary — all the way she sat entranced, looking out of the window at the landscape flying past in the spring light; also, she had all the fun in the world observing her fellow-passengers and their ways. But the journey's end held pain: at the Dublin hospital she and Paddy had to say goodbye.

I reached Dublin from London two days later. Sarah's treatment, with its alarming strangeness, had started — but as I walked down the ward to her bed her smile came to meet me, gay as ever. Lying there in a striped jacket, with sun falling on to the fluffy curls around her face, she looked young, almost schoolgirlish. At the same time, she was already the queen of her surroundings. She sent me up and down the beds, distributing the flowers and fruit I had brought her among the other patients. From left and right, I saw poor exhausted faces turned her way, as though imbibing strength. 'Mrs Barry's a treat for us all,' said the nurse to me. Sarah praised the hospital, saying she could not have run it better herself. During my daily visits we never, by her clear wish, spoke of her ordeal: instead, we chatted and laughed over little things. She said, 'Don't you want to know how I like Dublin?' I reminded her I still owed her a Christmas present, and she said she'd like a length for a new dress — 'with a nice little clever pattern; not too bold'.

I brought the stuff, but she never wore the dress. Just when everyone was most optimistic, when plans for her return journey had begun to be made, her heart gave out under the treatment: Sarah died. It was now, at last, that she realized her wish to return forever to Tipperary. As she had asked her son, she was buried there. Her funeral drove past the farms and gates and hedges whose picture had always been in her heart. Through Paddy's mind, as he followed, ran all those Tipperary stories she had told him over their fire in County Cork.

At the start, I pictured Bowen's Court standing empty. But that is not the picture Sarah would want you to see — and more, it is not a true one. Her presence is still to be felt there, and from no place where Sarah reigns can life turn away for long. I believe in her power to magnetize people home again: in the rooms will be heard again the laughter she liked to hear. You may say she gave her genius to a forlorn hope — to a house at the back of beyond, to a dying-out family. But I think no gift goes for nothing. She never lowered her flag; and by that she alone could make me believe in greatness. If we can play our parts in building a better world in Sarah's spirit, we shall not do too badly.

Elizabeth of Bowen's Court
Molly Keane

It is impossible to divide my memories of Elizabeth Bowen from my memories of Bowen's Court, although I would remember her always as a person, quite apart from her writing. To her friends her death is always a blank loss — and a vast loss of entertainment pure and simple.

She was a gifted and a very generous hostess, and I *can't* understand the mean quibbles of ex-guests, alleging discomforts and cold in an earlier Bowen's Court. In the twenties one bathroom and two loos were the norm, even in a big house — successors to the era of huge cans of hot water, covered in big bath towels, standing beside the hip-bath in front of the fire in your bedroom.

I quote an impression of Bowen's Court from — of all people — Virginia Woolf: 'Elizabeth's house was merely a great stone block full of Italian mantlepieces and decayed eighteenth-century furniture . . . however, they insisted on keeping up a ramshackle kind of state . . . '

How a writer like Virginia Woolf could be so suburban in her attitude to Bowen's Court is hard to understand — oblivious to the quality of what she describes as a square block of a house; forgetful of the rooms steeped in sunlight — those wonderful spaces in Georgian rooms, the 'circle within the square' in their conception — rooms to *breathe* in. Rooms so responsive to decoration they set the mind clamouring to set the purse free — which is exactly what Elizabeth did for Bowen's Court, the love of her life.

As to the comment on the furniture — that 'decayed eighteenth-century furniture' — the furniture, the glass, the silver, still in Bowen's Court during Elizabeth's years, were made to the order of the Henry Bowen who built the house in 1775, made by Cork cabinet-makers and silversmiths then at the height of their powers; the furniture was — is — Irish Sheraton and Chippendale whose strong, slender grace needs no praise.

There is such industry, such a strong skeleton of information behind all Elizabeth's work. In Bowen's Court she brings her forebears into the centre of our attention. As we read we are fascinated witnesses of their lifestyles, its grandeur and its discomforts. From diaries and letters she extracts their personalities, and these are as complex, as good or bad or doomed as any character in her novels or short stories. They still exist, their virtues, faults and follies intact.

Elizabeth was haunted by her predecessors but she wrote of them impartially, without a shadow of snobbery. She saw them with their faults and failings, men and women appropriate to their times.

The building of Bowen's Court by Henry Bowen III was not undertaken through a dross of extravaganza and vanity. It was not a folly. There was for him a light beyond that — the then reasonable expectation of a perpetual and beautiful home for unborn descendants. Alas indeed for the death of a house; saddest of all to know it was not an inevitable tragedy — pressure and panic defeated Elizabeth on the day Bowen's Court was sold.

There is an eerie shiver in Elizabeth's absolute acceptance and understanding of the lives of her Bowen predecessors. In writing of them it is as though she laughed with them, wore their clothes, ate such food as they did, saw the same sunshine or belting rain through the same high-paned windows. She was possessed. How she rid herself of the possessive power of this house is an even stranger mystery than the strength of that possession.

Perhaps, in her writing of house and family, through all the research preceding the writing, she exorcised the possessive power. I sometimes think that if one writes, even obliquely, about something good or bad, something right or wrong that one has enjoyed, or suffered, the effect of that transmission evaporates the joy, or the grief, from one's memory — from the physical system too!

Elizabeth, thank goodness, was very happy and *very* successful in the later years of her life — and always so *funny*, so entirely worthwhile.

Writing of the detractors and misunderstandings of houses like Bowen's Court, Mark Bence-Jones says: 'Such people are insensitive. Such people have never known a tall Irish house, least of all Bowen's Court . . . . Unlike the sensible, solid, Georgian houses of England, houses like Bowen's Court seem, for all their squareness, rather frail . . . . There is something dream-like and impermanent about them . . . . they have a beauty that is unique, an elusive beauty.'

Putting aside nostalgia for the beauty of that house, I would like to say something about the earlier domestic routine of Bowen's Court which has had the 'put down' I mentioned already. Quite lately I was talking to Molly O'Brien, who worked at Bowen's Court from the age of fifteen until the day the house was sold. For many of these years she was Elizabeth's cook. We met one morning at the gates of Bowen's Court — iron gates to nowhere, rusting and faltering on their hinges now, but Molly's cottage is a deep and solid house, with thick walls and sash windows in their depths. (Elizabeth gave her the cottage when she married.)

On the morning when we talked Molly's shocked refutation of the idea of aridity and discomfort ever existing at Bowen's Court gave rein to wonderful memories of her practical experience regarding the inner workings of the big old house — a house without electricity — in the early days of Elizabeth's era.

Molly's pride in those days was offended when she thought of the beautiful hospitality, the foot-baths by the bedroom fires before dinner — yes, and carrying the slops down in the morning. Cold? How cold they were! A hot stone jar put in the beds late, and a fire blazing away in every room. And the silver candlesticks and the brass candlesticks laid out at the foot of the staircase for them to take up to bed.

She asked if I remembered the brown buns made early every morning. And the salmon mousse for parties? And the big silver sauce-boats with that special horse-radish sauce in them? And the small dooney little potato cakes the size of a two shilling piece — she drew their size with a finger on the kitchen table. And Mrs Cameron would stand at the head of the kitchen stairs and call down for salt to put on them — they were very appetising with the drinks. As for breakfast — it was a full breakfast for all, brown buns and sausages and bacon and eggs. And the lunch would be as big as a dinner — and the dinners were only magnificent . . . . and all the guests coming down the staircase in their lovely dresses . . . . Molly looked away from me and across the kitchen with ghosts in her eyes.

She is a marvellous person, Molly, pretty and ageless and able; her service to Elizabeth was given with deep affection, pride, and a lot of enjoyment. Leisure was there too, and fun — Molly kept greyhounds.

What I would most like to express, to make *live* (as Mark Bence-Jones has the house, with its 38 windows, full of changing light, and its silvery stone), is the immense quality of attraction that Elizabeth possessed in such a high degree. Her looks, like the looks of the house, were elusive. I always thought she had the air of an aristocratic Elizabethan adventurer — home from the sea with a rich prize, when she had finished a book, setting out on a voyage of discovery when she was starting one. She wasn't beautiful, strictly speaking, but she dressed as remarkably as any beauty dares to, and with a careless distinction. When she came into a room the atmosphere changed. Even should one have a companion with his interest nailed and focused (one hoped!) his eyes wandered. Attention failed. He wanted to be near Elizabeth.

It was the same with young and old, with literary men, or solid country gentlemen. Once in *her* orbit, the enchantment held them.

I remember a *very* non-literary country gentleman saying to me: 'I was rather *bovvered* what to talk about at lunch. But *she* was so easy I could have been talking to another member of White's!' I think that was a charming tribute to her versatility. But it was no special effort for her: she loved men. And men's company and love were necessary to her. So were good food, and drink, and good talk, and jokes with friends. She entered into every enterprise, whether she was looking at a fairy shoe found in the mountains, or the winner of the 2,000 Guineas (owned by her great friend, Ursula Vernon), she was equally involved, and never shy of asking questions.

One loved having a drink with Elizabeth: her wits absolutely flamed, whether the drink was just before a grand dinner party at Bowen's Court — and they could be very grand and formal parties — or in a dingy roadside bar, a magic sense of the absolute importance of *enjoyment* was equally present.

She was marvellous to her woman friends, generous, forgiving, tolerant even of their youngest children. I know my children loved and relied on her: I remember her sweeping through the Shelbourne Hotel one evening, wearing a big yellow straw hat on her then blonde hair, and stopping to talk with us. After she had gone, my daughter Sally, aged 5, asked: 'Who was the lady who looked like a lovely summer evening?' I suppose it was partly Elizabeth's large, happy assurance that evoked such a comparison from one so young.

The big yellow hat was typical of her sense of the importance of clothes. Elizabeth's junk jewellery, chosen and worn with some daring, was a tremendous build-up and facade on the fortress of her looks — her ears shrank behind beautiful and preposterous earrings. That sense of importance never left her.

The last time I saw her, we were having dinner with Stephen and Ursula Vernon in a restaurant in Kinsale. It was summer time, and she was wearing a stiff, white, silk coat, faintly reminiscent of old Vienna and Strauss waltzes and white uniforms. Next year she died. But that evening we discussed seriously the question of really good expensive 'wiggies', and how much time they might save at the hairdressers. She planned to buy herself one as soon as she got back to London. I expect she did, and wore it to enormous effect, in the same way that junk jewellery seemed right and enhancing on her. Only Angus MacBean, the great photographer, ever did her style proper justice.

Apart from her genius for people and her love of giving or taking entertainment of all sorts and kinds, Elizabeth had a strongly disciplined religious side. On Sunday mornings she came into the hall just before eleven o'clock, wearing definitely less country, but not exaggeratedly London clothes. She had clipped on less vibrant ear-rings and as she talked pulled leather gloves with long wrinkling wrists on to her hands. She often walked down the drive to the little church, built by her family, at the gates. She never pressed any guest to go with her. She prayed. She sang. She listened with polite attention to any sermon. Then, back to the library and pink gins before lunch — those unforgettable martinis or pink gins in those stemless, goldfish-bowl sized glasses.

After Elizabeth's death the church was abandoned, rain coming through the roof, and dead birds in the aisle.

The chief instigator in the church's restoration — a tribute and memorial from her friends — is the Rev Dr Robert McCarthy. Derek Hill is another friend deeply concerned with the project. With the support of Desmond Guinness and the Georgian Society, they have achieved a memorial in which, because of its strength and its beauty, above all because of its escape from gloom, we have a fitting and perpetual testimony to Elizabeth.

It was Derek Hill who produced her untypically straightforward Nativity play in Derry Cathedral — an adventurous Ecumenical event to undertake in war-ravaged Ulster; crowds came to see it there, and so did the strangely diverse audience of her fox-hunting, racing and literary friends when Stephen Vernon directed the cast — drawn from the above classes — at the play's first presentation in Limerick.

Elizabeth died far too young — and if she had lived to a hundred, she would still have been too young to die. Sometimes overworked and over-stressed, she was never lonely or alone in her life, and I imagine that, if she still endures, though she is beyond her living friends, she is never short of a companion her equal in wits and stature. She is not wandering companionless among the stars that have a different birth. Companionless? Never — in this, or any, life.

Portrait of Youth III

for Lizzie Hennessy

Liam Ó Muirthile

Translated by: Ciaran Carson

An eternal cork-tipped
Craven 'A' cigarette drooped from your lips.
Trailing after you
Through your spotless palace of a house,
It was my job to look out for dust.
I liked the time — you didn't thank me for it —
When I pointed out the little mound of ash
That had fallen from your mouth.
We spent Sunday afternoons in the Morris Minor
With another childless couple.
Your husband Tom would nudge me in the ribs
For every girl we passed by.
You were given your head in our house.
Not so much a word of excuse
When, in the early hours, you'd put
Us children out of bed.
I went blackberry picking with you once,
Perched with the can on the back of your bike.
I felt ashamed when I had to get off,
As you struggled up a small hill.
When we reached the epic berries
I got stuck in a bramble of fear.
It was the grounds of a school for cripples,
Children floating in a pool together,
Arms and legs a tangle of lame branches
Hauled out by the brothers.
Yet back in the water, they are lithe as beavers,
The sap rose in their new-found healing;
I prised the nightmare bramble loose.
Perhaps I didn't care much for your company,
With your outmoded red smock and frizzy hair,
But Lizzie, for this one thing I am grateful —
You started me on this long apprenticeship,
Seeing how those scars could heal.

Seán Ó Riada in Cúil Aodha

Tomás Ó Canainn

from: *The Achievement of Seán Ó Riada* (1981)

One fine day in Dublin, when Seán, Ruth, Peadar and Rachel were
sunning themselves in the garden of their house in Galloping Green,
Seán said 'We're going to speak Irish in this family from now on'.
Ruth protested that she didn't know enough Irish. Peadar remembers accepting it (he was already going to Scoil Lorcain, the all-Irish
Dublin school). But Seán had his way and the family had been put
on a course that was to lead almost inevitably to Dún Chaoin and
Cúil Aodha and to a rural, Gaelic way of life that was to prove, I
think, intensely satisfying and productive for all of them.

Cúil Aodha is in the parish of Ballyvourney, some ten miles west
of Macroom in County Cork. It has its own chapel, school and
shops. There are approximately 1,500 people in the whole parish
and some 500 of these live in the townland of Cúil Aodha.

It was never a rich area, except in the cultural sense. There is a
school of native poetry (Daimhscoil Mhúscraí) which meets in bardic
contention annually, on the first day of the year; it is attended by
the local poets and by many others from the Munster region. They
vie with each other in producing new poems on a topic suggested
by the President of the school and already published in the local
newspapers. There has always been a great interest in singing: Cúil
Aodha has produced many famous traditional performers, some of
whom were composers of well-known songs in Irish.

One might think now that it was the natural place for Seán to
live, since he had relations there on his mother's side. (She was one
of the Creedons from near Macroom, and could play melodeon and
fiddle and sing a fine song too.) In fact, the local priest, an t-Athair
Donncha Ó Conchuir, who was involved in Seán's decision to move
to Cúil Aodha, sees it as almost fortuitous.

He gave Seán a lift one day near Ballyferriter, during the period
that the family were staying in Seán de h–Óra's house in Clochar.
Ó Riada was walking back to the house with a parcel of meat under
his arm. About a week later Seán contacted him and told him that
he had a teaching post in University College, Cork, but did not want
to live in the city. He said that Dublin hadn't suited him when he

lived in it and he was quite sure that Cork wouldn't either — he wanted to be somewhere in the country. He said he would love to stay where they were in Kerry, but it was too far from Cork. He wanted to know if there was any chance of a house for rent or sale in Cúil Aodha.

An t-Athair Donncha remembered that Máire Ní Cheocháin of Ballincollig was selling their house in Cúil Aodha (her father was the late Dónal Ó Ceocháin, regarded by many as the saviour of the Irish language in the region). Next day Seán went to Cork with Seán de h–Óra and Seán Ó Ciomháin; when he returned that evening he was the proud owner of the house in Cúil Aodha.

Their entry into the new house was not without a certain drama, though they were not aware of it themselves until the man concerned — Seán Sweeney — gave them the details a long time afterwards. They had stopped to ask directions from him where he was working on the road. They asked if this was Cúil Aodha and where Dónal Ó Ceocháin's house was. After a short conversation, they went to take possession of their new abode.

It was well that they had put their questions in Irish, for Seán Sweeney, who was somewhat of a Republican and a staunch Irish language man, told them later, when he became a valued friend of the family, that only for the fact that Seán Ó Riada was the man he was and had spoken to him in Irish he would have carried out his original intention, which was to make sure that they did not stay more than one night in Dónal Ó Ceocháin's house!

Becoming a part of the local community took a long time. The five children attended the local school and impressed everyone by speaking Irish all the time. The area, of course, was in the Gaeltacht, but some families did not speak Irish to the children. It is ironic that many people credit Seán with being largely responsible for the swing back to Irish among the present younger generation. Ruth got to know many of the locals while shopping and looking after the children, but Seán did not really mix with the community in the first year. He would have a drink in Williams' bar during the day, but would not appear there at night when the locals frequented it.

Some of them knew him already through meeting him at the Oireachtas in Dublin — people like singers Pádraig Ó Tuama, Diarmuid Ó Riordáin and Seán Ó Duinnín. Others were distant relations on his mother's side — the Ó Súilleabháins, for example, who were staunch supporters of all his musical involvements with the Cúil Aodha community. One of the Ó Riadas' first friends, and a regular visitor to the house, was their neighbour, Tadhg Ó Mulláin. He was a lonely old man when they came, living by himself, his wife dead and his family gone. Their arrival seemed to give him a new lease of life. Seán and Ruth were very fond of him and he taught Seán a lot about the place, its people and folklore. He came to be regarded as a mixture of 'ganger' and agricultural adviser when jobs were to be done by the Ó Riadas — such as setting potatoes. He was always brought to the house for the weekly practice of the choir — Cór Chúil Aodha — and was chairman of the evening's proceedings.

The formation of the choir, and Seán's involvement with it, was undoubtedly his most important step in coming to terms with the local community. An t–Athair Donncha Ó Conchúir remembers Seán suggesting to him that he should collect some of the 'lads' and form a choir to sing in the chapel in Cúil Aodha. He suggested that they could practise in the Ó Riada house and might begin the following Thursday. An t–Athair Doncha sought out the singers — Seán had said that ten would be plenty — and was surprised when they agreed to come to the house. He realized later that it was not so much the music that inspired them, but a considerable curiosity about the Ó Riada house and the rather unusual 'fear an tí', Seán himself. This would have been about a year after Seán's arrival — that is, in the winter of 1964.

The first night was devoted to good talking, and drinking too. It was so successful that all agreed to return the following week. Their primary aim was to sing at benediction, which was held once a month. They learned 'O Salutaris' and 'Tantum Ergo' and Seán went to great pains to ensure that they all understood every word. Some of the time was spent in discussing a nice Irish turn of phrase to translate the Latin and all the experts joined in the discussion. This was the pattern of the weekly practice over a few months.

It was easy to get them to sing in Ó Riada's house — it was quite another thing to get them into the chapel to sing. Eventually about ten o'clock on a winter evening they made their way there and had their first practice in the proper setting. 'Mo Ghrá–sa mo Dhia' was then added to their repertoire and singing at Mass was suggested. They learned a new entrance hymn composed by Seán and wanted one for the end of mass. It was Tadhg Ó Mulláin who suggested that Seán put music to a prayer which he then recited — 'Réir Dé go nDéanam'. A Communion hymn was suggested, too, and this really marked the beginning of the first Ó Riada Mass, 'Aifreann Sheáin Uí Riada', though a year or more was to elapse before the Mass was in the complete form that is now so familiar. It was all done bit by bit; he made sure that they learned each new hymn well before they sang it at Mass and then let them familiarize themselves with it before bringing forward the next new piece.

I can remember getting a Christmas card from Seán at this time with his newly composed 'Ár n–Athair' reproduced on it. I think he was very proud of it and of the choir; I remember him talking enthusiastically about both.

Two of the hymns from the Mass illustrate Seán's desire to make it a true 'Mass of the people'. The first is 'Gile Mo Chroí', which uses the air of the traditional song in Irish 'Sa Mhainistir Lá'. The story of its adoption by Seán Ó Riada was told to me by Seán Ó Sé and is worth retelling here.

On one of Seán Ó Sé's visits to Cúil Aodha to practise for a radio programme, Seán Ó Riada played him tapes of what he considered to be outstanding Munster singers. One of them was Muiricheartach Ó Sé of Adrigoole. Ó Riada was astonished and delighted when Seán told him that the singer was his uncle. They arranged immediately to pay him a visit and had a great day of seanchas and song. Seán Ó Riada recorded a number of the songs, including 'Sa Mhainistir Lá' and spoke highly of Muiricheartach's knowledge and musicality.

Some years later Seán and Ruth attended Muiricheartach's funeral and in conversation with Seán Ó Sé afterwards it transpired that Ó Riada had used Muiricheartach's version of 'Sa Mhainistir Lá' for his setting of 'Gile Mo Chroí'. Seán Ó Riada was making the point that even though his uncle's songs were no more, one of them still lived in 'Aifreann Uí Riada'. Seán Ó Sé had not, till then, been aware of this. In fact, the song had been recorded from the same singer some twenty years previously by Liam de Noraidh, in a version which is almost identical with the air of 'Gile Mo Chroí'.

I think Seán Ó Riada was profoundly influenced by his sojourn in Dún Chaoin, particularly when he stayed with the singer Seán de h–Óra. He used the air of one of that singer's songs, 'An Brianach Óg', for the well known hymn from his Mass, 'A Rí an Domhnaigh'. This air itself is related to that of the jig 'Túirne Mháire'. The air used by Ó Riada is somewhere between that of the song and the jig. As in the case of 'Gile Mo Chroí', the love-song text about the meeting of the singer with the beautiful lady and his invitation to her to join him

in a drink as he promises marriage is replaced by Tomás Rua Ó
Súilleabháin's noble lines in 'A Rí an Domhnaigh':

An Brianach Óg

Is lá breá gréine, 'smé dul ar aonach
Ag ceannach béabhair de'n fhaisiún nua,
Do chuala an spéirbhean, sí ag caoi ina h–aonar
I mbriathraibh Gaoluinne, ó is deise beol.
A chuid 'sa lao ghil suigh síos taobh liom
Se chughainn daorphuins is beam ag ól
Is go deimhin más féidir ár gcol do réiteach
Go mbeair mar chéile ag an mBrianach Óg

A Rí an Domhnaigh

A Rí an Domhnaigh tar le cabhair chugham
Is tóg in am ón bpéin mé.
A Rí an Luain ghil bí-se buan liom
Is ná lig uait-se féin mé.
A Rí na Máirte, a chroí na páirte
Déan díonadh lá an tSléibh' dhom,
A Rí Céadaoine saor ó ghéibhinn mé,
Cé fad óm' chaoimh-ghein féin mé.

Young O'Brien

On a bright sunny day, as I was going to a fair
To buy a beaver hat of the latest style,
I heard a beautiful lady lamenting all alone
In words of Gaelic that she knew well.
'My sweetest darling sit down beside me
Here's the best of punch and let us drink
And if we can settle our differences, love,
You will be the wife of young O'Brien.'

King of Sunday

King of Sunday, come to my aid
And take me in time from pain.
King of bright Monday, stay with me always
And never let me be parted from Thee.
King of Tuesday, my gentle heart,
Be my protection on the Day of Judgment.
King of Wednesday, free me from bondage
Though I am far now from my own gentle birth.

(translated by Bernard Harris)

There was some early local opposition to the singing at Mass. The congregation was not used to it and some of them would have preferred to be allowed to say their Rosary in peace as they had always done. The vernacular was not yet completely acceptable. In fact, Cúil Aodha, in using the Ó Riada Mass, was away ahead of most places in adopting the vernacular. The composition of the Mass continued, an t–Athair Doncha suggesting a poem he had learned at school, 'Ag Críost an Síol', as an offertory hymn. Seán set it to music and followed it with 'Is naofa, naofa' and 'A Uain Dé'. Eventually the Mass was complete and I remember Seán's undisguised pleasure a considerable time later as he showed me the very first copy of 'Aifreann Uí Riada', which he had just that day received.

Seán was unusually conscientious about being on time for the Mass and hardly ever missed a Sunday. It happened on a certain occasion that he was unavoidably absent on two consecutive Sundays and a woman started the rumour that the bishop had forbidden the singing at Mass. She was one of those who felt that it was all some sort of blasphemy! But it did continue, and as people got used to it they made their own of Seán's Mass. I can remember being pleasantly surprised, on a number of visits there, by the involvement of the congregation in the singing. It was something I had not experienced elsewhere. Séamus Ó Morain, one of the older members of the choir, could always be heard. He could not resist joining in when the singing started.

Seán became very interested in the Easter ceremonies and told an t–Athair Donncha that he had not realized before just how rich they were — particularly those of Good Friday. The choir would sing 'Caoineadh na dTrí Muire' at the adoration of the cross and 'Regina Coeli' was always sung on Easter Sunday, as Seán was very keen on having something in Latin.

An t–Athair Donncha, who visited regularly and had long nights of chat with Seán by the fireside, feels that Seán had a deep faith and that his atheism or agnosticism was almost a pose for the benefit of his Dublin friends. Coupled with his faith was an almost equally deep superstitiousness. This was an inheritance from both his mother and his father. In her early days of marriage his mother visited a fortuneteller in Adare, who told her that she would lose a lot of children; that childbearing would bring her great pain and sorrow; that she would eventually have two children, one of whom she would see become famous, and, finally, that she would live to see one of her children die.

Seán himself had a *fís* or *aisling* (a 'vision') when he was young, of a woman approaching him along a road in the evening. It was only as she passed him that he noticed she was walking a few feet above the ground. He ran home in terror and his mother later said that his hair started to turn grey from that day.

In Cúil Aodha his superstitions were maintained and he was always very careful to arrange who would enter their door first at New Year, so that it wouldn't be a red-head; his son Eoin (who could be described as a kind of red-head) incurred his wrath on one occasion by straying outside just before midnight to answer a call of nature and returning by the back door just before the pre-arranged 'good luck' visitor entered. He was also nervous about whom he might meet as he started a journey, in case there was a bad omen involved.

Death was something he seemed to think a lot about. I can remember talking to him the day he had been in to say goodbye to his very good friend, the singer Pádraig Ó Tuama. Pádraig himself knew that he was dying. It was a noble death — he had his friends coming to take their farewells for the last few days and he was giving them all good advice. Seán went in to see him and was trying on the one hand to prevent him dying and on the other, to find out what he could see before him on the other side. Seán was deeply impressed by Pádraig's philosophy about the insecurity of life. 'Cá bhfuil do léas, a dhuine; (where is your lease, man?)' was Pádraig's question when Seán tried to convince him that he could live. This lack of tenure was always at the back of Seán's thinking about life.

Peadar remembers seeing him crying at the death of Tadhg Ó Mulláin, his friend and neighbour.

There was singing at the funeral of Pádraig Ó Tuama: Gobnait Bean Uí Dhuigneáin told me how it came about. She met Seán Ó Riada at Pádraig's wake and in conversation she confessed to being disappointed that there had been no singing at the funeral of her father, Seán Eoin a' Bhab, a famous singer who had died recently. Seán asked her what could be sung at a funeral and she suggested 'Seán Ó Duibhir a' Ghleanna'. That in fact was what Seán played at Pádraig's funeral. It was at Séamus Ó Muineacháin's funeral that 'Gile Mear' was sung for the first time locally. It was also sung at Seán's own funeral and at Ruth's as well.

People in Cúil Aodha could see two Seán Ó Riadas — one who hob-nobbed with ministers of state and even the President of the country, and the other who joined with them in having a drink or a session of music or perhaps being host to all of them in his house for the 'station'.

It would be difficult to catalogue all the ideas and schemes he was a part of in Cúil Aodha. The only common denominator was that Ruth accepted them all and joined in them where she could, even though she knew they might not last too long and could even put herself and the family in the poorhouse. She was his support at all times.

The advancement of Cúil Aodha was behind most of the schemes. At one time he had Government ministers interested in aerial spraying of land and crops; at another time he formed a local gun club and was going to restock the lands — this last caused tremendous local opposition among the farmers, which has hardly yet subsided. He had the Government plagued with requests for factories in the area and had even planned an extensive hotel with the most modern amenities. There was no doubt that Seán saw himself in many ways as the leader of the local community and felt a responsibility to help. This provoked a mixed reaction — one of pride in his achievements coupled with a certain native suspicion of him at times. In the early days there was also some envy among those families who felt that their own stars were being eclipsed by this talented newcomer.

He founded a film company, Draíon Films, employing a number of people and building a studio on to his house. The idea was to make television films. In fact some of the 'Aililiú' series, in which he was involved as presenter, were made in Cúil Aodha. Equipment was bought or hired and at one stage there was a large crane in the

Ó Riada front garden. It was never too clear to us what its function was!

His attempted 'coup' of the school of poetry — Damhscoil Mhúscraí — was intended to bring it up to date and involve young people and poets from outside the area. He invited musicians from Dublin and Cork with the idea of changing its atmosphere of staidness to one of life and merriment. RTE came along as well to film the proceedings.

My own memory of the Ó Riada household is of a place which always had a welcome, whether you dropped in unexpectedly or had an invitation. I remember an early visit our family made on Seán's invitation. We had a fine tea and chat around a large table. I can remember his talk of maintaining contact between Cúil Aodha and Irish-speaking families like ours in Cork. We had a few tunes then — Seán on fiddle and myself, surprisingly, on accordion. I say surprisingly, because Seán had delivered himself of a tremendous attack on the accordion in Irish music in his radio programme 'Our Musical Heritage', some time before that. In the circumstances our duet was 'interesting'.

I remember another visit after the Damhscoil. Seán Ó Riordáin and myself were in the sitting room and Seán Ó Riada was pouring us both a drink of a local, pretty unmentionable brew. I refused it and they were both quite angry with me. They were even more angry when I pointed out to them the mark the bottle was making on the piano varnish. I indicated that I was not keen to have that sort of damage done to my inside. Their anger surprised me a lot at the time, as I was normally on very friendly terms with both of them, but time has a way of making some things clear.

I attended a lecture/recital given by Seán in the hall in Cúil Aodha. The occasion was a kind of festival to celebrate the memory of Martin Freeman who had collected songs in the area some forty years before. I knew Seán was very excited by the Freeman collection. It was his friend (and collector) Seán Ó Cróinín, who then lived in Macroom, who had introduced him to it. Seán played various pieces from it. One of them stands out in my memory; it was 'Aisling Gheal', which I had not heard before then. There was considerable discussion after the lecture. I thought the most sensitive request of the evening was made by the man who had travelled from Cork with me — Mícheál Ó Ceallácháin. He simply asked that Seán play 'Aisling Gheal' again, which he did. It was a perfect end to the evening. Most of the audience were from Cúil Aodha and Seán was very much at his ease among his own people.

Seán Ó Sé remembers Ó Riada's first reference to his West Cork background when they were in Dublin recording 'Rhapsody of a River', with the RTE Symphony Orchestra. They had made a first recording of a song — not very satisfactorily — and Seán Ó Riada leaned across from the rostrum he was on and said encouragingly to Seán (who was singing with a full orchestra for the first time) 'Don't mind this shower (pointing to the orchestra) — just remember that your grandfather and mine sold *bonavs* together in Ballyvourney Fair'.

There are many stories of Seán Ó Riada's procrastination, followed by the most tremendous panic to make a deadline. Seán Ó Sé was involved in one of these and told me the story. It seems that Ó Riada was commissioned to write the music for an American film called *John F. Kennedy's Ireland* and asked Seán Ó Sé to sing a few songs for it. He showed a rush of the film which he had been sent from America and it started with a couple separating on a beach as the man went off to America. The theme song selected by the Americans was 'Goodbye Mick and goodbye Pat, goodbye Kate and Mary — the anchor's weighed and the gangplank's up and I'm leaving Tipperary'.

They were in Cúil Aodha rehearsing this song when Seán Ó Riada put his hands down on the piano and said that it wouldn't do as it was too stage-Irish; he wouldn't have it. The problem was, of course, that it was to be recorded next day in Dublin with full orchestra.

Seán had no phone then, so they went back in the car to Cúil Aodha Post Office. Dónal Ó Scanaill was inside and Seán asked him rather casually to get this number in Palm Springs in America. Dónal, equally casually, asked Macroom for the Palm Springs number and got it very quickly. Everybody, including Seán Ó Riada, was enjoying the drama of it all. The contact-man in the hotel was wakened, to be told by Seán that 'Goodbye Mick, Goodbye Pat' would not do and he explained why. The American replied that, in fact, they were thinking of 'The Shores of Amerikay'. Seán said 'fine', put down the phone and negotiations were ended.

It was only when they were back in the car that Ó Riada suddenly said 'Íosa Críost, what's the Shores of Amerikay?' This was before it had been re-popularized. Seán Ó Sé did not know it either, but felt that Johnny Murphy's father might know it. Johnny lived about 25 miles away at the Blackstone Bridge in Cork. It was now about ten o'clock at night and Seán Ó Sé was despatched with a tape recorder to see if the song could be found. The Murphy's were all in bed when Seán reached the house. Johnny was awakened first and then his father, Mike, a very old man. He thought they were all mad to be wakening people up in the middle of the night for a song.

He said he knew the song and began to sing into the tape, much to Seán's delight — only to stop after one verse. He had forgotten the rest and couldn't recall it. Still, the problem was half-solved. Johnny suddenly remembered a bundle of *Ireland's Own* that they had in the bedroom. These were searched and sure enough, 'The Shores of Amerikay' was there.

Seán Ó Sé borrowed it and set off for Cúil Aodha again, reaching it about one o'clock in the morning. The song was played and Seán Ó Riada liked it. He wrote it out for Seán, who had the job of learning it for the next day.

Seán reached home in Cork about half past two in the morning and aroused the household as he played the piano and learned 'The Shores of Amerikay' before going to bed for a few hours. He then drove to Dublin and made his way to the St Francis Xavier Hall where the orchestra were rehearsing. As he walked in the door he could hear the strains of 'The Shores of Amerikay' in a full orchestral setting coming at him.

Ó Riada had spent the night doing the arrangement for orchestra. He then drove at speed to Cork to catch the early train to Dublin, where the copyists were waiting to write out the parts.

The film was shown, I think, at the Cork Film Festival, but never went on general release, thus frustrating another of Seán's dreams of riches and comfort for the rest of his life. He had similar dreams about buying a hotel in Killarney and playing the piano for the thousands who would throng to hear him. Peadar remembers him coming home one evening and discussing with him how he could tell Ruth that he was about to buy the hotel.

But, 1971 came unexpectedly. I visited Seán that summer in the Bon Secours Hospital in Cork as a member of our small B. Mus. class. He was in good form and was enjoying our visit. His mother, who lived nearby, came in to tidy up the place and rearrange his pillows. He joked about her fussiness and it was obvious that they got on well together. We were shocked to hear some time later that he was very seriously ill.

An t–Athair Donncha remembers being called to the hospital in Cork to be told that Seán was very ill and wanted to see him.

The family were there already. Seán sent out for him and said to him very simply: 'Déir siad liom go bhfuilim go h-olc, ach nílim ag géilleadh fós. Déanfadsa mo dhícheall teacht as. Ach téir-se anois go dtí an séipéal, faigh an naomh-shacraimint, tabhair faoistin agus comaoine dom. Cuir an ola dhéanach orm agus is cuma sa diail liom ansin.' (They tell me I'm not well, but I'm not giving up yet. I'll do my best to come out of it. But go to the chapel; get the blessed sacrament; give me confession and communion. Give me the last rites and I don't care then what happens.)

Peadar and an t-Athair Donncha spent a week together in the hospital in London with Seán. An t-Athair Donncha then had to return home. It was obvious to both him and Peadar that Seán knew he would not be coming back alive to his beloved Cúil Aodha, though he did not say so explicitly; it was clear nevertheless, from some of the directions he gave to Peadar.

Seán Ó Sé was asked to go to Seán's parents early on Sunday morning, October 3rd 1971, to tell them the sad news. His mother came to the door and before Seán could speak she said 'I know; he's gone.' Her first worry was for her husband who was at Mass. They took him from the Church and they all attended Mass in Ballinlough, which was Seán Ó Sé's parish. They arranged to have Seán Ó Riada prayed for at the Mass there. After breakfast they went to Cúil Aodha, saying the Rosary for their dead son as they travelled.

Séamus Murphy, the sculptor, had been asked to make Seán's death-mask. He asked me if I could give him a lift to Cúil Aodha from the Airport with the funeral and assist him with the death-mask. After the ceremony that evening we went back with the undertaker who opened the coffin for us and locked us into the chapel. When the death mask was made he returned to close the coffin.

I had the very last look at Seán Ó Riada, back again with his own people.

Eoin 'Pope' O'Mahony

Hubert Butler

from: *Escape from the Anthill* (1985)

There is still every year a commemorative service and a dinner in
Dublin for Eoin O'Mahony. He was known to everyone from his
schooldays onward as 'the Pope', but why this was so no one knew.
He was a great Irishman whose greatness lay in a field that he had
made peculiarly his own.

When he died in 1970 I wrote an appreciation of him in *The
Irish Times* and, as he is still remembered, I will repeat it here. I had
a special reason for admiring him which I did not express at the
time. He had seen in the extended family a blueprint for what life
might one day be like. Perhaps some generations or centuries from
now groups of people, linked together maybe as kinsmen, maybe as
neighbours, will feel a special responsibility for each other, based on
a closer knowledge and affection than is possible in our faceless and
centralized society.

In forming the O'Mahony Society, Eoin was following an ancient
pattern. The O'Mahonys had been a closely knit Irish clan, which
history had dispersed. In contrast the Butlers were merely a group
of families, sometimes closely, sometimes remotely, sometimes not
at all related. Yet when the Butler Society was formed we discovered
for ourselves French and German cousins, and there were inter-
marriages. We had the advantage of the O'Mahonys in the abundance
of our historic records, which reach back to the first coming of the
Normans. The Butler Society started when the sixth Marquess of
Ormonde gave Kilkenny Castle to the Irish nation, the O'Mahony
Society much earlier. Yet despite all their differences the two societies
developed along parallel lines. We felt we were exploring the past in
order to illuminate the future. Eoin wanted to restore richness and
variety and friendship to lives that our civilization has sterilized and,
within the compass of one man's powers, he succeeded.

Eoin never had any great triumphs or disasters and yet he liked
pomp and ceremony and relished life's vicissitudes. But he kept his
celebrations small and personal and on a do-it-yourself scale, and he
used pomp and ceremony not to magnify the great but to make
ordinary people interesting. If one went to one of his gatherings or

one of those dead parties which he brought to life by attending, nobody was a spectator, everyone was a participant. Nobody came away feeling he had surrendered to mass banality, as can happen at those public functions where everything proceeds smoothly towards a well-regulated climax. At any event that Eoin organized, the Organization Man, whom American sociologists rightly regarded as the Satan of the sixties, was sure to be routed ignominiously, and the Natural Man would take over. Eoin had such faith in him that he could make the sketchiest of plans, change them at the last moment and sweep on, not to the anticipated conclusion, but to an even better one.

I only attended one O'Mahony rally, but it had a wild spontaneity, a happy, confident chaos that must have had years of practice, megatons of spiritual buoyancy, behind it. Only a great artist in social intercourse could have brought it off.

Eoin had issued hundreds of gold-embossed invitations to the O'Mahony rally at Dunmanus Castle in the name of the Vicomte and Vicomtesse de O'Mahony, a nice young barrister and his wife, who lived at Orleans. The Vicomte was the elected Chieftain of the Clan, and probably owed his election to Eoin, who did not bother to tell him about the invitations.

A shower of them fell on Fleet Street and a reporter from the *Daily Express*, attracted by the idea of an invitation from a vicomtesse to dance in an ancient castle on a remote promontory in West Cork (he swore that the word 'Dancing' was written in the left-hand bottom corner), had packed his white tie and tails and, taking a day off his holidays and a ticket to Cork, had arrived at Dunmanus at the same time as ourselves. An English family with a tent and a caravan were encamped within the castle ruins and had just before been astounded by the arrival of an advance detachment of clansmen, bearing on long staves the banners of the O'Mahonys, and of all the nations that had given them refuge in the days of their exile.

They had planted their flags all around the caravan, and very soon a thousand other O'Mahonys had followed them and the small alien encampment, amazed but entertained, had been politely and totally submerged. Soon Eoin was in the thick of it all, booming eloquently in three languages, kissing continental hands, explaining and introducing. The O'Mahony rank-and-file and their friends were then planted on one side of a broken-down moat and the Vicomte stood on the other with Eoin beside him to interpret.

'I have to apologize,' began the Vicomte in high good humour and in French, 'that this is not my castle, and that it has not any roof, and that we are not able to dance in it, and that it wasn't I sent out that invitation.' Eoin translated all this jovially, and then we quickly passed on to serious matters, the long history of the O'Mahonys of Carbery and Kinelmeaky, their kinship and rivalries with the O'Sullivans and MacCarthys. Only the journalist sulked. When there was a pause in the narrative he went up to Eoin and said: 'I understood there was to be a dance.'

'Well,' said Eoin, 'there's an excellent hotel in Skibbereen. Very nice people indeed, and, if you tell them you want to dance, I am sure they'll be delighted.' Eoin was then swept away by his kinsmen, and the journalist went and sulked on a lump of fallen masonry. He grumbled to some bystanders that he had been brought to West Cork on false pretences, that this was his holiday, not a job. But soon he observed that the O'Mahonys were entertained rather then touched by his misadventure. They were pointing him out to each other — 'Do you see that fella? Did you hear what he has in his suitcase?' — and he saw that he was becoming a stock character in a new version of a traditional Irish story, the innocent Englishman, who had never heard of Pope O'Mahony.

So he moved off to Skibbereen and, drinking himself into a good humour in the hotel, wrote a charming account of the rally for the London daily.

That was a typical O'Mahony occasion. It was an everyday setting, the ruined castle, the rocky shore, the drifts of bog asphodel, the gorse, the pools of water lilies, white as well as orange. And there were everyday people there. There were solicitors from Cork and a garage proprietor from Killarney and hospital nurses and a camp counsellor from Massachusetts. More notable was Rev. Jeremiah O'Mahony from Palm Beach, who was President Kennedy's chaplain and pronounced his name O'Mahóney. The most surprising clansman from America was coal-black. Or could he have been like myself a mere O'Mahonyphile?

Without the magic of Pope O'Mahony to fuse us and transmute us, it would have been the dullest of sea-side outings. But like a watchful cook stirring the jam, Eoin was introducing them all to each other the whole time. He could glamorize even the dullest. This one's aunt had swum the Channel, that one's brother had been in the San Francisco earthquake or as a girl she had known

Fanny Parnell. Sometimes a stray sentence expanded into an immense anecdote, breeding other anecdotes, startling and complex but never malicious. If one of them were to end sadly like 'then the poor fellow took to drink and fell down a lift shaft in Las Vegas', it was like a wreath laid on a tomb. To be remembered by Eoin was to be honoured.

His great genius was to use the splendid in the service of the simple. Once I made myself hugely unpopular by flouting received opinion and became a local pariah. My friends rallied to me, but Eoin's support was the warmest and characteristic of him. He packed a shirt the next day (I think it was a shirt, not pyjamas, in that small, odd brown paper parcel), bussed to Naas, and hitch-hiked the rest of the way. He came out from Kilkenny on a creamery lorry, whose driver, he found, was a distant cousin of his. I do not think that we talked about the row at all. He was not much interested whether I was right or wrong. As with the prisoners, whom he was always trying to release, he had his own way of judging matters and always liked official verdicts to be reversed, and personal ones substituted. The next morning he spent at a table in the porch writing about thirty letters on notepaper headed with the address of a smart Dublin hotel, at which he often entertained his friends. For even if it meant starving himself later he liked to be hospitable in the grand manner.

One, I observed, was to a Cardinal, one to Her Serene Highness Somebody. He was asking them no doubt to use their influence, either for the prisoners or for building a bridge to Valentia Island, and some may have been letters of introduction for friends going abroad. (He once gave me a package of eleven.) Then he put the letters in the brown paper parcel and hitch-hiked back to Dublin. A day or two later an announcement appeared at the very top of the Social and Personal section of *The Irish Times*: 'Mr Eoin O'Mahony, B.L. K.M., has been staying with Mr Hubert Butler, B.A., in Kilkenny.' He probably sent it to the London *Times* as well. I have never before or since appeared in that illustrious column, and I have always made a special thing of *not* being a B.A. But I immediately saw the point. Eoin was showing his solidarity, not with my opinions, but with me, in the most public and ceremonious way he could contrive.

I have just been listening to the Radio Éireann recording of an earlier O'Mahony rally at Castlemore Castle. It was so clear and characteristic, it was almost as though Eoin and his wonderful personality had been embalmed for eternity. But ten years from now, how would it sound to those who never knew him? I think, though he left so little published writing, Eoin may wear better than most of us. For the Faceless Organization Man, whom Eoin combated, though he looks so vigorous, is really already a deader. Very soon we shall be searching for the scraps of the human personalities which he has pounded juggernaut-wise into the dust, and trying to piece them together. That is where Eoin and those he influenced will come into their own again. The seeds he sowed will begin to germinate in the vast and mouldering technological rubbish heap.

Being proud of him, we can be proud of Ireland too, for it is one of the few countries in which so eccentric a genius could be so warmly appreciated and so deeply regretted.

Jack Lynch
Dermot Keogh

A distinguished scion of Fianna Fáil once told me that campaigning with Jack Lynch was like 'walking into a town with Cú Chulainn'. This might be readily dismissed as the comment of a partisan who was close to the former Taoiseach in cabinet for many years. But that is not how I evaluate such a source. A shrewd judge of humanity, in all its manifestations, the source went on to say that the Irish people do not fully realize the debt owed to him: 'In the early 1970s he stood as a single individual in front of a stampede which threatened Irish democracy'. That was a reference to the years 1969–72 when Fianna Fáil faced its own internal civil war over Northern Ireland. The evaluation of my anonymous informant is broadly shared by the former British ambassador to Dublin (1970–73), Sir John Peck. Describing Jack Lynch as 'pure whip-cord', he added in his memoirs:

> My personal view of Mr Jack Lynch . . . remains . . . that while his government made their share of miscalculations and mistakes during that turbulent period [1969-72], all those

concerned with, and committed to peace with justice in the North owe a very great deal to his courage and tenacity in pursuing what he believed to be the right policy.

Now whipcord is a thin, tough kind of hempen cord of which whip-lashes, or the ends of them, are made. Is that a popular memory of Jack Lynch as Taoiseach — a Cú Chulainn as tough as whipcord? The reverse image predominates. Lynch is seen as having been weak and indecisive in those vital years. That image has been reinforced by two factors. In the first instance, there have been numerous accounts of the years 1969/70 by partisans and activists on the opposite side to Lynch. Secondly, Jack Lynch has remained singularly silent about those years, refusing to explain his side of events other than what he has put on the record of Dáil Eireann. But this historian has arrived at a much more positive conclusion after examining the available records of the period and interviewing a number of people. Jack Lynch ought not to be viewed as a hiatus between Seán Lemass and Charles Haughey. He was a person who kept his head at a time when many of those around him were losing theirs. His coolness under pressure won the admiration of many of his contemporaries. His resolute refusal to support the use of violence in Northern Ireland almost certainly saved many thousands of lives.

Jack Lynch was born on 15 August 1917 and was reared near Shandon, in Cork. He was educated at St Vincent's Convent, Peacock Lane, Cork, and later at the North Monastery. Like many of the best and brightest of his generation, he competed for every scholarship during his final year in school. He was called to teacher training, but chose instead to enter the civil service as a clerical officer and worked for the Dublin District Milk Board. He was transferred back to Cork where he worked as a court official and studied for the bar. He took night classes at University College, Cork in 1942 and 1943. Returning to Dublin, he was private secretary to the secretary of the Department of Justice, Stephen A. Roche. He studied at King's Inns and was called to the bar in 1945. Lynch resigned his permanent and pensionable job that year. Had he chosen to remain, he was likely to have reached the top in the civil service.

Jack Lynch had combined his law studies and work as a civil servant with a very successful sporting career. He won hurling all-Ireland medals in 1941, 1942, 1943, 1944 and 1946. He won a football championship medal in 1945. In 1946 he married Mairín and settled down to a life in the law. However, his legendary feats on the sporting field during the grim war years were no burden when he was first approached to stand in a by-election for Fianna Fáil in 1946. But he was newly married and had just begun to try to earn a living at law, so he turned down the offer. But his rejection was not definitive. He told Fianna Fáil that he might consider such an invitation for the next general election which he felt was a safe distance off.

Lynch rejected an overture to stand for Seán MacBride's Clann na Poblachta. He recalled being in the Teachers' Club, in Parnell Square, with his friend Paddy O'Donovan on the morning before a Railway Cup final after the end of the bitter national teachers' strike of 1946. This had resulted in defeat for the Irish National Teachers' Organization. On that occasion, Lynch overheard somebody remark that a new political party should be formed. The person in question was a friend of Seán MacBride and Con Lehane — two prime movers in the setting up of Clann na Poblachta. Lynch's initial reaction, despite the fact that he would have known a number of the people who helped set up Clann na Poblachta, was that it was not likely to last as a party and it was not for him.

He accepted the invitation by Fianna Fáil to stand in the 1948 general election and he was elected, despite the fact that Eamon de Valera lost power that year to a five-party coalition. He became a junior minister (then called a parliamentary secretary) when Fianna Fáil returned to power in 1951. After the fall of the country's second inter-party government (1954–1957), Lynch became Minister for Education. He was made Minister for Industry and Commerce when Seán Lemass succeeded de Valera as Taoiseach in 1959. After the 1965 election, he was named Minister for Finance.

Jack Lynch was the surprise choice to replace Lemass as the leader of the party in 1966. The latter had invited him to take over the leadership. Others wanted George Colley while another group pushed Seán Lemass's son-in-law, Charles Haughey, to take over. It appears that Lemass may have compelled Haughey to withdraw from the race. Lynch won the contest with ease. But there were those in the party who felt that he was an interim Taoiseach. The Minister for Finance, Charles Haughey, and the Minister for Agriculture, Neil Blaney, would have seen themselves as far more suitable material to provide the party with authentic republican leadership in the latter years of the 1960s when Northern Ireland was convulsed with violence. If there were those who thought that Lynch could be casually pushed aside after a year or so, in a surgically executed putsch, they were seriously mistaken.

Blaney failed to heed the 'yellow card' shown to him by Lynch while both men were on their way into the Dáil. He had made a speech in Letterkenny, Co. Donegal, on 8 December 1969 which had defied party policy. He said that 'no-one has the right to assert that force is irrevocably out' in order to achieve the unity of Ireland. A few days later he indicated that he would seriously consider putting his name forward were the position of Taoiseach to become available. A few weeks later, in a forceful speech, Lynch reiterated outright government opposition to the use of force. It is not expedient for many to consider in the 1990s just how much ambivalence there was during the late 1960s and early 1970s over the question of the use of violence. The Irish Republican Army had been reconstructed as so-called defenders of the people and there were those in Irish politics who thought in apocalyptical terms about the need to shed blood once and for all in order to bring about 'unity'. The IRA had its benefactors in the South — a story that remains to be documented.

Lynch lived in a Kafkaesque world during the early months of 1970. He would have had great sympathy with the main protagonist in Leonardo Sciascia'a *Il Contesto*; Inspector Rogas pursues a murder investigation only to discover that the conspiracy goes to the very core of the state itself. There were times when Lynch must have felt that he was actually dealing with a rival, parallel government. 'How can I trust anyone ever again', he said to a friend in the middle of 1970. But he was fortunate to have a number of strong supporters with sound judgment in the cabinet at that time of unprecedented crisis for the modern Irish state. They included the Minister for External Affairs, Patrick Hillery, and Erskine Childers, Tánaiste and Minister for Health. Lynch's wife, Mairín, was always a rock of good sense and her alleged influence in political affairs had given rise to the mean-spirited quip of 'petticoat power'.

Why did Lynch not move more swiftly in 1970 to halt the alleged freelancing in government? The radical uncertainty of the times made it difficult for him to act. It was also hard to believe the reports and the rumours about what was actually going on inside government and on the periphery of power. Lynch needed definitive proof and he had to wait to get it in order to act decisively. His apparent 'inaction' was not a result of procrastination. It was not a question of weakness. In the end, it was a question of timing. As a hurler, Lynch had not been known to retaliate when fouled, no matter how bad the provocation. However, the next time the two teams met, in the twinkling of an eye the offender usually received his retribution in good measure.

In the early months of 1970, Lynch suspected that he was being 'fouled'. But he chose to build up his own parallel network of reliable informants. He had to wait. He certainly could have been faulted for not having sacked the Minister for Justice, Michael Ó Morain, earlier in the year. Ó Morain had a serious drink problem and worse. Did that mean that Lynch was not handed, on a regular basis, important intelligence briefings during those vital months in early 1970? That was the reality. Lynch saw nothing of the detailed reports which had landed on the Minister for Justice's desk for transfer to the Taoiseach's office. For that reason, the Secretary of the Department of Justice, Peter Berry, felt that even Lynch was indifferent. Berry found it impossible to believe that such detailed information could not have been acted upon sooner. Eventually he took the unusual step of going to see the President, Eamon de Valera, only to be promptly told to see the Taoiseach immediately and hand over the information which he had in his possession.

The Kafkaesque atmosphere of those months placed Irish democracy under serious threat. Lynch could not afford to act precipitously. Ó Morain was sacked on 4 May 1970 and Blaney and Haughey were dismissed two days later. The Minister for Local Government, Kevin Boland, resigned in sympathy, as did Paudge Brennan, Blaney's parliamentary secretary. It was the moment when Lynch felt that he had optimum authority to act decisively. Rather than being seen as a ditherer, Lynch was displaying that he was made of whipcord, rather than straw as his opponents assumed. The extraordinary events of the 'Arms Trial' followed as Lynch was accused of 'felon setting' by a leading disaffected member of Fianna Fáil. The charge was conspiracy. In October 1970 Haughey was cleared of the charge and emerged from the court to cheers of 'We want Charlie' and 'Lynch must go'.

In the first flush of triumph, Haughey was reported as having called for the resignation of the Taoiseach: 'I think those who are

338

responsible for this debacle have no alternative but to take the honourable course that is open to them.' While that press conference was in progress in Dublin, Lynch was in New York to address the 25th session of the General Assembly of the United Nations. Lynch said in the course of his remarks, 'no one can deny that there was this attempt to import arms illegally' and added 'Republicanism doesn't mean guns. It doesn't mean using guns.' Returning to Dublin on 26 October 1970, Lynch was met at the airport by the cabinet (two were absent because they were out of the country at the time), some fifty TDs and senators and by the surviving founding fathers of the party, Frank Aiken, Seán MacEntee, Paddy Smith and Mick Hilliard. *The Irish Times* political correspondent, Michael McInerney, wrote that 'if anyone, after that display, wishes to say that they are better Republicans than Mr Lynch in Fianna Fáil, then they have a formidable task . . . . It was the Republic *par excellence*.' Lynch went on to win the overwhelming endorsement of the parliamentary party. He had survived the upheaval. While he had the support of a handful of close colleagues throughout the crisis, the lead up to the Arms Trial and its aftermath shook his confidence in human nature to the foundations.

Lynch went on to help win popular acceptance for Irish membership of the European Economic Community in 1972. Fine Gael also played a prominent part on the 'yes' side in the campaign. Meanwhile, his government had taken the stiffest action against the IRA and its political fellow travellers that year. Lynch had the Dáil carry emergency legislation in December 1972. He might have been faulted for not having gone to the country immediately after that tense Dáil debate when bombs in the capital had persuaded the opposition not to block the passage of the legislation. That was certainly the view of some members of his cabinet at the time. However, once Fine Gael had decided to support the Bill, there was no reason to call an election which would have had to be held during the week before Christmas.

The popular climate had turned against Fianna Fáil when Lynch finally decided to go to the country some weeks later. 'We had been in power for 16 years and the people wanted a change', said Brian Lenihan. That defeat of Fianna Fáil in 1973 was later eclipsed by the effective manner in which Lynch led his party to victory in 1977. That election has been seen as Lynch's finest political victory. It was a presidential-style campaign and Lynch was asked to play the role of populist leader of a resurgent Fianna Fáil. A complacent coalition — badly shaken by the circumstances surrounding the resignation of President Cearbhall Ó Dalaigh on 22 October 1976 — felt that Fine Gael and Labour would be returned to power. Fianna Fáil took no chances and presented an attractive election manifesto. Lynch won convincingly and he was back in power. In retrospect, Lynch may have had cause to regret the pledge to remove car tax given during the election. The decision to lift rates off private dwellings was, he would argue, supported by Fine Gael. It was an inequitable tax to have two families living beside each other paying the same rates. One home may be owned by an elderly widow and the other by a family with four wage packets coming into the house each week. But the support for local government was contingent after 1977 upon being given funding from the national exchequer. In the early 1980s such funds were cut down.

Lynch spent two further bruising years in politics before resigning as Taoiseach. Why did he go at that time in view of who was to succeed him? Perhaps he felt that he had lost the edge for politics. He was not being pushed and he would never have allowed himself to have been intimidated into resigning his position as Taoiseach. The Northern troubles had caused him to become embroiled in a major dispute within his party over the permission which had been granted to the British to overfly Irish territory when in 'hot pursuit'. That could be done only by the British following the receipt of permission from a senior Irish army officer of specific rank. There were question marks over whether the cabinet had formally given permission for such an arrangement. That episode led to very harsh anti-Lynch comments by backbenchers. The overflight imbroglio blew up again while the Taoiseach was on a visit to Washington and led to uncharacteristic exchanges with the press.

Returning to Ireland, Lynch was made aware that there was a campaign afoot to get rid of him. A number of caucus meetings had been held in his absence. At a party meeting he confronted those who were plotting against him and challenged them to make themselves known. Only one, Padraig Flynn, did so. Lynch encouraged the others to bring their grievances onto the floor of a party meeting. He knew who many of them were because he had been tipped off by a backbencher who had mistakenly entered a room while the caucus was having a meeting during Lynch's absence in America.

Lynch found himself to be back again in that Kafkaesque world towards the end of 1979 prior to the visit of Pope John Paul II. Rumours swept the capital and the country about the imminent resignation of President Patrick Hillery. It was relatively easy to dismiss such rumours out of hand, but they persisted and were connected by some to the leadership struggle inside Fianna Fáil. That scenario was the following: Hillery would be forced to resign through a series of orchestrated rumours; Lynch would be obliged to resign as Taoiseach in order to take over the vacant position of President; the way would then be clear for the various factions in Fianna Fáil to fight for the leadership of the party. Lynch must have known that his arch-rival Charles Haughey had become a strong contender for the position of Taoiseach. He had not been in a position to keep Haughey out of the cabinet after the 1977 election. Haughey had served as Minister for Health and had made quite an impression as usual. He was a success and was perceived — if one were to judge by the number of photocalls and sound bites — as being an outstanding minister. Haughey had spent nine years preparing for his eventual return as leader of Fianna Fáil. He had traversed the country during the time of the coalition rebuilding his constituency inside the party. Haughey was prepared to bid for the leadership of Fianna Fáil in 1979.

Lynch had already decided to resign from his position as Taoiseach before he had gone to the United States. He had picked 7 January 1980. However, Lynch allowed himself to be persuaded to resign earlier on the categorical assurance that he would be succeeded by George Colley. Lynch ought to have been more sceptical of confident predictions of victory. He received a number of delegations of backbenchers who tried to persuade him not to go. Charles Haughey was a formidable opponent and he had had nearly nine years to prepare his return. Colley ran a fatally flawed campaign and by the end of 1979 Charles Haughey was leader of Fianna Fáil and Taoiseach. It is virtually certain that Lynch would have remained in office had he been in a position to predict the outome.

In the 1980s Fianna Fáil was riven by internal civil strife which ultimately resulted in schism. Lynch has always been a strong admirer of Desmond O'Malley, the founder of the Progressive Democrats. He had made him Minister for Justice in 1970 after the sacking of Ó Morain, but he had felt obliged to not reappoint him to that position in 1977 because of the kidnap threats which

O'Malley's family had been receiving. At that stage O'Malley had a very young family and there had been rather ugly threats against the young Minister, indicating that the movements of his children were being watched. With O'Malley out of Fianna Fáil, Haughey had no real rival for the leadership of the party.

The legacy of Jack Lynch in Irish politics is disputed. There are those who argue that his alleged lack of authority inside government contributed to the arms crisis of 1970. This article rejects that interpretation and has argued that Lynch, on the contrary, did not lack authority. His handling of the unprecedented events leading up to the arms crisis of 1970 has to be set in the context of the times. Lynch had at no time authorized the supplying of arms to elements in Northern Ireland. He had placed the Irish army on the border to provide medical aid to refugees. The troops acted as a deterrent against anyone wishing to try to smuggle arms into Northern Ireland. At no time did he contemplate that Irish troops should cross the border into Derry or into Newry. That would have constituted an act of war. It would also have endangered the lives of thousands of Catholics in inner city Belfast. Lynch remains scathing of those who argue that the crossing of the border by Irish troops in 1969/70 would have helped solve the problem of partition. The world is not that simple.

It is usually inadvisable to compare modern politicians to mythological figures. But during the months of April, May and June 1970 Lynch may have felt as alone as Cú Chulainn when the latter was defending Ulster. However, Lynch was never in any sense a warrior Taoiseach. The mystique of violence held no appeal for him. Lynch helped to keep the gun out of Irish politics and Irish democracy is all the safer for his having been Taoiseach.

The Vegetable Seller
Nell McCafferty

She was as fresh as the vegetables she sells and more deeply rooted. Eileen Ahern's mother worked there before her, her daughter Deirdre will work there after her, her sister Siobhan stands in a second stall alongside her in Cork's 'English Market'; a family tree offering sustenance and sweet succour to all who linger by their banked rows of nature's own produce.

She is a confident Cork presence in a cosmopolitan world of shiny brown dates from Saudi Arabia, cheeky tangerines from Spain, Indian peppers sweet and strong, courgettes, celery and carrots. Eileen is at home with them all. Spinach does not daunt her, salsify satisfies, cabbage red or green presents no problem. A potato is not necessarily a potato, there are yams — she points proudly — from America. Aubergines, artichokes, asparagus, broccoli, beetroots and beans, corn, courgettes or cucumber, parsnips, peas and Swedish turnips, the wealth and wonders of the natural world form a peaceful phalanx around a woman faced with gutted fish and sliced flesh in the marketplace.

All the same, she confided to me when I was first drawn to her, did you ever taste anything as nice as a pig's foot on a Saturday night? She was driving to Dublin on the Sunday for a hurling match. She invited me home to see the medals Deirdre had won for Irish dancing. I could swap Northern names with her husband, she said, who used to organize a yearly bus tour for Ulster people around the ambush spots of West Cork. Now he organizes holidays for children of the North, from Shankill and the Falls.

She drew my attention to the fruit. Green apples, blueberries, yellow bananas, eponymous oranges, plummy plums, passion fruit — did they work or just grow on trees, like money — Eileen has no time for fantasy, though she wages merry war against reality, morning noon and evening six days a week. When Cork Corporation wanted to remove the fountain that had not worked for ages she held out for an aesthetic that surpassed articulation. She sensed that it was lovely. The fountain, its song silenced, holds mute court still before her eyes.

An English visitor proferred a sterling pound note. Eileen sent him round the corner looking for punts. Her soul is not for sale; one link at least had been broken and she was glad to leave the chain gang.

I brought her a cutting from my spider plant; she met me in an ice-cream shop, pressed upon me reacquaintance with a melting Dream-boat in a glass dish; thereafter I used sit upon her sacks of potatoes, lulled by her lullabies in the harsh caucus of commerce. Did I know the Montagues were in India? That young one there, talking about honey, was a daughter of Ó Riada. Had I been to Coolea? She told me of the Tailor's grave in Gougane Barra and gave me an avocado for a picnic there.

I asked her how to make coleslaw and Eileen said she preferred her cabbage boiled; I complained about my Renault and she said she bought her car from Fords, where her brother worked; I met her in Crosshaven one summer's evening as she strolled by the sea with her husband and daughter, and we retired to a pub for a civil libation. Eileen drinks Babycham.

In the marketplace every day I met her, at her stall, among the vegetables and fruit, and she let me look and listen while Cork passed by.

Eileen Arún.

VI THE WEIGHT OF HISTORY

The Battle of the Starlings, 1621
Anonymous

About the seventh of October last, Anno 1621, there gathered together by degrees, an unusual multitude of birds called stares, in some Countries knowne by the name of Starlings. . . . It is and hath been an old proverbe, that, *Birds of a feather hold and keep together*, which hath ever beene a common custome in these as much as in any other kind whatsoever, but now the old proverb is changed, and their custome is altered cleane contrary. For at this time, as these birds are in taste bitter, so they met to fight together the most bitterest and sharpest battell amongst themselves, the like, for the manner of their fight, and for the time the battell did continue, never heard or seene at any time in any country of the world. . . .

Now to come to the flight of our birds, the stares or starlings, they mustered together at this above named Citie of Corke some foure or five daies, before they fought their battells, every day more and more encreasing their armies with greater supplies, some came as from the East, others from West, and so accordingly they placed themselves, and as it were encamped themselves eastward and westward about the citie, during which time their noise and tunes were strange on both sides to the great admiration of the citizens and the inhabitants near adjoining, who had never seen for multitude, or ever heard for loud tunes which they uttered, the like before. Whereupon they more curiously observing the courses and passages they used, noted that from those on the East, and from those on the West, sundry flights, some twenty or thirty in a company, would passe from the one side to the other, as it should seeme imployed in embassages, for they would fly and hover in the ayre over the adverse party with strange tunes and noise and so return back again to that side from which as it seemed they were sent. . . .

These courses and customes continued with them until the XII of October, which day being Saturday, about nine of the clocke in the morning, being a very faire and sunshine day, upon a strange sound and noise made as well on the one side as on the other, they forthwith at one instant took wing, and so mounting up into the skyes encountered one another, with such a terrible shocke, as the evening was somewhat dark and the battle was fought over woods more remote off, but for more assured proof of this fight the Sunday before named, there are at this time in London divers persons of worth and very honest reputation, whom the Printer of this Pamphlet can produce to justifie what they saw, as cause shall require upon their oaths.

Now to return to the last battell fought at Corke by these stares. Upon Munday the XIV of October, they made their return again, and at the same time, the day being as faire a sun-shine day as it was the Saturday before, they mounted into the aire and encountered each other with like violent assaults as formerly they had done, and fell into the city upon the houses, and into the river, wounded and slaughtered in like manner as before is reported, but at this last battell there was a kite, a Raven and a Crow, all three found dead in the streets, rent, torn and mangled.

Battle and Aftermath:
The Beast of Ballynagrumoolia
Aidan Higgins
from: *Helsingør Station & other Departures* (1989)

If the wholesale slaughter that was the Battle of Kinsale finished off the rough princely world of Latinists and gallowglasses in three hours in the Ballinamona bog, had it not been lost already when McMahon sold out O'Neill in return for a bottle of the hard stuff on that miserable wet late December day 387 years ago? No?

Neap tides flooded 9,288 times into Ballymacus Creek where as a difficult young thing you liked to retire, to sulk. Our independence won with jigs and reels God knows how many church collections later, and the national flag raised jerkily aloft in mismatching shades of dandelion orange (leaves, stalk and root containing a bitter milky juice) and septic green, divided by neutral white, and complemented by a national anthem that was never any great shakes, 'composed' by a north Dublin housepainter, a bowsy by the name of Carney reputedly related to the roistering Behans.

Years later, out walking with you on another soft December day beyond the ramparts, we spotted the Beast of Ballynagrumoolia beyond a denuded winter hedge. Pale and plump, the deep-set piggish eyes red-rimmed like an anus, the flaccid cheeks soiled with mud, immemorial slobber, shit and tears. The Beast's stiff yellow hair was erupting from under nodding headgear, fore-hooves rooting in the driveway, the twin enraged nostrils aflare; while from the deep barrel chest stormily rising and subsiding came grievous sighs and the most heartfelt groans. Great sods of earth were being hurled about; an apparition as alarming as a she-gorilla enraged — the very stuff of nightmares.

Scavengers, looters and pillagers, the extreme poor of Munster arrived with the wild dogs and birds of prey to cover the battlefields now become graveyards, a thousand of O'Neills and O'Donnell's men become shades, in an unforgettable day that would be for Ireland what Kossovo would be for Hungary. But the poison was already being prepared and the wild geese scattered, soon to become extinct. Something was broken so that something else could begin.

And sure enough, scarcely had a year passed than there came yet another in the long roster of our betrayal; this one by the name of Jamsey Blake, turncoat and native of Galway who was said to be in the pay of Sir George Carew the Lord High President of Munster. It was he who arranged that poison be laid out for Red Hugh at a dinner in Simancas, watched him sample wine of the Palomino grapes, swig and swallow; take *percebes*, which are goose barnacles, now stuffed with death, take his portion with a slow easy hand. Blake, hidden, watched, and so did some ruffed and bearded Spanish grandees, not comprehending; saw him swallow it in a place now outside of time, wiped out by time, frozen within time.

As the Scots troops crouched miserably all night in corn-stooks in freezing rain, their powder damp, their spirits low, awaiting Cromwell's fearful attack at sun-up, time stopped. At daybreak the Scots troops began shuffling into line.

Elsewhere in other times and places in different darkness St Elmo's fire was glinting on damp Irish lances (not to be used much that day) and Panzer tank engines coughing into life at sun-up were rolling towards Kusk. These fields, Kossovo and its crows, the tank battle of Kusk, the graveyard of Kinsale, a drenched cornfield in Scotland. *Jamais deux sans trois*; never four without more.

Shrapnel tore through the grey insentient air, bees with their hives knocked over. From the enemy lines the machine-gun fire was reaching out, stuttering, probing, stitching the air. Somewhere in the murk ahead lay the pierced barbed-wire entanglements. Juss trod on something soft and yielding — flayed human flesh not yet dead, himself dragged along by the current of time. His face felt stiff as a death-mask, from generous tots of three-star Hennessy. The thought flew unsoberly through his head: *Schicksal* had become *Schnicksal*, both British and Germanic destiny become ridiculous and dirty, become piercing red-hot. The ordinary expectation of suffering was one thing; this was something else again.

The Beast of Ballynagrumoolia had come via Ballinspittle through all the intervening gardens of Munster, breaking down clapboard fences, trampling vegetables patches, grunting and sweating, to Kippagh.

The Battle of Kinsale was fought and lost one vile wet Sunday on the 24th of December 1601 and over in barely three hours. Within a period so brief a large force was destroyed by a smaller one, the English horse under Wingfield pursued the fleeing Irish as far as Innishannon fives miles distant, killing at will. The Spanish presence within the town had been more a hindrance than a help. Trust not foreign friends; the old adage had a cruel ethnic twist to it. The River Bandon snaked about the small port, a walled town of two hundred houses, as duodenum and colon, lower bowel and anus. Spared the shame of defeat, the Spanish were flushed down the river and out to sea. Don Juan de Aquila was in command. The Armada had sunk only thirteen years before. For the Irish, crippling defeats at the Yellow Ford and Benburb, and now Kinsale, the final setback. The ancestors had begun to seem strange. *Kolkrabe the Raven greets you!* Shaking out sodden feathers, stropping its beak on the bars of the cage. Hiding its food, first under this stone, then under that. Swearing profusely, e'er all be over and done with. Ever since the sixteenth century the wind had been blowing against European Catholicism.

The Sack of Baltimore

Thomas Davis

This poem by Thomas Davis commemorates the events of 20 June 1631. On that day, two Algerian galleys, guided by a County Waterford fisherman, anchored at Baltimore. The crews attacked the village and captured many of the people. [Ed.]

I

The summer sun is falling soft o'er Carbery's hundred isles,
The summer sun is gleaming still through Gabriel's rough defiles;
Old Inisherkin's crumbled fane looks like a moulting bird,
And in a calm and sleepy swell the ocean tide is heard.
The hookers lie upon the beach; the children cease their play;
The gossips leave the little inn; the households kneel to pray;
And full of love, and peace, and rest — its daily labour o'er —
Upon that cosy creek there lay the town of Baltimore.

II

A deeper rest, a starry trance, has come with midnight there;
No sound, except that throbbing wave, in earth, or sea, or air.
The massive capes and ruined towers seem conscious of the calm;
The fibrous sod and stunted trees are breathing heavy balm.
So still the night, these two long barques round Dunashad that glide
Might trust their oars — methinks not few — against the ebbing tide.
Oh! some sweet mission of true love must urge them to the shore:
They bring some lover to his bride, who sighs in Baltimore!

III

All, all asleep within each roof along that rocky street,
And these must be the lover's friends with gently gliding feet —
A stifled gasp! a dreamy noise! 'the roof is in a flame!'
From out their beds, and to their doors, rush maid, and sire, and dame,
And meet upon the threshold stone the gleaming sabre's fall,
And o'er each black and bearded face the white or crimson shawl;
The yell of 'Allah' breaks above the prayer, and shriek, and roar —
Oh, blessed God! the Algerine is lord of Baltimore.

IV

Then flung the youth his naked hand against the shearing sword;
Then sprung the mother on the brand with which her son was gored;
Then sunk the grandsire on the floor, his grand-babes clutching wild;
Then fled the maiden moaning faint, and nestled with the child.
But see, yon pirate strangled lies, and crushed with splashing heel,
While o'er him, in an Irish hand, there sweeps his Syrian steel:
Though virtue sink, and courage fail, and misers yield their store,
There's *one* hearth well avengèd in the sack of Baltimore!

V

Mid-summer morn, in woodland nigh, the birds began to sing;
They see not now the milking maids — deserted is the spring!
Mid-summer day — this gallant rides from distant Bandon's town;
These hookers crossed from stormy Skull, that skiff from Affadown:
They only found the smoking walls, with neighbours' blood besprent,
And on the strewed and trampled beach awhile they wildly went;
Then dashed to sea, and passed Cape Cléire, and saw five leagues
    before
The pirate galleys vanishing that ravished Baltimore.

VI

Oh! some must tug the galley's oar, and some must tend the steed;
This boy will bear a Scheik's chibouk, and that a Bey's jerreed.
Oh! some are in the arsenals, by beauteous Dardanelles;
And some are in the caravan to Mecca's sandy dells.
The maid that Bandon gallant sought is chosen for the Dey:
She's safe — he's dead—she stabbed him in the midst of his serai;
And when, to die a death of fire, that noble maid they bore,
She only smiled — O'Driscoll's child — she thought of Baltimore.

VII

'Tis two long years since sunk the town beneath that bloody band,
And all around its trampled hearths a larger concourse stand,
Where, high upon a gallows tree, a yelling wretch is seen —
'Tis Hackett of Dungarvan, he who steered the Algerine!
He fell amid a sullen shout, with scarce a passing prayer,
For he had slain the kith and kin of many a hundred there;
Some muttered of MacMurchadh, who brought the Norman o'er;
Some cursed him with Iscariot that day in Baltimore.

General Wonder in Our Land

Anonymous

General wonder in our land,
    And general consternation;
General gale on Bantry strand,
    For general preservation.

General rich he shook with awe
    At general insurrection;
General poor his sword did draw,
    With general disaffection.

General blood was just at hand,
    As General Hoche appeared;
General woe fled through our land,
    As general want was feared.

General gale our fears dispersed,
    He conquered general dread;
General joy each heart has swelled,
    As General Hoche has fled.

General love no blood has shed,
    He left us general ease,
General horror he has fled,
    Let God get general praise.

To that great General of the skies,
    That sent us general gale,
With general love our voices rise
    In one great general peal.

The Lament for Arthur O'Leary

Eibhlín Dhubh Ní Chonaill

Translated by: Eilís Dillon

In his inaugral lecture as Professor of Poetry at Oxford in 1984, Peter Levi referred to 'Caoineadh Airt Ui Laoghaire' (Lament for Arthur O'Leary) as 'the greatest poem written in these islands in the eighteenth century'. The poem was composed by Eibhlín Dhubh Ní Chonaill after her husband, Airt Ó Laoghaire, a Catholic, was shot while on the run in 1773. Earlier, he had refused to sell his horse for five pounds (the maximum legal worth of a horse owned by a Catholic) after he had won a race against Abraham Morris, the High Sheriff of Cork. Airt Ó Laoghaire is buried in Kilcrea Abbey, a few miles from Ballincollig on the western side of Cork city. The epitaph on his tomb was composed by his wife:

Lo! Arthur Leary, generous, handsome, brave,
Slain in his bloom, lies in this humble grave.

I

Eileen speaks:

My love forever!
The day I first saw you
At the end of the market-house,
My eye observed you,
My heart approved you,
I fled from my father with you,
Far from my home with you.

II

I never repented it:
You whitened a parlour for me,
Painted rooms for me,
Reddened ovens for me,
Baked fine bread for me,
Basted meat for me,
Slaughtered beasts for me;
I slept in ducks' feathers
Till midday milking-time,
Or more if it pleased me.

III

My friend forever!
My mind remembers
That fine spring day
How well your hat suited you,
Bright gold banded,
Sword silver-hilted —
Right hand steady —
Threatening aspect —
Trembling terror
On treacherous enemy —
You poised for a canter
On your slender bay horse.
The Saxons bowed to you,
Down to the ground to you,
Not for love of you
Bur for deadly fear of you,
Though you lost your life to them,
Oh my soul's darling.

IV

Oh white-handed rider!
How fine your brooch was
Fastened in cambric,
And your hat with laces.
When you crossed the sea to us,
They would clear the street for you,
And not for love of you
But for deadly hatred.

V

My friend you were forever!
When they will come home to me,
Gentle little Conor
And Farr O'Leary, the baby,
They will question me so quickly,
Where did I leave their father.
I'll answer in my anguish
That I left him in Killnamartyr.
They will call out to their father;
And he won't be there to answer.

VI

My friend and my love!
Of the blood of Lord Antrim,
And of Barry of Allchoill,
How well your sword suited you,
Hat gold-banded,
Boots of fine leather,
Coat of broadcloth,
Spun overseas for you.

VII

My friend you were forever!
I knew nothing of your murder
Till your horse came to the stable
With the reins beneath her trailing,
And your heart's blood on her shoulders
Staining the tooled saddle
Where you used to sit and stand.
My first leap reached the threshold,
My second reached the gateway,
My third leap reached the saddle.

VIII

I struck my hands together
And I made the bay horse gallop
As fast as I was able,
Till I found you dead before me
Beside a little furze-bush.
Without Pope or bishop,
Without priest or cleric
To read the death-psalms for you,
But a spent old woman only
Who spread her cloak to shroud you —
Your heart's blood was still flowing;
I did not stay to wipe it
But filled my hands and drank it.

IX

My love you'll be forever!
Rise up from where you're lying
And we'll be going homewards.
We'll have a bullock slaughtered,
We'll call our friends together,
We'll get the music going.
I'll make a fine bed ready
With sheets of snow-white linen,
And fine embroidered covers
That will bring the sweat out through you
Instead of the cold that's on you!

X

Arthur
O'Leary's
sister speaks:

My friend and my treasure!
There's many a handsome woman
From Cork of the sails
To the bridge of Toames
With a great herd of cattle
And gold for her dowry,
That would not have slept soundly
On the night we were waking you.

XI

Eileen speaks:

My friend and my lamb;
You must never believe it,
Nor the whisper that reached you,
Nor the venomous stories
That said I was sleeping.
It was not sleep was on me,
But your children were weeping,
And they needed me with them
To bring their sleep to them.

XII

Now judge, my people,
What woman in Ireland
That at every nightfall
Lay down beside him,

357

That bore his three children,
Would not lose her reason
After Art O'Leary
That's here with me vanquished
Since yesterday morning?

XIII

Arthur
O'Leary's
father speaks:

Bad luck to you, Morris! —
May your heart's blood poison you!
With your squint eyes gaping!
And your knock-knees breaking! —
That murdered my darling,
And no man in Ireland
To fill you with bullets.

XIV

My friend and my heart!
Rise up again now, Art,
Leap up on your horse,
Make straight for Macroom town,
Then to Inchigeela back,
A bottle of wine in your fist,
The same as you drank with your dad.

XV

Eileen speaks:

My bitter, long torment
That I was not with you
When the bullet came towards you,
My right side would have taken it
Or a fold of my tunic,
And I would have saved you
Oh smooth-handed rider.

XVI

Arthur
O'Leary's
sister speaks:

My sore sharp sorrow
That I was not behind you
When the gun-powder blazed at you,
My right side would have taken it,

358

Or a fold of my gown,
And you would have gone free then
Oh grey-eyed rider,
Since you were a match for them.

XVII

Eileen speaks: My friend and my treasure!
It's bad treatment for a hero
To lie hooded in a coffin,
The warm-hearted rider
That fished in bright rivers,
That drank in great houses
With white-breasted women.
My thousand sorrows
That I've lost my companion.

XVIII

Bad luck and misfortune
Come down on you, Morris!
That snatched my protector,
My unborn child's father:
Two of them walking
And the third still within me,
And not likely I'll bear it.

XIX

My friend and my pleasure!
When you went out through the gateway
You turned and came back quickly,
You kissed your two children,
You kissed me on the forehead,
You said: 'Eileen, rise up quickly,
Put your affairs in order
With speed and with decision.
I am leaving home now
And there's no telling if I'll return.'
I mocked this way of talking,
He had said it to me so often.

XX

My friend and my dear!
Oh bright-sworded rider,
Rise up this moment,
Put on your fine suit
Of clean, noble cloth,
Put on your black beaver,
Pull on your gauntlets.
Up with your whip;
Outside your mare is waiting.
Take the narrow road east,
Where the trees thin before you,
Where streams narrow before you,
Where men and women will bow before you,
If they keep their old manners —
But I fear they have lost them.

XXI

My love and my treasure!
Not my dead ancestors,
Nor the deaths of my three children,
Nor Domhnall Mór O'Connell,
Nor Connall that drowned at sea,
Nor the twenty-six years woman
Who went across the water
And held kings in conversation —
It's not on all of them I'm calling
But on Art who was slain last night
At the inch of Carriganima! —
The brown mare's rider
That's here with me only —
With no living soul near him
But the dark little women of the mill,
And my thousand sorrows worsened
That their eyes were dry of tears.

XXII

My friend and my lamb!
Arthur O'Leary,
Of Connor, of Keady,
Of Louis O'Leary,
From west in Geeragh
And from east in Caolchnoc,
Where berries grow freely
And gold nuts on branches
And great floods of apples
All in their seasons.
Would it be a wonder
If Ive Leary were blazing
Besides Ballingeary
And Guagán of the saint
For the firm-handed rider
That hunted the stag down,
All out from Grenagh
When slim hounds fell behind?
And Oh clear-sighted rider,
What happened last night?
For I thought to myself
That nothing could kill you
Though I bought your habit.

XXIII

Arthur
O'Leary's
sister speaks:

My friend and my love!
Of the country's best blood,
That kept eighteen wet-nurses at work,
And each received her pay —
A heifer and a mare,
A sow and her litter,
A mill at the ford,
Yellow gold and white silver,
Silks and fine velvets,
A holding of land —
To give her milk freely
To the flower of fair manhood.

361

XXIV

My love and my treasure
And my love, my white dove!
Though I did not come to you,
Nor bring my troops with me,
That was no shame to me
For they were all enclosed
In shut-up rooms,
In narrow coffins,
In sleep without waking.

XXV

Were it not for the small-pox
And the black death
And the spotted fever,
That powerful army
Would be shaking their harness
And making a clatter
On their way to your funeral,
Oh white-breasted Art.

XXVI

My love you were and my joy!
Of the blood of those rough horsemen
That hunted in the valley,
Till you turned them homewards
And brought them to your hall,
Where knives were being sharpened,
Pork laid out for carving
And countless ribs of mutton,
The red-brown oats were flowing
To make the horses gallop —
Slender, powerful horses
And stable-boys to care them
Who would not think of sleeping
Nor of deserting their horses
If their owners stayed a week,
Oh brother of many friends.

XXVII

My friend and my lamb!
A cloudy vision
Came last night to me
In Cork at midnight
Alone in my bed:
That our white court fell,
That the Geeragh withered,
That your slim hounds were still
And the birds without sweetness
When you were found vanquished
On the side of the mountain,
Without priest or cleric
But an old shrivelled woman
That spread her cloak over you,
Arthur O'Leary,
While your blood flowed freely
On the breast of your shirt.

XXVIII

My love and my treasure!
And well they suited you,
Five-ply stockings,
Boots to your knees,
A three-cornered Caroline,
A lively whip,
On a frisky horse —
Many a modest, mannerly maiden
Would turn to gaze after you.

XXIX

Eileen speaks: My love forever!
And when you went in cities,
Strong and powerful,
The wives of the merchants
All bowed down to you
For they knew in their hearts
What a fine man in bed you were,
And what a fine horseman
And father for children.

363

XXX

Jesus Christ knows
I'll have no cap on my head,
Nor a shift on my back,
Nor shoes on my feet,
Nor goods in my house,
Nor the brown mare's harness
That I won't spend on lawyers;
That I'll cross the seas
And talk to the king,
And if no one listens
That I'll come back
To the black-blooded clown
That took my treasure from me.

XXXI

My love and my darling!
If my cry were heard westwards
To great Derrynane
And to gold-appled Capling,
Many swift, hearty riders
And white-kerchiefed women
Would be coming here quickly
To weep at your waking,
Beloved Art O'Leary.

XXXII

My heart is warming
To the fine women of the mill
For their goodness in lamenting
The brown mare's rider.

XXXIII

May your black heart fail you,
Oh false John Cooney!
If you wanted a bribe,
You should have asked me.
I'd have given you plenty:
A powerful horse
That would carry you safely

Through the mob
When the hunt is out for you,
Or a fine herd of cattle,
Or ewes to bear lambs for you,
Or the suit of a gentleman
With spurs and top-boots —
Though it's sorry I'd be
To see you done up in them,
For I've always heard
You're a piddling lout.

XXXIV

Oh white-handed rider,
Since you are struck down,
Rise and go after Baldwin,
The ugly wretch
With the spindle shanks,
And take your revenge
For the loss of your mare —
May he never enjoy her.
May his six children wither!
But no bad wish to Máire
Though I have no love for her,
But that my own mother
Gave space in her womb to her
For three long seasons.

XXXV

My love and my dear!
Your stooks are standing,
Your yellow cows milking;
On my heart is such sorrow
That all Munster could not cure it,
Nor the wisdom of the sages.
Till Art O'Leary returns
There will be no end to the grief
That presses down on my heart,
Closed up tight and firm
Like a trunk that is locked
And the key is mislaid.

XXXVI

All women out there weeping,
Wait a little longer;
We'll drink to Art son of Connor
And the souls of all the dead,
Before he enters the school —
Not learning wisdom or music
But weighted down by earth and stones.

She is Far From the Land

Thomas Moore

*This song commemorates Sarah Curran, a native of Newmarket, County Cork.
She was the beloved of Robert Emmet who was hanged for his part in a rebellion
in 1803. Her father, John Philpot Curran, was a famous advocate. This song is
still sung frequently in north Cork. [Ed.]*

She is far from the land where her young hero sleeps,
    And lovers are around her, sighing;
But coldly she turns from their gaze, and weeps,
    For her heart in his grave is lying!

She sings the wild song of her dear native plains,
    Every note which he lov'd awaking; —
Ah! little they think who delight in her strains,
    How the heart of the Minstrel is breaking.

He had liv'd for his love, for his country he died,
    They were all that to life had entwin'd him;
Nor soon shall the tears of his country be dried,
    Nor long will his love stay behind him.

Oh! make her a grave where the sunbeams rest,
    When they promise a glorious morrow;
They'll shine o'er her sleep, like a smile from the West,
    From her own lov'd island of sorrow.

The Hunger

An tAthair Peadar Ó Laoghaire

from: *Mo Scéal Féin* (1915)

Translated by: Cyril Ó Céirín

As soon as understanding comes to a child, it is usual for people to be asking him what would his vocation in life be, when he would be big. I well recall that question being put to me very often. I don't recall having any other answer to give to it but the one, solitary answer: that I would be a priest. From the beginning that much was settled in my mind and I don't recall that there was ever anything other than that. Neither do I recall when my mind first settled on my becoming a priest when I would be grown up.

I know well that people used to be making fun of the story, for it was clear to everyone that my father had nowhere near the necessary capital to set about such an undertaking. As soon as I got any sense, I also knew that he hadn't got the capital, but that did not prevent me from being steadfast in my mind about becoming a priest, whatever way this would come about. If it were not for the blight coming on the potatoes and the bad times that came afterwards, I don't say that he would not have been able to give me the necessary amount of schooling. But the bad times turned everything upside down.

A strange thing — it was the big, strong farmers who were the first to fall! The man who had only a small farm, the grass of six or seven cows, kept his hold; the man with the big, broad, spacious farm was soon broken when the changed times came. He who had only a little, lost only a little. Before this, this was no big rent or big demands on him. He was accustomed to living without much extravagance. It wasn't too difficult for him to tighten his belt a little bit more, and to answer the small demands on him without too much hardship. But he, who had a big farm, was accustomed to the expensive way of life. He was independent as long as his farm responded. When the change came, the returns from the farm came to a sudden stop. The loss, the extravagance, the demands were too great. It was impossible to meet them and they swept him off his feet. I well recall how I would hear the latest news and how it caused amazement: 'Oh! Did you hear? Such a person is burst! His land is up for sale. He's gone. He slipped away. His land is up!'

You would often hear 'His land is up!' — but you wouldn't hear at all that time, 'His land has been taken by another person'. Nobody had any wish to take land. Things used to be very bad for those who had lost their land. They'd have neither food nor credit and there was nothing they could do but go looking for alms. They would not be long begging when they used to go into a decline and they'd die. As they were not accustomed to hunger or hardship, they couldn't stand it long when the hunger and hardship would come on them. Often, when the hunger was very severe, thev'd have to rise and move out and head for the house of some neighbour (who, perhaps, would be as needy as themselves, or close to it) to see if they could get a mouthful of something to eat, which might take the frenzy of hunger off them.

One day, when I was eight years of age (I seem to remember that I was standing at the corner of the haggard), I saw a woman coming towards me up the hill. She was barefoot, walking very slowly and panting, as if she had been running. She was blowing so much, her mouth was wide open, so that I had a sight of her teeth. But the thing that amazed me altogether was her feet. Each foot was swollen so that, from the knee down, it was as big and as fat as a gallon-can. That sight took such a firm grip on my mind that it is before my eyes now, every bit as clear-cut as it was that day, although it is around three score years and five since I saw it. That woman had been fairly independent and free from adversity until the blackness had come upon the potatoes.

Another day — I can't tell if it was before or after that — I was inside in our house, standing on the hearthstone, when a boy came in the door. I saw the face that was on him and the terror that was in his two eyes, the terror of hunger. That face and those two eyes are before my mind now, as clear and as unclouded as the day I gave them the one and only look. Somebody gave him a lump of bread. He snatched the bread and turned his back to us and his face to the wall and he started right into eating it so ravenously that you would think he would choke himself. At the time I did not realize that I was so amazed by him or by his voracity, but that sight has stayed in my mind, and will stay as long as I live.

I remember one evening during the period, when the people were running in and out and they talking away. In the winter, it was. The night was after falling. I heard someone saying, 'It was down by Carriginanassey I heard the shout!' 'There it is again!' said another, and they all ran out. A while afterwards, they came back in with a poor, old fellow between them. They put him standing on the floor — he was hardly able to stand. I was facing him and I had a view of his features. His mouth was wide open and his lips, upper and lower both, were drawn back, so that his teeth — the amount he had of them — were exposed. I saw the two, big, long, yellow eye-teeth in his mouth, the terror in his eyes and the confusion in his face. I can see them now as well as I could see them then. He was a neighbour. It is how the hunger drove him out to see if he could find anything to eat and the poor man went astray in the bog that was below Carriginanassey. When he found himself going astray, he became afraid that he would fall into a hole and be drowned. He stopped then and began to shout. That was a custom — there was a certain shout for the purpose — for anyone going astray. Each one knew how to send up that *liúgh*, so that, when they heard it, everybody would know the meaning of it, and the people would gather and seek the person who was going astray.

There was a little stable at the head of the house. A poor person by the name of Patrick Buckley came and shelter was given to himself, his wife and two children in the stable. They stayed for some weeks there, but they had a small cabin for themselves after that. Sheila was the name of the elder of the two children. We had a serving-boy — Conor was his name — and I overheard Sheila talking to him one day.

'Con,' she said, in Gaelic.

'Coming, Sheila,' Con said.

'I have no speech now,' she said.

'*Airiú*, what else have you, Sheila?' Con said.

'English,' says she.

'*Airiú*, what English could you have?' Con said.

'Peter's English and Seáinín-Philib's English.' (Seáinín-Philib was another poor person, who lived in a cabin beside the place.)

'But surely English is speech, Sheila?'

'English speech?' she said in amazement. 'If it was, surely people would understand it!'

One day, Sheila's mother had a handful of gravel in the little broad-bottomed pot, the griddle-oven they used to call it, as she was going to bake a cake; she was scouring and scraping the inside of the griddle-oven with the gravel.

'Oh, Mam!' Sheila said, 'is it how you'll put gravel in the cake?'

'It is,' said her mother.

Out went Sheila. She saw Con.

'Oh, Con' says she, 'What'll we do? What'll we do at all?'

'What's on you now, Sheila?' Con said.

'The grey-green gravel my mother's putting in the cake for use and I don't know how in the world we'll be able to eat it. All our teeth'll be broken. Some of the stones in the gravel are very big. Not one of us will have a tooth left in his head. It's all right for little Jeremiah he hasn't got any teeth at all yet.'

Little Jeremiah was Sheila's small, young brother. In with Con until he'd see what Sheila's mother was doing. When he saw what the gravel was being used for, they had a great laugh.

The famine came. Sheila and her father and mother and little Jeremiah had to go down to Macroom into the poorhouse. No sooner were they inside than they were all separated from each other. The father was put among the men. The mother was put among the women. Sheila was put among the small girls. And Jeremiah was put among the very young children. The whole house, and all the poor people in it, was smothered in every kind of evil sickness; the people, almost as fast as they'd come in, falling down with a malady and — God bless the hearers! — dying as fast as the fever came on them. There used not be room for half of them in the house. The amount that would not be able to get in could only go and lay themselves on the bank of the river, on the lower side of the bridge. You would see them there every morning, after the night was over, stretched out in rows, some stirring, some quiet enough without any stir at all out of them. In a while, certain men would come and they would take those who were not stirring, and they would put them into trunks. They would take them to a place beside Carrigastyra, where a great, wide, deep hole had been opened for them, and they would put them altogether down into the hole. They would do the same with all who had died in the house after the night.

It was not too long, after their going in and after his separation from his mother, that death came to little Jeremiah. The small body was thrown up on the truck and taken to the big hole, and it was thrown in along with the other bodies. But it was all the same to the child: long before his body was thrown in the hole, his soul was in the presence of God, in the joys of the heavens. It was not long until Sheila followed little Jeremiah. Her young body went into the hole, but her soul went up to where little Jeremiah was, in the presence of God, in the joy of the heavens, where she had solace and the company of the saints and angels, and the company of the Virgin Mary, and speech that was better by far than 'Peter's English and Seáinin-Philib's English'.

The father and mother were asking and questioning as often as they were able about Sheila and little Jeremiah. The children were not long dead when they heard about it. All the poor people had Gaelic. The superiors hadn't got it, or else they spoke it poorly. The poor people could often get word about each other without the superiors knowing it. As soon as the father and mother found out that the pair of children had died, such a grief and a brooding came over them that they could not stay in the place. They were separated from each other, but they found the opportunity of sending word to each other. They decided to steal away from the place. The wife's name was Kit. Patrick first slipped out of the house. He waited for Kit at the top of the Road of the Wisps. In a while, he saw her coming, but she was walking very slowly. The sickness was on her. They pushed on towards Carrigastyra. They came to the place where the big hole was. They knew that the two children were down in the hole with the hundreds of other bodies. They stood beside the hole and they wept their fill. Up on Derryleigh to the east of the Caharin was the cabin in which they had been living before they went into the poorhouse. They left the big hole and they headed north-west for Derryleigh, where the cabin was. The place was six miles of a journey from them, and the night was coming, but they pushed on. The hunger was on them and the sickness on Kit. They had to walk very slowly. When they had put a couple of miles of the journey past them, Kit was forced to stop. She was not able to walk any further. A neighbour came across them. Drink and some little bit of food was given to them, but fear would not allow anyone to give them shelter since they were only just after coming out of the poor-house and the evil sickness was on the woman. Patrick only lifted the woman onto his back and pushed on north-westwards for the cabin.

The poor man himself was weak enough. It would have been hard on him to put the journey by him without having any load. With the load, he was forced to stop and to leave his load down on the ditch of the road for a while. But whatever weariness was on him, he continued to put that journey by him. He did not part with his load. He reached the cabin. The cabin was cold and empty before him, without fire nor heat.

The morning after, some neighbour came to the cabin. He went inside. He saw the pair there and they both dead, and the feet of the woman in Patrick's bosom, as if he had been trying to warm them. It would seem that he had felt the weakness of death coming over Kit and her feet cold, and he put the feet into his own bosom to take the cold from them.

'He was a good, loyal, noble man!' some person might say, perhaps, 'and the deed he did was a noble one!'

It is true. But I will tell you this much. Thousands of deeds of the same kind were done in Ireland during that period, and nobody was one whit amazed at the excellence of the deeds. According to everyone, Patrick Buckley had only done a thing that any man, who was worth calling a Christian, would have done.

That little man-een, whose name was Michael O'Leary, was living in a cabin not far from that in which Patrick Buckley and his wife died. Black Michael was a nick-name they had on him. Cathleen Purcell was his wife's name. They had the full of the house of children. There wasn't as much as one word of English in themselves or in the children. The famine came hard on them. Tadhg was the name of their eldest son. He saw his father and mother growing weak with the hunger, and the youngest member of the family stretched dead in a corner of the cabin. At nightfall, he took an axe and a knife with him and out he went. He went into the cowhouse of one of the neighbours and he killed a beast. He took some of the skin from it, stripping the amount of meat he wanted to bring with him. He took away the two hind quarters and came home. They all had a good meal that night. When the hunger had been taken from them, Tadhg took out the body that was in the corner, and he made a hole out in the garden and put the body in it.

When the morning came, the people who owned the cow rose and found the cow dead out in the shed, with its two hind quarters gone. The owner went to Macroom and got a search warrant. He had an idea where the meat was brought. He and whatever law-officer he had with him came to Black Michael's cabin. The bones and some of the meat was found. Tadhg was taken prisoner and brought to Macroom and put into prison. When the time came for it, he was tried. He was sentenced without much hesitation and transported. I never heard any report since then of what happened him afterwards nor of what end befell him.

Michael and Cathleen and those of the family who still lived left the cabin and took to the roads.

Some days after they had gone away, a neighbour was going past the cabin. He saw a hound, with something in his mouth, in the garden; the hound threw down the thing he had in his mouth and ran away. The neighbour came over and he nearly fell with the shock and the horror when he saw that it was a person's hand that the dog had in his mouth! Tadhg hadn't made the hole deep enough before he had put the body down into it.

The Great Irish Famine

N. Marshall Cummins

from: *Some Chapters of Cork Medical History* (1957)

The great Irish Famine of 1845–47 was perhaps the greatest calamity that ever afflicted the Irish race, not only because of the many thousands who died, but also from the far-reaching consequences this dreadful visitation caused. It is impossible to mention here more than a fraction of what happened in the South of Ireland, as every town and hamlet had its own particular horror. I can only record some of the more dramatic episodes that occurred and a few of the leading figures who filled the stages of Irish life in those terrible years.

The first signs of the famine, due to the failure of the potato crop, were dramatically portrayed by Father Mathew, writing to Mr. Trevelyan, Secretary of the Treasury: 'On the 27th July, 1846, I passed from Cork to Dublin and this doomed plant bloomed in all the luxuriance of an abundant harvest. Returning on the 3rd August I beheld one wide waste of putrefying vegetation. In one week the chief support of the masses was utterly lost. The famine had an immediate and devastating effect on the Irish people. The destitute rushed to the workhouses, which soon became crowded to excess by those who had been able-bodied men and women, whilst the aged, the sickly and the children were left to starve. Overpowered by hunger they lay down helpless, the ready victims of the pestilence that followed close upon the footsteps of famine, and died in thousands.'

The following heart-rending letter† sums up all the horrors of the famine in a few short words. It was published by Mr M.T. Moriarty, of Ventry Cottage, Dingle, who saw the whole pitiful drama enacted before his eyes: 'Near my house there lately lived a house of eight persons. One by one did one of the daughters, alone and unassisted, carry her father and sisters to their long home, merely covered in the rags they died in, and then, worn out and unable to reach her wretched house where the last member of the family was at the moment expiring, she laid down her weary limbs and aching head beside a ditch and there her tired spirit obtained the wished for release.'

On the 4th February, 1847, Fr. Mathew wrote to Mr Trevelyan: 'We are in a deplorable state in Cork from the influx into the city of more than 10,000 foodless, homeless people, young and old. The Workhouse has been closed and there is no refuge for these miserable creatures.' Mr. J.F. Maguire, M.P., writes of 1847: 'The famine was raging in every part of the afflicted country, and starving multitudes crowded the thoroughfares of the large towns. Death was everywhere — in the cabin, on the high seas, in the garret, in the cellar, and even on the flags of the most public streets of the city. In the Workhouse the carnage was frightful and it was increasing at a prodigious rate. More than 100 Workhouse officers fell victims during this fateful year to the famine fever. For three months in 1847 the number of human beings that died in the Cork Workhouse was 2,130. In Father Mathew's cemetery alone, within nine months, 10,000 bodies were buried. At the Church of St Ann Shandon, under a kind of shed attached to a guard house, lay huddled in their filthy, foetid rags, about forty-two human creatures — men, women and children, and infants of the tenderest age — starving and fever stricken, most of them in a dying state, some dead, and all gaunt, yellow, hideous from the combined effects of famine and disease. Under this open shed they had remained during the night until about 10 o'clock in the morning, when the funeral processions were passing by, and their indescribable misery was beheld by the leading citizens of Cork, including the Mayor. The odour which proceeded from that huddled-up heap of human beings was of itself enough to generate a plague. As the procession reached the Church of St Ann Shandon a cry of horror was raised at the spectacle which was there beheld.'

†*'Cork Constitution'*, 13/4/1847.

A correspondent[†] writes: 'I would wish to direct the attention of the city to the danger they are in from those who have died, and who are interred in the open vaults under our city churches, particularly St Finbarr's and St Ann Shandon. There is no danger at the present time of the doctors wanting subjects for dissection, but the congregations attending these churches are exposed to danger by the offensive smells, especially at the Cathedral, by the great numbers interred there.'

Cork City and County suffered more severely than most places in Ireland. Dr. Callanan reports: 'From the commencement of 1847, fate opened her book in good earnest here, and the full tide of death flowed on everywhere around us. During the first six months of that dark period, one-third of the daily population of our streets consisted of shadows and spectres, the impersonation of disease and famine, and crowding in from the rural districts and stalking along to the general doom — the grave — which appeared to await them, but at the distance of a few steps or a few short hours. And so in sad truth it was, for the obituary of our Workhouse here for 1847 gives the appalling return of 3,329 deaths. Within the month of March, 757 inmates of that dismal abode perished from famine and fever.'

In the workhouse, the inmates were put 3, 4 and 5 in a bed, and in the convalescent ward there were 45 beds for 120 patients.

J.T. Collins[*] writes: 'Fr. Augustine Maguire, a young priest, had as his first mission to aid the chaplain in ministering to the sick in the Cork Workhouse in the famine. In later years he acted as chaplain at Scutari Hospital during the Crimean War. Looking back upon the 50 years of his priesthood, he said then that what stood most vividly in his memory were his early experiences in the Cork Workhouse. As compared with them his experiences in the Crimean War were but trivial. The smoke of battle, the blood, the sight of maimed and dying, never affected him like the sight of his fellow countrymen dropping dead by the roadside, carried off by the starvation and the fever that came on suddenly and gave them no chance to fight against it. "I remember one day," continued Monsignor Maguire, "when no less than 80 people were brought up to the Workhouse in a body. They filled a long line of cars, and as rapidly as I could I gave Absolution and anointed these poor creatures before they died." '

[†]'*Cork Constitution*', 6/7/1847.
[*]'*Cork Evening Echo*,' 10/11/1954

In a population of 80,000 in Cork in 1847 there were seven to eight hundred patients under daily treatment for fever. In the three years — 1845, 1846 and 1847 — there were 12,805 cases of fever, with 583 deaths in the Cork Fever Hospital.

The following temporary fever hospitals were opened in 1847:

The Cat Fort Hospital treated 1,477 patients, with 99 deaths.

The Barrack Street Hospital treated 2,529 patients, with 444 deaths, and of these, 214 deaths were due to cholera.

The North Fever Sheds admitted 839 patients, with 48 deaths.

The North Infirmary was taken over as a fever hospital. Fever cases kept coming in until the very lobbies were filled with beds; 1,602 fever patients were admitted, with 156 deaths.

Dr W. Beamish reported* that: 'Even the Cork County Jail, which was built for 240 inmates, at one time held 959 persons, chiefly fever cases.'

The Cove Fever Hospital: In the two years, 1847 and 1848, Dr Cronin reported 1,239 cases of fever, with 75 deaths.

In all these hospitals, each physician was responsible for over 125 patients and was paid the princely salary of 5/- a day.

The south-western coastal districts of County Cork suffered terribly severely. 'In the middle of December, 1846' Mr W. O'Brien writes, 'a visit of inquiry was undertaken to near Skibbereen by Mr Nicholas Marshall Cummins, J.P., a well-known and leading Cork merchant. Strongly moved by what he had himself seen, he lost no time in communicating to the British public the results of his visit. This he did in the shape of an urgent and most impressive appeal addressed by him in a published letter to the Duke of Wellington, which I can distinctly recall, produced everywhere an immediate and most powerful effect in attracting general attention and much munificent relief to this remote and, then, sorely stricken region:

'To His Grace, Field Marshal, the Duke of Wellington: My Lord Duke,

Without apology or preface I presume so far to trespass on Your Grace as to state to you and, by the use of your illustrious name, to present to the British public the following statement of what I have myself seen within the last three days:

Having for many years been intimately connected with the western portion of the County of Cork, and possessing some small property

*'*Cork Constitution*,' 1/4/1847.

there, I thought it right personally to investigate the truth of the several lamentable accounts which had reached me of the appalling state of misery to which that part of the country was reduced. I accordingly went on the 15th instant to Skibbereen and, to give the instance of one townland which I visited as an example of the state of the entire coast district, I shall state simply what I there saw.

It is situated on the eastern side of Castlehaven Harbour and is named South Reen, in the parish of Moyross. Being aware that I should have to witness scenes of frightful hunger, I provided myself with as much bread as five men could carry, and on reaching the spot I was surprised to find the wretched hamlet deserted. I entered some of the hovels to ascertain the cause, and the scenes that presented themselves were such as no tongue or no pen can convey the slightest idea of. In the first, six famished and ghastly skeletons, to all appearance dead, were huddled in a corner on some filthy straw, their sole covering what seemed to be a ragged horse-cloth and their wretched legs hanging about, naked above the knees. I approached with horror and found by a low moaning they were alive; they were in fever — four children, a woman, and what once had been a man. It is impossible to go through the details, suffice it to say that in a few minutes I was surrounded by at least 200 of such phantoms, such frightful spectres as no words can describe. By far the greater number were delirious, either from famine or from fever. Their demoniac yells are still ringing in my ears, and their horrible images are fixed upon my brain. My heart sickens at the recital, but I must go on. In another case — decency would forbid what follows, but it must be told — my clothes were nearly torn off in my endeavours to escape from the throng of pestilence around when my neckcloth was seized from behind by a grip which compelled me to turn. I found myself grasped by a woman with an infant, *just born*, in her arms and the remains of a filthy sack across her loins — the sole covering of herself and babe. The same morning the police opened a house on the adjoining lands, which was observed shut for many days, and two frozen corpses were found lying upon the mud floor, *half devoured by the rats*.

A mother, herself in fever, was seen the same day to drag out the corpse of her child, a girl of about twelve, perfectly naked and leave her half covered with stones. In another house, within 500 yards of the cavalry station at Skibbereen, the dispensary doctor found seven wretches lying, unable to move, under the same cloak — one had been dead many hours, but the others were unable to move either themselves or the corpse.

To what purpose should I multiply such cases? If these be not sufficient, neither would they hear who have the power to send relief and do not, even 'though one came from the dead'.

Let them, however, believe and tremble that they shall one day hear the Judge of all the earth pronounce their tremendous doom, with the addition: 'I was hungered and ye gave Me no meat; thirsty and ye gave Me no drink; naked and ye clothed Me not.' But I forget to whom this is addressed. My Lord, you are an old and justly honoured man. It is yet in your power to add another honour to your age; to fix another star and that the brightest to your galaxy and glory. You have access to our young and gracious Queen — lay these things before her. She is a woman, she will not allow decency to be outraged. She has at her command the means of at least mitigating the sufferings of the wretched survivors of this tragedy. They will soon be few, indeed, in the district I speak of if help be longer withheld.

Once more, my Lord Duke, in the name of starving thousands, I implore you, break the frigid and flimsy chain of official etiquette and save the land of your birth — the kindred of that gallant Irish blood which you have so often seen lavished to support the honour of the British name — and let there be inscribed upon your tomb, *Servata Hibernia*.

> I have the honour to be,
> My Lord Duke,
> Your Grace's obedient humble servant,
> N.M. Cummins, J.P.

Ann Mount, Cork
   December 17th, 1846.'

Immediately following publication of this letter he journeyed to London, and with his uncle, James John Cummins, the banker, collected £10,000 for famine relief.

To the Editor, *Cork Constitution*:

'I have abounded satisfaction in being able to assure you that nine names alone in London have this day subscribed for the truly noble amount of £8,000. Surely her merchants are princes, and her traders

378

the honourable of the earth. The names are as follows: Barings, Rothschilds, P. J. Smiths, Overends, Truman, Hanbury & Co., Duke of Devonshire, Jones Lloyd, a £1,000 each; Bruce Buxton, £500; Lord John Russell, £300; Roberts & Co., £200. Small sums, £200. — N.M.C.'

The Editor replied:

'We have seldom published a letter with more satisfaction than the above. The English do not want willingness — that they have proved a thousand times. All that they want is to be rightly called. They are ready to love, but must have the invitation. Let some recognised person lead and he won't lack followers. What is described in the letter has been done without meeting or appeal. It is the result of a mere consciousness that aid was needed, and it would be unjust to withhold from Mr Cummins the credit in having in no small degree contributed to create that consciousness. Indeed, we are persuaded that his single letter did more for it than anything else that has been said or written, and the blessings of thousands that are 'ready to perish' will, we hope, reward him.'

N.M. Cummins was much criticized in the Press by people who stated that the conditions described by him were very much exaggerated. But these criticisms were refuted by Mr McCarthy Downing and Rev. Moloney, C.C., who visited the locality and made a most minute examination of the state of the inhabitants. The result was that the statement of N. M. Cummins was found to fall far short of giving the full and real state of wretchedness to which the people had been reduced. Later the following letter from a resident at Castletownshend was published: 'I have now to mention the lamentable fact that out of 60 houses and 320 inhabitants on the farm of South Reen, two years since, there now remain after the ravages of dysentery and starvation eight houses and about 50 persons. The houses were pulled down for firing and the people carried off by fever.' A man of superb physique, N. M. Cummins survived the famine years, but soon after 1847 he was compelled to leave the country a ruined and bankrupt man, having sacrificed his fortunes for the people when they were in dire need.

In 1847, 'The Jamestown,' a man-of-war, was fitted out by the American Government and loaded with provisions and sent over to Cork for famine relief. She arrived in the outer harbour on 12th

April, where Capt. Parker of the 'Sabrina,' en route to Bristol, took her in tow and brought her alongside Haulbowline. A public meeting was held in the County Courthouse, and the following deputation, consisting of the High Sheriff, the Dean of Cork, M. J. Barry, Wm. Fagan, T. R. Sarsfield, Rev. Theobald Mathew and Nicholas Cummins were appointed to express thanks to Captain Forbes and the American people for their kindness and sympathy. The gentlemen were severally introduced by Mr Nicholas Cummins, of the firm of Messrs. Nicholas and Joseph Cummins of this city, who had started for Cove on the previous evening with dispatches for Mr Forbes on board 'The Jamestown,' off the harbour, and accompanied him to Haulbowline. The following Committee, 'The American Relief Committee,' was immediately formed to make arrangements for the distribution of the foodstuffs through Cork City and County: Lord Bernard, Chairman; Major N. Ludlow Beamish, Vice-Chairman; The Dean and Archdeacon of Cork, R. C. Vicar Capitular; Collector Troy, Francis Lyons, M. D.; T. Jennings, R. Dowden, Rev. Father Mathew, J. Lyons, Acting Mayor; Wm. Clear, J. Jennings, P. McSweeney, Sir Robert Lane, Caesar Otway. The Secretaries were the two cousins, Nicholas and Nicholas Marshall Cummins. In addition, Nicholas Cummins was Secretary to the British Relief Association in Cork. One hundred and fifty localities in the county, well-known to the Committee as possessing the strongest claims for relief, were selected for five tons of provisions apiece, the local distribution of which was left to the clergy of the various denominations rather than to the official relief committees. That Captain Forbes had ample evidence of how sadly needed were these provisions is shown by his description of the gruesome sights he witnessed during his brief stay in Cork:

'I went with Father Mathew only a few steps out of one of the principle streets of Cork into a lane — the valley of the shadow of death was it? Alas, no, it was the valley of death and pestilence itself. I saw enough in five minutes to horrify me: houses crowded with the sick and dying, without floors, without furniture, and with patches of dirty straw covered with still dirtier shreds and patches of humanity; some called for water to Father Mathew, and others for a dying blessing. From this very small sample of the prevailing destitution we proceeded to a public soup kitchen under a shed guarded by police officers. Here a long boiler containing rice, meal, etc., was at work, while hundreds of spectres stood without, begging for some of the soup which I can readily conceive would be refused by well-bred pigs in America. Every corner of the streets is filled with pale, careworn creatures, the weak leading the weaker; women assail you at every turn with famished babies imploring alms.'

Dr James McCormack wrote* from Crookhaven in January, 1884: ' Nothing can so truly depict our miserable condition as the deserted state of our religious houses of worship. Attendances a few months ago were about 400, last Sunday week about 50, and yesterday 20.' Skibbereen was described by one correspondent as 'one mass of famine, disease and death, the poor rapidly sinking under fever, dysentery and starvation. It was one of the longest to suffer and the slowest to recover.' Mr T. H. Marmion opened a soup kitchen which kept 600 persons alive and only supplied those who were most destitute.

On 13th February, 1874, Mr James Mahony, of Cork, wrote in the *London Illustrated News* : 'Neither pen nor pencil could ever portray the misery and horror witnessed in Skibbereen. I saw the dying, the living and the dead lying indiscriminately upon the same floor, without anything between them and the cold earth, save a few miserable rags upon them, Not a single house out of the 500 could boast of being free from death and fever, though several could be pointed out with the dead lying close to the living for the space of three, four and even six days, without any effort being made to remove the bodies to a last resting place.'

Dr O'Donovan continues the grim story: 'We next went to see the "hut". This shed is seven feet long and six feet in breadth. The hut is surrounded by a rampart of human bones which have accumulated to such a height that the threshold, which was originally on a level with the ground, is now two feet beneath it. In this horrible den, in the midst of a mass of human putrefaction, males and females with most malignant fever were huddled together as closely as were the dead in the graves around.' Before reaching Skibbereen, Mr Mahony visited Clonakilty. 'Here the horrors of povetry became visible in the vast number of famished poor who flocked around the coach to beg alms.'

In Bantry Workhouse, human beings were sleeping 4, 5 or even 6 in a narrow bed, and 'Medico' writes:† 'I visited fifty hovels, in every one of which there existed six or eight human beings, the greater part

---

Cork Constitution January, 1847
†*Cork Constitution*, 1847

so reduced by emaciation from famine, fever and dysentery as scarcely to appear human. In one house, the first deserving the name that we visited, there were six families in six rooms, in all 35, the greater part dead or dying, the only distinguishing marks being the agonizing shrieks of the latter for help to save them from starvation. If you can imagine an unconscious form in the agonies of death summon all the ebbing energies of life in one fearful scream and then relapsing back on the bed, dead, you can form a very slight idea of the most awful sound that ever met the ears or conscience of men, a sound that will ring in my memory till the oblivion of the grave overcomes it.'

In Bantry, 900 bodies were interred in a plot of ground only 40 ft. square. 'Frightful and fearful,' writes Rev. Dr Traill, Rector and Chairman of Schull Relief Committee, 'is the havoc around me. Our medical friend, Dr Sweetnam, informed me yesterday that if he stated the mortality in Schull at an average of 35 daily he would be within truth. The children in particular, he remarked,* were disappearing with awful rapidity. And to this I may add the aged, who with the young — neglected perhaps amidst the widespread destitution — are almost, without exception, swollen and ripening for the grave. Out of 18,000 persons in Schull, 5,000 have not a morsel more than charity supplies. My house is more like a beleaguered fortress besieged. Ere the day has dawned, the crowds are gathering; my family and I all are perfect slaves. Ourselves and our servants are worn out with attending to them. I would not wish, were it possible, for one starving creature to leave my doors without giving something to allay the cravings of hunger.' And later he wrote: 'I may say of a truth that the plague has begun. They could not count the bodies which were brought for interment yesterday. Every house is filled with fever and its attendants — dysentery, dropsy, death.'

Dr Traill died shortly afterwards, completely worn out from his exertions on behalf of the poor. He used his large fortune liberally for their relief.

A curious experience of a friend of the author is here recorded. I can vouch for this lady's absolute honesty and one must accept her story as she told it to me: 'I was motoring on a winter's evening on a lonely country road between Forrest and Nettleville and near Carrigadrohid, in Co. Cork, when coming down a hill I saw in the lights of the car about 50 yards ahead a tall gaunt figure standing

*Cork Constitution, February 2nd, 1847.

382

motionless by the roadside. Drawing nearer, I beheld an emaciated woman with a death-like face. She was almost naked, except for a piece of greenish black cloth hanging from her shoulders. Her legs and arms were bare and thin as drumsticks. I was about to stop the car and offer her some assistance, when I suddenly became afraid and hurried home, intending to inform the Guards of her plight.

I, however, first of all asked the advice of my groom, who came from the locality. He exclaimed in an agitated voice: "Do nothing, ma'am; do nothing, ma'am! That road is a bad road, and many queer people have been seen there." I subsequently made further inquiries and discovered that a soup kitchen had been located near there in the great famine, and also that there had been much distress at that time and that many had died from starvation and typhus fever.'

Father Mathew wrote to Sir Charles Trevelyan, Assistant Secretary, on 16th December, 1846: 'I deeply regret the abandonment of the people to corn and flour dealers. They charge 50% to 100% profit. Cargoes of maize are purchased before their arrival and are sold like railway shares, passing through different hands before they are ground and sold to the poor.' Rev. Nicholas Martin wrote:* 'People are completely dependent for means of subsistence upon provisions which have been raised to an exorbitant price by merchants and speculators who take advantage of this trying emergency to enrich themselves at the expense of every humane and noble consideration.'

One firm alone in Cork made a profit of £80,000, another £40,000. In four days the price of Indian meal was raised by £3 5s. 0d. in speculations in the Cornmarket. Mrs Woodham Smith writes:‡ 'Flight or death was the choice. The people tramped to the ports and for as little as 2/6 were transported across the channel. 278,000 Irish poured into Liverpool; 90,000 into Glasgow. Mr. Trevelyan gives the names of 19 relieving officers and 30 Catholic priests who caught the cholera and died. In Liverpool alone, 10,000 persons died of typhus in 1847. In 1847, 75,000 Irish emigrated to British North America, of whom nearly 10,000 died from fever either on the voyage or in the quarantine hospitals after arrival. Four ships from Cork and six from Liverpool had 804 deaths on the voyage and 876 on arrival.

'No faintest apprehension of the fatal results crossed the minds of landlords, statesmen and philanthropists as the "coffin ships"

* *Cork Constitution*, February 2nd, 1847.
‡ *The Reason Why*, p. 126

made their slow voyage across the Atlantic, a voyage said by men who had experienced both to transcend in horror the dreaded middle passage of the slave trade, and bore with them a cargo of hatred. In that new world, which had been called into being to redress the balance of the old, there was to grow up a population among whom animosity to England was a creed; whose burning resentment could never be appeased, who, possessing the long memory of Ireland could never forget. The Irish Famine was to be paid for by England at a terrible price; out of it was born Irish America.'

Mrs Woodham Smith describes the utter ruthlessness of some of the Irish landlords in dealing with their tenants in Co. Mayo in her remarkable book, *The Reason Why.* As a contrast, we turn to A. M. Sullivan, who wrote: 'No adequate tribute has ever been paid to those Irish landlords — and they were of every party and creed — who perished, martyrs to duty, in that awful time; who did not fly from the plague-reeking workhouse, or fever-tainted court.' Amongst those he singled out for mention, Mr Martin of Ballinahinch, and Mr Nolan of Ballinderry (father of Col. Nolan, MP), the latter died of typhus caught in Tuam Workhouse. Mr Richard White, nephew of the Earl of Bantry, whose memory will be long cherished by the people of Bantry, died at Inchiclogh of fever. J. T. Collins continued:[†] 'Others who died at that time administering to the stricken people were Rev. J. R. Cotter of Innishannon, who died from fever. He was the second son of Sir James Cotter of Rockforest, near Mallow. At Bandon, of fever, caught in discharge of his duties as Poor Law Guardian, John Lovell, Esq., also Maskelyne Alcock, of Roughgrove, Bandon. At Ballindeasig House, near Minane Bridge, of fever caught in attendance on the poor of her neighbourhood, died Mrs. Kenefick. At Robert's Cove, of fever contracted in discharge of his duties as Poor Law Guardian, Edward Galway, Esq. The Rev. Daniel Horgan, C. C., Donoughmore, caught the fever and died, aged 34 years. Also died, Mr. Samuel Lane, of Frankfield House. He is said to have fed over 900 individuals who had neither food nor money to buy it. On June 1st, died of fever, Mr. Richard Coppinger, of Camden Quay, Cork; on July 30th, at Clonakilty, of illness brought about by his exertions to relieve the poor, died John O'Hea, J. P., bank manager, leaving a widow and 10 children. On August 12th died Abraham Beale of fever. He was Secretary to the Friends'

† *'Cork Evening Echo',* 10/11/1954

Committee in Cork and had travelled throughout the country distributing relief in money and food.'

A.M. Sullivan* writes: 'no pen nor tongue can trace nor relate the countless deeds of heroism and self-sacrifice which the dreadful visitation called forth on the part, pre-eminently, of two classes in the community, the Catholic clergy and Dispensary doctors.' The fatality amongst these two classes was lamentable. A very careful summary was made by Drs Stokes and Cusack: 'During the 25 years up to 1843, out of 1,220 medical practitioners in Ireland in charge of 406 medical institutions, 300 or nearly one-quarter died, and of these 132 died of typhus fever alone, while the remaining 168 deaths include cholera, scarlet and other fevers. One out of 2.29 deaths of doctors died from typhus fever. Dr John Popham, in his presidential address to the Cork Medical Society in 1861, states: 'We, in the famine years, became painfully accustomed to the mournful reiteration of the ill-boding words, "died of fever in the course of his medical duties."' And, he said, it was found in 1847 that one in fifteen of the whole medical community had been swept away. And that while the mortality from fever compared to deaths from all other causes for the whole community was 1 in 10, for the medical faculty it was 1 in 2¼; a mortality far exceeding that of army surgeons amidst the chances and privations of war.

> 'Christian heroes, martyrs for humanity, their names are blazoned on no courtly roll; yet shall they shine upon an eternal page, brighter than the stars.'

* 'New Ireland,' p. 137.

Emigration
Mr and Mrs Hall
from: *Hall's Ireland* (1841)

Cork is the great outlet of emigrants from the south of Ireland and the Australian Emigration Society have an agent here.

In the month of June, we stood on the quay of Cork to see some emigrants embark in one of the steamers for Falmouth on their way to Australia. The band of exiles amounted to two hundred and an immense crowd had assembled to bid them a long and last adieu. The scene was very touching, and it was impossible to witness it without heart-pain and tears. Mothers clung upon the necks of their athletic sons, young girls clung to elder sisters, fathers — old, white-haired men — fell upon their knees with arms uplifted to heaven, imploring the protecting care of the Almighty on their departing children. Amid the din, the noise, the turmoil, the people pressing and rolling in vast masses towards the place of embarkation, there were many such sad episodes. Men, old men too, embracing each other and crying like little children. Several passed carefully bearing little relics of their homes; the branch of a favourite hawthorn bush or a bush of meadow-sweet. Many had a long switch of witch-hazel to encircle the ground whereon they were to sleep in the foreign land, so as, according to the universal superstition, to prevent the approach of any venomous reptile or poisonous insect.

On the deck of the steamer there was less confusion than might have been expected. The hour of departure was at hand, the police had torn asunder several who at the last would not be separated, and as many as could find room were leaning over the side of the craft speechless yet eloquent in gesture, expressing their adieus to their friends and relatives on shore. In the midst of the agitation, a fair-haired boy and girl were sitting tranquilly, yet sadly, watching a very fine white Angora cat that was carefully packed in a basket.

'We are going out to Papa and Mama with nurse,' they said in an unmitigated brogue, 'but we are very sorry to leave dear Ireland for all that.' Their father had, we imagine, been a prosperous settler.

It is impossible to describe the final parting. Shrieks and prayers, blessings and lamentations mingled in one great cry from those on the quay and those on shipboard until a band stationed in the forecastle struck up 'St Patrick's Day'. The communicating plank was with-drawn, and the steamer moved majestically forward on her way. Some, overcome with emotion, fell down upon the deck, others waved hats, handkerchiefs and hands to their friends and the band played louder.

We left the vessel and her crowd of clean, well-dressed and per-fectly sober emigrants with deep regret, reminding ourselves that while there are in Ireland so many miles of unreclaimed land, it is a sad loss that such a freight should be conveyed from her shores.

The evening that succeeded this agitating morning was calm and balmy. We desired to examine the scene of the morning's turmoil and drove along the quay which was lonely and deserted save for a few stragglers. We continued our voyage until the signs of immediate traffic were wildly scattered. We drove through the village of Douglas, once famous for its sail cloth manufacture and proceeded until the Cork river widened into a mimic sea, called Lough Mahon. We drove slowly, enjoying the rare and exquisitely varied landscape.

Old Skibbereen
Anonymous

Oh, father dear, I often hear you speak of Erin's Isle,
Her lofty scenes and valleys green, her mountains rude and wild,
They say it is a lovely land wherein a prince might dwell,
Oh, why did you abandon it? the reason to me tell.

Oh, son! I loved my native land with energy and pride,
Till a blight came o'er my crops — my sheep, my cattle died;
My rent and taxes were too high, I could not them redeem,
And that's the cruel reason that I left old Skibbereen.

Oh, well do I remember the bleak December day,
The landlord and the sheriff came to drive us all away;
They set my roof on fire with their cursed English spleen,
And that's another reason that I left old Skibbereen.

Your mother, too, God rest her soul, fell on the snowy ground,
She fainted in her anguish, seeing the desolation round,
She never rose, but passed away from life to mortal dream,
And found a quiet grave, my boy, in dear old Skibbereen.

And you were only two years old and feeble was your frame,
I could not leave you with my friends, you bore your father's
    name —
I wrapt you in my cotamore at the dead of night unseen,
I heaved a sigh and bade good-bye, to dear old Skibbereen.

Oh, father dear, the day may come when in answer to the call
Each Irishman, with feeling stern, will rally one and all;
I'll be the man to lead the van beneath the flag so green,
When loud and high we'll raise the cry — 'Remember Skibbereen'.

Waifs

Canon P. A. Sheehan

from: *Glenanaar* (1905)

Glenanaar, the glen of slaughter, is a deep ravine, running directly
north and south through a lower spur of the mountains that divide
Cork and Limerick. The boundary line that separates these counties,
and also the dioceses of Cloyne and Limerick, and the parishes of
Ardpatrick and Doneraile, runs right along the top of the glen, and
close to that boundary line on the southern side was the farm of
Edmond Connors, one of the men who had been put back on the
second trial in the Doneraile Conspiracy, of which we have just
written. His farm lay along the slope of the valley, facing directly
east. It extended right over the slope, and was terminated there by
the wild heather of the mountain; and it stretched downwards to
the river, always full even in summer, but a fierce, angry torrent in
winter; and which took its name, Avon, or, as it is pronounced,
Own-anaar, from the same terrific battle after which the glen is
named. The house, a long, low building, thatched with reed, fronted
the south; and, although very remote from village or town, the
whole place — farm, field, and river, were as cosy and picturesque as
could be found in Ireland. Edmond Connors, the proprietor, as we
have said, a man of Herculean strength, broad-shouldered, deep-
chested, strong-limbed; but you needed only to look at that calm,
clear face, and those mild, blue eyes, that looked at you with a half-
pitying, half-sorrowful glance, to see, as every one said, that
Edmond Connors 'would not hurt a child.' He was in fact, a superb
type of a very noble class of peasants, now, alas! under modern
influences, dying away slowly in the land. They were all giants,
largely formed, strongly thewed. They rarely touched meat. At
Christmas and Easter it was a luxury. Their dietary was simple and

ascetic — meal, milk, and potatoes. But their constant exposure to rough weather, their incessant labour, and the iron constitutions they inherited from their forefathers and conserved by the purity and temperance of their lives, were better adapted than the feeble helps civilization gives to create a hardy and iron race. It was of such men and their forefathers that Edmund Spenser, a rabid exterminator, wrote in despair to Queen Elizabeth, that they were quite hopeless — these attempts that were made to destroy or root out such a people; for they were so hardy, so fearless of death, so contemptuous of fatigue and wounds, that even the savage efforts of Elizabethan and Cromwellian freebooters failed to destroy what Providence evidently intended to maintain and preserve. With these strong peasants, too, modern worries and vexations had no place. They had their trials; but they relied so implicitly on the maxims of their religion, which was also their philosophy, that they bore every reverse of fortune, and sickness and death, with the most profound and tranquil equanimity. A few times during their long and laborious lives, they might flash out in some sudden flame of anger, and it was bad for those who crossed their path. But that died away in remorse immediately, and the old, calm, patient way of life was resumed again. It was really pathetic the way these gentle giants used to look out from their clear blue eyes, in which there was always a depth of sorrow hidden under their strongest bushy eyebrows; and how patiently they took the events of life, and calmly the wildest vagaries of destiny. You could not disturb their equanimity. Tell them of the most wonderful or dreadful thing, and they accepted it without surprise or alarm. They would be the despair of a dramatist. He could not astonish them, or excite their enthusiasm. To sleep, to wake, to work, to pray, to die — that was the programme of existence. To wonder, to admire, to be angry, to be enthusiastic — they knew not the secret of these things. All things are ordered by a Supreme Will, of whom we are the puppets — that is all! Who does not remember them in their strong frieze cutaway coats, their drab or snuff-coloured vests and knee-breeches, the rough home-woven stockings, and the strong shoes — all made, like themselves, for hard work and wild tempestuous weather? No Wordsworth has yet sung the praises of these Irish dalesmen; but this, too, will come in the intellectual upheaval that we are witnessing just now.

Since the time of the trial, and his merciful escape from a horrible death, old Edmond Connors was accustomed to remain even more alone than was his usual wont. Always of a solitary turn of mind, he began now to haunt the mountains continually. Sometimes he was seen sitting on the low parapet of a bridge that crossed the mountain stream, sometimes on a great boulder deep down in some primeval valley, visited only by sun and moon and stars; and sometimes his great form was seen outlined against the wintry sky, as he knelt and prayed on one of those immense stones that form cairns on the crest of the hills looking down into the glens and dales of Limerick. What were his thoughts no one knew, for like all his class he was a silent man, and rarely spoke but in monosyllables.

There was a heavy fall of snow a few days before Christmas of this year; and, as the weather was intensely cold, there were none of the usual thaws, but the frost knit the snow-flakes together and crusted them all over with its own hard but brilliant enamelling. The whole landscape was covered with this white, pure surface, except where the river, now blackened by the contrast, cut its cold, dark way between the clefts it had made for itself out of the soft sand of the hills. The bleak, dreary appearance of the landscape, however, did not deter Edmond Connors from his daily ramble in the mountains. His strong gaiters and boots defied the wet of the snow-clad heather; and he trudged along through slushy bog and across wet fields, only stopping from time to time to look down across the white, level plain that stretched its monotone of silver till it touched the sky-line, and was merged in it. One evening, just as dusk fell, about four o'clock, and the atmosphere became sensibly colder, he turned his footsteps homeward. His way led across the little bridge down beyond the plantation of fir-trees on the main road. As he came in sight of it he saw in the twilight a woman sitting on the low parapet, with a child in her arms. His footsteps were so completely muffled by the soft snow that she was unaware of his approach, until he came quite close to her, and she woke up from her reveries and stared at him. She was quite young, but the child in her arms told that she was married. Her face would have been very beautiful, except that it was now drawn tight as parchment; and two great black eyes stared out of the pallor, as if in fright at some undefined but yet unrealized sorrow that was haunting her with its shadow. On seeing the great, tall figure near her, she drew up her black shawl hastily and covered her head, and turned away. The old man seeing this, and thinking that she had been suckling her child, and had turned away in modesty, approached and said, kindly:

'God save you, honest 'uman! Sure 'tis a cowld evening to be out; and a cowld rest you have got for yerself.'

The woman did not answer.

'Wisha, thin, me poor 'uman,' said the old man, kindly; 'you ought to seek shelter tonight, if not for yerself, at laste fer yer little child.'

The woman remained silent, with averted face. He fumbled in his pocket and drew out a silver piece.

'Here, me poor 'uman,' he said, extending the coin toward her. 'I haven't much; but the Lord has been good to me, and we must be good to every poor crachure that wants it.'

She put the hand aside with an angry gesture; and rising up to her full stature, she looked at the old man with blazing eyes.

'Edmond Connors,' she said, 'I know you, and you don't know me. But you go your ways, and lave me go mine. It will be better for you in the ind.'

'Wisha, thin, agragal,' he said, humbly, 'sure I meant no harrum; but I thought it 'ud be murdher intirely to see you and your little *gorlach* on the road a night like this.'

'Why do you talk to me of murdher?' she said.

'Haven't you murdher on your own sowl? And isn't the rope swinging for you a-yet?'

'I have not murdher, nor any other crime on my sowl,' he said, meekly, 'though, God knows, I am a sinful man enough. But you're out of your mind, me poor 'uman, and you don't undershtan' the words you're spakin'.'

'I wish 'twas thrue for you, Edmond Connors,' she said. 'I wish to God tonight that I was mad out intirely; and thin I could do what I was goin' to do, whin God or the divil sint you acrass my path.'

'I don't know what you mane,' said the old man, now very anxious, 'but if you wor thinkin' of doin' any harrum to yerself or yer child, may God and His Blessed and Holy Mother privint you. Sure that's the last of all.'

'Wouldn't it be betther for me to be dead and buried,' she said, somewhat more calmly, 'than be harried from house to house, and from parish to parish, as I am, wid every dure slammed in me face, and a curse follyin' me on me road?'

'That's quare,' said the old man, 'sure haven't you the ring on your marriage-finger as well as the best of thim?'

'I have so,' she said. 'More bad luck and misfortune 'tis to me. 'Tis I'd be the happy 'uman if I could brake that ring, and put the pieces where they couldn't be found.'

391

'At laste,' said the old man, compassionately watching the blue eyes that stared up at him from the pinched, starved face of the child, 'you should consider the child that God sint you; and if you cannot do anything to help yourself, or if you wor thinkin' of somethin' bad agin it —— '

'What could I be thinkin' of?' she said, defiantly. 'If you have murdher in your own heart, Edmond Connors, that's no rayson ye'd suspect me of the same.'

'I see, me good 'uman,' said the old man, moving slowly away, 'you're not from this neighburhood, tho' ye seem to know me name. No body in this parish 'ud spake as you have done. And,' he said, with some little temper, 'it 'udn't be safe for thim if they did.'

It seemed to touch some latent sensibility in the wretched woman, for after some hesitation she called after him.

'I ax your pardon,' she said, 'for the hard words I said agin you just now. You didn't desarve them; and no wan knows that betther than me. If I could say all I'd like to say, Edmond Connors, there 'ud be short work wid your next thrial. But me mout' is shut. But only for this little crachure, me Annie, me only tie on airth, I'd very soon put the says betune me and thim you know. An' I suppose t'was God sint you this cowld, dark night, to save me sowl from hell; for, Edmond Connors, the murdher I said wos on your sowl, and 'twas a lie, was very near bein' on me own.'

The old man looked at her sorrowfully in the growing twilight. There was something in her aspect, something in her words with their mysterious allusions, that attracted and interested him. And the blue eyes of the child seemed to haunt him, and ask for protection.

'Now, me poor 'uman,' he said, 'you're back in yer sinses agen. Sure I know well how the hardship and distress dhrive people out of their mind sometimes. But it may come on ye agen; and remimber this is a Christian counthry, where any wan would be glad to take from ye that purty, weeshy little crachure in yer arms, and save it from the cowld river. Here, now, take these few shillings, and buy somethin' warm for yourself, for ye need it; and keep God and His Blessed Mother ever afore yer sight.'

She stretched out her hand, and it lingered long in his great rough palm, whilst she fixed her glowing eyes, shaded with anxiety, upon him. Then, in a sudden impulse, she raised the big, strong hand to her lips; and, dragging her wretched shawl more closely around her, strode away. The old man stood and watched her tall, girlish figure, as it swayed along the road, darkly outlined against the white background of the snow. Then he moved slowly homeward. As he reached the crest of the hill through a short cut across the heather, he turned round, and looked back. The woman's figure stood forth clearly outlined against the darkening sky. She, too, had stood still, and was looking toward him. Seeing him still watching, she raised her hand, and waved a farewell, and passed out of his sight as he thought for ever.

He was more than usually silent, as he sat by the fire that night, and watched the red turf and blazing wood, as they poured from the open hearth great volumes of smoke up through the wide chimney that yawned darkly above. The eyes of that little child haunted him. He was troubled in conscience about it. He thought he should have asked the poor, lone woman to allow him and his *vanithee* to be her protector. One mouth more was not much to feed; and He who giveth food to the sparrows on the house-top would help to feed a little child. He was quite angry with himself, and once or twice he was about to rise and go out, and follow the waifs. But, he argued, they are gone too far on their way now. Yet when he came to the Fifth Joyful Mystery, as they recited the Rosary that evening, the remorse came back, and choked his voice with the emotion.

from: **At the Trial of the Galtee Boy, 1877**
Anonymous

In 1877, John Sarsfield Casey, known as the Galtee Boy, went on trial in Dublin as a result of allegedly libellous letters he had written concerning the conditions of the tenantry on the Galtee Castle Estate. In 1870, Casey, from Mitchelstown, had returned to Ireland after he and a number of other Fenian prisoners were sent back from Australia. One of those called to give evidence for the defence at the libel trial was Denis Murphy, a tenant on the estate. Cross-examined by Issac Butt, Murphy gave a vivid account of the appalling conditions in which he and his family lived. Such conditions were not unusual in the parts of north Cork and Tipperary bordered by the estate. In fact, they were commonplace in many parts of Ireland. Casey was found innocent and acquitted of the libel charge. In 1897, he became coroner in County Limerick. [Ed.]

Denis Murphy, a tall, gaunt man, who gesticulated excitedly when giving his evidence, was next called and examined by Mr Butt.

Are you a tenant on Mr. Buckley's estate? — I am.

How much land do you hold? — Mr Bridge told me I had 10¾ acres.

What old rent did you pay? — At the time that the Land Company bought this property from the Right Hon. the Earl of Kingston we were in unity and peace. (*Laughter*)

What rent did you pay to the company? The company's agent, my lord, which was Mr. Langford Rae, Esquire, came in the year 1854, my lord, and gave me and my partners notices to quit. Well, that was a thunderbolt to me, indeed, because to the Right Hon. George, Earl of Kingston, I or my father never was one farthing in debt. (*Laughter*)

Well, what rent did he make you pay? Because I was not able to stand law with him I submitted, and said he might take my case into his sympathy and humanity. (*Laughter*)

Just answer my question, and then I will ask my Lord Chief Justice to let you say something for yourself. (*Laughter*) What did you pay to the land company? £3 7s. 6d. per year ——

Mr W. O'Brien — That will do; now stop.

Mr. Butt — Has Mr Bridge asked you to pay more now? Oh! goodness me, sir, he broke my neck and my back. (*Loud laughter*)

What rent is he asking from you? £6 15s., double £3 7s. 6d., and must be paid or the crow-bar will be applied to the corner stone and level it, and leave me like a raven in the world. (*Laughter*)

Have you paid that increased rent? Ah, sure God help me, I have, and neglected myself in every form, through raiment and food.

What effect has the payment of that increased rent had; you said something about your raiment and food? I will tell you that.

Tell it quietly? That when this rent was doubled upon me I knew the result, and I pawned my body coat, a frieze coat, my lord, in order to be up to the rent, and there it went from that day until this from me, in the year 1874, and I never saw it since. (*Laughter*)

You have never been able since to get your coat out of pawn? No, sir; because when the terms fixed by the pawn-office was passed it was sold.

Was it to pay the increased rent that you pawned your coat? It was just as I told you; I am on my oath.

Could you have paid that increased rent without pawning your coat? I could not unless I mortgaged the land.

How many have you in family? I have my wife, and I had nine children. There are three of my children in America. When they saw this charge made upon me, they said that when they were in their youthful bloom (*Laughter*) they would never suffer such destitution, and they advised me to go to America. But after the hardships and destitution of myself and my brother and my father, who is in the grave, bringing the limestone in a basket on his back, I would not. And there is not a man, my lord, in the world that is able to describe mountain land like a man who toils on it, neither a Walker nor a Bridge (*Laughter*), and it is a scrupulous thing, my lord, that any gentleman, of decent appearance, should see hungry and naked creatures (*with great energy*), because, my lord, I am as healthy as any man in the courthouse, and my visage can show I am starving from want of food.

Since you agreed to pay that increased rent have you yourself had sufficient food? Upon my oath, I had nothing but Indian meal stirabout, and I would be very glad to subsist upon Swedish turnips, that it was never decreed by Almighty God a human creature should subsist on it. After eating a bellyful of it I would not be able to go 10 perches through weakness.

Have your family been living on the same? On part they have, and not as much as I have, because many is the journey and the toil and the hardship that I should go through; but still and all my food was insipid and weak.

Where did you get turnips?' In 'Febry'.

Where is that? The month of 'Febry'. (*Loud laughter*)

What I asked was where did you get them? I go to a friend of mine in Coolegarrauroe. I live in Skeheenarinky, and descend from the precipice into the mainland, and go to my brother-in-law and take a donkey-load of them.

He made you a present of them? What else? I could not buy them.

Do you mean to tell me that was the ordinary subsistence of your family for the last three years? Indeed it was.

Had you ever a meal of meat? Musha, God help me and my meat (*Laughter*), I did not. I did not eat it at the last festival — that was in September. It is a doleful thing to tell you, I did not taste a bit of meat, because I had not money to buy it.

Had your wife been out at service? When I was put to this difficulty — surrounded, my lord — I said, 'Well, after my father's sweat and my own, God is good,' said I; 'and now,' said I, 'you may go for a year in service, in order that we may keep it sooner than be turned away into the workhouse, and while you are able to work you can get better food there in this farm.' She condescended, my lord to my advice, and went into service.

Is she at service now? She is at home in her own cabin.

What kind of a house have you — how many rooms? None but the one.

Is the roof a good one? It is, but the thatch is wrecked, and reed is too dear, and my land don't grow corn.

Is your land high up on the mountain? Oh, then, it is so high, and the cliffs and glens getting into it, that if you stayed in it and looked down, 'Niagara megrims' would come in your head, and you would fall down. (*Laughter*)

You are a good way up the mountain? Oh, I am too far up.

You remember when your father took this land? No.

How long do you remember it? I remember it since the year 1821.

In what state was this land? Oh, dear knows; with the exception of two fields he reclaimed I saw heath that grew up to my knees.

I suppose you heard from your father who reclaimed the two fields? It was himself; there is not a house or a home there, only just as there is on Mount Ararat. (*Laughter*)

Will you tell me how you reclaimed that land? To go to the limestone quarry that was on the lowland and to fill, my lord, a little donkey car; to fill about 6 cwt; to drive on until we began to get against the steep hill; to unload a portion until we get into another cliff; to unload a portion again, and in the long run you would not know what colour was the horse, only white, like the day he was foaled, with sweat; and, upon my oath, there would not be more than 1 cwt. when it reached the kiln. To reclaim this barren mountain we had nothing but a spade and a pickaxe, and we had to get powder to blast the rocks. I would be willing to forfeit the ten acres three-quarters (*slapping his hand*) for the gentlemen of the jury to see one glimpse of the place I am living in. (*Laughter*)

Are there stones there? Upon my oath, man, there are — stones bigger than the bench the Chief Justice is sitting on. (*Laughter*)

How did you do with the rocks? A crowbar should raise them, and a stout man with an iron sledge in his hand, and the greatest bully of a man had enough to do to make quarters of three big rocks in a day, and indeed, my lord, it was not on Indian meal stirabout he could do it.

After having removed the stones, what did you do with the heath? To dig it with a spade and turn it into the ground, to come then with the quicklime burnt in the kiln, and to shake a little dust of that on it. Well, then, with a quantity of little manure, by pulling some heath and lying it opposite the door of the barn and then spreading it over the ground. Then to go — and, so help me God, if you dug a sod of that stuff, and were strong enough to throw it over this great building, where it would fall it would be as stiff as when you cut it out of the farm.

Sergeant Armstrong — That is the process of reclamation, I suppose.

Mr Butt — I think it is a perfect description; it would be very much admired in Irving, I know. (*To witness*) — How long should you work? Dear knows, from the rising of the sun until the going down. I have as much stones to do as even Mr Buckley and the company joined together would get tired of it. When they tried to subsoil, by cripes! when they saw the money Mr Rae had sunk in it —— (*Loud laughter*)

Did you get any assistance from the landlord? No, no more than you did.

Or from the company? Ah! nonsense; no more than we got from God and our own industry.

You were not able to give it as much lime as it required! Yes, that is it.

You say your three children went to America? Steered to America.

Was that in consequence of your condition by being made pay the increased rent? Sure it was, unless they went about the country with their spades on their shoulders, but now I ask you where would they get hire?

Were you going to America yourself at the time? No, nor I won't today. I would sooner die where I am today. If I had the courage of a man, it would be better for me; but now, when I am worn down, let me sink or swim, I have no chance now, while God leaves me the life.

Cross-examined by Sergeant Armstrong — Would you like your rent to be reduced? Of course I would.

How much? To the former rent — £3 7s 6d, and I tell you in this state of Ireland, on this day, I would not be able to pay it.

Had you ever any other farm but this? I possessed a farm a short time. I married a widow woman who had a farm.

Is that the present wife? I never was married but once.

Is that the farm you sold to John Slattery? Yes. My brother-in-law.

What did you get from Slattery? Something about £19.

How many acres in it? Thirty-two acres some perches.

And he is living on it now? He is. He has no other place.

Is he not a very well-to-do man? I think he is fair enough, unless the times and health would shake him.

Why could you not keep it? I was not able to keep it.

Why was he able to keep it? Because he was a rich man.

Where did he get the money? I don't know.

He had no other way of living? I don't think he had.

And you could not keep it? He got a fortune with the wife that enabled him to keep it. I got no fortune but the farm, and it was embarrassed.

Had you any cows that you got with the wife? Not a cow, nor a hen, nor a goose, nor a pig, nor an ass, nor a horse, but land that was in arrear with fifteen years. Thomas Slattery got a fortune and a wife.

How long was it since your wife was at service — whom was she with? With her uncle, Thomas Slattery.

What wages did she get? She got £6.

With her uncle, Thomas Slattery? During the three years that she served £2 a year.

Did you get anything when your father-in-law died? I did, £20.

How long ago is that? Well, I will give you day and date, if you wait — that was in the year 1869, just on December 27th.

How much did it cost you to send the three boys to America? A boy and two daughters.

Did you pay their passage? No, nor I was not able to pay. Their friends paid their passage from America — their first cousins.

And how many in family have you at home? One in service, and another little child seven years old, and my wife.

Sergeant Armstrong — That will do.

Witness — And I have further to tell you that my younger son, that I was trusting to him alone, ran away from me on the 25th of March on the free emigration, and I never saw him since, and I wish to God I never had any of them, because I have no one now to bury me when I fall.

Johanna Fitzgerald, who had a baby in her arms, deposed that she was the wife of William Fitzgerald, and lived at Skeheenarinky. Her husband was in England working with his brothers. She held the farm. The old rent was £2 10s 4d; the new rent, four guineas. She was not able to pay the new rent, and had gone into debt under the old rent, but the neighbours were very good to her. She held fourteen or fifteen acres of land. She had four children, and they lived on Indian meal, and eat dry, because she could not afford often to buy a pennyworth of milk.

Cross-examined by Mr Heron — My husband paid the new rent up to March last, but he got time until he earned it. My husband sent me money from England, and he sent money to them that he owed debts. I wanted my husband not to pay the rent if I could hold it. My husband spent three-quarter of a year away in England altogether without coming back, this is the fourth year with him now.

Mr. O'Brien — Did your husband come home that time? He did, and stopped three months at home.

The Court then adjourned.

Christmas Day in Mitchelstown Workhouse
William O'Brien
from: *Christmas on the Galtees* (1878)

Christmas on the Galtees, *subtitled* An Inquiry into the Condition of the Tenantry of Mr Nathaniel Buckley, *was published in Dublin in 1878. It followed upon the trial of the Galtee Boy, John Sarsfield Casey. It was written by William O'Brien whose stark descriptive powers predate many modern examples of realistic, investigative journalism. Patten Bridge was the hated land agent for the Galtee Castle Estate. In this excerpt, O'Brien describes a visit to Mitchelstown workhouse on the Kingston Estate where he found that the conditions were better than those experienced by the tenantry at nearby Skeheenarinka in south Tipperary. [Ed.]*

Two things have forced themselves into notice at every step of my progress through the Buckley estates. One is that I have not heard from high or low, in town or country, from tenants or dependants, a single good word for Mr Bridge, nor a single violent one against him. The other is that the tenants who have 'settled' — at least the great majority of those whom I have spoken with — are even more crushed in hope and spirit than those over whom eviction is impending. They do not cloak their passionate interest in the stand made by their sturdier brethren. They speak of themselves in tones of misery and shame. They hail the Rev. Dr Delany with welcomes, and part with him with prayers, because they think (and think truly) that he has not yet abandoned hope. They reiterate in many a variation upon the same woful plaint, that they have bowed under a rent which will crush them. Their apology, put in plain terms, is that, in order to keep the roofs over them for the present, they have bandaged their eyes to the future. In reference to Mr. Bridge again, strangers, who have been horrified with blood-stained pictures of the tenantry, might have looked for vengeful fury of language on the part of some, and tenderness, or at least caution, on the part of semi-dependants with whom he is presumed to be in peace. The converse is my experience. Not even the language of outrage from men doomed to ejectment, and words of wringing bitterness from those whom prudence ought to have silenced. The strongest term of vituperation I have heard used, even in heat, by the men under notice was 'That man,' with a significant nod towards Galtee Castle, and the best wish, that his shadow had never fallen across the estate. If there is anything more obvious than the utter inoffensiveness and peaceable longings of the tenantry it is the eagerness with which they look for redress to the newly discovered powers of law and public opinion — rare visitants hitherto to those sequestered glens. The names of their counsel and champions are constantly on their lips with blessings. They have got dim revelations that courts and newspapers are made for mountaineers as well as citizens. Their visit to the capital has given them other material for fireside talk than how Din Murphy got the better of the Serjeant on the 'cross' or how Shawn Shaughnessy's body-coat was the wonder of Sackville Street. I have generally lighted on them in their cabins in one of two moods — listless dejection or picturesque vehemence; and in either phase there is a resistless fascination in their sorrow, emphasized as it is in so many cases by worn cheeks and hungry eyes, by bare walls and barren heaths.

I went to Mitchelstown workhouse today to see the paupers eat their Christmas dinner. The prospects I had seen of the festive season at Skeheenarinka excited a curiosity to learn how much worse off an idle pauper could be than a farmer who has spent all his days creating soil upon the breast of a mountain. Now, the Mitchelstown Guardians do not feast their charge with roast beef and plum-pudding, and currant cake and tea, nor are the rooms wreathed with holly, nor do kind ladies distribute toys and sweetmeats among the children, as is done within other workhouse walls of my acquaintance. But they give the paupers a breakfast of bread and coffee, and a solid dinner of one pound of prime boiled beef and vegetables, with an inexhaustible cauldron of appetising soup. I saw the old people attack their trenchers, and right heartily demolish their contents. They were cleanly and warmly clad and shod. I saw parties of infirm men and women lolling before bright fires in their dayrooms, or basking in the sun in the exercise yards. I passed through the pure white dormitories, with floors scrupulously scrubbed and windows half opened to admit the bracing air from the hills. The mattresses of clean straw were, in the infirmary ward, extended on wooden stretchers, and in the able-bodied department upon a raised flooring at wide intervals. The bedding was two pairs of woollen blankets, a pair of sheets, a warm rug, and a pillow. I passed through the children's quarters, where about a hundred healthy-looking little children are neatly clothed, and fed, and educated, and, I was glad to hear, admitted almost daily to breathe the air of the free fields. I saw old, bed-ridden people, whom the order of the doctor might elevate to a diet of wine or porter, beefsteak or arrowroot. It was not very splendid as a prospect in life; but, there were no dripping walls, no scanty clothes, no clamorous creditors, no hungry stomachs, though these people toiled not, neither did they spin. I am not going to say that Christmas on the Galtees was gloomier than in the workhouse. In many homes on the estate, I have no doubt, there were whatever Christmas comforts humble means could buy. In the very poorest, as far as I know, by whatever pinch or device, some scrap of meat was foraged out in honour of the first of festivals. The custom that it should be has the spell of a superstition. But I mean to say that the dryness, and cleanliness, and warmth, the indolence and fare, of the workhouse would have been luxury if transferred to two dozen of the cottier homes of Skeheenarinka, where men have delved all their lifetime for bread with twice the industry that would have cleared a settlement in the American backwoods. Not a sprig of holly was to be seen in any house I visited. I looked up once towards where, in the obscurity, I thought I saw a flitch of bacon hanging up opposite the chimney-corner, as I had seen in happier spots; it was a horse collar. Sweetmeats would be like sending one ruffles who wanted a shirt. It would be almost a levity to speak of the ordinary Christmas adjuncts of merry-making. A meal of bread and tea and pork was the average Christmas banquet. In one house there were 6lb. of pork among ten; in another 3lb. of mutton among five. A goose or a bit of bacon was the mark of superior station. As I drove past the base of the hill after nightfall, when no cheerful twinkle lighted the cabin windows, and when a snowstorm breaking over the Galtees overspread it like a shroud, there seemed to be few spots in Christendom that had less business with a happy Christmas.

The Last Garden Party
Elizabeth Bowen
from: *Bowen's Court (1942, 1964)*

At the beginning of August 1914 Henry VI and I were at Bowen's Court. My cousin Audrey Fiennes was staying with us, and Aunt Sarah had come over from Mitchelstown, for that summer holiday, to keep house. She reassumed her born role with dignity. To signalize my beginning to grow up, or to comfort me on this return to the house, my father had had several rooms redecorated: my former nursery was now a stylish bedroom with light-grey walls and a lilac frieze. August having opened in heavy rain, my cousin and I spent the time indoors, constructing furniture for the dollshouse out of matchboxes and scraps of silk. I remember no concern but the dollshouse, also, the hope that the weather might clear up in time for the Mitchelstown Castle garden party, to be held on August 5th. Also, what hat was I to wear? What my father thought about I do not know: in breaks of the rain he walked up and down the avenues, hands behind his back, sometimes pausing to look reflectively at the house. Or, he talked to his sister Sarah — their voices pitched much on the same note, their very alike faces turned to each other. News in those days travelled slowly to Ireland: I do not even remember the word War.

August 4th passed: in the course of it the rain stopped. August 5th was a white-grey, lean gritty day, with the trees dark. The newspaper did not come. A wind rose, and, as about eleven o'clock that morning we drove down the avenue in the large pony trap — the only conveyance Bowen's Court now had: but for the pony the carriage-stables were empty — my cousin and I held on the hats we had elected to wear. We were to go round by Rockmills, pick up the youngest Oliver — a girl, but christened Silver after her ancestor — then on to Mitchelstown, where we were to eat lunch at Aunt Sarah's house in King-square. Aunt Sarah remained at Bowen's Court: her friend Lady Kingston was now dead, and she did not care for Castle parties without her.

At Rockmills my father — whose manner, I do remember, had been growing graver with every minute — stopped the pony and went into the post office. There was a minute to wait, with the pony stamping, before I again saw him framed in the low dark door. He cleared his throat and said: 'England has declared war on Germany.' Getting back into the trap he added: 'I suppose it could not be helped.' All I could say was: 'Then can't we go to the garden party?' . . . We picked up Silver Oliver and drove on to Mitchelstown — Henry, with his whole mind, courteously answering a rattle of questions from us girls. If at ten or twelve I had been precocious, at fifteen I was virtually idiotic. The bye-roads had dried in the wind and were glaring white; the War already gave them an unreal look.

That afternoon we walked up the Castle avenue, greeted by the gusty sound of a band. The hosts of the party were the late Lady Kingston's second husband Mr Willie Webber, and his companion Miss Minnie Fairholme. They were not young, and, owing to the extreme draughtiness everywhere, they received their guests indoors, at the far end of Big George's gallery. In virtue of this being a garden party, and of the fact that it was not actually raining, pressure was put on the guests to proceed outside — people only covertly made incursions into the chain of brocade saloons. Wind raced round the Castle terraces, naked under the Galtees; grit blew into the ices; the band clung with some trouble to its exposed place. The tremendous news certainly made that party, which might have been rather flat. Almost everyone said they wondered if they really ought to have come, but they *had* come — rightly: this was a time to gather. This was an assemblage of Anglo-Irish people from all over north-east County Cork, from the counties of Limerick, Waterford, Tipperary. For miles round, each isolated big house had disgorged its talker, this first day of the war. The tension of months, of years — outlying tension of Europe, inner tension of Ireland — broke in a spate of words. Braced against the gale from the mountains, licking dust from their lips, these were the unmartialled loyalists of the South. Not a family had not put out, like Bowen's Court, its generations of military brothers — tablets in Protestant churches recorded deaths in remote battles; swords hung in halls. If the Anglo-Irish live on and for a myth, for that myth they constantly shed their blood. So, on this August 1914 day of grandeur and gravity, the Ascendancy rallied, renewed itself. The lack — it was marked — of one element at that party made us feel the immediate sternness of war: the officers from Kilworth, Fermoy and Buttevant had other things to do with the afternoon. They were already under orders, we heard. We few young people got together in groups — would the war prevent our return to England, to school? My father's overcoat blew about; his head rose above the crowds on the terrace. I heard several people say, 'Let us ask Mr Bowen,' I have, now, some notion what he may have been asked. For through the grown-up talkers ran and recurred one question — Will *this* having happened stop Home Rule?

It was an afternoon when the simplest person begins to anticipate memory — this Mitchelstown garden party, it was agreed, would remain in every one's memory as historic. It was, also, a more final scene that we knew. Ten years hence, it was all to seem like a dream — and the castle itself would be a few bleached stumps on the plateau. Today, the terraces are obliterated, and grass grows where the saloons were. Many of those guests, those vehement talkers, would be scattered, houseless, sonless, or themselves dead. That war — or call it now that first phase of war — was to go far before it had done with us. After 1918 came the war in Ireland, with the burning down of many of the big houses — some already futureless, for they had lost their heirs. For Ireland, between 1918 and 1939, 'peace' contracted into a shorter space than people in England realize — in fact, perhaps one does not say of Ireland that war began again, but that war resumed. North of the Galtees, south of the Galtees, familiar military movement was to announce itself; and that landscape known to so many generals, was soon mapped for other campaigns. Once more the old positions were fought for; once more, bridges were blown up; limestone valley walls rang with the old echoes, and flames were making people run through the night when, in their beds in the peaceful darkness of England, people dreamed that war would not occur again.

Even in the little area I have covered, the few miles of country between the Galtees and the Blackwater, even in the little society — Anglo-Irish settler society — whose evolution, being also that of the Bowens, I have tried to describe, the events and plans and passion of the years between 1914 and 1941 would make a book that should be as long again as the book that I have written by now. In — the life of what we call the new Ireland — but is Ireland ever new? — the lives of my own people become a little thing; from 1914 they began to be merged, already, into a chapter of different history. So, on the terrace of Big George's castle, I shall say goodbye to the society that he once so very fittingly led, and which, perhaps, in idea he continued to dominate — say goodbye at the start of one war that War as we now know it encloses in its immense Today. The unseen descent of the sun behind the clouds sharpens the bleak light; the band, having throbbed out God Save the King, packs up its wind-torn music and goes home. From different points of the terrace, most of the landscape of which I have written is to be seen. So from here I say goodbye to the landscape too — for this book only, not for myself.

Salonika
Anonymous

My husband's in Salonika, I wonder if he's dead
I wonder if he knows he has a kid with a foxy head.
So right away, so right away,
so right away Salonika
right away me soldier boy.

And when the war is over
what will the slackers do?
They'll be all around the soldiers
for the loan of a bob or two.

And when the war is over
what will the soldiers do?
They'll be walking around with a leg and a half
and the slackers will have two.

Now they taxed their pound of butter
and they taxed their ha'penny bun,
But still with all their taxes
they can't bate the bloody Hun.

They taxed the Coliseum,
they taxed St Mary's Hall:
Why don't they tax the bobbies
wi' their backs agin the wall?

And when the war is over,
what will the slackers do:
For every kid in America
in Cork there will be two.

For they takes us out to Blarney,
they lays us on the grass:
They puts us in the family way
and leaves us on our ass.

Now there's lino in the parlour
and in the kitchen too:
There's a glass-backed cheffoneur
that we got from Dicky Glue.

Now never marry a soldier,
a sailor or a marine,
But keep your eye on the Sinn Féin boy
with his yellow white and green.

The Boys of Kilmichael

Anonymous

Whilst we honour in song and in story the mem'ry of Pearse and
    MacBride,
Whose names are illumined in glory with the martyrs who long
    since died.
Forget not the boys of Kilmichael, those brave lads so gallant and true,
They fought 'neath the green flag of Erin and they conquered the
    red white and blue.
Then here's to the boys of Kilmichael, those brave lads so gallant
    and true,
They fought 'neath the green flag of Erin and they conquered the
    red white and blue.

On the twenty-eighth day of November the Tans left the town of
    Macroom:
They were armed in two Crossley tenders, which led them right
    into their doom.
They were out on the road to Kilmichael, they never expected to
    stall,
And they met with the boys of the Column who made a clean
    sweep of them all.
Then here's to the boys of Kilmichael, those brave lads so gallant
    and true,
They fought 'neath the green flag of Erin and they conquered the
    red white and blue.

The sun in the west it was sinking, 'twas the eve of a cold winter's day,
When the Tans we were wearily waiting sailed into the spot where
    we lay.
And over the hills went the echo, the peal of the rifle and gun,
And the flames from the lorries gave tidings that the boys of the
    Column had won.
Then here's to the boys of Kilmichael, those brave lads so gallant
    and true,
And the Irish Republican Army they made bits of the red white and
    blue.

The lorries were ours before twilight and high over Dunmanway
town
Our banners in triumph were waving for to show the Tans had
gone down.
We gathered our rifles and bayonets and soon left that glen so
obscure,
And we never drew rein till we halted at the faraway camp of
Glenure.
Then here's to the boys of Kilmichael, those brave lads so gallant
and true,
They fought, neath the green flag of Erin and they conquered the
red white and blue.

Terence MacSwiney: The End

Moirin Chavasse

from: *Terence MacSwiney* (1961)

As the middle of October approached, his condition was visibly
changing for the worse. One great source of suffering was that he
felt he could not get enough air, he could not breathe, it seemed to
him that if people were near him they took away his air. Bed-sores
made him wretched, and for some time past he had found the
weight of the bedclothes almost unendurable, the least thing left on
his bed tortured him. The effort to continue his fight must have been
extreme, for all that he never let the least sign of this appear. 'Beidh
mé dílis duit, beidh mé dílis duit go deo,' he was heard murmuring
to himself. ('I will be faithful to you, I will be faithful to you forever'.)

On Monday morning, October 18, the three doctors came to see
him. They told him that scurvy was breaking out all over his body
and if he did not take some lime juice he would suffer great pain.
He replied that he would take whatever pain God sent him.

The next day, Tuesday, the 69th day of his fast, Dr Griffith
returned, and endeavoured to make him give in, finally saying that
he would have to take the lime juice, that he would compel him to
take it. MacSwiney replied that if he attempted to do this he would
refuse to swallow anything, even water, and added: 'Can't you let

me die in peace?' Dr Griffith retorted: 'You won't die in peace, you'll die in pain.' Yet when he saw the doctor turn to the door to leave, he held out his hand to him, saying: 'Well, you think you are doing your duty, I suppose; I would like to thank you for anything you have done for me and say goodbye: I won't see you again. We may differ on principles but we can still part friends.'

In a short time the disastrous effects of this scene appeared. He grew terribly excited, insisted on the Governor being sent for and in a long interview complained to him about Dr Griffith's behaviour and threats. When the Governor had left he told his brother that he had been unable to see him very well, and thought he had not made himself very clear, and for several hours he remained in a very disturbed condition, going over and over what he had said to the Governor. Towards evening he became a little quieter, but by next morning he was struggling desperately on the verge of delirium. At one time he made his sister Annie show him her watch and he read the time to show her he was not delirious; then he told her to repeat after him, or to write down, that she was a witness that he was dying a soldier of the Republic; he made her promise to do this on the crucifix of his beads. Hardly had she complied than delirium returned — caused by the terror of the doctor's threats and the fear that they would use his unconsciousness to injure his honour and the honour of Ireland. In all these periods of delirium he thought he was struggling against people who were trying to force food on him, striking out with both hands, shouting and trying to get out of bed. The two doctors attached to the prison seemed to think that since the British Government had accepted the fact that he was on a hunger strike and had stated in the House of Commons that he was taking no food, it was not right to force it on him. Dr Griffith thought otherwise. MacSwiney that day was given an injection of morphia and he was calmer after it. For a few moments he recognized where he was. 'I must keep clear,' he murmured, 'I must keep clear.' Then the delirium closed down on him again.

That evening Dr Griffith told Mary MacSwiney that he was going to feed her brother forcibly. She protested; he replied that all his relations were only allowed there on sufferance, and if a word was said they would all be turned out of prison. She thereupon sent telegrams to Asquith, Shortt, Adamson and Commander Kenworthy that the doctor was about to feed her brother forcibly. That night he was very ill, delirious and struggling.

Early the next morning, Thursday, the nurse forced some tea-spoonfuls of meat juice and water between his lips. A little later he regained a moment's consciousness and found the taste of it in his mouth. 'They've tricked me! They've tricked me!' he cried. 'How did they do it?' and at once passed into violent delirium, striking at invisible people on each side of his bed. A few minutes later he vomited all that had been given him, with great pain and struggling. After an hour or so, while unconscious, he was given brandy and milk; this was followed by a terrible fit of vomiting, more than half a bowl of green liquid coming up. The nurse continued to feed him. When he felt the spoon he would clench his teeth and move his head away even though unconscious, but it was easy for her to get the spoon between his lips and let the liquid trickle into his mouth. On one occasion he cried: 'No. No! Take it away!' before falling back unconscious; on another he struck the cup out of her hand so that its contents were spilt over the bed. At one time when she started to feed him she said: 'Won't you take a little more?' and Peter MacSwiney, who was present, burst out: 'It's a shame for you to ask an unconscious man that — you know if he were conscious he would say "No".' Mrs MacSwiney, who was sitting in the room, came up to stop any more being said, but the nurse was deeply offended and complained to Dr Griffith. From time to time that day there were lucid intervals. Once he asked Annie MacSwiney where he was and why he was there. She replied he was in Brixton, 'for the Republic'. His whole face lit up and he said: 'So it is established?' She replied, 'Yes' After a moment he said: 'Oh, we did grand marching in the night.'

That afternoon, Friday, Dr Griffith came as usual to see him, and refused to let Mrs MacSwiney and Peter, who had meanwhile retired into the passage, to go back into the room or even to wait outside. During a long argument Mrs MacSwiney protested that she was the only one who never interfered with anyone, and he at last gave permission for her to stay, but no-one else. However, when Annie MacSwiney arrived she was allowed to stay for an hour. When her sister Mary returned she went to Dr Griffith and asked him the meaning of the order. He said it was an order from the Home Office and refused to concede anything more.

Next morning, Saturday, both sisters were forbidden to go near his room. They refused to leave the prison and stayed in the waiting room all day. That night, after a prolonged argument with the

Deputy Governor they left only when the police began to eject them by force, acting, so they said, according to an order from the Home Office. The others, however, Peter and Seán MacSwiney, Fr. Dominic, and Fred Cronin, who had lately come to London, were sometimes allowed in for short periods. The next day, October 24, the two sisters were not permitted to pass the outer gates, and remained outside the prison throughout the day. Mrs MacSwiney, who had not been well all night, drove up and was told she must wait to see her husband till the nurse was ready. She refused to wait saying she was not well, and left without seeing him. Later on Art O'Brien went with her to the Home Office and saw Mr Shortt's Secretary. They were told that they were refused admittance to the Lord Mayor's room owing to medical reasons, and that under no circumstances would his sisters be allowed to enter the prison.

That night, as the seventy-fifth day of his fast began, Fr. Dominic and Seán MacSwiney, who were sleeping in the prison, were awakened at 4.35 a.m. and told that the Lord Mayor was dying. Seán wished to telephone to his relations, but Dr Griffith would not allow him to use the prison telephone or to leave the prison. He could do nothing but join Fr. Dominic, who was praying at his brother's bedside, and watch him die. They could not afterwards speak of the hour that then passed by. All that could be told was that he struggled for air. The doctors at last left him, powerless to keep him or to torment him any longer. He appeared to be unconscious, but Fr. Dominic, wishing to give him the plenary indulgence sent by Pope Benedict, asked him, since he could no longer speak to shut his eyes if he could still hear. This he did. Having given him the indulgence Fr. Dominic then began to recite the prayers for the dying:

'Depart, Christian soul, out of this world, in the name of God the Father Almighty Who created thee, in the name of Jesus Christ, Son of the Living God, Who suffered for thee; in the name of the Holy Ghost Who sanctified thee. . . . Remove, O merciful Father, whatever is corrupt in him through human frailty, or by the snares of the enemy. . . . Have compassion, O Lord, on his tears and admit him to reconciliation with Thee who has no hope but in Thee. . . . I recommend thee, dear brother, to Almighty God and leave thee in His mercy Whose creature thou art, that, having paid the common debt by surrendering thy soul, thou mayest return to thy Maker who formed thee out of the earth. Let therefore, the splendid Company of the Angels meet thy soul at its departure; let the

court of Apostles receive thee, let the triumphant army of glorious
martyrs conduct thee. . . . We pray that it may be thy happy lot to
behold thy Redeemer face to face, to be ever in His Presence and
in the vision of that Truth which is the joy of the blessed, and thus
placed among those blessed spirits mayest thou be ever filled with
heavenly sweetness.'

The prayers ceased. For a few moments they listened to the
gasping breath of the dying man. Then Fr. Dominic took up his
beads once more. In a little while the painful breathing faltered, and
stopped; and that splendid Company received him.

Victory at Crossbarry

Tom Barry

from: *Guerilla Days in Ireland* (1949)

By the middle of March, 1921, the British invariably operated in
West Cork in units of not less than three hundred. Consequently
the Brigade Flying Column was brought to its greatest possible
strength by the addition of every available rifle in the area and it
now totalled one hundred and four officers and men. Unfortunately
we had only forty rounds of ammunition for each rifle and there
were no reserves. It was with the greatest reluctance we departed
from our fixed policy of not putting all our eggs in one basket, and
risking practically all our best officers and all our armament in one
Flying Column. It was also no easy matter to manoeuvre, conceal,
billet and feed a Flying Column of that strength over a long period,
in an area that was then holding down at least five thousand British
troops. But where was the alternative? We could not hope to engage
the strong British forces with a smaller force, and in addition
wanted men, who, if captured, would be killed by the British, had a
far better chance of survival in a Flying Column, than if left to evade
capture and death in small groups in the various Battalion areas.
The officers with the Column then were Liam Deasy, Adjutant,
Tadhg O'Sullivan, Quartermaster, Dr Con Lucey, Medical Officer,
and Eugene Callanan, Assistant Medical Officer. The M.O. and his
Assistant did not wear the Red Cross insignia as the British would

not recognize our rights to use it, so Lucey and Callanan were active fighting soldiers who carried First Aid equipment in addition to their rifles. There were seven Sections of fourteen riflemen in each including the Section Commander. Those numbering One to Seven were commanded respectively by Sean Hales, John Lordan, Mick Crowley, Denis Lordan, Tom Kelleher, Peter Kearney and Christy O'Connell. The strength of Sections in other armies usually varies between seven and ten riflemen, but ours was organized to a strength of fourteen, mainly because as we were completely unsupported, the Column had always to be ready to stem a flank or rear attack or both at one time, and a section of a lesser strength would be ineffective for that purpose. We could not model our fighting unit on other armies or according to textbooks, but only in the manner which the prevailing circumstances demanded. A piper now accompanied our Flying Column. He was Florence Begley, an Assistant to the Brigade Adjutant, a well-known player of the bagpipes. This was an innovation and we were soon to test an opinion I had formed, that the best of soldiers will fight even better still to the strains of their traditional war songs, and that the harsh wild music of the bagpipes would have a demoralizing effect on the Sassenach foes.

On the morning of March 16th, information reached us that three hundred enemy troops were being sent on the following day from Kinsale to Bandon as reinforcements. That night the Flying Column marched to intercept them at Shippool, half-way between Kinsale and Bandon. An hour before dawn on St Patrick's Day we occupied ambush positions on the roadside which ran close by and parallel to the railway line and Bandon River in the lovely wooded valley of Shippool. We lay all day vainly waiting until four o'clock when our scouts, who had been sent to Kinsale to watch the enemy movements, returned. They reported that the enemy had set out as scheduled, travelled over a mile, were then halted and later returned to barracks. Obviously they were recalled because of information received that our Brigade Column had moved across their line of march. Incidentally we were never able to trace their source of information. Immediately I received this news, the Column was withdrawn to retire on to Skough, east of Innishannon. Twenty minutes later a British reconnaissance plane, flying low, zoomed along the valley, searching for us as we lay flat and still in extended order, hidden in the dykes, pressed close to the ditches,

The following day we remained in billets waiting for an enemy move which I knew was now inevitable. The British would surely attempt a large scale operation against the Column, but we could only attempt to anticipate the tactics they would employ. It was an uneasy day and the most stringent security measures were adopted by the Flying Column. Reports from some of the garrison towns around us, including one brought by Seán MacCarthy, Upton, Chairman GAA, regarding Cork City, that all was exceptionally quiet, did not ease the tension, for such a lull in their activities was unusual and even ominous. It was easy to imagine General Strickland's Divisional Headquarters Staff in the city, twelve miles away, feverishly at work preparing the troop movements, which would eventually encircle, compress and destroy our Flying Column. In an inky darkness the Column moved again northwards to cross the two Cork–Bandon main roads into Ballyhandle, six miles away. Kelleher's Section was detailed as the Advance Guard with instructions that half of the Section was to travel inside both ditches of the road, to prevent surprise by British ambushing units. At 1 a.m. the Column arrived at John O'Leary's, Ballyhandle, and this house became Column Headquarters. The son of the house, Paddy, was a member of the Column and Captain of the Upton Company, and the daughter was a member of the Cumann na mBan. The Column moved off to billet at the surrounding houses. Crowley and Kelleher left to mobilize the local Company as an outer ring of unarmed scouts, while Deasy, a few others and I went into John O'Leary's. I felt so sure action was imminent that I refused to go to bed and lay down fully dressed on a sofa in a room off the kitchen. Just before 2.30 a.m. Crowley and Kelleher returned hurriedly to report seeing the lights and hearing the noises of lorries some miles to the west. I immediately ordered the assembly of the Flying Column. Ten minutes later a similar report was received of enemy movements to the east, and at 2.50 a third report came in of occasional glares of lorry lights and of dogs barking excitedly away to the south. By then there was no doubt that an extensive operation against the Column was in full swing, but it was not until later, of course, that the details were confirmed.

At 1 a.m. on the morning of March 19th, four hundred troops left Cork, two hundred Ballincollig, three hundred Kinsale and three hundred and fifty Bandon. Later one hundred and twenty Auxiliaries left Macroom. Still later, troops left Clonakilty and more left Cork.

They proceeded by lorries to four points, approximately four miles north-north-east, south-south-east and west of Crossbarry. There they dismounted and formed up in columns. About half of each column then moved on foot as they raided the countryside and converged on Crossbarry. The remainder again mounted the lorries and were moved slowly onwards after the raiding columns. Their tactics were apparently those of motorized infantry who could be rushed to any point where the IRA were contacted. This arrangement also allowed for the changing over of raiding troops on foot for the fresh men on the lorries.

They raided and closely searched every house and out-house in the countryside. Each column took many civilians and some unarmed Volunteers prisoners. One of the eastern columns came to the house three miles north of Crossbarry, where Commandant Charles Hurley was recuperating from a bullet wound. They killed him, but he died fighting as he tried to break through. Two unarmed scouts had been sent on earlier to bring Charlie Hurley down to the Column, but had been intercepted on the way and had been taken prisoners. The Column clearly heard the shots that killed him at about 6.30 a.m. Thus the British made very slow progress as they moved on to where the Column was waiting.

When the Column mobilized at 2.30 a.m. it had full knowledge of the fact that the enemy was moving to attack it from several sides. Although the numbers of the enemy were not then known the IRA had no doubt that they were outnumbered by ten to one at least. I had to decide without delay whether to fight or to retire and attempt to evade action. The decision to fight was made immediately. Each and all of the following factors governed the decision:

(a) It was extremely doubtful if the IRA Column could retire in any direction without being met by numerically superior forces. The only direction from which the British were not known to be advancing was north-west. But there was no guarantee that they were not coming that way also. Had the Column retired that way and met an enemy force they would have held the high ground and their tactics need only have been to man the ditches in a 'holding' operation, while the other British columns closed in on the IRA

(b) The IRA Column had only forty rounds per rifle. This shortage demanded initially a swift and intensive fight at

415

close quarters, which, if not in itself decisive, would have the effect of upsetting the carefully planned enemy deployment. If the Column retired, this objective could not have been achieved, and the best the Column could hope for would be an all-day series of skirmishes with the British, who would harass it continually, even if it did not corner it. The IRA ammunition would not last several hours of this warfare, much less a full day.

(c) A heavy and successful attack on those large British rounds-up was an overdue strategic necessity. Hitherto they had not been attacked and there was a grave danger that by their wholesale arrests of Volunteers, captures of dumped arms, and intimidation of the civilian population, they would seriously interfere with the Volunteer organization and damage the morale of the people.

(d) From observations of enemy movements it was clear that the British force from the west would reach Crossbarry some time before the other British columns. That would even up the opening fight and the Column was supremely confident of being able to defeat it and thus smash one side of the encircling wall of troops. This would leave the IRA Column free to pass on to the west where it could, according to circumstances, turn either north or south with the practical certainty of avoiding for that day further contact with the British. In addition there was the expectation of the Column increasing its armament, particularly its ammunition, from such an attack. At 3 a.m. I spoke to the Flying Column giving them an outline of the situation and our plan of attack. The following action orders were stressed:

(1) No Section was to retire from its position without orders, no matter how great the pressure. Arrangements for rapid reinforcement of any point had been made. Even though Sections saw no enemy they were not to move to the aid of other Sections, as the enemy were operating on various sides.

(2) No volunteer was in any circumstances to show himself until the action started, for the plan entailed allowing the British forces to move right through the ambush position until the leaders were over the eastern mine, when it was to be set off. The order was then to attack the nearest enemy, whilst the second mine was to be set off if any of the enemy came near it.

(3) Communication between the Column Commander and the various Sections was to be made by runners. The Command Post was movable between the centre Sections.

(4) The direction of retirement would not be given until the move-off, but whatever Sections were engaged on advance, rear and flank guards, were to keep moving in extended order not nearer than three hundred yards to the main Column.

The Column marched off to Crossbarry at 3.30 a.m., and positions were occupied by 4.30. Crossbarry is situated twelve miles south-west of Cork City. It is about nine miles from Ballincollig, twelve from Kinsale and eight from Bandon. The old road from Bandon to Cork which was and is quite a good road passes through Crossbarry. Here it is met by two roads from the north and two from the south, and they form a double crossroads only thirty yards apart. It was west of those crossroads that all our Sections were posted. Hales' Section was placed at the western entrance to the ambuscade inside the northern ditch of the road. An old boreen ran up on this flank, and this was now blocked with a small stone wall to prevent armoured cars from entering and enfilading the Column. As well as being able to fire on the enemy immediately in front, this Section could also enfilade the approach road. Stretched along east from Hales' Section for several hundred yards inside this northern ditch, and in the two roadside farmhouses, Beasley's and Harold's, were the riflemen of the Section commanded by John Lordan, Mick Crowley, Peter Kearney and Denis Lordan. This last Section on the extreme left was capable of enfilading the approaches to Crossbarry Cross in addition to frontal fire. Just beyond it, around the bend, another stone wall was erected to prevent any enemy lorries from racing through. Between Crowley's and Kearney's, and between Kearney's and Denis Lordan's Sections, two observation mines were embedded in the road. The piper was in the centre of the attacking Sections in Harold's yard, with instructions to play Irish war songs from the first crack of the rifles. Tom Kelleher's Section was placed in the 'Castlefield' six hundred yards directly to the rear of Denis Lordan's Section, to cover the left flank and the left rear approaches. Christy O'Connell's Section was posted about two hundred yards north of the approach road, and six hundred yards to the west of Hales' Section to cover our right flank. From its position it could also fire on any enemy on the approach road as well as stemming a flank attack. Three riflemen were detached from the main attacking Sections to patrol a half mile in the rear of our positions. Even though this small group was not strong enough to stop an enemy force of any strength, it would delay them and give the Flying Column time to change deployment. Thus, seventy-three officers and men were deployed for an attack, and thirty-one others were protecting their flanks and rear. By 5.30 a.m. all these preparations were completed and I was perfectly confident that we could not be surprised.

After hearing the shots that had killed Charlie Hurley at 6.30 a.m. we waited immovable and silent. The quietness of the breaking dawn was disturbed only by the sounds of the enemy transport which crept nearer and nearer. About 8 a.m. a long line of lorries carrying troops came slowly on past O'Connell's flanking Section and into our main ambush positions. Twelve lorries were between Crowley's Section in the centre and O'Connell's flankers, but many more stretched back along the road. Liam Deasy and I flattened against the ditch as the leading lorry came on, but suddenly it halted and the soldiers started shouting, for unfortunately, despite the strictest orders, a Volunteer had shown himself at a raised barn door and was seen by many of the British. The British started to scramble from their lorries but the order to fire was given and Crowley's Section opened up at them. Immediately John Lordan's and Hales' Sections also attacked the enemy nearest them and away on our flank Christy O'Connell's men blazed at the enemy on the road below. Begley played martial airs on his warpipes as four of our Sections attacked. Volley after volley was fired mostly at ranges from five to ten yards at those British and they broke and scattered, leaving their dead, a fair amount of arms and their lorries behind them. The survivors had scrambled over the southern ditch of the road and were running panic-stricken towards the south. Three of our Sections were ordered out on the road to follow them up. Using rapid fire they chased the enemy who lost many men. These British troops did not stop running until they reached the main Cork–Bandon Road, a mile and a half away. Even then they did not attempt to reform but straggled back in disorganized groups to Bandon, nearly seven miles away.

Within ten minutes of the opening of our attack we had smashed the British encircling lines wide open. We could have marched away to the south without fear of interference had I wished to do so. But now confidence in ourselves to meet the attacks we knew were coming from other British units was mixed with contempt for our enemy's fighting ability. The three Sections were ordered back to collect the arms of the British dead. Helping them now was a man named White of Newcestown, who although not a Volunteer, had been arrested that morning and carried as a hostage in the leading lorry. He had a doubly lucky escape from death as after escaping our first volley, he was nearly shot dead when I came on the road, before he shouted that he was an Irishman and a prisoner of the British. Now he was staggering under the load of a new British Lewis gun and eight fully loaded pans which the enemy machine-gunners, dead on the road, never had a chance of using. The captured rifles were slung across the backs of Volunteers and the captured ammunition was distributed immediately amongst all our riflemen. It was a welcome addition to half empty bandoliers. Then the lorries were prepared for burning and the British dead pulled away from their vicinity. The first three were burning when heavy rifle fire broke out on our left flank and all Volunteers were ordered back to their original action stations. Another British Column of about two hundred had advanced from the south-east. They were attacked by Denis Lordan's Section. Kearney's men were moved up to reinforce Lordan's and after heavy fighting the enemy retreated leaving a number of dead. This unit was not again seen on that day. Those troops too, like those on the lorries, had evidently had enough.

We had not long to await the third phase of the engagement, for shortly afterwards the sounds of rifle fire came from our right flank. Here about a platoon of British tried to come in across country but were met by O'Connell's Section. This party had apparently been left behind the main British column to complete the raids. O'Connell's riflemen surprised them and the British hurriedly withdrew. The firing had died down so quickly that our reinforcing Section which had started out was recalled.

Ten minutes later the fourth development of the action opened. Still another British column came in on our left rear. Numbering about two hundred they had entered an old boreen about a mile back, and keeping close to the ditch as they crept in, they were unobserved for some time. Their manoeuvre did not, as they had hoped, bring them in on the rear of an unsuspecting Flying Column, as when they emerged on to the Castlefield, Kelleher's riflemen were waiting for them. Kelleher's Section allowed them to come to within fifty yards of its position before opening fire and knocking over a number of them. The remainder hurriedly retired to cover from where they continued to engage our men. Immediately this action started I sent Jim Murphy (Spud) and eleven riflemen to reinforce Kelleher. Spud had his arm in a sling, the result of a bullet wound received a few weeks previously in a fight with the British, but he was such a fine fighter and Section Commander that I had no hesitation in detailing him for the job. There were now twenty-six officers and men facing this British Column and our line was extended northwards to counter an anticipated enemy flanking movement. This soon came and again the enemy was met with such heavy fire that they hurriedly retreated once more. The fighting had gone on here for about ten minutes and as there were no British in sight anywhere but those being attacked by Kelleher and Murphy, I moved the whole Flying Column back, except O'Connell's Section, to strike at this enemy unit with our full strength. But when I reached Kelleher's position all the British had gone and we saw no more of those either.

British corpses were strewn on the Crossbarry road, in the fields south of it, in front of Denis Lordan's Section, near Christy O'Connell's Section, and now here were several more of them lying around Kelleher's position. But we, too, had not escaped unscathed. Three of our soldiers lay dead and several others were wounded. Volunteer Peter Monahan, Volunteer Jeremiah O'Leary, Leap, and Volunteer Con Daly, Ballinascarthy, had died fighting for Ireland that morning. We laid our three dead comrades close together in a field, and placing the most seriously wounded, Dan Corcoran of Newcestown and Jim Crowley of Kilneatig, Kilbrittain, in our midst, moved back to the old boreen which flanked Hales' Section, and Christy O'Connell's flankers were drawn in. About two hours had elapsed since the opening of the fight; we were in possession of the countryside; no British were visible; and our task was completed. The whole Column was drawn up in a line of Sections and told they had done well. Those British units were finished, but other fresh troops might be encountered as we retired to billets at Gurranereigh. These were fourteen miles due west of Crossbarry, but twenty miles as we would have to travel. Flankers would have to travel cross-country for at least twelve miles, where we would halt to look for breakfast. Strict march discipline would have to be observed, but the Column would move at an easy pace so that it would be fresh and fit to fight again at any stage of our retirement.

Shortly after the order to march was given we spied a gathering of British away in the distance; evidently groups of disorganized units. They appeared to be leaderless, as they were standing around in the centre of a small field in the sloping hillside east of Crossbarry. Through field glasses I could see them gesticulating as if they were arguing as to what to do next. We helped them to make up their minds, for although the distance was a bit far, the Column was halted and deployed along a ditch. The range was given and three volleys from nearly a hundred rifles were fired at them. A few staggered and fell, others broke in all directions, and soon the West Cork hillside was clear of the khaki clad troops. Crossbarry was over.

A Civil War Diary
P. F. Quinlan

This is an extract from a diary kept during the Civil War by P. F. Quinlan, a lieutenant in the pro-Treaty forces. Quinlan later became secretary of Ireland's first Young Farmers' Club which was formed in Mitchelstown in the 1920s. He became prominent in Macra na Feirme and, in later years, he was president of the Irish Agricultural Organisation Society (now ICOS), a director of the Agricultural Credit Corporation, and he was also an agriculture columnist with The Irish Times. *In this excerpt, Quinlan has been engaged in military action (or 'stunt') close to the graveyard at Shanrahan where his friend Seán O'Donoghue is buried. O'Donoghue fought on the anti-Treaty side in the Civil War and he was killed near Dublin Hill in Cork on 28 September 1922. (Ed.)*

Friday 26th. Rose pretty early and had breakfast. Great hubbub over Doc. not visiting post. Bad cases sent away and Red Cross came up. Crossley going with Corporal G when stunt came on then off for we knew not where terrible secrecy. Got to Mtown [Mitchelstown]. Knocked up digs. Sgt. Mc falling out exhausted on the way. Went into POBs had a few drinks and to bed.

Sat. 27th. Up again with scarcely a doze in bed and on for Ballyp [Ballyporeen] met several neighbours and lots of suspicious 'good days.' Spread out at [Meany's] and on for the open country. Got nothing so swung on for village. Had row with some of the boys. Called into Kennedys and had some chat on again for the village. Into MOBs and had some grub called down to Aunties with Jim Finn. Had tea and out at dark for the night on B-C. [Ballyporeen–Clogheen] road. Called into J. Ph's and got on fine had some tea etc. again in the morning — off again after great talk and horse lore.

Sun 28th. Through Bally. [Ballyporeen] spread out and on for the 'home of the irregulars' as it has come to be known not much of an appearance of irregulars about it as we moved on for the first hour. But hark a little shot. A pause. Another shot. Three almost together. How the sound of those death messages makes a chap's blood boil. What queer characteristics they bring to light in a bloke. How a man longs for blood at the sound of firing. What totally savage beings so called civilized men are. How near the polished surface is the bald proof of sheer savagery I have often seen proved on such occasions. Then on for our stunt. Stealth of movement passing along orders punctuated by the crack of skirmishing fire. *Nuf* said now. I shall not forget the rest of the scrap. But now that it is over I remembered I was near the burying place of Seán O'D. (Seán O'Donoghue) so I called in to see his grave. Heavens how small a little place we all can fit in some day but in that small place decorated by wreaths and tokens of sorrow from heartbroken friends lay my life-long friend poor Seán that I loved since I was so wee that I cannot remember and that everybody loved that ever met him. Ah how sorrowful. The bare bald tombstones seemed to fling scornful glances at me. The dove in the ivy-clad poplar which spread its apron of branches over that lonely grave cooed in such a manner as to mock my prayers for my poor friend as if he needed them for where else could he be but with his God, poor saint and the poplar branches solemnly beckoning their bare branches as if to token my attention to his grave. All, each, and everything seemed to mourn for him but seemed as if by mutual consent to exclude me from the circle of mourners. How deep down in my heart (if indeed I have such a thing) I felt the irony of my behaviour. Coming in the green uniform to pray for him that was done to death by men wearing same. But I was alone with the dead and I wanted no more. As I prayed and thought over his life and our associations I showed the woman. Try how I might I could not stop. Circumstances are indeed cruel here am I praying for poor Seán with the uniform of those that murdered him and I still cannot throw it off. I explained to him my friend. Gallant. Shapely boy. Gay and buoyant in the bloom of his youth now lying stiff and cold several feet down in the damp cold clay by the hand of a cowardly drunken parasite who would not dare to face him on equal terms. Yes, Seán, my old friend you told me long ago you would be shot but in that manner why who should have thought it possible? Very well I have made thee a promise. Sean death has made it impossible for us to shake hands upon it. But your ideals I shall strive to attain. Your death I shall revenge aye if I shall suffer death a thousand times over for it that man shall fall whatever the cost. I will send him before his God to account for his deeds and to be judged on his merits and your ideal. 'A Republic' I will fight for by my method different to yours. But Sean if I had misgiving as to a republic once when the path to such is rendered sacred by the blood of brave and noble souls more especially by your blood, then it is *the* path for me.

The Tomb of Michael Collins

Denis Devlin

from: *Collected Poems* (1989)

To Ignazio Silone

Much I remember of the death of men,
But his I most remember, most of all,
More than the familiar and forgetful
Ghosts who leave our memory too soon —
Oh, what voracious fathers bore him down!

It was all sky and heather, wet and rock,
No one was there but larks and stiff-legged hares
And flowers bloodstained. Then, Oh, our shame so massive
Only a God embraced it and the angel
Whose hurt and misty rifle shot him down.

One by one the enemy dies off;
As the sun grows old, the dead increase,
We love the more the further from we're born!
The bullet found him where the bullet ceased,
And Gael and Gall went inconspicuous down.

II

There are the Four Green Fields we loved in boyhood,
There are some reasons it's no loss to die for:
Even it's no loss to die for having lived;
It is inside our life the angel happens
Life, the gift that God accepts or not,

Which Michael took with hand, with harsh, grey eyes,
He was loved by women and by men,
He fought a week of Sundays and by night
He asked what happened and he knew what was —
O Lord! how right that them you love die young!

He's what I was when by the chiming river
Two loyal children long ago embraced —
But what I was is one thing, what remember
Another thing, how memory becomes knowledge —
Most I remember him, how man is courage.

And sad, Oh sad, that glen with one thin stream
He met his death in; and a farmer told me
There was but one small bird to shoot: it sang
'Better Beast and know your end, and die
Than Man with murderous angels in his head.'

III

I tell these tales — I was twelve years old that time.
Those of the past were heroes in my mind:
Edward the Bruce whose brother Robert made him
Of Ireland, King; Wolfe Tone and Silken Thomas
And Prince Red Hugh O'Donnell most of all.

The newsboys knew and the apple and orange women
Where was his shifty lodging Tuesday night;
No one betrayed him to the foreigner,
No Protestant or Catholic broke and ran
But murmured in their heart: here was a man!

Then came that mortal day he lost and laughed at,
He knew it as he left the armoured car;
The sky held in its rain and kept its breath;
Over the Liffey and the Lee, the gulls,
They told his fortune which he knew, his death.

Walking to Vespers in my Jesuit school,
The sky was come and gone; 'O Captain, my Captain!'
Walt Whitman was the lesson that afternoon —
How sometimes death magnifies him who dies,
And some, though mortal, have achieved their race.

Heffernan's Cow: A War Incident

Robert C. Cummins

from: *Unusual Medical Cases:
A Cork Physician's Memories* (1962)

It was at the height of the second world war. I was subpoenaed to
attend a medico-legal case at the country assize. It was irritating, it
meant a long day, petrol was both precious and scarce. There would
be the inevitable tedious delays, that always occur in medico-legal
bottlenecks, the most exasperating waiting, and a day wasted in a
draughty Courthouse. The law is the law.

I had been quite pleased with the patient too, not that he had
recovered, he had died, but I had succeeded in placing him amongst
those obscure toxic anaemias that are grouped under the name of
Lederer, for which no exact cause has as yet been found, and that
are said to be frequently fatal.

The Court assembled, I was called, and I was about to be examined by the opposing Counsel. At this point a shock-headed Civic

Guard thrust his head into the Court, and he took off his hat. With quite complete disregard for his Lordship and considerable excitement, he shouted 'There's a Halifax landing in Heffernan's field, my God she is right over against us, she. . . .' At this point his lordship insisted on silence and the maintaining of proper legal dignity, and that the case should be proceeded with, although the dust of generations was rising up in the Court, and the door was jammed by the rush of people trying to empty it! During the turmoil that followed I heard in the distance, piercing the roar of the aeroplane, the unperturbed voice of the Counsel asking 'Dr. W. can you tell me if the cause of Lederer's anaemia is known?' As I was replying that no cause had as yet been discovered, the same shock-headed Civic Guard again thrust his head in, and took off his hat, this time he did not hesitate and again shouted 'She is over against the off wall. My God, she's killed Heffernan's cow, the best milker in all west Cork! . . . she is down safe, no! She is coming right up against the public house wall. Oh my God she. . . .' Again and at this most critical point his Lordship re-established order, and the opposing Counsel with amazing composure and proper legal dignity proceeded to address the Court. 'My Lord, as no cause for this rare condition of Leader's anaemia is admitted to be known, I submit, My Lord, that this unfortunate man's illness must have been initiated when he fell off Mr Foley's outside car, on August the 7th. when the condition originated, there was no petrol in the town at the time. In spite of Dr W's. well-known skill and care, nothing could prevent this unfortunate accident, from proceeding to a fatal issue, in the well known Cork Hospital, as Dr W. has so ably explained to the Court.'

His Lordship agreed with the Counsel's argument, admitted liability, fixed damages, at the reasonable sum of £150, and adjourned the Court, in one single breath or less, and just as the shock-headed Civic Guard announced 'She's stopped right over against the wall itself, thank God they are all saved!' And then without the least remorse at his gross final breach of Court etiquette he replaced his hat, and he proceeded to conduct his Lordship and his distinguished legal and medical colleagues, with exemplary dignity through a milling crowd, which had already been roped off. His Lordship, in his robes, inspected every inch of the machine, even the cockpit. The crew were being entertained lavishly elsewhere.

The aeroplane slipped out quietly, in the evening light, to the cheers of the onlookers. No press report ever appeared.

426

It was a great day, one still remembered after 15 years.

One feels that Heffernan's cow must have been well compensated for; at least this famous milker died in a good cause, and I felt some reflected glory in being associated with so distinguished a Beast.

Index